ATLAS OF MEXICO

ATLAS OF MEXICO

James B. Pick, Edgar W. Butler,
and Elizabeth L. Lanzer

Westview Press
BOULDER, SAN FRANCISCO, & LONDON

This Westview softcover edition is printed on acid-free paper and bound in softcovers that carry the highest rating of the National Association of State Textbook Administrators, in consultation with the Association of American Publishers and the Book Manufacturers' Institute.

Published in 1989 in the United States of America by Westview Press, Inc., 5500 Central Avenue, Boulder, Colorado 80301, and in the United Kingdom by Westview Press, Inc., 13 Brunswick Centre, London WC1N 1AF, England

Library of Congress Cataloging-in-Publication Data
Pick, James B.
  Atlas of Mexico.
  Includes index.
  1. Mexico—Maps. 2. Mexico—Economic conditions—
1970–   —Maps. 3. Mexico—Social conditions—
1970–   —Maps. I. Butler, Edgar W. II. Lanzer,
Elizabeth L. III. Title.
G1545.P5 1989   912′.72   88-675255
ISBN 0-8133-7695-5

Printed and bound in the United States of America

The paper used in this publication meets the requirements of the American National Standard for Permanence of Paper for Printed Library Materials Z39.48-1984.

10   9   8   7   6   5   4   3   2   1

To my parents, Louis and Tibby Lanzer,
for teaching me to pursue my dreams

E.L.L.

To my mother, Josephine Bowen,
and to Don Bowen

E.W.B.

To Rosalyn Laudati and the entire Laudati family

J.B.P.

Contents

Figures

Maps

Tables

Acknowledgments

A project such as this one involves the cooperation, assistance, support, and expertise of many people to bring it to a successful conclusion. The authors accept full responsibility for the contents of this book, but wish to recognize the important contributions of others.

Appreciation is hereby expressed to all of the people who made this project possible; this includes people at the Mexican Census Bureau, Secretaria de Turismo, and other agencies in the Mexican government, Mexican political parties, El Colegio de Mexico, and University of California, Riverside.

At UCR, we are especially appreciative to the members of the Mexico Database Project over the past several years, Glenda Tellis and Hiroshi Fukurai in Sociology, and Swapan Nag, John Chow and Suhas Pavgi in Management. Without their great talent and abilities to handle the information systems complexity of this project, this book would not have been possible. Thanks to Glenda Tellis and Hiroshi Fukurai also for review of some of the contents of this volume.

Also at UCR, we thank Bill Vanore, Alex Ramirez, and Larry Sautter of Computing and Communications, Steve McRae, Corey La Mar, and Claude Johnson, formerly of the UCR Geography Research Laboratory, office staffs in the Graduate School of Management and Sociology, and the staff of the Rivera Library. We appreciate the interest in our project of professors Robert Singer, Adalberto Aguirre, and Arturo Gomez-Pompa. Thanks to the project funding support of UC-MEXUS, UCR Collaborative Research and Training Group, and Dean Stepan Karamardian of the Graduate School of Management.

In Mexico, special thanks to Carlos Jarque Uribe, Carlos Camacho Gaos, Juan Manual Herrero, and Edmundo Berumen Torres at INEGI, as well as to Franciso Alba of El Colegio de Mexico, and Francisco Javier Gutierrez of CONAPO.

Also, we appreciate the assistance of the Westview Press, in particular Dean Birkenkamp, Lynn Arts, Michelle Starika, and former editor Amos Zubrow. We thank anonymous reviewers for their helpful comments and suggestions. Finally, the Atlas would not have been completed if it had not been for the outstanding efforts and dedication of our research assistants Glenda Tellis in Sociology and John Chow from the Graduate School of Management.

Elizabeth L. Lanzer
Edgar W. Butler
James B. Pick

1

OVERVIEW

Introduction

This atlas was developed as part of a larger project devoted to developing a database of the population of Mexico. We became aware that no extensive atlas of the states of Mexico had utilized the 1980 Mexican Census and later governmental data. Furthermore, a limited amount of systematic mapping and analysis of socioeconomic data on the states had been accomplished using prior censuses and other available information. Accordingly, we decided to make available some of the material from our larger U.S.-Mexico Database Project in the form of an <u>Atlas of Mexico</u>.

The atlas is a descriptive volume that we hope will enhance understanding of Mexico, broaden U.S. perspectives on Mexico, and interest others in using the data and maps that we have brought together into one information system (Butler et al., 1987d). The data used in this atlas are available to the public in the form of census publications, annual statistical volumes (anuarios), and in a variety of other publications and reports, although the logistics of gathering the information are difficult. The only information included in this atlas available on computer tape as of 1988 are data from the World Fertility Survey or WFS (SPP, 1978, 1979a,b,c; WFS, 1980).

To our knowledge no one else has systematized into one database such comprehensive information on Mexico. Most of the data in the atlas are from the 1980s, and are the most recent available. The detailed data from the Mexican Census of 1980 were only made available to the public in 1985. The detailed data from the Mexican Census of 1990 will not be processed and available until about 1993 or 1994. At that time, the atlas may be revised into a subsequent edition incorporating census and other data from the early 1990s.

The atlas data set is part of a larger database on Mexico, which has been utilized by us in a variety of research projects. Results of many of these projects are cited in the atlas text. Most data and maps presented are for the 32 Mexican federal entities, which are also referred to as states. The only federal entity which is not also a state is the Federal District. In addition, there are several maps for geographical units smaller than the state level. Other maps are for municipios within states. The municipio is a geographical unit analogous to a county in the United States, and is defined by the Mexican Census as the base unit of territorial division and political/administrative organization in the nation (SPP, 1982-85; Pirez, 1981). The municipio was established by the 1917 Constitution with the intent of giving more emphasis to regions and localities. Partly because municipio boundaries have not been substantially altered since 1917, there is an unequal number of municipios among states. For instance, there are 571 municipios in Oaxaca and 222 in Puebla, versus only four in Baja California and 38 in Coahuila.

The atlas is divided into an introductory chapter and nine descriptive chapters, each containing a set of maps. With each map we have included the data used to generate the maps, the data source, and the exact definition of the characteristic being mapped. Each map is also accompanied by text describing the data and its spatial distribution, and offering some interpretation and reference to selected scholarly publications. This text is to assist understanding of the basic trends portrayed. This comprehensive atlas serves as reference source for academic, government, and business researchers and practitioners. A beneficial side effect of this atlas may be to stimulate research.

We are convinced that this atlas will be of use to planners, researchers, and business analysts, as well as to laypersons. We have discovered that even the most knowledgeable person about Mexico can be surprised at some of the data and spatial distributions.

Sections of the Atlas

The atlas is divided into ten major sections. This overview chapter describes the overall atlas, its data sources, and methodology. This section also includes base maps that are valuable in understanding subsequent sections of the atlas.

The base maps are useful in delineating state and regional boundaries which are referred to in many other maps in the atlas. Base Map 1.1 outlines the state boundaries of Mexico. This base map is used for producing all other maps at the state level found in the atlas. These state boundaries were delineated from the official 1979 Turista Map (Secretaria de Turismo, 1979). The second base map (Map 1.2) identifies regions of Mexico, to facilitate discussion. The regions shown are those used by the World Fertility Survey of 1976-1977 (SPP, 1979b). They are (1) northwest, (2) north, (3) northeast, (4) west, (5) central, (6) gulf, (7) pacific south, and (8) southeast. These regions are very similar to those proposed by Bassols (1961). The states included in each region are listed on Table 1.1. While these regions are adopted consistently in discussion, individual states within regions often differ radically from each other and these individual state differences are noted. The regional map should be viewed only as a very rough guide for three reasons. First, there are others who have divided Mexico into different socioeconomic regions (Scott, 1982; J. Wilkie, 1970; R. Wilkie,1984; Fukurai et al., 1988), as well as others at earlier points in time, such as Rodriguez (1960). Second, some researchers of Mexico argue that regions vary by dimension, character, or the variable under analysis. Third, many other people familiar with Mexico believe that states vary so much from each other that it does not make sense to delineate regions because regionalization in Mexico does not exist. After studying this atlas, the reader may come to his/her own decision regarding the utility of base regions for particular purposes.

In addition to the eight base regions, shown in Map 1.2, two other unique regions are referred to in the text. One is the border region, which cross-cuts the northern base regions. It consists of the states of Baja California, Sonora, Chihuahua, Coahuila, Nuevo Leon, and Tamaulipas. These states are discussed as a unique region in order to identify and interpret communalities and trends relevant to states bordering the United States in phenomena such as income levels, fertility, etc. (Stoddard, 1983). A second unique region is comprised of two federal entitities, the Federal District and the state of Mexico, at the heart of the base central region, and is referred to as the central metropolitan zone, or more simply, the central zone. In 1980, this region had a population of 16,395,414, of which perhaps 14 million lived in the Mexico City metropolis. This region is distinguished to emphasize the overwhelming importance of the Mexico City metropolis for many phenomena, such as economic output, finance, communications, transportation, etc.

The second chapter of the atlas, focusing on Population and Urbanization, first features maps of total population in 1900 and 1980, and a summary table and graph of the historical sequence of population data from the 1900, 1930, 1950, 1970, and 1980 censuses. While this atlas is primarily descriptive, several maps in this section analyze growth and change: (1) percentage growth in population between 1970 and 1980, and (2) urbanization change between 1950 and 1980. Also, major cities in Mexico for 1980 are shown. The age structure of population in 1980, and dependency and sex ratios further illuminate several important population dimensions. In addition, population density is presented, both for the nation and for areas within the Federal District. The final part of this chapter focuses on the U.S.-Mexico borderlands. The northern border between Mexico and the U.S. and the various cities along both sides of the border are shown. Finally, a map is presented of borderlands urbanization at the municipio level.

Marriage and Fertility constitutes the next atlas section. These are important components of any population and this is especially true for Mexico. Over the past thirty years Mexico has had a fertility rate at about the median for the world's major nations. For instance, in 1987 its total fertility rate of 4.0 was the sixth lowest among the eleven most populous nations (Population Reference Bureau, 1987). Over the past two decades fertility dropped substantially in Mexico, along with other major developing nations. Maps presented in this chapter were generated primarily from the Mexican census, the World Fertility Survey data tape, and various anuarios. Marital status maps focus on typical measures but also include information on common law marriages (union libres), number of times married, and divorce/separation.

We have included several maps illustrating the fertility experiences of Mexican women. Some of them focus on fertility rates, while others illustrate cumulative fertility, that is, the number of children ever born to married women or women of particular age categories. Finally, a series of maps shows the extent of knowledge about and actual use of family planning in various Mexican states.

While fertility is a very important dimension of population growth, another major aspect of population change is what proportion of the population remains in the state of birth or moves elsewhere. Thus, the fourth chapter of the atlas examines Migration. The description of raw migration flows emphasizes the population that is native to the state (e.g., born in the state) and the largest 1979-80 interstate migration streams (Fukurai et al., 1987b). Another set of maps shows outmigration, inmigration, and net migration divided by the population of the sending or receiving state for lifetime and 1979-80 migrants, as measured in 1980. Population studies often examine Mortality in addition to fertility and migration. Mortality for Mexico is shown in the fifth chapter along with several different health indicators. The maps show infant mortality rates, and indirectly standardized mortality rates for a variety of causes of death. Indirect standardization adjusts each states age-specific population by the age-specific mortality rates for Mexico. Health indicators shown are hospitals and clinics and children who have no meat or eggs to eat.

The sixth chapter of the atlas presents a variety of Social Characteristics. Two maps show 1980 literacy and literacy change, 1930-70. A map series shows various measures of education in 1980. A map of 1980 indigenous population is presented, along with an historical graph showing the population speaking indigenous languages by region from 1900 to 1980. Non-Catholics are shown and then consumption, crime, and housing dimensions of Mexican society are illustrated.

Two chapters deal with the Economy and Population Economics. In the economy section, emphasis is on the labor force in various industries while another part examines various primary production activities, including mineral, animal, agricultural, and energy production. The last two parts focus on corporations and economic development. The Population Economics chapter examines the economically active population by sex, illustrates various occupational categories, and shows underemployment and unemployment. The last part of this section presents information on low and medium incomes in 1980.

The next chapter focuses on Transportation and Communication. A series of maps show various aspects of highways and vehicles in Mexico, including vehicle registrations and fatal accidents. Airport and passenger measures follow and then major seaports are presented. An historical series on the development of railroads is illustrated by maps showing the railroad network at important dates from 1880 through 1980. These maps are presented because of the importance of the railroads to historical growth and change in population and urbanization. The latter part of this section focuses on telephones, radios, and television stations.

The final chapter of the atlas presents data and maps on Miscellaneous characteristics that do not conveniently fit other sections but yet are important in describing contemporary Mexico. Maps in this section cover a variety of dimensions, including hotels, tourism, and political elections. Maps illustrate state results for the 1988 presidential election and mid-80s municipio and gubernatorial elections in Sonora and Chihuahua, along with a graph presenting national presidential election results by party from 1934 to 1988.

Methodology

This Atlas of Mexico utilizes data from a variety of sources. Major data sources are the Mexican censuses of 1895 through 1980, the Mexican portion of the World Fertility Survey of 1976-77, and miscellaneous government data sources especially Anuarios Estadisticos (SPP, various years). Several data sources required special effort and permission to obtain. The complete set of censuses, 1895-1970, is available in very few U.S. libraries, but fortunately it was available as of 1987 in a combination of microfiche and hard copy through the library of the University of California, Riverside. Through the assistance of several people in Mexico, the 1980 Mexico census was made available to us. None of these censuses, not even in 1980, was available as of 1988 in computerized media, necessitating data entry by us for all information regardless of source. The Resumen General sections from each census were of especial value to the data collection effort due to the presence in summary form of statistics on important variables consolidated by state. In some cases, these were not available using state volumes only.

The World Fertility Survey data are from the Mexican part of a worldwide survey undertaken in the late 1970s, which eventually compiled fertility data from 42 developing nations and 20 developed nations covering 39 percent of the world's population. The survey was conducted under the supervision of the International Statistical Institute in conjunction with statistical interviewing teams in collaborating nations (WFS, 1980). The Mexican survey, known as the Encuesta Mexicana de Fecundidad, was undertaken in 1976-77 and surveyed women members of households. Of the 7,672 respondents in Mexico who were surveyed, 7,310 (93.5%) were successfully interviewed. The survey covered individual attributes in fertility, family planning, migration, health, and socioeconomic characteristics. The computer tape for this survey was obtained by special permission of the Mexican government.

Additional data covering 1981-85 were obtained from the Anuario Estadistico, an annual statistical almanac containing a wide variety of information collected by the Mexican government and published by the Mexican Census (SPP, various volumes). Anuario data were gathered by various federal government agencies and therefore vary in accuracy due to the variety of data gathering techniques utilized. Also, some data were utilized from Florescano (1983), the Anuario Estadistico of Pemex (1986), and miscellaneous cited federal government publications.

The text emphasizes simple interpretation and comparisons. If there are regional differences and/or major differences among states, these are pointed out. Simple descriptive statistics are often referred to. For longitudinal data series, trends and change over time are discussed. At times, textual material may also refer to other maps showing similarities or contrasts. To assist in our comparions, a correlation matrix was computed for the full set of atlas variables; this matrix is available by request from the authors. Generally, the correlation coefficient examines the relationship between two variables with a range from -1.0 to 1.0 (Afifi and Azen,1972; Blalock, 1979). Also reported in the atlas for many dimensions is the arithmetic average for the states, or the mean. Finally, to present some idea of relative homogeneity among variables, the coefficient of variation (CV) is reported. The CV is a measure of related variables that takes into account deviation relative to the mean (Afifi and Azen,1972; Blalock, 1979). The coefficient of variation is defined as 100 times the ratio of the standard deviation to the mean. The CV thus allows a relative comparison of variation among all variables. In the text, a CV of less than 20 is treated as small or narrow; a CV between 21-99 is considered middle-range; while a CV of 100 and greater is considered as large.

Mapping Methodology

Once data from various sources were gathered, they were processed for statistical and mapping purposes using several software packages, especially ARC/INFO, SPSS-X, and SAS. The processing was done on a VAX 8700 at the University of California, Riverside. ARC/INFO (ESRI, 1985) is a comprehensive geographic information system package designed to develop and manipulate spatially oriented data-bases by linking attribute information to geographic entities represented as points, lines, or polygons. SPSS-X (SPSS Inc., 1986) and SAS (SAS Statistical Institute, 1985) are well known generalized statistical packages.

State and municipio level maps were automated using conventional cartographic techniques on a digitizing board at a scale of approximately one inch to 58 miles. Besides the coverage of the state boundary base map, several other map coverages were digitized including the international boundaries and the historical railroad network. These coverages are currently maintained in digitizing board inches.

Data were entered and manipulated and maps created by the following steps:

1. Data were input and tested for accuracy in a text editor data file.

2. An INFO file was defined specifically for each text editor data file. The raw data values from Step 1 were then loaded into the INFO template and reviewed for accuracy again.

3. The unique state or municipio identification code from the geographic state or municipio coverage file was joined to the raw INFO data files using ARC/INFO functions.

4. Many raw data values were transformed using the CALCULATE command in INFO to produce final ratio variables which were utilized for many maps.

5. These ratios for final variables were sorted to determine the range of the variables among the states.

6. For state maps, states were grouped approximately into quintiles from lowest to highest values of the variable being mapped, and assigned shading symbols. For municipio maps, municipios were similarly grouped into sextiles. Legend information was gathered manually at this time.

7. The INFO data files were re-sorted by the unique state or municipio identification code before further processing to assure appropriate shading for each variable.

8. Text editor files required by ARC/INFO for producing legends were created.

9. Text editor files of ARC/INFO ARCPLOT commands were created.

10. VAX batch queues were utilized to submit the files from Step 9 to ARC/INFO and produce ARC/INFO plot files for each variable.

11. Finally, plot files were spooled from the VAX to a high resolution CALCOMP plotter to produce hardcopy maps.

12. Statistical analyses were performed by transferring data from the INFO data-base into data

files, which were then accessed by the SPSS-X and SAS packages, to produce sorts, descriptive statistics, correlations, etc.

13. A systematic set of files was built to include all variables in the atlas. Computerized documentation was maintained to keep track of variable definitions, variable names, publication sources of each variable, and mapping codes. Also, a computerized codebook was maintained and updated in a file to keep track of the organization of the statistical files.

Overall, the methodology relied on well-known, large scale packages, which were integrated together through file connections. Such a complex project is most effectively created on a minicomputer. However, simplified versions of the present project could be accomplished on a large micro with appropriate digitizing and plotting equipment.

The Base Maps

Two base maps are presented. These base maps are essential for an understanding of the other material presented in the atlas. The numbers attached to the states in Map 1.1 are referred to throughout the remainder of the atlas -- that is, state 1 is always Aguascalientes, etc. The Base Map 1.2 outlines regions often referred to in the textual material accompanying each map subsequently presented in the atlas. As we indicated earlier, there is no consensus regarding regions of Mexico, but in order to reduce textual material, these regions will be referred to when it seems appropriate to do so. That is, if the distribution of certain variables being examined fit these regions it will be indicated. For other variables, there may not be a fit and thus the dimension will be discussed state by state.

Atlas Variables

The variables presented in this atlas are only a few of the multitude available in numerous Mexican government publications and reports and from private agencies. The atlas primarily utilizes the 1980 Mexican census and subsequently published Anuarios up through 1987. However, available in these and a variety of other sources is information covering lengthy time periods of Mexican history, especially beginning in 1895. In addition to the dimensions and time periods presented in this atlas, the UCR Mexico Database Project contains a substantially larger computerized database of Mexico. This atlas, then, is only illustrative of the range of variables and time periods actually contained in the Mexico database. Plans are for subsequent editions of this atlas to contain other dimensions as well as over varying time periods.

The range of variables and time periods contained in this edition of the atlas were constrained by cost considerations rather than database limitations. For those who are interested in obtaining the computerized state database for the variables included in this atlas, or who would like to obtain maps, computer graphics, data analysis, etc. from the larger database, information may be obtained by writing to the following address :

Butler/Pick, Mexico Database Project
Department of Sociology,
University of California, Riverside, CA 92521
Tel : (714)787-5444

Table 1.1 Mexican Regions

Region Number	Name	States
1.	NORTHWEST	Baja California Baja California Sur Sinaloa Sonora Nayarit
2.	NORTH	Coahuila Chihuahua Durango San Luis Potosi Zacatecas
3.	NORTHEAST	Nuevo Leon Tamaulipas
4.	WEST	Aguascalientes Colima Guanajuato Jalisco Michoacan
5.	CENTRAL	Distrito Federal Hidalgo Mexico Morelos Puebla Queretaro Tlaxcala
6.	GULF	Tabasco Veracruz
7.	PACIFIC SOUTH	Chiapas Guerrero Oaxaca
8.	SOUTHEAST	Campeche Quintana Roo Yucatan

SOURCE: 1976-77 World Fertility Survey.

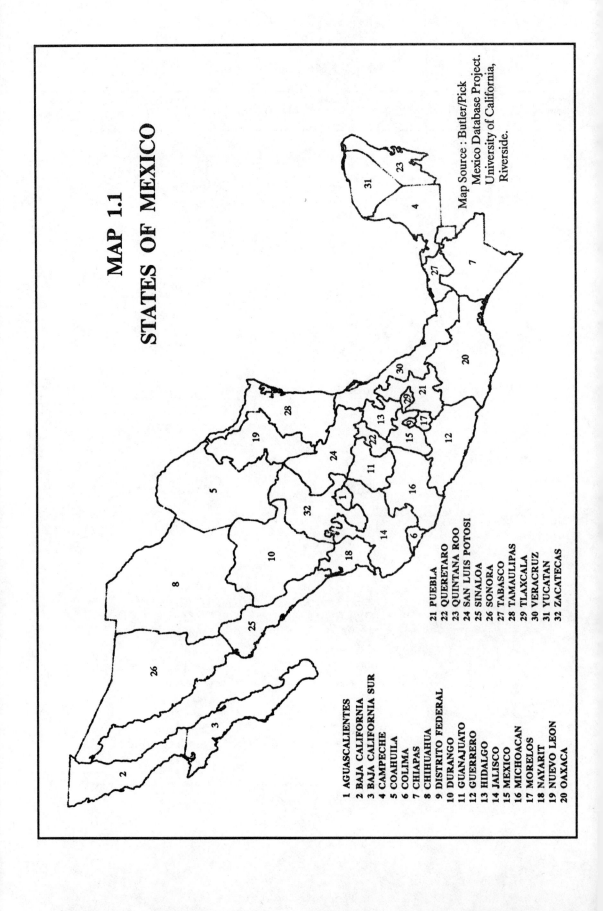

MAP 1.1
STATES OF MEXICO

1 AGUASCALIENTES
2 BAJA CALIFORNIA
3 BAJA CALIFORNIA SUR
4 CAMPECHE
5 COAHUILA
6 COLIMA
7 CHIAPAS
8 CHIHUAHUA
9 DISTRITO FEDERAL
10 DURANGO
11 GUANAJUATO
12 GUERRERO
13 HIDALGO
14 JALISCO
15 MEXICO
16 MICHOACAN
17 MORELOS
18 NAYARIT
19 NUEVO LEON
20 OAXACA

21 PUEBLA
22 QUERETARO
23 QUINTANA ROO
24 SAN LUIS POTOSI
25 SINALOA
26 SONORA
27 TABASCO
28 TAMAULIPAS
29 TLAXCALA
30 VERACRUZ
31 YUCATAN
32 ZACATECAS

Map Source : Butler/Pick
Mexico Database Project.
University of California,
Riverside.

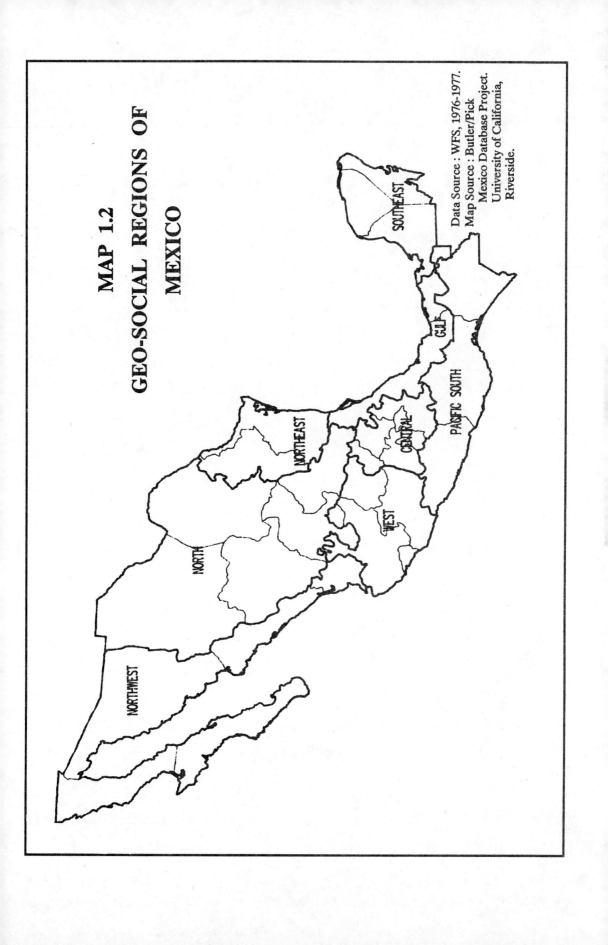

MAP 1.2
GEO-SOCIAL REGIONS OF
MEXICO

NORTHWEST

NORTH

NORTHEAST

WEST

CENTRAL

PACIFIC SOUTH

GULF

SOUTHEAST

Data Source : WFS, 1976-1977.
Map Source : Butler/Pick
Mexico Database Project.
University of California,
Riverside.

2

POPULATION AND URBANIZATION

Introduction

This chapter covers topics related to Mexican population, population age structure, population density, and urbanization. It presents the data and describes geographic distributions. Although focus is at the state level for Mexico as a whole, the population and urbanization of the U.S.-Mexico border region are analyzed in more detail by focusing on municipios. Municipios are units in Mexican states somewhat comparable to U.S. counties. Historical trends are analyzed by means of several maps, tables, and graphs for population and urbanization in the 20th century. The data in this chapter are primarily from various Mexican census volumes and <u>anuarios</u>. Rates and other statistics were calculated utilizing data abstracted from these volumes.

Total Population

From 1900 to 1980, the Mexican population increased by about five-fold to total 66.8 million in 1980. Tables 2.1A and 2.1B present population data by state, for census years 1900, 1930, 1950, 1970, and 1980, as well as percentage population change between 1970 and 1980. Map 2.1A portrays population distribution in 1980.

The Mexican population grew at an increasing rate over the eighty year period. Average decennial population growth rates for the nation increased from 6.5 percent for the 1900-30 period to 24.8 percent for 1930-50, 36.7 percent for 1950-70, and 39.8 percent between 1970-80. The rate of increase slowed in the latter 1970s, due to lowering in age-adjusted fertility rates. Nevertheless, population increased in the 1970s by a total of about 19 million, at an average annual rate of 3.3 percent. Figure 2.1 illustrates population changes by region from 1900 to 1980.

As shown on Maps 2.1A and 2.1B, both in 1900 and 1980, the geographic distribution by state of the Mexican population was rather consistent, although the following four regional patterns of change are apparent:

Population Concentration in the State of Mexico. Although it contained substantial population in 1900, the state of Mexico increased in importance over the eighty years. In fact, the proportion of population in Mexico state increased from 6.9 percent in 1900 to 11.2 percent in 1980. Recent decades' increase has been due in large part to growth of the central metropolis outside of the Federal District boundaries into adjoining states.

Not apparent on the maps is the rapid population increase of the Federal District itself. The District was not formed in 1900, so its population must be estimated. The smaller city, versus metropolitan, population of Mexico City was 419,304 in 1900, 3.1 percent of the national population. By 1930, the Federal District's population accounted for 7.4 percent of Mexico, and in 1980 had increased to 13.2 percent.

Increasing Importance of the Northern Border States. The borderlands region increased in overall importance from 1900 to 1980. This region, consisting of the six states of Baja California, Coahuila, Chihuahua, Nuevo Leon, Sonora, and Tamaulipas, grew from 10.6 percent of the national population in 1900 to 15.9 percent in 1980. Over the full eighty year period, especially rapid growth took place in Baja California (25-fold increase), Tamaulipas (9-fold) and Nuevo Leon (8-fold). Looking at the border cities in 1980 (Map 2.10A), Baja California and Tamaulipas each contained several large border cities, which grew rapidly in the 60s and 70s. The rapid growth of Nuevo Leon stems mainly from Monterrey urban area growth.

Population Change in Certain Central States. It is clear from the maps that states in the southern north region, plus Guanajuato and Hidalgo just to the south, decreased substantially as a percent of national population from 1900 to 1980. While the five states comprised 22.6 percent of Mexico's 1900 population, they accounted for only 12.7 percent of its 1980 population. The decrease stemmed in part from rural-to-urban outmigration to Mexico City as well as from the relative weakness in the economies of the five states.

Population Change in Oaxaca. Oaxaca's national population proportion decreased from 7.0 percent in 1900 to 3.5 percent in 1980. Oaxaca's slower growth vis-a-vis the nation is mostly due to a large volume of net outmigration especially to the Federal District (Fukurai et al., 1987b) as well as to higher standardized mortality rates in the region. (See Map 5.1C.)

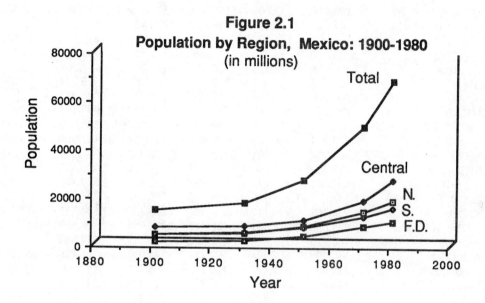

Figure 2.1
Population by Region, Mexico: 1900-1980
(in millions)

SOURCE: Estadisticas Historicas de Mexico, 1985.

Table 2.1A Total Population, 1900-1980

No.	State	1900	1930	1950	1970	1980	Population Growth 1970-80
1	AGUASCALIENTES	102,416	132,900	188,075	338,142	519,439	0.5362
2	BAJA CALIFORNIA	47,624	48,327	226,965	870,421	1,177,886	0.3532
3	BAJA CALIFORNIA SUR	*	47,089	60,864	128,019	215,139	0.6805
4	CAMPECHE	86,542	84,630	122,098	251,556	420,553	0.6718
5	COAHUILA	296,938	436,425	720,619	1,114,956	1,557,265	0.3967
6	COLIMA	65,115	61,923	112,321	241,153	346,293	0.4360
7	CHIAPAS	360,799	529,983	907,026	1,569,053	2,084,717	0.3286
8	CHIHUAHUA	327,784	491,792	846,414	1,612,525	2,005,477	0.2437
9	DISTRITO FEDERAL	541,516	1,229,576	3,050,442	6,874,165	8,831,079	0.2847
10	DURANGO	370,294	404,364	629,874	939,208	1,182,320	0.2588
11	GUANAJUATO	1,061,724	987,801	1,328,712	2,270,370	3,006,110	0.3241
12	GUERRERO	479,205	641,690	919,386	1,597,360	2,109,513	0.3206
13	HIDALGO	605,051	677,772	850,394	1,193,845	1,547,493	0.2962
14	JALISCO	1,153,891	1,255,346	1,746,777	3,296,586	4,371,998	0.3262
15	MEXICO	934,463	990,112	1,392,623	3,833,185	7,564,335	0.9734
16	MICHOACAN	935,808	1,048,381	1,422,717	2,324,226	2,868,824	0.2343
17	MORELOS	160,115	132,068	272,842	616,119	947,089	0.5372
18	NAYARIT	150,098	167,724	290,124	544,031	726,120	0.3347
19	NUEVO LEON	327,937	417,491	740,191	1,694,689	2,513,044	0.4829
20	OAXACA	948,633	1,084,549	1,421,313	2,015,424	2,369,076	0.1755
21	PUEBLA	1,021,133	1,150,425	1,625,830	2,508,226	3,347,685	0.3347
22	QUERETARO	232,389	234,058	286,238	485,523	739,605	0.5233
23	QUINTANA ROO	**	10,620	26,967	88,150	225,985	1.5636
24	SAN LUIS POTOSI	575,432	579,831	856,066	1,281,996	1,673,893	0.3057
25	SINALOA	296,701	395,618	635,681	1,266,528	1,849,879	0.4606
26	SONORA	221,682	316,271	510,607	1,098,720	1,513,731	0.3777
27	TABASCO	159,834	224,023	362,716	768,327	1,062,961	0.3835
28	TAMAULIPAS	218,948	344,039	718,167	1,456,858	1,924,484	0.3210
29	TLAXCALA	172,315	205,458	284,551	420,638	556,597	0.3232
30	VERACRUZ	981,030	1,377,293	2,040,231	3,815,422	5,387,680	0.4121
31	YUCATAN	309,652	386,096	516,899	758,355	1,063,733	0.4027
32	ZACATECAS	462,190	459,047	665,524	951,462	1,136,830	0.1948
	Mean	453,575	517,271	805,595	1,507,039	2,088,964	0.4312
	S.D.	337,039	409,423	669,863	1,395,786	1,993,948	0.2610
	C.V.	74.31	79.15	83.15	92.62	95.45	60.5288
	Minimum	47,624	10,206	26,967	88,150	215,139	0.1755
	Maximum	1,153,891	1,377,293	3,050,442	6,874,165	8,831,079	1.5636
	National Total	13,607,272	16,552,722	25,779,254	48,225,238	66,846,833	

DEFINITION: Population Growth 1970-80 is the ratio of total population 1980 minus the total population 1970 to the total population 1970.

SOURCE: 1900 Mexican Census of Population; 1930, 1950 and 1970 Mexican Censuses of Population, Resumen General; 1980 Mexican Census of Population, Volume 1, Table 2.

* Baja California Sur was a territory and included with Baja California in 1900.
** Quintana Roo was a territory and included with Yucatan in 1900.

Table 2.1B Population by Region, 1900, 1930, 1950, 1970, 1980 (in thousands)

A. Region	1900	1930	1950	1970	1980
NORTHWEST	716	975	1,724	3,908	5,483
NORTHEAST	543	762	1,458	3,151	4,438
NORTH	2,033	2,371	3,718	5,900	7,556
WEST	3,319	3,486	4,799	8,470	11,113
FEDERAL DISTRICT	542	1,230	3,050	6,874	8,831
CENTRAL	3,125	3,390	4,712	9,058	14,703
GULF	1,141	1,601	2,403	4,584	6,451
SOUTHEAST	396	481	666	1,098	1,710
SOUTH PACIFIC	1,789	2,256	3,248	5,182	6,563
TOTAL	13,608	16,552	25,778	48,226	66,848
B. Region					
NORTH (Consolidated)	3,296	4,108	6,900	12,959	17,477
CENTRAL (Consolidated)	6,444	6,876	9,511	17,528	25,816
FEDERAL DISTRICT	542	1,230	3,050	6,874	8,831
SOUTH (Consolidated)	3,326	4,338	6,317	10,864	14,724
TOTAL	13,608	16,552	25,778	48,225	66,848

NOTES: Population for Quintana Roo in 1900 was included in Yucatan. Population for Baja California Sur in 1900 was included in Baja California. In panel B, north consolidated includes the northwest, northeast, and north regions from panel A. The central region in panel B includes the west and central regions from panel A. The south region in panel B includes the gulf, southeast, and south pacific regions from panel A.

SOURCE: Mexico Census of Population, 1900-1980.

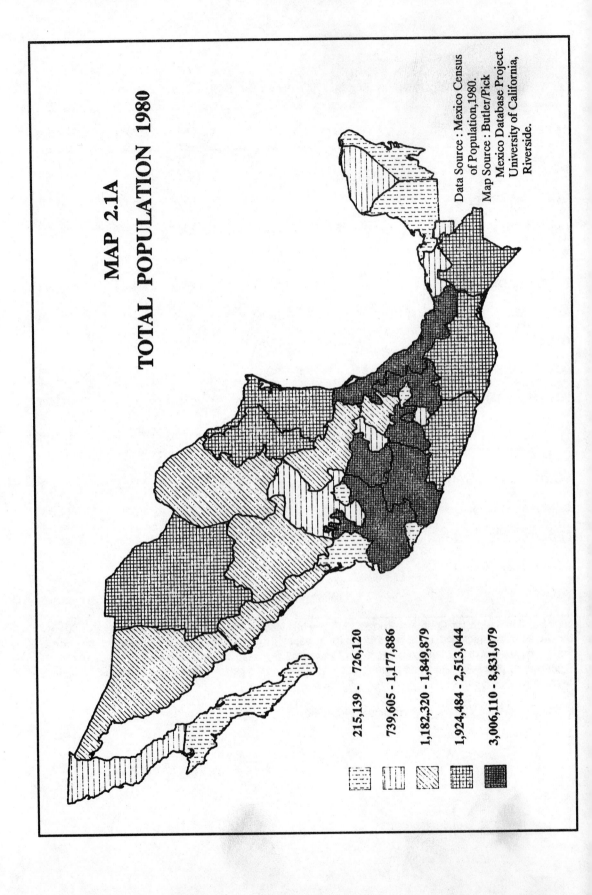

MAP 2.1A

TOTAL POPULATION 1980

215,139 -   726,120

739,605 - 1,177,886

1,182,320 - 1,849,879

1,924,484 - 2,513,044

3,006,110 - 8,831,079

Data Source : Mexico Census
    of Population, 1980.

Map Source : Butler/Pick
    Mexico Database Project.
    University of California,
    Riverside.

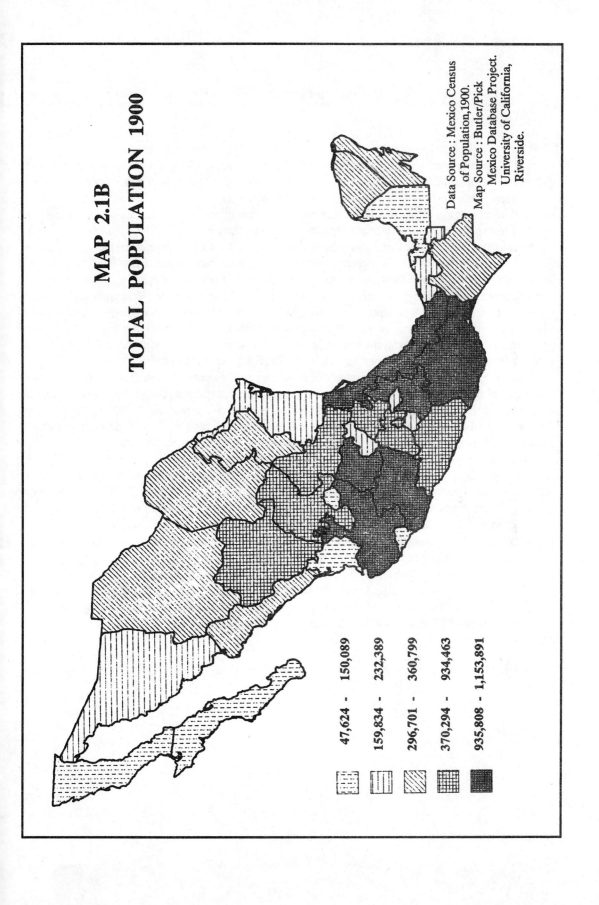

MAP 2.1B

TOTAL POPULATION 1900

47,624 - 150,089

159,834 - 232,389

296,701 - 360,799

370,294 - 934,463

935,808 - 1,153,891

Data Source : Mexico Census
of Population,1900.

Map Source : Butler/Pick
Mexico Database Project.
University of California,
Riverside.

Population Growth, 1970-1980

Poulation growth between 1970 and 1980 is shown on Table 2.1A and Map 2.2. From 1970 to 1980 Mexico's population grew by 38.6 percent, at an average compound annual growth rate of 3.26 percent. This compares to compound rates of 3.23 percent in the 1960s and 1.99 percent from 1900 to 1980. The mean 1970-80 state percentage change was 43.1 percent, with a moderate coefficient of variation of 61. No state lost population between 1970 and 1980.

State percentage changes reveal areas of rapid and slow growth, which on the whole do not correspond to the boundaries of standard regions. Although the Federal District had slow growth, the surrounding states of Mexico and Morelos grew rapidly, reflecting metropolitan overspill from the Federal District. Nuevo Leon's high percent increase (48 percent) primarily reflected continuing growth in the metropolis of Monterrey. Aguascalientes' rapid growth (54 percent) largely reflected population expansion and economic growth in the city of Aguascalientes. Very high growth rates for Baja California Sur (68 percent) and Quintana Roo (156 percent) were indicative of small states which had substantial economic growth in the 70s (both have high 1980 per capita gross state products) as well as increases in the tourist industry. These states and Campeche (67 percent) represent a type of Mexican phenomenon similar to "Sunbelt" growth in the U.S.

Areas of slow growth encompass most of one region and scattered states. The north region, excepting Coahuila, grew in the 70s by 25 percent, reflecting a compound growth rate at two thirds the mean state rate. Its slow growth stems partly from the economic weakness of the region, as shown by low to medium per capita gross state products. The Federal District (28 percent) exhibited reduced growth, due in part to low fertility and economic and environmental constraints related to its highly urbanized, congested, and polluted nature. The slow growth rates of Tamaulipas (32 percent) and Hidalgo (30 percent) were due in part to weaknesses in the state economies. In the pacific south and west, Oaxaca (18 percent), Guerrero (32 percent), and Michoacan (23 percent) had slow growth. These states have historically been among Mexico's poorest states, as reflected in low per capita gross state products (except Oaxaca) and low income levels. In addition, Oaxaca and Guerrero sent substantial numbers of migrants to the central zone in the 70s (Fukurai et al., 1987b).

It is important to note that in the 70s the geographical distribution of absolute population increase differs from the distribution of percent population increase. Absolute growth 1970-80 was centered in the big five populous, urbanized states of the Federal District, Mexico, Jalisco, Puebla, and Veracruz, plus Nuevo Leon containing the metropolis of Monterrey. In 1980, together these six states contained 47 percent of the Mexican population but accounted for 52 percent of absolute population growth 1970-80.

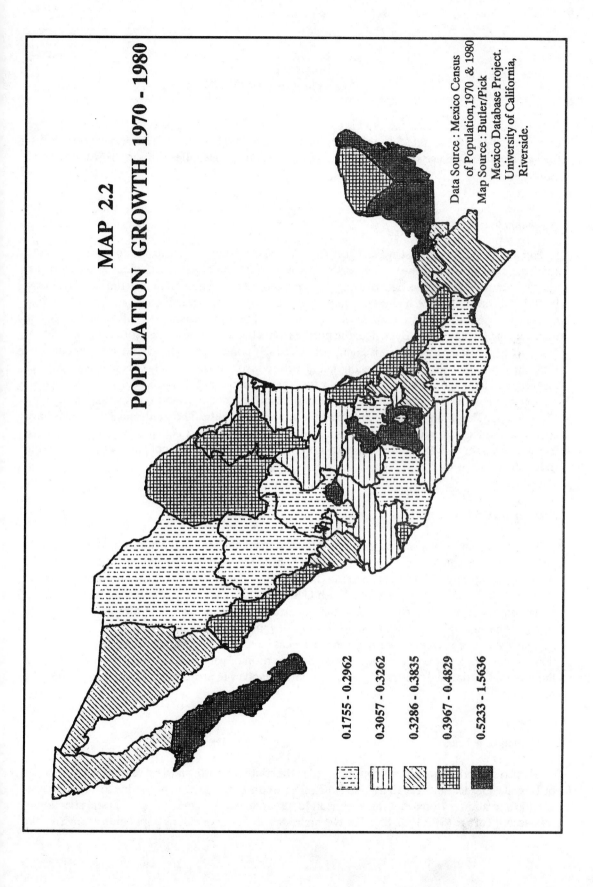

MAP 2.2

POPULATION GROWTH 1970 - 1980

Data Source : Mexico Census
of Population,1970 & 1980

Map Source : Butler/Pick
Mexico Database Project.
University of California,
Riverside.

0.1755 - 0.2962

0.3057 - 0.3262

0.3286 - 0.3835

0.3967 - 0.4829

0.5233 - 1.5636

Age Structure, 1980

Population age structure for 1980 is measured by percent of the total population in three age categories, 0-17, 18-64, and 65+, and by the dependency ratio (see Table 2.2). Mexico reveals distinct areal patterns in age structure, with the most variegated state differences in the southeast and gulf regions.

Population 0-17 Years

Population in the youngest age category (Map 2.3A) is concentrated in an area encompassing the southern parts of the northwest and north regions, plus the states of Aguascalientes, Guanajuato, and Queretaro. These areas had relatively high annual and cumulative fertility in the late 70s (Maps 3.2B, 3.2C, and 3.2E). The highest proportion of young population is in Zacatecas. This may be related to the rural nature of the state, which was only 38 percent urbanized in 1980, and to higher than average fertility rates. By region, the northeast has the lowest proportion of young population (49 percent). Not surprisingly, it is highly urbanized (81 percent) with low standarized annual fertility rates in 1979. Also, its urban economic structure favors smaller family size, lower proportion married, and later age at marriage especially for Nuevo Leon (Maps 3.1A, 3.1C).

Among the federal entities, the Federal District has the lowest proportion of young population (44 percent). This is largely due to historically low rates of fertility. The south and gulf regions have an inconsistent age structure pattern. For instance, Tabasco has a very high percentage young, while Yucatan has a very low percentage. These age structural differences do not appear directly related to fertility differences.

Population 18-64 Years

The proportion of working population of 18-64 years is elevated in the borderlands, the Federal District, and the state of Yucatan (Map 2.3B). Substantial working population contributes to the economic prosperity of the first two areas (Map 8.4B). The border states contain prosperous job markets which often adjoin and interact with U.S. urban job markets. In the case of Yucatan, there is high urbanization (75 percent) and a major metropolitan labor market in Merida. These three areas, not surprisingly, are low in the percentage of young population. The western region and its adjoining states of Nayarit, Durango, and Zacatecas have low proportions of working age population. Again, this is the converse side of a high proportion of young. The central region, excepting the Federal District, and south regions have generally moderate proportions of working age population.

Population 65+ Years

Mexico's elderly population is concentrated in the southern north and west regions, plus the states of Tlaxcala, Oaxaca, and Yucatan (Map 2.3C). These concentrations are partly due to historical age-specific migration patterns, but this is difficult to research because census migration statistics do not take account of age (SPP, 1982-85). The two highest proportions of elderly population are in Yucatan

(5.1 percent) and Tlaxcala (4.6 percent). Quintana Roo's lowest level in proportion elderly of 2.1 percent may be due in part to its explosive growth in the 70's, attracting typically younger migrants.

Dependency Ratio, 1980

The dependency ratio measures the ratio of dependents, i.e. children, adolescents, and elderly, to working age population. It is important to note that in Mexico the age structure is such that dependents consist mostly of the young rather than the elderly (compare Maps 2.3A and 2.3C). The mean state dependency ratio of 1.23 is nearly double that of the U.S. in 1980 (Bogue, 1985). Although there is low overall variation in dependency ratio (coefficient of variation equals 9), the percentage range between the lowest value for the Federal District and highest value for Zacatecas is 65 percent. The Federal District's dependency ratio of 0.92 is the result of an age structure weighted towards working age population. From a social welfare standpoint, the District's low dependency is fortunate in counteracting some already unmanageable problems (Schteingart, 1988). At the high end, Zacatecas's dependency ratio results from very high proportion of both the young and elderly.

As shown on Map 2.3D and Table 2.2, border states have low dependency ratios, which is the result of a low proportion of young people, combined with a low proportion of elderly in Baja and Chihuahua. Baja's dependency ratio of 1.06 is the second lowest in the nation. Additional factors reducing dependency in Baja may be a prosperous economy -- second only to the Federal District in high income per capita, and the presence of unattached, working-age males, awaiting opportunities to migrate to the U.S. In the gulf, southeast, and south regions, dependency ratios vary considerably. The ratio is highest in Tabasco and impoverished Guerrero, and lowest in the more urban Yucatan. Regional and state differences in dependency call for further research study as well as attention by the Mexican government, in order to optimize social benefits in economic, health, and other programs.

Table 2.2 Age Structure, 1980

No.	State	Age 0 - 17 Population	Ratio	Age 18 - 64 Population	Ratio	Age 65+ Population	Ratio	Dependency Ratio	Total Population
1	AGUASCALIENTES	274,506	0.5285	223,885	0.4310	20,827	0.0401	1.3191	519,439
2	BAJA CALIFORNIA	568,671	0.4828	570,451	0.4843	37,464	0.0318	1.0626	1,177,886
3	BAJA CALIFORNIA SUR	107,955	0.5018	100,034	0.4650	7,020	0.0326	1.1494	215,139
4	CAMPECHE	214,071	0.5090	192,356	0.4574	13,735	0.0327	1.1843	420,553
5	COAHUILA	783,452	0.5031	713,843	0.4584	58,876	0.0378	1.1800	1,557,265
6	COLIMA	178,036	0.5141	154,598	0.4464	13,460	0.0389	1.2387	346,293
7	CHIAPAS	1,051,222	0.5043	923,406	0.4429	61,860	0.0297	1.2054	2,084,717
8	CHIHUAHUA	990,960	0.4941	933,050	0.4653	53,142	0.0265	1.1190	2,005,477
9	DISTRITO FEDERAL	3,885,898	0.4400	4,593,743	0.5202	347,581	0.0394	0.9216	8,831,079
10	DURANGO	633,392	0.5357	495,734	0.4193	46,618	0.0394	1.3717	1,182,320
11	GUANAJUATO	1,588,595	0.5285	1,287,191	0.4282	125,083	0.0416	1.3313	3,006,110
12	GUERRERO	1,105,178	0.5239	916,098	0.4343	82,232	0.0390	1.2962	2,109,513
13	HIDALGO	800,274	0.5171	681,542	0.4404	63,500	0.0410	1.2674	1,547,493
14	JALISCO	2,213,050	0.5062	1,925,890	0.4405	192,968	0.0441	1.2493	4,371,998
15	MEXICO	3,908,022	0.5166	3,440,265	0.4548	204,721	0.0271	1.1955	7,564,335
16	MICHOACAN	1,509,122	0.5261	1,232,161	0.4295	123,879	0.0432	1.3254	2,868,824
17	MORELOS	472,569	0.4990	434,604	0.4589	38,486	0.0406	1.1759	947,089
18	NAYARIT	385,083	0.5303	309,873	0.4268	30,937	0.0426	1.3426	726,120
19	NUEVO LEON	1,229,559	0.4893	1,189,939	0.4735	92,350	0.0367	1.1109	2,513,044
20	OAXACA	1,183,191	0.4994	1,070,295	0.4518	103,627	0.0437	1.2023	2,369,076
21	PUEBLA	1,701,258	0.5082	1,480,667	0.4423	143,394	0.0428	1.2458	3,347,685
22	QUERETARO	396,788	0.5365	314,618	0.4254	27,911	0.0377	1.3499	739,605
23	QUINTANA ROO	117,368	0.5194	103,465	0.4578	4,764	0.0211	1.1804	225,985
24	SAN LUIS POTOSI	874,557	0.5225	723,571	0.4323	74,042	0.0442	1.3110	1,673,893
25	SINALOA	965,143	0.5217	816,500	0.4414	65,187	0.0352	1.2619	1,849,879
26	SONORA	745,363	0.4924	714,189	0.4718	53,042	0.0350	1.1179	1,513,731
27	TABASCO	567,377	0.5338	462,187	0.4348	32,462	0.0305	1.2978	1,062,961
28	TAMAULIPAS	943,497	0.4903	901,926	0.4687	77,690	0.0404	1.1322	1,924,484
29	TLAXCALA	289,816	0.5207	240,042	0.4313	25,728	0.0462	1.3145	556,597
30	VERACRUZ	2,671,252	0.4958	2,499,413	0.4639	208,413	0.0387	1.1521	5,387,680
31	YUCATAN	498,698	0.4688	508,273	0.4778	54,655	0.0514	1.0887	1,063,733
32	ZACATECAS	634,112	0.5578	450,213	0.3960	50,578	0.0445	1.5208	1,136,830
	Mean	104,650	0.5099	956,376	0.4491	79,257	0.0380	1.22567	2,088,964
	S.D.	953,118	0.0225	974,239	0.0234	73,534	0.0065	0.11374	1,993,948
	C.V.	91,076	4.41	101,868	5.21	92,779	17.11	9.280	95.452
	Minimum	107,955	0.4400	100,034	0.3960	4,764	0.0211	0.92160	215,139
	Maximum	3,908,022	0.5578	4,593,743	0.5202	347,581	0.0514	1.5208	8,831,079

DEFINITION: Ratio is the population age 0-17 and age 65+ to age 18-64.

SOURCE: 1980 Mexican Census of Population, Volume 1, Table 1.

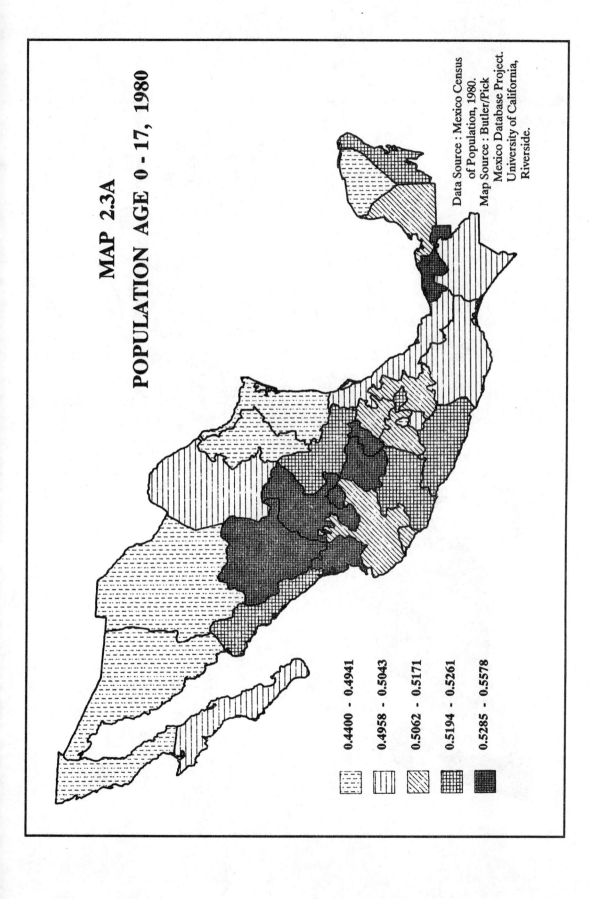

MAP 2.3A
POPULATION AGE 0 - 17, 1980

Data Source : Mexico Census
of Population, 1980.
Map Source : Butler/Pick
Mexico Database Project.
University of California,
Riverside.

0.4400 - 0.4941

0.4958 - 0.5043

0.5062 - 0.5171

0.5194 - 0.5261

0.5285 - 0.5578

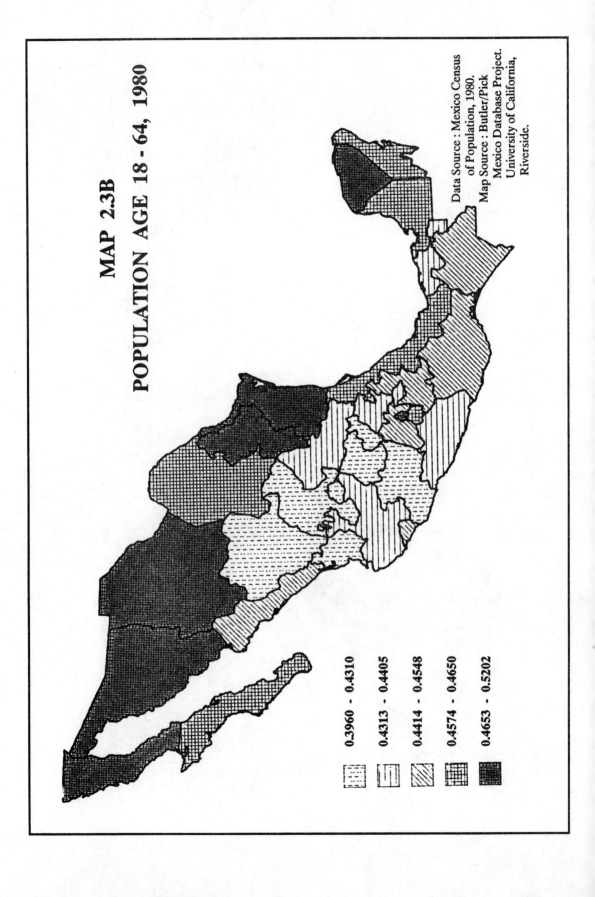

MAP 2.3B

POPULATION AGE 18 - 64, 1980

Data Source : Mexico Census
of Population, 1980.

Map Source : Butler/Pick
Mexico Database Project.
University of California,
Riverside.

0.3960 - 0.4310

0.4313 - 0.4405

0.4414 - 0.4548

0.4574 - 0.4650

0.4653 - 0.5202

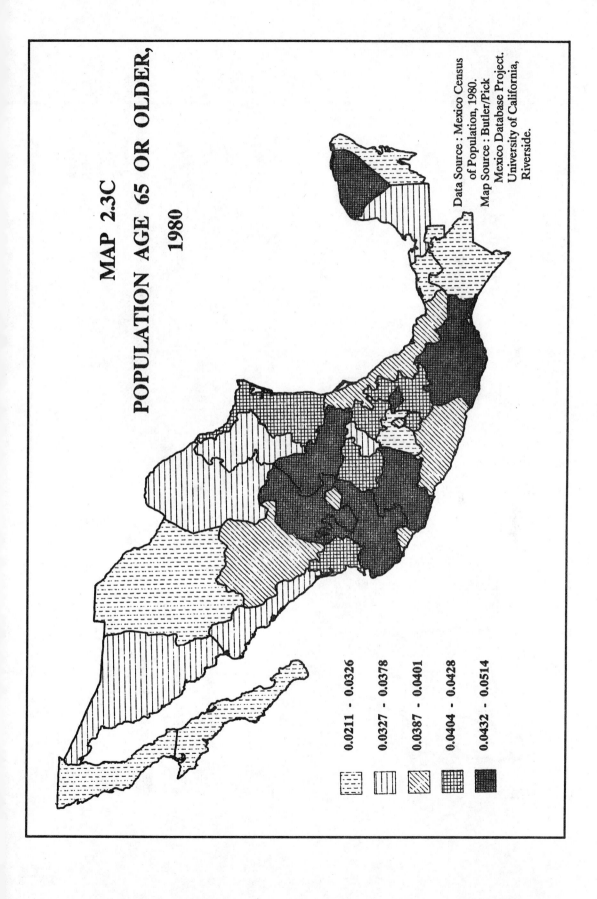

MAP 2.3C

POPULATION AGE 65 OR OLDER,

1980

Data Source : Mexico Census
of Population, 1980.
Map Source : Butler/Pick
Mexico Database Project.
University of California,
Riverside.

0.0211 - 0.0326

0.0327 - 0.0378

0.0387 - 0.0401

0.0404 - 0.0428

0.0432 - 0.0514

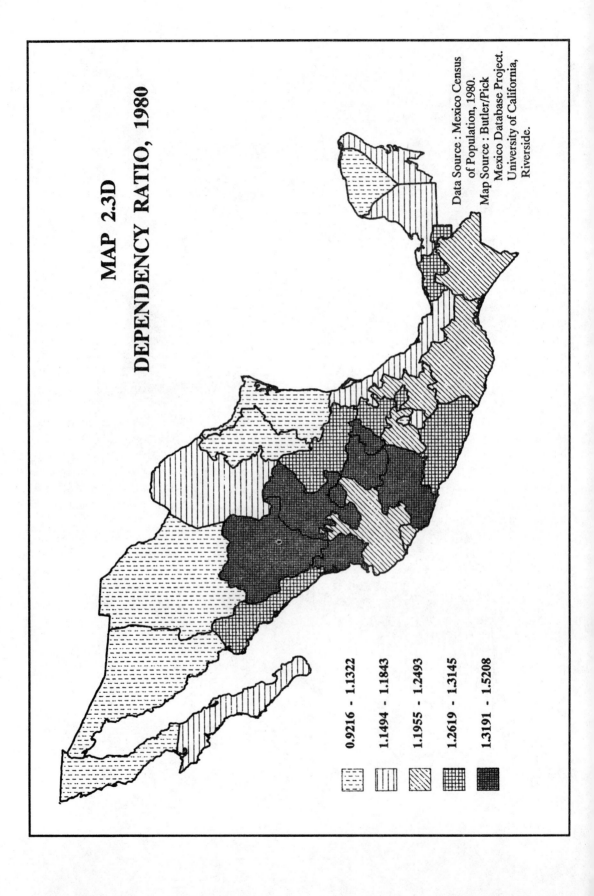

MAP 2.3D

DEPENDENCY RATIO, 1980

Data Source : Mexico Census
  of Population, 1980.
Map Source : Butler/Pick
  Mexico Database Project.
  University of California,
  Riverside.

0.9216 - 1.1322

1.1494 - 1.1843

1.1955 - 1.2493

1.2619 - 1.3145

1.3191 - 1.5208

Sex Ratio, 1980

The sex ratio is defined as the ratio of the number of males to females. A sex ratio above 1.0 indicates a preponderance of males, while one below 1.0 indicates more females. Sex ratios showed a slight coefficient of variation of three among Mexican states. As shown in Table 2.3, the mean sex ratio is 0.99, which compares to a 1980 U.S. sex ratio of 0.95 (Bogue, 1985). This difference is not surprising, since the U.S. population is substantially older, reflecting greater influence of higher male mortality rates at older ages. There is a positive correlation of the sex ratio with male economic activity and a negative one with female economic activity, both highly significant. This is consistent with a higher sex ratio implying that more males are available for economic participation. Fairly consistent regional patterns are apparent in the northwest, northeast, and west (see Map 2.4). In the northwest there is a high sex ratio, except for Baja California. In contrast to its neighboring states, Baja has very low male economic activity and very high female economic activity (see Tables 8.2 and 8.3). Part of this effect may stem from the influence of industries with differential hiring by sex. An example of such opposite appeal in Baja California is maquiladora industry, where it is much more prevalent than in the rest of the northwest. Maquilidora industry refers to factories which use large numbers of semiskilled or unskilled workers in production and assembly processes (Stoddard, 1987). Studies have shown that the maquiladora industry has a very low sex ratio, perhaps as low as 0.25 (Stoddard, 1987). The presence of maquiladora industry in Baja may contribute to Baja's low sex ratio.

The northeast is characterized by moderate sex ratios. In Nuevo Leon male and female economic activity are about average. In Tamaulipas male economic activity is relatively higher than female, but this is balanced by a high proportion of aged. The west has a low to moderate sex ratio.

In the central region, the Federal District has the nation's lowest sex ratio (0.92). This corresponds to the nation's lowest male, and highest female economic activity. The Federal District's "spillover" states of Mexico and Morelos and, more distantly, Queretero and Puebla, have low sex ratios, with higher male economic activity levels, except for Queretero.

The sex ratio pattern in the rest of the central and southern part of the north regions are inconsistent and less easily explained by economic activity and age effects. In the remaining regions, gulf, southeast, and north, regional patterns are inconsistent. In the gulf and southeast, a variegated pattern corresponds well to age effects but not to economic activity.

Table 2.3 Sex Ratio, 1980

No.	State	Male Population	Female Population	Sex Ratio
1	AGUASCALIENTES	254,783	264,656	0.9627
2	BAJA CALIFORNIA	580,727	597,159	0.9725
3	BAJA CALIFORNIA SUR	109,550	105,589	1.0375
4	CAMPECHE	209,823	210,730	0.9957
5	COAHUILA	774,010	783,255	0.9882
6	COLIMA	172,453	173,840	0.9920
7	CHIAPAS	1,053,577	1,031,140	1.0218
8	CHIHUAHUA	992,132	1,013,345	0.9791
9	DISTRITO FEDERAL	4,234,602	4,596,477	0.9213
10	DURANGO	589,892	592,428	0.9957
11	GUANAJUATO	1,484,934	1,521,176	0.9762
12	GUERRERO	1,050,308	1,059,205	0.9916
13	HIDALGO	776,233	771,260	1.0064
14	JALISCO	2,133,088	2,238,910	0.9527
15	MEXICO	3,755,869	3,808,466	0.9862
16	MICHOACAN	1,413,567	1,455,257	0.9714
17	MORELOS	468,285	478,804	0.9780
18	NAYARIT	364,459	361,661	1.0077
19	NUEVO LEON	1,251,286	1,261,758	0.9917
20	OAXACA	1,176,733	1,192,343	0.9869
21	PUEBLA	1,647,616	1,700,069	0.9691
22	QUERETARO	368,367	371,238	0.9923
23	QUINTANA ROO	116,360	109,625	1.0614
24	SAN LUIS POTOSI	834,380	839,513	0.9939
25	SINALOA	932,702	917,177	1.0169
26	SONORA	761,047	752,684	1.0111
27	TABASCO	534,793	528,168	1.0125
28	TAMAULIPAS	949,996	974,488	0.9749
29	TLAXCALA	277,476	279,121	0.9941
30	VERACRUZ	2,679,431	2,708,249	0.9894
31	YUCATAN	529,716	534,017	0.9919
32	ZACATECAS	561,112	575,718	0.9746
Mean		1,032,478	1,056,485	0.9905
S.D.		956,333	1,022,760	0.0252
C.V.		92.63	96.81	2.5442
Minimum		109,550	105,589	0.9213
Maximum		4,234,602	4,596,477	1.0614

DEFINITION: Sex Ratio is the male population to the female population.

SOURCE: 1980 Mexican Census of Population, Volume 1, Table 1.

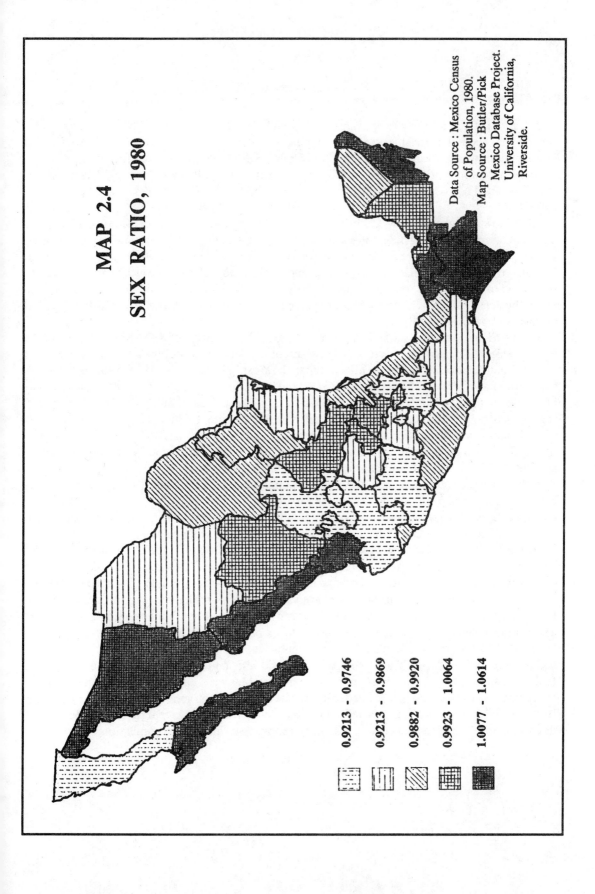

MAP 2.4
SEX RATIO, 1980

0.9213 - 0.9746

0.9213 - 0.9869

0.9882 - 0.9920

0.9923 - 1.0064

1.0077 - 1.0614

Data Source : Mexico Census
of Population, 1980.

Map Source : Butler/Pick
Mexico Database Project.
University of California,
Riverside.

Population Density, 1980

The states of Mexico reveal large variation in population density, measured by persons/km2. Excluding the Federal District, mean state population density is 56.4 persons/km2. The Federal District's density is by far the highest at 5,971 persons/km2. This density reflects the population concentration of the world's largest metropolis. Mexico and Morelos, "overspill" states from metropolitan Mexico City, are next in density levels, with 354 and 191 persons/km^2 respectively (Table 2.4).

At the low extreme are Baja California Sur and Quintana Roo, having densities of 2.9 and 4.5 persons/km^2 respectively. These states are the two lowest in 1980 population, and lack major cities. On the other hand, they were among the top three states in population growth rates, 1970-80. Such high growth may in part reflect the environmental attractiveness of low density land areas, as well as the impact of tourism. The extent of these density extremes is revealed by a 75-fold differential between the density levels of Mexico and Morelos (ignoring the Federal District) and the density levels of Baja Sur and Quintana Roo.

If the nation is viewed as a whole, it may be divided into four zones of decreasing density: (1) the Federal District, Mexico, and Morelos; (2) the rest of the central flank of the country running from Veracruz and Tabasco in the East to Michoacan in the West; (3) portions of Mexico above and below the central flank (states of Coahuila, Zacatecas, and San Luis Potosi), consisting of the eastern part of the north, the northeast, and south regions; and (4) the southeast and a modified "northwest" region, consisting of Baja California, Baja California Sur, Sonora, Chihuahua, and Durango.

Explanations of these differences stem from combinations of historical settlement patterns, location of cities, climate, agriculture, and topographical features such as mountains and deserts. These are briefly discussed for the four density zones (see Map 2.5).

Federal District/Mexico/Morelos. This is the urbanized core of the nation which developed in pre-colonial Mexico and is continuing to increase rapidly.

The Rest of the Central Flank. This region generally has adequate rainfall and reasonable temperatures. It has many major cities which developed for a variety of historical reasons.

Portions of Mexico Above and Below the Central Flank. In the north, the climate is generally of mediocre attractiveness and agriculture is often limited by dryness. In addition, density is reduced by the presence of the Sierra Madre Oriental mountains along its eastern side. The northeast region is near the median in density. Its topographic and climatic features have average attractiveness, allowing a moderate agricultural production, largely irrigated. The south is heavily agricultural with a substantial indigenous population, limiting the development of larger cities. In this zone, there are fewer larger cities for equivalent land area than in the central flank.

Northwest and Southeast. The northwest is quite arid with limited natural or irrigated agriculture. It also has substantial mountainous areas. Its states are physically larger than the smaller states of the central flank, contributing to lower densities. The southeast is an area with a hot, tropical climate. In recent Mexican history, it has lacked substantial city development except for Merida because of its remoteness, lack of transportation, and high proportion of indigenous population.

Table 2.4 Population Density, 1980

No.	State	Area (Square Kilometers)	Total Population	Density
1	AGUASCALIENTES	5,471	519,439	94.9
2	BAJA CALIFORNIA	69,921	1,177,886	16.8
3	BAJA CALIFORNIA SUR	73,475	215,139	2.9
4	CAMPECHE	50,812	420,553	8.3
5	COAHUILA	149,982	1,557,265	10.4
6	COLIMA	5,191	346,293	66.7
7	CHIAPAS	74,211	2,084,717	28.1
8	CHIHUAHUA	244,938	2,005,477	8.2
9	DISTRITO FEDERAL	1,479	8,831,079	5,971.0
10	DURANGO	123,181	1,182,320	9.6
11	GUANAJUATO	30,491	3,006,110	98.6
12	GUERRERO	64,281	2,109,513	32.8
13	HIDALGO	20,813	1,547,493	74.4
14	JALISCO	80,836	4,371,998	54.1
15	MEXICO	21,355	7,564,335	354.2
16	MICHOACAN	59,928	2,868,824	47.9
17	MORELOS	4,950	947,089	191.3
18	NAYARIT	26,979	726,120	27.0
19	NUEVO LEON	64,924	2,513,044	38.7
20	OAXACA	93,952	2,369,076	25.2
21	PUEBLA	33,902	3,347,685	98.7
22	QUERETARO	11,449	739,605	64.6
23	QUINTANA ROO	50,212	225,985	4.5
24	SAN LUIS POTOSI	63,068	1,673,893	26.5
25	SINALOA	58,328	1,849,879	31.7
26	SONORA	182,052	1,513,731	8.3
27	TABASCO	25,267	1,062,961	42.1
28	TAMAULIPAS	79,384	1,924,484	24.2
29	TLAXCALA	4,016	556,597	138.6
30	VERACRUZ	71,699	5,387,680	75.1
31	YUCATAN	38,402	1,063,733	27.7
32	ZACATECAS	73,252	1,136,830	15.5
Mean		61,194	2,088,964	241.2
S.D.		53,702	1,993,948	1,031.3
C.V.		87.80	95.45	427.6
Minimum		1,479	215,139	2.9
Maximum		244,938	8,831,079	5,971.0

DEFINITION: Population density is the ratio of total population to total area in square kilometers.

SOURCE: <u>1980 Mexican Census of Population</u>, Volume 1, Table 1 and associated adjunct information cards.

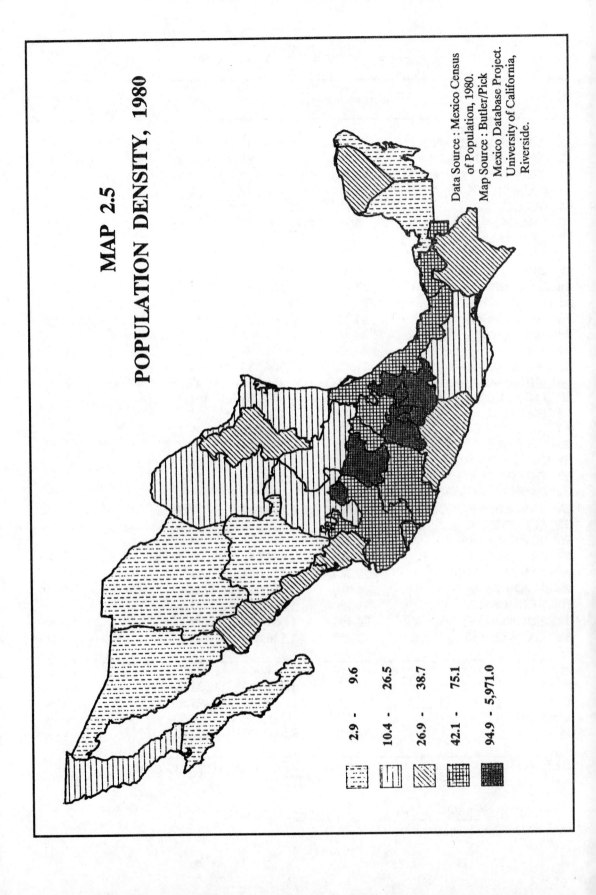

MAP 2.5
POPULATION DENSITY, 1980

Data Source : Mexico Census
of Population, 1980.
Map Source : Butler/Pick
Mexico Database Project.
University of California,
Riverside.

2.9 - 9.6

10.4 - 26.5

26.9 - 38.7

42.1 - 75.1

94.9 - 5,971.0

Urbanization

Urbanization, 1900-1980

Urbanization is defined as the ratio of population living in places of 2,500 population or more to total population. This definition was the one adopted by the Mexican Census for longitudinal comparisons (SPP, 1985), although other investigations have utilized places of 15,000 or more population as the criterion (Unikel, 1977). However, for purposes of the present atlas, the two definitions are so highly correlated that it makes little difference which one is chosen for geographic mapping and comparisons.

Over the eighty year period, both the urbanization ratio and urban population have increased greatly (see Table 2.5). The percent urban increased from 28.3 in 1900 to 66.3 in 1980, while the total urban population increased from 5.54 million in 1900 to 44.30 million in 1980. Figure 2.2 illustrates percent change in urbanization as opposed to percent rural. The turning point occured around 1960 when Mexico began to become more urbanized than rural. The total urban population increased over 80 years at an average compounded rate of 2.60 percent. In spite of such a great increase, the geographic distribution of urbanization has remained remarkably stable. This is reflected in highly significant positive longitudinal correlations, for example r=0.80 between urbanization ratios, 1930 and 1950.

Within the overall stable pattern, individual regions reveal several major changes in geographical distribution over time (see Map 2.6A):

(1) Over the period, the border region increased substantially in urbanization, relative to the nation, to become by 1980 the most highly urbanized region besides the central zone. The states of Baja and Sonora had especially large increases.

(2) The western region was consistently high in urbanization over 80 years. This may have stemmed from the development in the 19th century of major western cities, which retained their importance from 1900 to 1980 (SPP, 1985).

(3) Over the period, the central region showed considerable change. Foremost of these was the major increase in the central zone and contiguous state of Morelos. Comparison is hampered slightly because the Federal District was not counted as a federal entity in 1900. However, if for 1900 the central zone's population is approximated at about 540,000 by substituting Mexico City for the Federal District (SPP, 1985), the 1900 urban population in the central zone would have accounted for an estimated 14 percent of the nation's urban population. This percentage increased to 29.6 percent in 1950 and 33.5 percent in 1980. The state of Mexico grew extremely rapidly, increasing 30-fold, from 1930 to 1980, at a compounded annual rate of 6.8 percent. Likewise, the urban population of Morelos, bordering the Federal District to the south, increased 21-fold from 1930 to 1980. Balancing out the added importance of Mexico and Morelos, Queretaro and Puebla decreased substantially in relative urbanization over the eighty year period.

(4) The gulf and pacific south regions were consistently low in urbanization over eighty years, except for Chiapas's relatively high value in 1900. The southeast revealed inconsistent trends by state -- Yucatan was consistently high; Campeche decreased while Yucatan increased modestly.

The overall consistent geographic pattern of urbanization is strongly related to other atlas variables. Regardless of year, urbanization is highly and positively correlated with the economic variables of gross state product and value of corporation: the transport variables, personal vehicles, gasoline consumption, and length of railways; and variables reflecting "urban lifestyle", telephones,

34

televisions, movies, sports events, and trials. Urbanization variables show significant negative cor-relations with standardized annual fertility, dependency ratio, and agricultural labor force. The strength of these relationships corroborates urbanization's importance as one of Mexico's key social and population indicators.

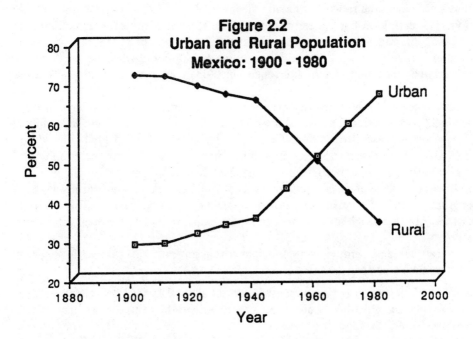

Figure 2.2
Urban and Rural Population
Mexico: 1900 - 1980

SOURCE: Estadisticas Historicas de Mexico, 1985.

Urbanization in Oaxaca, 1980

As Map 2.6B illustrates, the majority of the 570 municipios in Oaxaca are rural. Urbanization here being defined as the percentage of population residing in localities with a population of 2500 or more. Of 570 municipios, 473 have no urbanized areas. In Oaxaca the percentage of the popula-tion who speak an indigenous language, although quite varied, is higher than elsewhere in Mexico; however, there is no relationship between urban and rural residence and speaking a native language, and with many other social and demographic variables. Urbanization in Oaxaca is negatively corre-lated with persons reporting no/low incomes and positively associated with medium and high incom-es. Urbanization in Oaxaca also is negatively related to literacy and to the economically active population. An evaluation of the 1980 Oaxaca census data indicates that the data should be used cautiously since some variables have relatively high levels of no response (Butler et al., 1987c).

Table 2.5 Urbanization, 1930-1980

No.	State	1930 Population Places 2500+	1930 Urban Ratio	1950 Population Places 2500+	1950 Urban Ratio	1980 Population Places 2500+	1980 Urban Ratio	% Change Urbanization 1950-80
1	AGUASCALIENTES	72,735	0.5473	103,262	0.5490	365,545	0.7037	0.1547
2	BAJA CALIFORNIA	26,268	0.5435	146,391	0.6450	1,004,194	0.8525	0.2075
3	BAJA CALIFORNIA SUR	16,979	0.3606	20,022	0.3290	149973	0.6971	0.3681
4	CAMPECHE	38,155	0.4508	70,069	0.5739	292,006	0.6943	0.1204
5	COAHUILA	227,276	0.5208	413,978	0.5745	1,204,971	0.7738	0.1993
6	COLIMA	27,402	0.4425	67,559	0.6015	258,586	0.7467	0.1452
7	CHIAPAS	92,627	0.1748	209,133	0.2306	702,969	0.3372	0.1066
8	CHIHUAHUA	162,099	0.3296	373,357	0.4411	1,410,799	0.7035	0.2624
9	DISTRITO FEDERAL	1,135,123	0.9232	2,884,133	0.9455	8,831,079	1.0000	0.0545
10	DURANGO	94,248	0.2331	180,486	0.2865	595,544	0.5037	0.2172
11	GUANAJUATO	336,663	0.3408	552,516	0.4158	1,771,604	0.5893	0.1735
12	GUERRERO	97,336	0.1517	199,251	0.2167	883,394	0.4188	0.2021
13	HIDALGO	114,933	0.1696	179,892	0.2115	506,275	0.3272	0.1157
14	JALISCO	494,452	0.3939	836,124	0.4787	3,304,635	0.7559	0.2772
15	MEXICO	202,956	0.2050	367,679	0.2640	6,007,404	0.7942	0.5302
16	MICHOACAN	275,330	0.2626	455,789	0.3204	1,530,083	0.5333	0.2129
17	MORELOS	33,219	0.2515	118,354	0.4338	699,331	0.7384	0.3046
18	NAYARIT	58,703	0.3500	99,008	0.3413	414,528	0.5709	0.2296
19	NUEVO LEON	172,175	0.4124	413,911	0.5592	2,197,288	0.8744	0.3152
20	OAXACA	195,901	0.1806	293,953	0.2068	757,871	0.3199	0.1131
21	PUEBLA	319,524	0.2777	539,233	0.3317	1,899,938	0.5675	0.2358
22	QUERETARO	46,276	0.1977	69,196	0.2417	350,623	0.4741	0.2324
23	QUINTANA ROO	2,790	0.2627	7,247	0.2687	133,511	0.5908	0.3221
24	SAN LUIS POTOSI	158,712	0.2737	260,452	0.3042	786,023	0.4696	0.1654
25	SINALOA	90,651	0.2291	177,522	0.2793	1,049,545	0.5674	0.2881
26	SONORA	116,225	0.3675	231,424	0.4532	1,067,861	0.7054	0.2522
27	TABASCO	38,790	0.1732	79,558	0.2193	405,950	0.3819	0.1626
28	TAMAULIPAS	147,367	0.4283	380,281	0.5295	1,445,960	0.7513	0.2218
29	TLAXCALA	56,632	0.2756	110,315	0.3877	320,480	0.5758	0.1881
30	VERACRUZ	392,926	0.2853	679,380	0.3330	2,743,286	0.5092	0.1762
31	YUCATAN	185,867	0.4814	285,567	0.5525	782,041	0.7352	0.1827
32	ZACATECAS	110,291	0.2403	166,678	0.2504	426,432	0.3751	0.1247
	Mean	173,143	0.3355	342,866	0.3993	1,384366	0.6137	0.2144
	S.D.	211,127	0.1575	503,820	0.1676	1,788,363	0.1732	0.0916
	C.V.	121.94	46.94	146.94	41.97	129.19	28.21	42.72
	Minimum	2,790	0.1517	7,247	0.2068	133,511	0.3199	0.0545
	Maximum	1,135,123	0.9232	2,884,133	0.9455	8,831,079	1.0000	0.5302
	Total Urban Population	5,540631		10,971,720		44,299,729		
	Total Population	16,552,722		25,779,254		66,846,833		
	Percent Urban	33.5		42.6		66.3		

DEFINITION: Urbanization is the ratio of population living in localities of the stated population total to the total population of the state.

SOURCE: 1930 and 1950 Mexican Census of Population, Resumen General; 1980 Mexican Census of Population, Volume 2, Table 2.

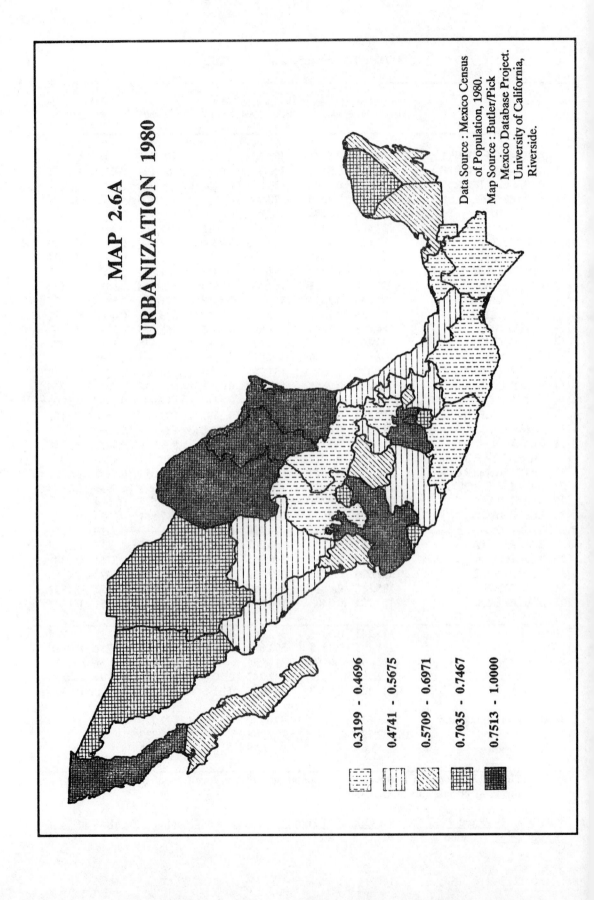

MAP 2.6A
URBANIZATION 1980

Data Source : Mexico Census
of Population, 1980.
Map Source : Butler/Pick
Mexico Database Project.
University of California,
Riverside.

0.3199 - 0.4696

0.4741 - 0.5675

0.5709 - 0.6971

0.7035 - 0.7467

0.75513 - 1.0000

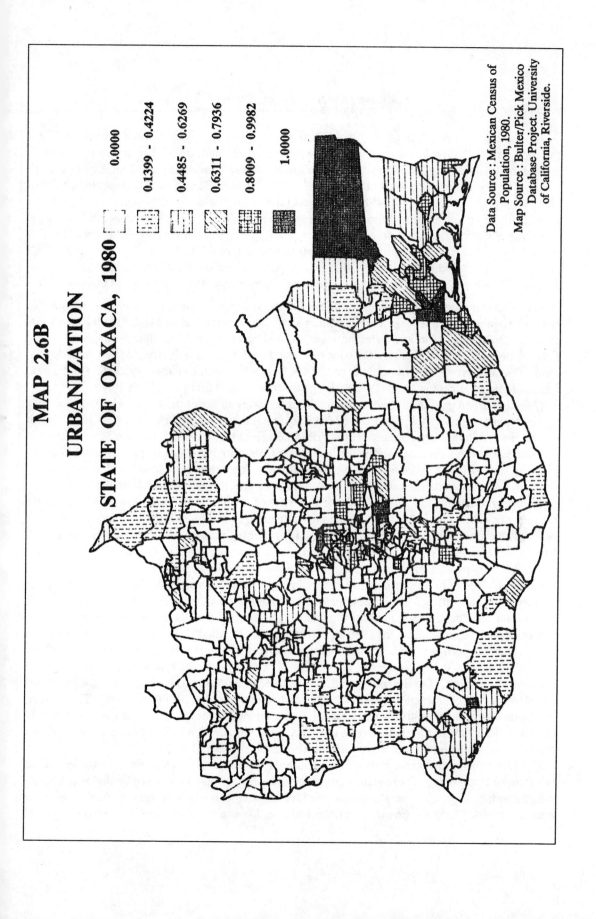

MAP 2.6B

URBANIZATION

STATE OF OAXACA, 1980

0.0000

0.1399 - 0.4224

0.4485 - 0.6269

0.6311 - 0.7936

0.8009 - 0.9982

1.0000

Data Source : Mexican Census of
    Population, 1980.
Map Source : Bulter/Pick Mexico
    Database Project. University
    of California, Riverside.

Urbanization Change: 1950-1980

As shown in Figure 2.2, beginning in 1940, Mexico became significantly more urbanized. Here the focus is on change in urbanization levels between 1950 and 1980. Urbanization change is measured by subtracting 1950 from 1980 urbanization. National urbanization change from 1950 to 1980 was 24 percent versus 9 percent for the 1930-50 period (see Table 2.5). The large change, 1950-1980, took place concomitantly with national population increase of 159 percent. The principal cause of the huge urban growth was massive rural-to-urban migration. This redistribution of the Mexican population took place despite higher standardized fertility rates in rural as opposed to urban areas. The geographic distribution of urbanization was remarkably stable from 1950 through 1980 (see Map 2.7). Excluding the Federal District and state of Mexico, state urbanization changes between 1950 and 1980 ranged from 11 to 37 percent. Major regional trends were as follows:

(1) With the exception of the Federal District, there was a very large urbanization increase in states containing the three largest metropolitan areas: Monterrey, Nuevo Leon; Guadalajara, Jalisco; and Mexico and Morelos, states adjacent to, and receiving metropolitan overspill from the Federal District. This overspill for the state of Mexico has been carefully studied (Van Arsdol et al., 1976). Mexico, in fact, experienced the nation's highest urbanization change, 1950-80. The Federal District's minor percent increase 1950-80 is due to its near-total urbanization by 1950.

(2) High urban growth in Queretaro and Puebla, states adjacent to Mexico and Morelos, may again be partly an overspill from the Federal District, albeit at a greater distance. Cities in both Queretaro and Puebla are connected by major railroad and highway links with the Federal District and serve as alternative destinations for inmigrants from outlying states to the center of Mexico. Likewise smaller towns and cities in these two states are alternative rural to urban destinations.

(3) A low rate of urban growth in Hidalgo and Zacatecas stemmed in part from these states' low economic productivity and income. These two states are among the three lowest in gross state revenue per capita (Map 7.7A) and have high percentages of low monthly income (Map 8.4A). Weak state economies lower the job attraction for potential inmigrants, decreasing urban growth rates.

(4) Medium or high urban growth change, is seen especially in Nuevo Leon, Chihuahua, and Tamaulipas. Nuevo Leon's urban growth has already been discussed, in the framework of its large metropolis of Monterrey. In addition, smaller cities in Nuevo Leon, although not directly on the border, may have benefitted by border proximity. The general stimulating effect on city growth of border location or proximity in the 1950-80 period has been detailed elsewhere. Sonora's high urban growth rate was partially due to growth in the border city of Nogales (population 66,000 in 1980). To a greater extent, it grew as a result of an influx of population to the interior cities of Hermosillo and Ciudad Obregon. On the other hand, Tamaulipas' high urban growth rate was significantly affected by the border cities of Reynosa (195,000) and Nuevo Laredo (202,000 in 1980). The remaining border states, Baja California and Chihuahua, experienced average urban change between 1950 and 1980. Baja's average growth may be explained by its already high 1950 urbanization rate of 64.5 percent; such a high initial rate limits further urbanization potential.

(5) Low urban growth characterized the south pacific states of Oaxaca and Chiapas and in the gulf state of Campeche. These states have a relatively high proportion of population speaking an indigenous language, which in Mexico usually is associated with a lack of urbanization. Quintana Roo, as explained below, is an exception. In addition, Oaxaca and Chiapas are Mexico's two most

highly agricultural states in terms of occupation. Strong agriculture also contributes to the small amount of urban increase.

(6) Large urban increases occurred in the states of Baja California Sur, Sinaloa, and Quintana Roo. The large increases in urbanization in these states had a variety of causes. In all of these states population growth was partially related to a substantial increase in the tourism industry. The emphasis on tourism is revealed by the presence of international airports in Baja California Sur, Quintana Roo, and Sinaloa, even though Baja Sur and Quintana Roo are the least populous in Mexico. Statistics on hotels and pensions/capita and international airport and air passengers/capita shown in Chapter 9 also substantiate the tourism effect. Baja Sur and Quintana Roo are consistently in the highest categories and Sinaloa has a high level of air passengers/capita and well-known tourism destinations, including Matzatlan. For Sinaloa and Sonora, another cause of urban growth, at least in the 70s, was concerted governmental planning for industrial growth. In Mexico, Sinaloa and Quintana Roo have been among the top states in planned towns, as percent of land area. Government planning emphasis does not, in Mexico or elsewhere, always lead to practical outcomes. But here it has to be assumed that for these two states planned development had significant results.

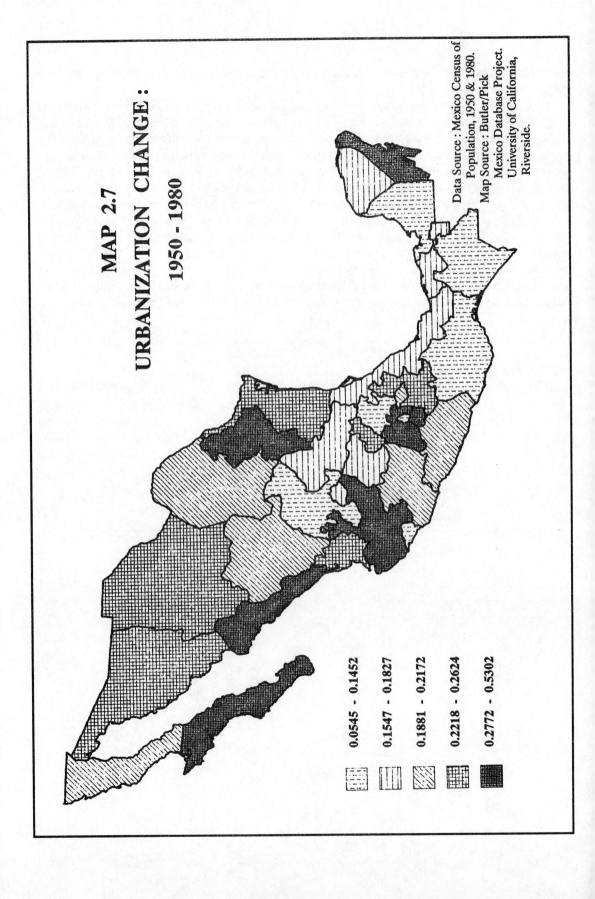

MAP 2.7

URBANIZATION CHANGE :

1950 - 1980

0.0545 - 0.1452

0.1547 - 0.1827

0.1881 - 0.2172

0.2218 - 0.2624

0.2772 - 0.5302

Data Source : Mexico Census of
Population, 1950 & 1980.
Map Source : Butler/Pick
Mexico Database Project.
University of California,
Riverside.

Large Cities, 1980

In 1980, there were 46 Mexican cities of over 100,000 population. Together, these cities accounted for 65 percent of the urban population and 43 percent of the total population of Mexico. The largest of these were Mexico City, Guadalajara, and Monterrey with populations of 13,354,271, 2,192,557, and 1,913,075 respectively. The three primary cities accounted for 26.1 percent of the population. Although the 46 large cities have a mean population of 625,000, when the three primary cities are excluded, the mean is only 263,000. Besides the three largest cities, eight other cities contain over 400,000 population -- Puebla, Leon, Ciudad Juarez, San Luis Potosi, Torreon, Tijuana, Tampico, and Merida. Regionally, these eight cities are located in the borderlands (Ciudad Juarez, Tijuana, and Tampico), the Yucatan peninsula (Merida), and the rest in the nation's central flank.

There was a large increase in large city population between 1970 and 1980 (see Table 2.6). In 1970 there were 35 cities with populations over 100,000, having a total population of 17,999,137. This total grew by 59.7 percent to 28,752,571 in 1980. By comparison, the national population grew by 38.6 percent from 1970 to 1980, and the national urban population grew by 56.5 percent. Mexico City grew by 51.7 percent, which represents an absolute increase of 4.5 million persons. This burgeoning of population placed great strains on government, services, health care, environment and many other aspects of the metropolis (Schteingart,1988).

Among the most rapidly growing cities were: Merida, the largest city in the Yucatan Peninsula and adjacent to Mexico's oil region and the rapidly growing state of Quintana Roo; Culiacan in Sinaloa near coastal tourist areas; Acapulco, the nation's largest tourist city; Saltillo, near the metropolis of Monterrey; and Queretaro and Toluca, cities just outside the urban reach of Mexico City. The six large border cities of Ciudad Juarez, Tijuana, Mexicali, Nuevo Laredo, Reynosa, and Matamoros experienced growth of 38.4 percent between 1970-80, a rate below the national city average (see Margulis and Tuiran, 1984 for explanation of slower border growth).

As shown on Map 2.8, Mexico's large cities are scattered throughout the country. Five states, however, do not contain a city of 100,000 or more; states without a large city are located in different regions, Baja California Sur in the northwest, Zacatecas in the north central, Colima in the south central, Tlaxcala in the south, and Quintana Roo in the southeast. These states are among the lowest in population. States with several large cities are Tamaulipas and Veracruz, with five each, and Baja California, Coahuila, Guanajuato, and Sinaloa, with three apiece. By region, the highly urbanized northern regions (northwest, north, northeast) contain 22 cities, as compared to only 5 in the southern regions (south, southeast). Mexico's central flank (gulf, central, west regions) contains 19 cities. There are six large cities, with total population of 1,900,724, adjacent to the U.S. border, but no large cities along the southern border.

Table 2.6 Large Cities, 1970-1980

No.	City	State	Population 1970	Population 1980	Rank	Percent Growth 1970-80
1	Acapulco de Juarez	GUERRERO	172,000	301,901	17	75.52
2	Aguascalientes	AGUASCALIENTES	181,000	293,152	20	61.96
3	Campeche	CAMPECHE		128,434	40	
4	Celeya	GUANAJUATO		141,675	37	
5	Ciudad Juarez	CHIHUAHUA	407,000	544,496	6	33.78
6	Cajeme	SONORA		165,572	33	
7	Ciudad Obregon/Victoria	TAMAULIPAS	114,000	140,161	38	22.95
8	Coatzacoalcos/Minatitlan	VERACRUZ	136,000	233,935	22	
9	Cuernavaca	MORELOS	134,117	192,770	29	43.73
10	Culiacan	SINALOA	168,000	304,826	16	81.44
11	Chihuahua	CHIHUAHUA	281,937	385,603	12	36.77
12	Durango	DURANGO	204,385	321,148	15	57.13
13	Ensenada	BAJA CALIFORNIA		120,483	43	
14	Guadalajara	JALISCO	1,491,085	2,192,557	2	47.04
15	Hermosillo	SONORA	176,596	297,175	19	68.28
16	Irapuato	GUANAJUATO	117,000	170,138	31	45.42
17	Jalapa	VERACRUZ	122,000	204,594	24	67.70
18	Leon	GUANAJUATO	365,000	593,002	5	62.47
19	Los Mochis/Ahome	SINALOA		122,531	42	
20	Matamoros	TAMAULIPAS	138,000	188,745	30	36.77
21	Mazatlan	SINALOA	120,000	199,830	26	66.53
22	Merida	YUCATAN	212,097	400,142	11	88.66
23	Mexicali	BAJA CALIFORNIA	263,000	341,559	14	29.87
24	Mexico City	D.F./MEXICO	8,799,937	13,354,271	1	51.75
25	Monclova	COAHUILA		115,786	44	
26	Monterrey	NUEVO LEON	1,246,181	1,913,075	3	53.52
27	Morelia	MICHOACAN	161,040	297,544	18	84.76
28	Nuevo Laredo	TAMAULIPAS	150,922	201,731	25	33.67
29	Oaxaca de Juarez	OAXACA	99,535	154,223	35	54.94
30	Orizaba	VERACRUZ		114,848	45	
31	Pachuca	HIDALGO		110,351	46	
32	Poca Rica de Hidalgo	VERACRUZ	121,300	166,799	32	37.51
33	Puebla	PUEBLA	546,430	772,908	4	41.45
34	Queretaro	QUERETARO	112,995	215,976	23	91.14
35	Reynosa	TAMAULIPAS	137,000	194,693	28	42.11
36	Saltillo	COAHUILA	161,000	284,937	21	76.98
37	San Luis Potosi	SAN LUIS POTOSI	301,896	471,047	7	56.03
38	Tampico/Ciudad Madero	TAMAULIPAS	260,000	400,401	10	54.00
39	Tepic	NAYARIT	111,300	145,741	36	30.94
40	Tijuana	BAJA CALIFORNIA	277,000	429,500	9	55.05
41	Toluca	MEXICO	114,079	199,778	27	75.12
42	Torreon/Gomez Palacio	COAHUILA/DURANGO	336,700	445,053	8	32.18
43	Tuxtla	CHIAPAS		131,096	39	
44	Uruapan	MICHOACAN		122,828	41	
45	Veracruz	VERACRUZ	258,605	367,339	13	42.05
46	Villahermosa/Centro	TABASCO		158,216	34	

	Total City Population	17,999,137	28,752,571		59.74
	National Population	48,225,238	66,846,833		38.61
	Percent in Cities	37.32	43.01		15.24
	Mean	514,261.0	625,055.8		21.54
	S.D.	1,450,093	1,937,720		
	C.V.	281.9761	310.0076		
	Minimum	99,535	110,351		10.87
	Maximum	8,799,937	13,354,271		51.75

SOURCE: Estadisticas Historicas de Mexico (1985).

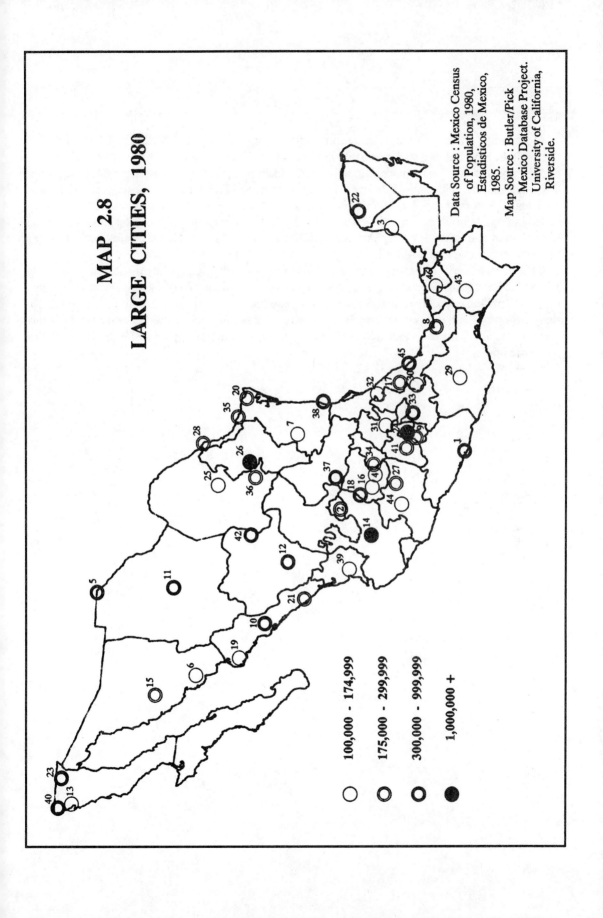

MAP 2.8
LARGE CITIES, 1980

100,000 - 174,999

175,000 - 299,999

300,000 - 999,999

1,000,000 +

Data Source : Mexico Census
of Population, 1980,
Estadisticos de Mexico,
1985.
Map Source : Butler/Pick
Mexico Database Project.
University of California,
Riverside.

Capital Cities, 1980

Most capital cities are among the nation's forty six large cities (see Table 2.6 and 2.7). Seven of the capitals, however, are under 100,000 in population. These consist of: La Paz, Baja California Sur; Colima, Colima; Guanajuato, Guanajuato; Chilpancingo, Guerrero; Chetumal, Quintana Roo; Tlaxcala, Tlaxcala; with only 18,437 persons; and Zacatecas, Zacatecas. In most cases, these were the original historical population centers of states. Guanajuato and Chilpancingo have been superceded in population by other cities in the state. In three other cases, large capital cities have been overtaken in size by other cities, Mexicali by Tijuana, Chihuahua by Ciudad Juarez, and Jalapa by Veracruz and Coatzacoalcos/Minatitlan.

The average size of capital cities is 598,000. However, when Mexico City is excluded, the mean size is 332,459, which reflects the generally large size of the capitals. The 1980 population of Mexico City at 8.8 million is smaller than the 13.4 million population listed in Table 2.3, since it only includes that portion of the metropolitan area located within the boundaries of the Federal District. Only one state capital, Mexicali, is located at the U.S. border, although there are six large Mexican cities along the border.

Table 2.7 Capital Cities, 1980

No.	State	City	Population
1	AGUASCALIENTES	Aguascalientes	293,152
2	BAJA CALIFORNIA	Mexicali	341,559
3	BAJA CALIFORNIA SUR	La Paz	91,453
4	CAMPECHE	Campeche	128,434
5	COAHUILA	Saltillo	284,937
6	COLIMA	Colima	86,044
7	CHIAPAS	Tuxtla	131,096
8	CHIHUAHUA	Chihuahua	385,603
9	DISTRITO FEDERAL	Mexico City	8,831,079
10	DURANGO	Durango	321,148
11	GUANAJUATO	Guanajuanto	48,981
12	GUERRERO	Chilpancingo	67,498
13	HIDALGO	Pachuca	110,351
14	JALISCO	Guadalajara	2,192,557
15	MEXICO	Toluca	199,778
16	MICHOACAN	Morelia	297,544
17	MORELOS	Cuernavaca	192,770
18	NAYARIT	Tepic	145,741
19	NUEVO LEON	Monterrey	1,913,075
20	OAXACA	Oaxaca	154,223
21	PUEBLA	Puebla	772,908
22	QUERETARO	Queretaro	215,976
23	QUINTANA ROO	Chetumal	56,709
24	SAN LUIS POTOSI	San Luis Potosi	471,047
25	SINALOA	Culiacan	304,826
26	SONORA	Hermosillo	297,175
27	TABASCO	Villahermosa/Centro	158,216
28	TAMAULIPAS	Ciudad Obregon/Victoria	140,161
29	TLAXCALA	Tlaxcala	18,437
30	VERACRUZ	Jalapa	204,594
31	YUCATAN	Merida	400,142
32	ZACATECAS	Zacatecas	80,083
		Mean	598,041
		S.D.	1,576,541
		C.V.	263.62
		Minimum	18,437
		Maximum	8,831,079

SOURCE: Estadisticas Historicas de Mexico (1985).

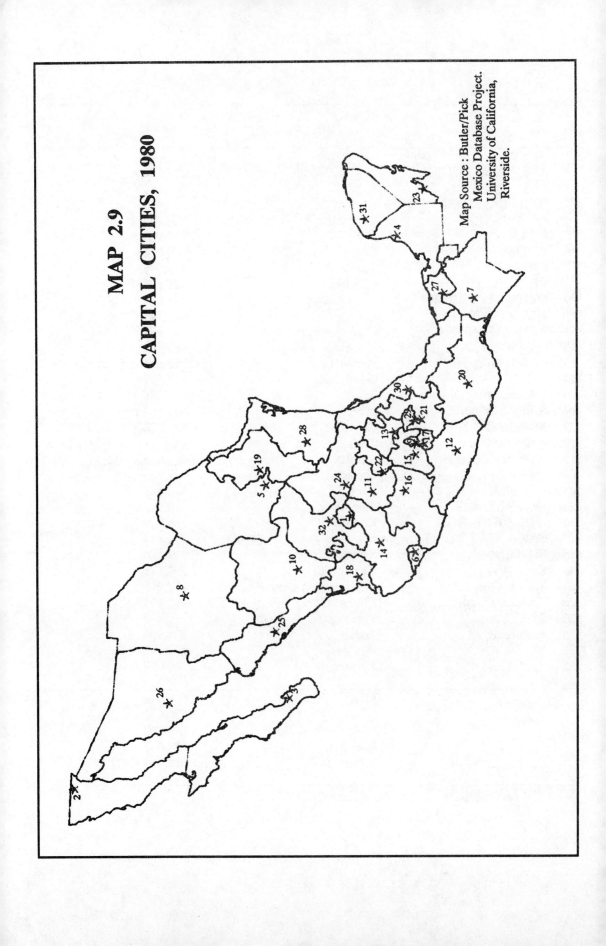

MAP 2.9
CAPITAL CITIES, 1980

Map Source : Butler/Pick
Mexico Database Project.
University of California,
Riverside.

United States-Mexican Border

United States-Mexican Border Cities and States, 1980

The United States-Mexican border is the world's longest land border separating high and low income countries (Dillman, 1983b). It extends along the four U.S. states of California, Arizona, New Mexico, and Texas, and the six Mexican states of Baja California, Sonora, Chihuahua, Coahuila, Nuevo Leon, and Tamaulipas. There is extensive interchange between Mexico and the U.S. along the border including maquiladora industry, retail trade, commuter workers, tourism, and international immigration. Parts of the Mexican border, especially the city of Tijuana, are used as jumping off places for undocumented immigration from Mexico into the U.S. (Stoddard, 1983), or for return of undocumented migrants back to Mexico (Cantu, 1986; Jones, 1984). On the U.S. side, border cities are generally less prosperous economically than comparable non-border cities, while Mexican border cities tend to have higher incomes and economic productivity than comparable interior cities (Dillman, 1983b).

Along the border are a series of twin cities; that is, there are adjacent cities on both sides of the border, which in many ways form bi-national metropolitan areas. As seen in Table 2.8 and Map 2.10A, there were eight pairs of twin cities in 1980, having a total population of 3.6 million. The population was 56 percent on the Mexican side. The size and importance of the Mexican border cities is underscored by the fact that 19.0 percent of the 1980 population of the six border states is in the ten border cities. In the U.S., the ten border cities are much less important relative to the four U.S. border states, comprising only 3.8 percent of the population of these states. Over the past thirty years, Mexican border cities have been growing at over double the rate of their U.S. twins (Dillman, 1983b). In the future, it is likely the twin cities' populations will be weighted even more heavily towards Mexico.

If the consolidated bi-national populations are considered, the Tijuana/San Diego is the largest twin city, with 1.3 million persons and accounting for 36 percent of the total. In second place is Ciudad Juarez/El Paso, having about 1 million persons and comprising 27 percent of the total twin city population. At the other extreme are the Piedras Negras/Eagle Pass and Nogales/Nogales twin cities, with 80-90,000 persons apiece.

Several Mexican twin cities are located in populous regions encompassing several municipios (Pick et al., 1987a). In particular, Tijuana and Mexicali form part of a five municipio region in Baja California and northwest Sonora having a total population of 1.2 million, while Matamoros and Reynosa are part of a six-municipio region in northeast Tamaulipas with a population of 627,000. It is likely that multi-municipio metropolitan regions will become more important in the future, as borderlands cities increase in size and area. There are other cities on both sides of the border or near the border, which do not qualify as border twin cities. These include Ensenada, Tecate, San Luis Rio Colorado, and Agua Prieta on the Mexican side and Douglas, Arizona on the U.S. side (see Dillman, 1983b).

Borderlands Population and Urbanization, 1980

The distribution of 1980 population for the 272 municipios in the Mexican borderlands is shown in Map 2.10B. Municipio population varies greatly in the region, from a high of 1,090,009 in Monterrey, Nuevo Leon, to 501 in Oquitoa, Sonora. Total population for the borderlands region is 10,687,887 (see Table 2.9.)

There are eight zones of high municipio population. A high population zone is selected to represent groups of municipios which are geographically continguous and belong to the highest quintile, i.e. share the highest range of values as seen on the map. As shown in Table 2.9, each zone corresponds to one or two high-population municipios. The percent column refers to percent of total borderlands population.

The largest population zone, Monterrey and seven other municipios, contains 21.3 percent of the borderlands population, in spite of its small area relative to the other zones. The next two most populous zones, Tijuana/Mexicali/others and Hermosillo/others, together constitute 20.3 percent of the borderlands population and over all of Baja California and about half of Sonora. These two adjacent urban zones may link together in the future. There are also eight zones of low population, i.e., with municipio population in the lowest quintile. Three are located in Coahuila, one in Nuevo Leon, and four in Sonora. These zones have means of 6,000 population and four municipios.

The population distribution of the entire borderlands gives the analyst a different outlook than just considering the twin cities along the border strip. Another view of the borderlands is a plot of urbanization by municipio, shown in Map 2.10C. This map illustrates urbanization by the ratio of persons in urban locations of 2,500 or more to total population.

The level of urbanization of borderlands municipios ranges from 0 to 100 percent. Mean urbanization is 34 percent. There are four major zones of urbanization. In this case a major zone is defined as consisting of at least five contiguous municipios in the fourth and fifth quintiles of urbanization and covering a large geographic area, except for Monterrey. The Monterrey urban zone consists of five small-area municipios and is 99.6 percent urbanized. The Tijuana, Mexicali, and San Luis Rio Colorado zone consists of five municipios with a population of over 1.1 million persons. The Hermosillo and Guaymas zone consists of six municipios. This zone stretches northward towards the border city of Nogales in an urban "strip" corresponding to a major highway. In the future the zone will likely connect to Nogales. The Monclava, Piedra Negras, and Acuna zone consists of eleven municipios in northern Coahuila. Along the border strip, Mexican twin cities are apparent, and tend to be highly urbanized, i.e. the twin cities vary from 92 to 99 percent urbanization.

Table 2.8   U.S. - Mexico Twin Cities, 1980

No.	Twin city, State	Population	Twin Cities Population	Percent
1.	Matamoros, Tamaulipas	188,745	273,742	7.543
2.	Brownsville, Texas	84,997		
3.	Reynosa, Tamaulipas	194,693	269,974	7.191
4.	McAllen, Texas	66,281		
5.	Nuevo Laredo, Tamaulipas	201,731	293,180	8.078
6	Lardo, Texas	91,449		
7.	Piedras Negras, Coahuila	67,455	88,862	2.449
8.	Eagle Pass, Texas	21,407		
9.	Ciudad Juarez, Chihahua	544,496	969,755	26.721
10.	El Paso, Texas	425,259		
11.	Nogales, Sonora	66,000	81,683	2.251
12.	Nogales, Arizona	15,683		
13.	Mexicali, Baja California	341,559	355,971	9.809
14.	Calexico, California	14,412		
15.	Tijuana, Baja California	429,500	1,305,038	35.959
16.	San Diego, California	875,538		
	Total	3,629,205		
	Mexico Total	2,034,179		56.050%
	U.S. Total	1,595,026		43.950%

SOURCE: 1980 Mexican Census of Population.

Table 2.9 Major Population Zones in the Mexican Borderlands, 1980

Rank	State Location	Municipios	Population	Percent of Borderlands
1.	W. NUEVO LEON	Monterrey and 7 others	2,279,980	21.3
2.	BAJA, N.W. SONORA	Tijuana, Mexicali Ensenada, San Luis, Rio Colorado	1,240,136	11.6
3.	S.W. SONORA	Hermosillo and 5 others	927,362	8.7
4.	N.E. TAMAULIPAS	Reynosa and 5 others	627,460	5.9
5.	S.W. COAHUILA	Torreon and 3 others	576,578	5.4
6.	N. CHIHUAHUA	Juarez	567,360	5.3
7.	CENTRAL CHIHUAHUA	Chihuahua	406,830	3.8
8.	S.E. TAMAULIPAS	Tampico, Ciudad Madero	400,401	3.7
	Population of Major Population Zones		7,206,112	65.7
	Total Municipio Population		10,689,887	100.0

SOURCE: 1980 Mexican Census of Population.

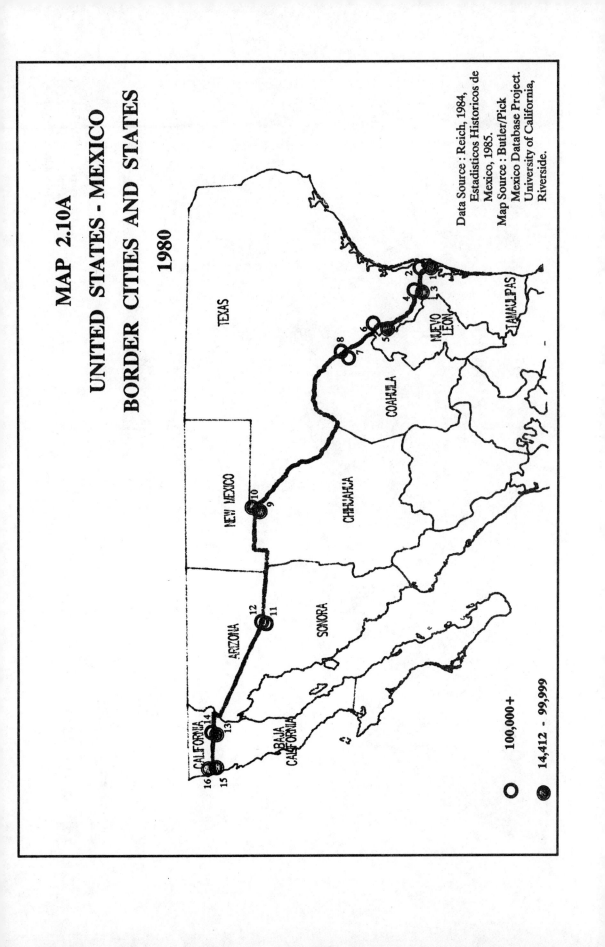

MAP 2.10A
UNITED STATES - MEXICO
BORDER CITIES AND STATES
1980

Data Source : Reich, 1984,
    Estadisticos Historicos de
    Mexico, 1985.
Map Source : Butler/Pick
    Mexico Database Project.
    University of California,
    Riverside.

○ 100,000+

● 14,412 - 99,999

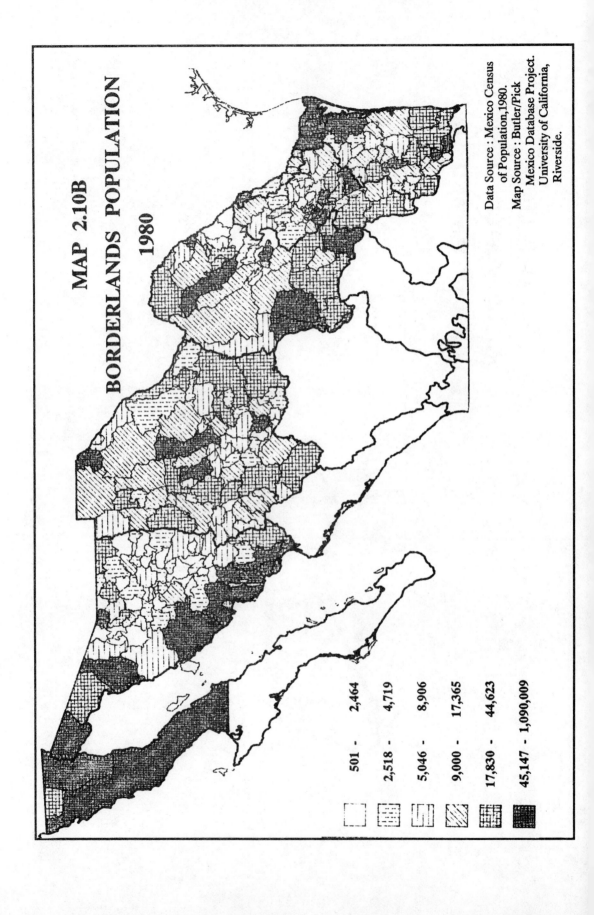

MAP 2.10B

BORDERLANDS POPULATION

1980

Data Source : Mexico Census
    of Population,1980.
Map Source : Butler/Pick
    Mexico Database Project.
    University of California,
    Riverside.

501 -   2,464

2,518 -   4,719

5,046 -   8,906

9,000 -   17,365

17,830 -   44,623

45,147 - 1,090,009

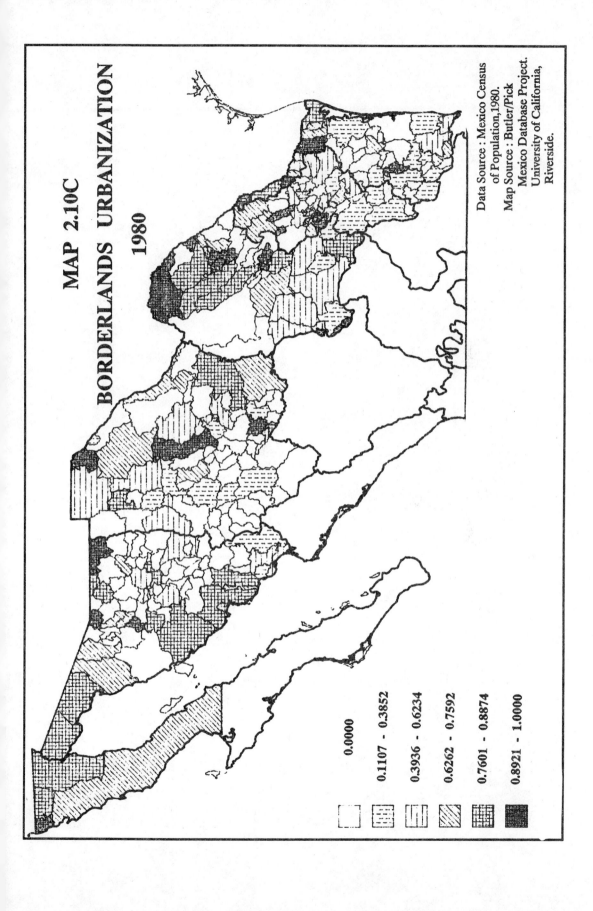

MAP 2.10C

BORDERLANDS URBANIZATION

1980

Data Source : Mexico Census
of Population,1980.
Map Source : Butler/Pick
Mexico Database Project.
University of California,
Riverside.

0.0000

0.1107 - 0.3852

0.3936 - 0.6234

0.6262 - 0.7592

0.7601 - 0.8874

0.8921 - 1.0000

3

MARRIAGE, FERTILITY, AND FAMILY PLANNING

Introduction

Chapter 3 examines various dimensions of marriage, fertility, and family planning. All data, maps, and discussion in this chapter focus on these dimensions at the state level. Data are from the World Fertility Survey (WFS) conducted in Mexico during 1976-77 and from the 1980 Mexican census. Rates and other statistics were calculated utilizing data from the WFS computer tape and from information computerized from the census.

Marriage variables included in the atlas cover women currently married, common law marriages, age at first union, and women currently divorced or separated. Fecundity and the fertility dimensions of the crude fertility rate, standardized fertility rate, and the cumulative fertility of women in various age categories are presented. Wasted pregnancies, induced abortions, women knowing an efficient birth control method, birth control pill use, and female sterilization constitute the family planning section of this chapter.

Marriage, fertility, and family planning attributes covered in this chapter are only illustrative of the many that are available from the WFS and 1980 and earlier Mexican censuses. In addition, statewide data from other more recent surveys are in process of being incorporated into the Mexico database so that they will be available for future editions of the atlas.

Marriage

Women Currently Married, 1976-77

The percent of women respondents in the World Fertility Survey currently married shows wide variation among regions and even between adjacent states. The mean percent of respondents currently married is 78.4. By comparison, the national average for percent currently married was 64.2 percent in the 1979 National Prevalence Survey (Martinez, 1982). The difference in values is due in part to differences in respondents' age ranges in the two surveys (see Table 3.1).

The highest rate of women currently married of 87.8 percent was in the state of Quintana Roo while the lowest was in the adjacent state of Yucatan with 63.2 percent.The geographic distribution reveals high values in the pacific south and gulf regions, and low values in the west and state of Chihuahua. The three states of the Federal District, Nuevo Leon, and Jalisco with the major metropolitan centers have low rates of women currently married. The highly rural pacific south and gulf regions have high rates. Except for Chihuahua's low value, the U.S.-Mexico border states all have intermediate rates of women currently married.

As shown on Map 3.1A, there is generally a disparity between north and south. Except for Nayarit with a relatively high percentage and the Federal District, and the anomaly of the Yucatan with lower percentages, there is substantial difference between the north and south of Mexico with the south having a higher percentage of women currently married. A similar north-south differential and very low Federal District value occurred in the 1979 National Prevalence Survey for women currently married (Martinez, 1982). This is further reflected in a significant negative correlation between women currently married and 1980 urbanization.

The data for women ever married 1976-77 are also presented in Table 3.1. This variable has a highly significant correlation with women currently married. Thus the conclusions drawn for women currently married also apply to women ever married.

Common Law Marriage (Union Libre), 1976-77

According to World Fertility Survey data, the average for the states of percent of common law marriages at first union in 1976-77 is 17.5 percent (Table 3.2). There is great variation in common law marriages, ranging from none reported in Aguascalientes to a high of 49 percent in Guanajuato. There are moderate state differences in the prevalence of common law marriages, as shown by the coefficient of variation of 77.

States with the highest values are Guanajuato, Hidalgo (45 percent), Veracruz (40 percent), and Nayarit (39 percent). Map 3.1B shows that these states are irregularly located across Mexico's central flank, and do not correspond to standard regions. In the populous Federal District, 11 percent of women have a common law first union. States with the lowest values are Aguascalientes (0 percent), Yucatan (25 percent), and Michoacan (4 percent). States with less than five percent common law marriage at first union are located in the west, excepting Guanajuato. In the border region, values are distributed along a gradient from high in the west to low in the east.

There is no significant relationship between common law marriage and non-Catholic religion (Map 6.4A). For instance, for both the heavily Catholic zone of the west region/Zacatecas/Queretaro and the heavily non-Catholic zone of southeast region/Tabasco/Chiapas, a full range of values for percent common law marriages is apparent. There is a significant inverse correspondence between common law marriage at first union and women currently married. This is partly the result of the definitions of the two variables, since women currently married excludes women in common law marriages.

Age at First Union, 1976-77

Age at first union is defined as the age at which respondents to the WFS entered in a first union of any type, i.e., common law (union libre) or legal marriage. As seen in Table 3.3, on the average for states, age at first union was 18.3 years in 1976-77. This compares to a median age of first marriage for U.S. females in 1980 of 22.0 years (Bogue, 1985). There is a low level of regional variation in average age at first union. The coefficient of variation is five and there is a range of four years between the highest age at marriage in Aguascalientes of 20.4 and the lowest mean age in Tabasco of 16.5.

The border region has a high age at first union. Excepting Coahuila with a moderate value, the five other border states have an average age of first union of 19.3(Map 3.1C). The Federal District has an even higher value of 19.7 years. The western region plus the neighboring states of Mexico and Guerrero have high values. States with low age at first union are concentrated in a zone comprising the gulf region plus Oaxaca and Chiapas to the south. Thus, while clearcut regions in mean age at first union are shown by the data and on the map, these regions only partly correspond to standard regions defined by a variety of investigators. In broad regional terms, there is strong similarity to results for age at first union in the Mexican National Prevalence Survey of 1979 (Martinez, 1982).

There is a strong correspondence between age at first union and total population in 1980 (see Map 2.1A), but lack of correspondence with urbanization variables. In addition, there is a positive relationship with cumulative fertility in 1976-77 (Map 3.2D), but a negative relationship with pill use, the nation's major contraceptive method in the late 70s (Map 3.3D). The former relationship is not surprising, since earlier marriage tends to raise total fertility. For the latter, women marrying earlier may be more exposed to use of the pill, versus other contraceptive techniques.

Number of Times in Union (Includes Common Law), 1976-77

This measure equals the mean number of consensual unions plus marriages for WFS respondents. The average state value is 0.95, or about one union per respondent at the time of the survey, with relatively small variation (see Table 3.4).

Map 3.1D reveals little regional consistency. Generally, the highest values are in the lower northwest states of Sinaloa and Nayarit, the pacific south and gulf states of Oaxaca, Chiapas, and Tabasco. Also, Quintana Roo in the Yucatan peninsula has the highest rate in the entire nation, yet its neighboring state of Yucatan has the country's lowest rate. This paradox also exists for women currently married. Other states with low rates are the Federal District, Zacatecas, as well as the west region. Border states are variable but generally in the intermediate range.

Number of times in union shows a strong opposite relationship with urbanization (see Map 2.6A); in other words there tends to be more marriages per woman in rural areas. Hence, it is not surprising that number of times married is associated with agricultural labor force (see Map 7.2A) but opposite in geographic distribution from such urban indicators as corporations, television, sports events, and movies (see maps in Chapters 6 and 7). It also shows a positive association with non-Catholicism (Map 6.4A), which is not surprising given Catholicism's tenets against divorce.

Women Currently Divorced or Separated, 1976-77

The percent of women currently divorced or separated in 1976-77 averaged 5.6 percent, with moderate variation among states(Table 3.5). This figure is very close to the 1979 national figure of 6.2 percent for proportion of women divorced, separated, or widowed reported in the National Prevalence Survey of 1979. The range is from 2.4 percent in Queretaro to 11.1 percent in Chiapas.

The percent of women currently divorced or separated in 1976-77 shows geographic patterns inconsistent with other marriage-related dimensions(see Map 3.1E). There are high rates in a three state northern region consisting of the states of Chihuahua, Durango, and Sinaloa, the Federal District (7.9 percent), the states bordering the Gulf of Mexico and pacific south states, and Yucatan and Quintana Roo on the Yucatan peninsula. States with the lowest rates of divorce/separation include Queretaro, Aguascalientes, Tabasco, and Nuevo Leon. Overall, the pattern does not conform to standard regions. Results are in general agreement with the 1979 National Prevalence Survey, which divided the nation into four regions, different from the present base regions (Martinez, 1982). That survey revealed highest rates in the "south," followed by "Federal District," "north," and "central."

The geographical pattern of divorce/separation shows moderate correspondence to the patterns for total population in 1970 and 1980 (Map 2.1A) as well as to certain urban-related variables such as electric lights and television. Its pattern also resembles that of non-Catholicism (Map 6.4A), since it is plausible that non-Catholic religions are more tolerant of divorce. However, several prominent exceptions are Tabasco and Nuevo Leon, having high non-Catholicism and low separation/divorce and the Federal District, having average non-Catholicism and high separation/divorce.

Table 3.1 Women Currently Married, 1976-77

No.	State	Percent Currently Married	Percent Ever Married
1	AGUASCALIENTES	73.2	82.9
2	BAJA CALIFORNIA	78.3	86.7
3	BAJA CALIFORNIA SUR	ND	ND
4	CAMPECHE	ND	ND
5	COAHUILA	79.5	87.5
6	COLIMA	ND	ND
7	CHIAPAS	81.0	96.3
8	CHIHUAHUA	72.1	82.2
9	DISTRITO FEDERAL	67.9	78.8
10	DURANGO	79.1	88.5
11	GUANAJUATO	75.3	80.5
12	GUERRERO	79.1	87.9
13	HIDALGO	81.3	90.1
14	JALISCO	72.9	79.7
15	MEXICO	80.6	88.0
16	MICHOACAN	77.5	84.4
17	MORELOS	83.3	90.7
18	NAYARIT	81.1	87.8
19	NUEVO LEON	73.9	81.5
20	OAXACA	83.7	94.2
21	PUEBLA	82.5	89.7
22	QUERETARO	86.2	90.7
23	QUINTANA ROO	87.8	94.9
24	SAN LUIS POTOSI	77.2	86.1
25	SINALOA	80.1	89.4
26	SONORA	77.3	83.1
27	TABASCO	84.6	92.3
28	TAMAULIPAS	76.2	83.5
29	TLAXCALA	ND	ND
30	VERACRUZ	82.5	91.4
31	YUCATAN	63.2	70.2
32	ZACATECAS	78.0	83.5

Mean		78.4	86.5
S.D.		5.4	5.6
C.V.		6.87	6.52
Minimum		63.2	70.2
Maximum		87.8	96.3

DEFINITION: The percentages of currently and of ever married women are based on the total number of respondents, and the respondents marital status at the time of the survey. Note that currently married repondents were also included as ever married.
NOTE: ND = no data.

SOURCE: 1976-77 World Fertility Survey.

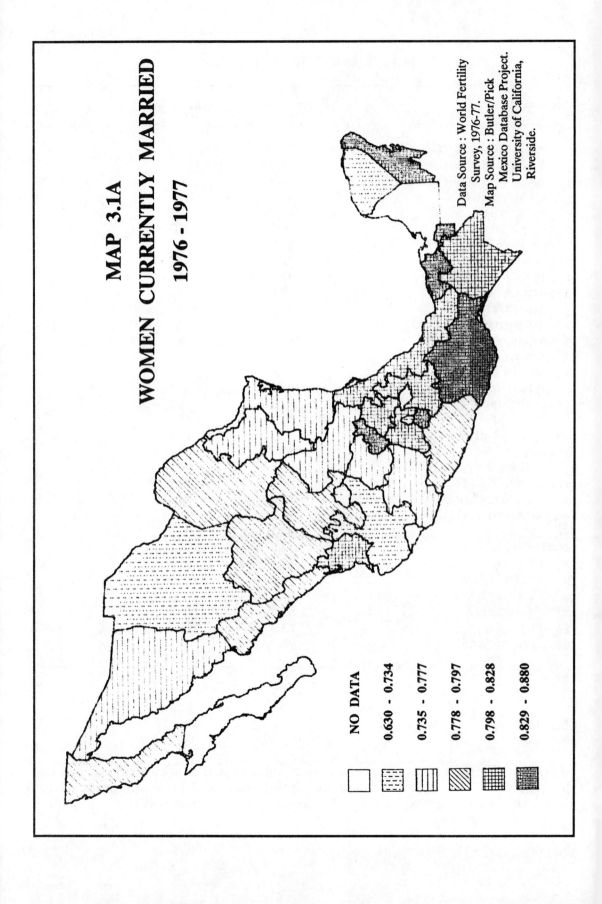

MAP 3.1A

WOMEN CURRENTLY MARRIED

1976 - 1977

Data Source : World Fertility
Survey, 1976-77.

Map Source : Butler/Pick
Mexico Database Project.
University of California,
Riverside.

NO DATA

0.630 - 0.734

0.735 - 0.777

0.778 - 0.797

0.798 - 0.828

0.829 - 0.880

Table 3.2 Common Law Marriage (Union Libre), 1976-77

No.	State	Percent Common Law Marriages
1	AGUASCALIENTES	0.0000
2	BAJA CALIFORNIA	0.2500
3	BAJA CALIFORNIA SUR	ND
4	CAMPECHE	ND
5	COAHUILA	0.1300
6	COLIMA	ND
7	CHIAPAS	0.3480
8	CHIHUAHUA	0.1370
9	DISTRITO FEDERAL	0.1100
10	DURANGO	0.1370
11	GUANAJUATO	0.4900
12	GUERRERO	0.0810
13	HIDALGO	0.4450
14	JALISCO	0.0510
15	MEXICO	0.1070
16	MICHOACAN	0.0380
17	MORELOS	0.1840
18	NAYARIT	0.3920
19	NUEVO LEON	0.0750
20	OAXACA	0.2570
21	PUEBLA	0.1570
22	QUERETARO	0.0540
23	QUINTANA ROO	0.0860
24	SAN LUIS POTOSI	0.1540
25	SINALOA	0.3020
26	SONORA	0.1560
27	TABASCO	0.1560
28	TAMAULIPAS	0.1050
29	TLAXCALA	ND
30	VERACRUZ	0.3960
31	YUCATAN	0.0250
32	ZACATECAS	0.0790

Mean	0.1751
S.D.	0.1316
C.V.	75.14
Minimum	0.0000
Maximum	0.4900

DEFINITION: Ratio is the percent of survey respondents with common law marriages for first union.

NOTE: ND = no data.

SOURCE: 1976-77 World Fertility Survey.

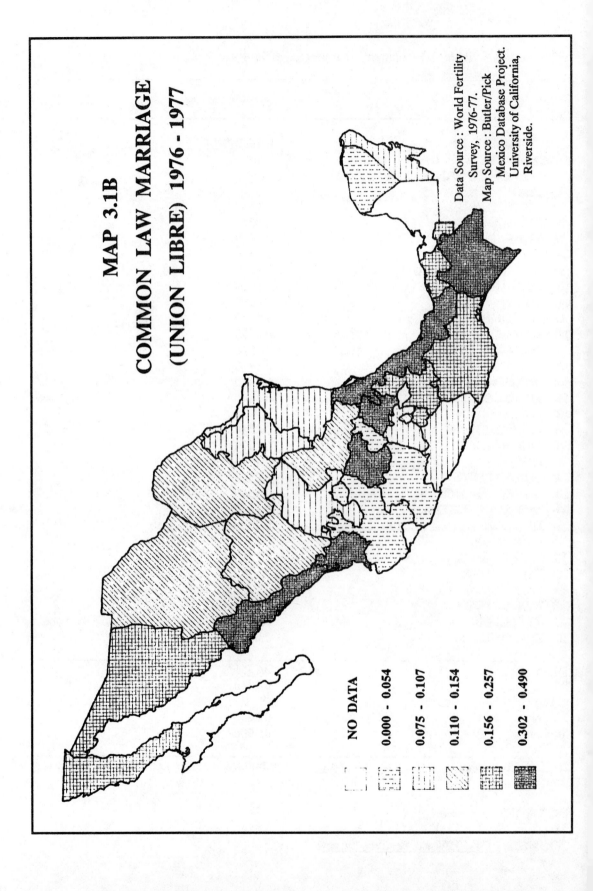

MAP 3.1B

COMMON LAW MARRIAGE

(UNION LIBRE) 1976 - 1977

Data Source : World Fertility
Survey, 1976-77.
Map Source : Butler/Pick
Mexico Database Project.
University of California,
Riverside.

NO DATA

0.000 - 0.054

0.075 - 0.107

0.110 - 0.154

0.156 - 0.257

0.302 - 0.490

Table 3.3 Age at First Union, 1976-77

No.	State	Average Age At First Union
1	AGUASCALIENTES	20.3500
2	BAJA CALIFORNIA	18.7400
3	BAJA CALIFORNIA SUR	ND
4	CAMPECHE	ND
5	COAHUILA	17.6900
6	COLIMA	ND
7	CHIAPAS	16.6100
8	CHIHUAHUA	19.9100
9	DISTRITO FEDERAL	19.6600
10	DURANGO	17.6000
11	GUANAJUATO	18.2400
12	GUERRERO	18.6200
13	HIDALGO	18.4700
14	JALISCO	18.9400
15	MEXICO	18.5700
16	MICHOACAN	18.5300
17	MORELOS	18.0600
18	NAYARIT	17.3300
19	NUEVO LEON	19.5100
20	OAXACA	16.8000
21	PUEBLA	17.7000
22	QUERETARO	18.2200
23	QUINTANA ROO	17.5400
24	SAN LUIS POTOSI	17.9000
25	SINALOA	17.8800
26	SONORA	19.6200
27	TABASCO	16.5400
28	TAMAULIPAS	18.7900
29	TLAXCALA	ND
30	VERACRUZ	17.0700
31	YUCATAN	18.1500
32	ZACATECAS	18.4600

Mean	18.2679
S.D.	0.9605
C.V.	5.26
Minimum	16.5400
Maximum	20.3500

DEFINITION: Values are the average of respondents age at first union.

NOTE: ND = no data.

SOURCE: 1976-77 World Fertility Survey.

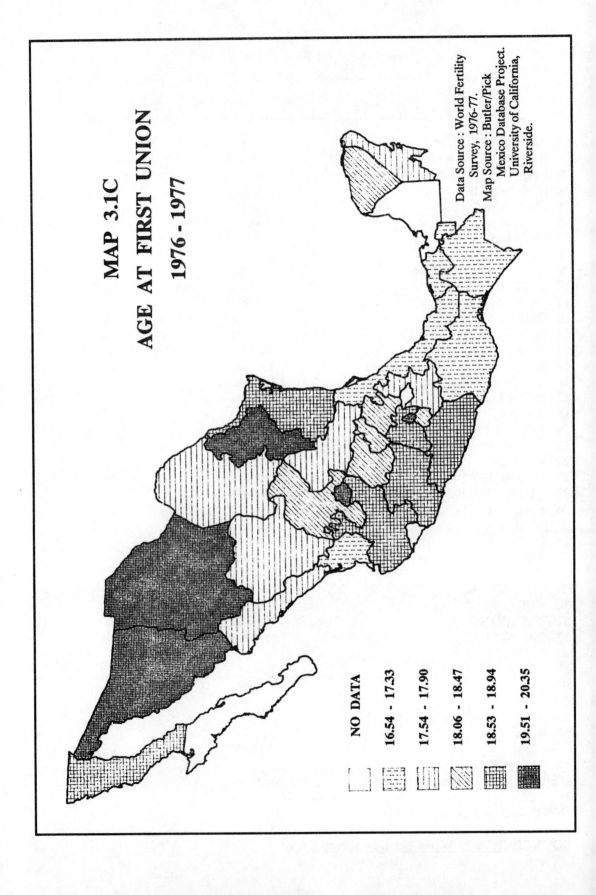

MAP 3.1C

AGE AT FIRST UNION

1976 - 1977

Data Source : World Fertility
Survey, 1976-77.

Map Source : Butler/Pick
Mexico Database Project.
University of California,
Riverside.

NO DATA

16.54 - 17.33

17.54 - 17.90

18.06 - 18.47

18.53 - 18.94

19.51 - 20.35

Table 3.4 Number of Times Married, 1976-77

No.	State	Average Number of Times Married
1	AGUASCALIENTES	0.90
2	BAJA CALIFORNIA	0.98
3	BAJA CALIFORNIA SUR	ND
4	CAMPECHE	ND
5	COAHUILA	0.98
6	COLIMA	ND
7	CHIAPAS	1.12
8	CHIHUAHUA	0.89
9	DISTRITO FEDERAL	0.85
10	DURANGO	0.96
11	GUANAJUATO	0.84
12	GUERRERO	0.94
13	HIDALGO	0.98
14	JALISCO	0.83
15	MEXICO	0.94
16	MICHOACAN	0.88
17	MORELOS	0.95
18	NAYARIT	1.09
19	NUEVO LEON	0.87
20	OAXACA	1.08
21	PUEBLA	0.93
22	QUERETARO	0.93
23	QUINTANA ROO	1.14
24	SAN LUIS POTOSI	0.94
25	SINALOA	1.05
26	SONORA	0.91
27	TABASCO	1.06
28	TAMAULIPAS	0.90
29	TLAXCALA	ND
30	VERACRUZ	1.04
31	YUCATAN	0.75
32	ZACATECAS	0.86

Mean		0.9496
S.D.		0.0929
C.V.		9.78
Minimum		0.75
Maximum		1.14

DEFINITION: Values are the average of the number of unions for respondents, including common law marriages.

NOTE: ND = no data.

SOURCE: 1976-77 World Fertility Survey.

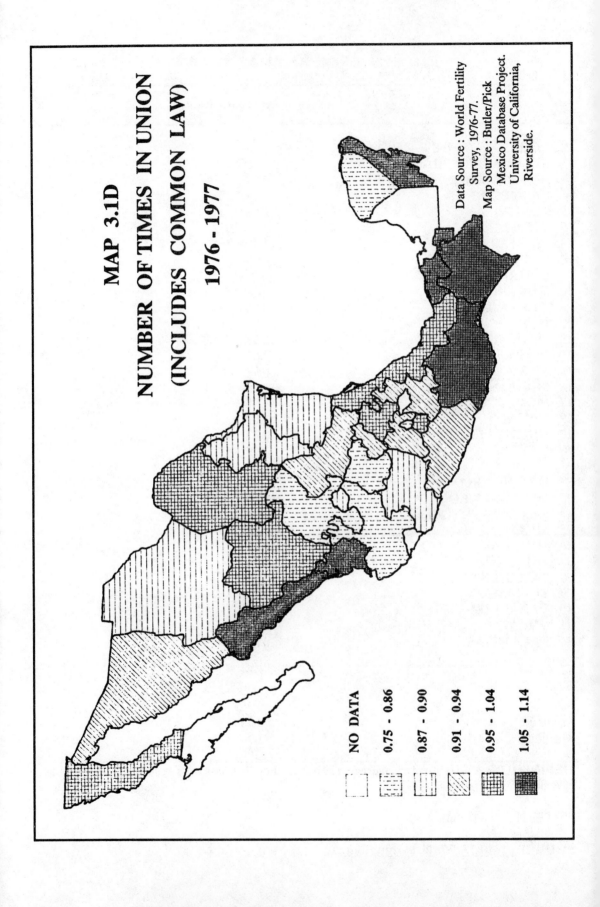

MAP 3.1D
NUMBER OF TIMES IN UNION
(INCLUDES COMMON LAW)
1976 - 1977

Data Source : World Fertility
Survey, 1976-77.

Map Source : Butler/Pick
Mexico Database Project.
University of California,
Riverside.

NO DATA

0.75 - 0.86

0.87 - 0.90

0.91 - 0.94

0.95 - 1.04

1.05 - 1.14

Table 3.5 Women Currently Divorced or Separated, 1976-77

No.	State	Percent Divorced or Separated
1	AGUASCALIENTES	2.4
2	BAJA CALIFORNIA	5.6
3	BAJA CALIFORNIA SUR	ND
4	CAMPECHE	ND
5	COAHUILA	5.1
6	COLIMA	ND
7	CHIAPAS	11.1
8	CHIHUAHUA	8.9
9	DISTRITO FEDERAL	7.9
10	DURANGO	7.1
11	GUANAJUATO	2.7
12	GUERRERO	6.3
13	HIDALGO	4.3
14	JALISCO	4.5
15	MEXICO	5.2
16	MICHOACAN	4.8
17	MORELOS	4.6
18	NAYARIT	4.4
19	NUEVO LEON	3.9
20	OAXACA	6.8
21	PUEBLA	4.4
22	QUERETARO	2.4
23	QUINTANA ROO	6.2
24	SAN LUIS POTOSI	5.7
25	SINALOA	8.4
26	SONORA	4.5
27	TABASCO	3.5
28	TAMAULIPAS	6.8
29	TLAXCALA	ND
30	VERACRUZ	6.4
31	YUCATAN	7.0
32	ZACATECAS	4.4
Mean		5.6
S.D.		2.0
C.V.		36.30
Minimum		2.4
Maximum		11.1

DEFINITION: Figures shown are the percent of all respondents who were divorced or separated at the time of the survey.

NOTE: ND = no data.

SOURCE: 1976-77 World Fertility Survey.

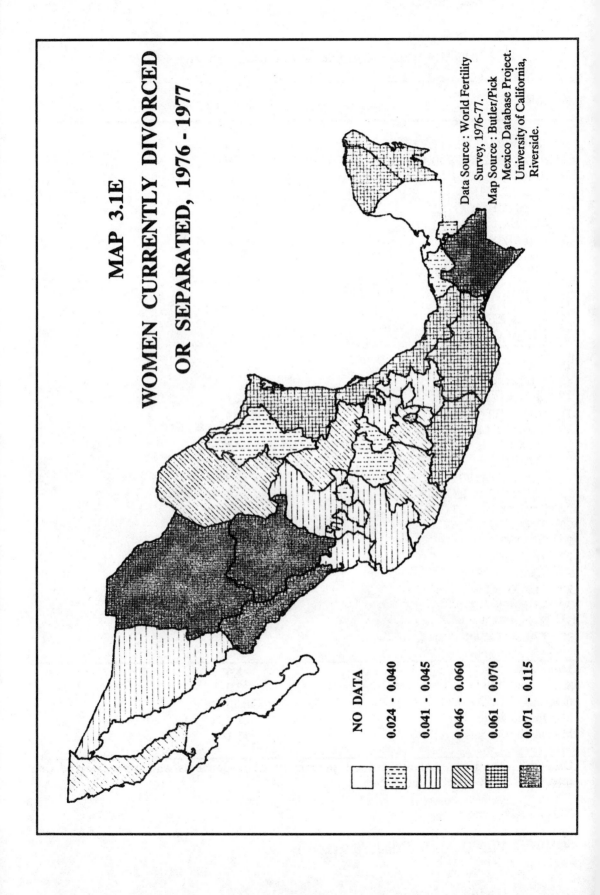

MAP 3.1E

WOMEN CURRENTLY DIVORCED
OR SEPARATED, 1976 - 1977

Data Source : World Fertility
Survey, 1976-77.
Map Source : Butler/Pick
Mexico Database Project.
University of California,
Riverside.

NO DATA

0.024 - 0.040

0.041 - 0.045

0.046 - 0.060

0.061 - 0.070

0.071 - 0.115

Fertility

Fecundity, 1976-77

Fecundity, measured as the percentage of women in a union and fecund, has a mean value of 68 percent. Thus about one third of married respondents have not borne a child for biological or other reasons. As seen in Table 3.6, there is little variation among states. Highest values are in Quintana Roo (84 percent) and Queretaro (77 percent), while the lowest values are in Aguascalientes (55 percent), the Federal District (60 percent), and Yucatan (60 percent). The west has low to medium values and the central region, excluding the Federal District, has medium to high values(Map 3.2A).

There are very significant negative relationships between fecundity and cumulative fertility, desired family size, and marriage, as measured by women ever married, women currently married, and age at first marriage. Fecundity also has a very significant positive association with wasted pregnancies and induced abortions. In addition, there are significant positive associations with common law marriage and number of times married, and, curiously, with major contraception forms of pill and IUD use. There is a strong positive relationship between fecundity and hospitals/clinics per 10,000 population. For instance, for the five states with high fecundity, Coahuila, Nayarit, Queretaro, Guerrero, and Quintana Roo, all except Coahuila have high per capita density of hospitals and clinics. The highest fecundity rate is for Quintana Roo, which is also the state with the highest per capita hospital/clinic rate.

Crude and Standardized Annual Fertility Rates, 1979

Crude annual fertility rates vary 72 percent between the lowest rate in the the state of Mexico of 27 and the highest rate for Guerrero of 4.6. The Federal District has a very low crude fertility rate of 32. This very low fertility, characteristic of about 20 percent of the Mexican population, exerts an attenuating effect on the overall national fertility rate. The capital's low fertility has been frequently reported in national studies (Garcia y Garma, 1979; Zambrano Lupi, 1979; Martinez et al., 1982).

As seen in Maps 3.2B and 3.2C, surrounding the central metropolitan zone is an eight state area of high fertility, including Michoacan, Guerrero, Oaxaca, Pueblo, and Morelos to the south and Hidalgo, Queretaro, and San Luis Potosi to the north. The first four of these have among the highest fertility in the nation (averaging 45.1). This high fertility is not surprising, given the generally low literacy, low income, and low gross state revenues, variables usually associated in Mexico with high fertility (Seiver, 1975; Holian, 1983, 1986; Pick, Butler, and Pavgi, 1988a). High fertility rates may be as a "push" factor in the massive net migration movement which occurred in the 60s and 70s from these states into the central zone (Fukurai, Pick and Butler, 1987a).

In the north, the border region has low to moderate fertility. Nuevo Leon's fertility rate of 31 is the lowest in the border region. This is not surprising given the presence of the metropolis of Monterrey. Tlaxcala's low fertility rate is surprising, since its urbanization and income levels are less than average (see Maps 2.6A and 8.4A). This is partly due to the above average youth of its age structure.

The standardized annual fertility rate was computed by indirect standardization (Shryock and Siegel, 1976, pp.242-3). In this method the crude annual fertility rate for each state is adjusted by a factor d/Summation($F_a p_a$), where d represents the total births in the state, F_a is the age-specific fertility rate for the nation and p_a is the population of a five-year age group in the state. It is important to indirectly standardize the crude rate, because otherwise the age structure of individual states can have an undue influence on the state's fertility, e.g. a young state's fertility rate may appear unduly high from a greater proportion of women in the highly fertile twenties age range. Both crude and standardized rates are presented in Table 3.7. The geographic distribution of standardized fertility rates is very similar to that for crude rates, mainly because variation among states in age structure is very small (see the age structure section in Chapter 2). As a result, interpretations given for crude fertility rates also apply to standardized rates.

Cumulative Fertility to Ever Married Women, 1976-77

Cumulative fertility to ever married women, 1976-77, measures the total number of births to WFS respondents. It includes women of various ages in the WFS sample. The mean value for the 28 states included in the WFS is 4.6, with quite low statewide differences as measured by the coefficient of variation(see Table 3.8). This value is considerably lower than in the early 1970s. For example, 1970 Mexican total fertility rate, a measure close to the present one, has been estimated at 6.5 (Martinez, 1982). Presently Mexico's total fertility rate is estimated at 4.0 (Population Reference Bureau, 1988).

In the WFS sample, cumulative fertility increases substantially by age of woman. The following information shows cumulative fertility rates, averaged for 28 states, for four age ranges of women.

Average Cumulative Fertility by Age of Respondent, WFS, 1976-77

Cumulative Fertility	Age<25	Ages 25-34	Ages 35-44	Age 45+
mean	1.76	4.27	6.81	7.21
standard deviation	0.18	0.50	0.83	1.74
coeff. of variation	10.44	11.75	12.21	24.12

SOURCE : 1976-77 World Fertility Survy (1978).

The geographic patterns of cumulative fertility for the four ages ranges are highly similar. Hence, the geographic distribution on Map 3.2D generally reflects cumulative fertility for the four age groups.

Among states, the Federal District has the lowest cumulative fertility of 3.6 children ever born. This corresponds to other studies which indicate that Mexico's lowest fertility is located in the Federal District (Martinez et al., 1982). The central region, surrounding the Federal District, varies from low to high cumulative fertility, and is generally higher in its northern part. The state of Mexico's cumulative fertility is average. This compares with low values for Mexico state's annual fertility rates in 1979 (see Maps 3.2B and 3.2C). Fertility in the state of Mexico lowered relatively in the 70s, probably as a result of the state's rapid growth, resulting in an increasing proportion of its population included in the Mexico City greater metropolitan area (Chapter 2 demonstrates its growth in the 1970s). Thus, it is likely its fertility will continue to decrease, approximating the Federal District level.

The west region has very high cumulative fertility, more so relatively than for the 1979 standardized fertility rate. This is especially surprising for Jalisco, since it includes the very large city of Guadalajara. The borderlands region has an inconsistent pattern of cumulative fertility, with high values in Baja California, Coahuila, and Tamaulipas. Overall, its values are relatively higher than for the other fertility variables in the atlas. The pacific south region has moderate to high cumulative fertility, which is similar for 1980 crude and standardized annual fertility rates. In the southeast region, cumulative fertility is low for Yucatan and moderate for Quintana Roo.

The overall pattern by regions agrees with results for cumulative marital fertility in the Mexican National Prevalence Survey of 1979 (Martinez, 1982). In that survey, for four broad regions of Mexico, cumulative marital fertility was 5.27 in the Federal District, 7.85 in the "central" region, 7.16 in the "north", and 7.20 in the "south."

Cumulative Fertility to Women, Age 20-29, 1980

Cumulative fertility for women, age 20-29 years, is calculated from the 1980 census question which asked women in households how many children they had given birth to. This measure of cumulative fertility differs from cumulative fertility to ever married women, 1976-77, by measuring cumulative fertility to all women, not just those ever-married, and by restricting women's age to 20-29 years. Results are shown in Table 3.9. The mean value of 1.8 children per woman, age 20-29, approximates the range for cumulative fertility by age groups in the World Fertility Survey (see text table for the previous variable). As is typical of Mexican fertility, variation among states is low.

The geographic distribution for cumulative fertility to women 20-29, seen in Map 3.2E, closely resembles the patterns for the crude and standardized annual fertility rates. As with annual fertility, cumulative fertility to women 20-29 is low in the borderlands, very low in the Federal District, and low in the state of Mexico. In the central and south regions, cumulative fertility age 20-29 has moderate to high values, versus annual fertility's distinctively higher values in the south compared to the central region. There are no consistent regional patterns in the gulf and southeast regions. Overall, the national pattern corresponds to the results for cumulative marital fertility in the Mexican National Prevalence Survey of 1979. Cumulative fertility for women age 20-29 is strongly correlated with annual fertility rate, standardized annual fertility rate, and cumulative fertility for women age 45-49. It varies inversely to urbanization 1980 (see Map 2.6A), as well as to urban-related variables, including value and number of SACVs (corporations), gross state product per capita, per capita gasoline expenditures, telephones per capita, and movies per capita. Not surprisingly, rural variables, such as percent agricultural workforce, 1980, and agricultural occupations, 1980, show strong direct relationship to cumulative fertility for women, age 20-29. The urban-rural effects on fertility in Mexico have been documented in a number of prior fertility studies (Pick et al., 1986, Pick et al., 1988a,c). Another set of variables which show strong negative relationships are the literacy and education variables (see Maps 6.1A-C, 6.2A-D). These effects have often been noted (World Fertility Survey, 1980; Holian, 1983, 1986; Pick et al., 1986; Pick et al., 1988a,d). Also, female economic activity and knowledge of effective birth control are inversely related to the present characteristic, while male economic activity and crowding are directly related to it. Similar economic activity ef-ffects were noted at the municipio level in the Mexican borderlands (Pick et al., 1986, 1988d).

Cumulative Fertility to Women, Age 45-49, 1980

Cumulative fertility to women, age 45-49, represents total number of births per woman and is cal-culated similarly to cumulative fertility for women age, 20-29 (again, see Table 3.9). It reflects fer-tility which largely took place in the 1950s and 1960s. The mean fertility value for the states is 6.6, a level which approximates WFS cumulative fertility for ever married women, 45 or older. This amount greatly exceeds recent fertility levels in Mexico. For instance, the closely related measure of total fertility rate was estimated at 6.7 for the year 1971 (Martinez et al., 1982) but dropped to an estimated 4.0 in 1988 (Population Reference Bureau, 1988). Although there is low variation in cumulative fertility to women, age 45-49, the range of 3.1 is considerable.

Map 3.2F reveals that the geographic pattern of cumulative fertility to women, age 45-49, resembles somewhat that for cumulative fertility to women, age 20-29, but differs from other fertility variables. There is an extensive zone of high fertility encompassing the west region, as well as the states of Zacatecas and Durango. The border region has low to moderate fertility. There is a large zone of low fertility in parts of the south, gulf, and southeast regions, not noted for other fertility variables. Overall, the geographic pattern differs from the pattern by regions of cumulative marital fertility in the 1979 Mexican National Prevalence Survey, in which there were nearly equal fertility levels in the "north" versus the "south."

Cumulative fertility to women, age 45-49, has weaker relationships than cumulative fertility to women, age 20-29, with education/literacy, urbanization, education/literacy, and urban-related vari-ables. It does, however, have significant resemblence to female economic activity and percent non-Catholic, and significant differences from male economic activity and crowding.

Table 3.6 Fecundity, 1976-77

No.	State	Fecundity
1	AGUASCALIENTES	0.5500
2	BAJA CALIFORNIA	0.6900
3	BAJA CALIFORNIA SUR	ND
4	CAMPECHE	ND
5	COAHUILA	0.7220
6	COLIMA	ND
7	CHIAPAS	0.7070
8	CHIHUAHUA	0.6240
9	DISTRITO FEDERAL	0.5970
10	DURANGO	0.6870
11	GUANAJUATO	0.6710
12	GUERRERO	0.7240
13	HIDALGO	0.7090
14	JALISCO	0.6310
15	MEXICO	0.7070
16	MICHOACAN	0.6790
17	MORELOS	0.7070
18	NAYARIT	0.7220
19	NUEVO LEON	0.6140
20	OAXACA	0.6740
21	PUEBLA	0.7200
22	QUERETARO	0.7650
23	QUINTANA ROO	0.8370
24	SAN LUIS POTOSI	0.6840
25	SINALOA	0.6990
26	SONORA	0.6820
27	TABASCO	0.6840
28	TAMAULIPAS	0.6700
29	TLAXCALA	ND
30	VERACRUZ	0.7210
31	YUCATAN	0.5960
32	ZACATECAS	0.6810
Mean		0.6841
S.D.		0.0550
C.V.		8.04
Minimum		0.5500
Maximum		0.8370

DEFINITION: Fecundity equals fecund respondents currently in union (including pregnant women) divided by total respondents currently in union.

NOTE: ND = no data.

SOURCE: 1976-77 World Fertility Survey.

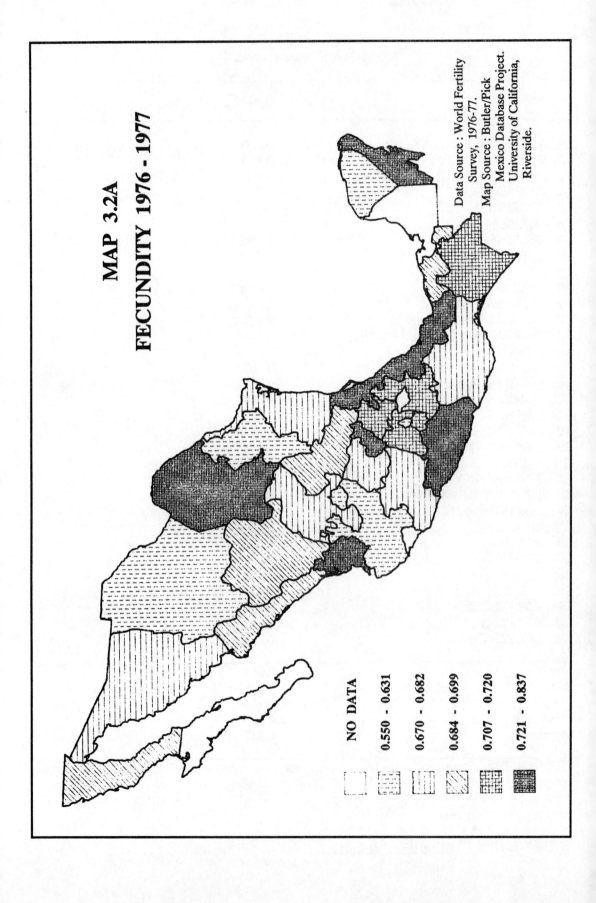

MAP 3.2A
FECUNDITY 1976 - 1977

NO DATA

0.550 - 0.631

0.670 - 0.682

0.684 - 0.699

0.707 - 0.720

0.721 - 0.837

Data Source : World Fertility
Survey, 1976-77.
Map Source : Butler/Pick
Mexico Database Project.
University of California,
Riverside.

Table 3.7 Fertility Rates, 1979

No.	State	Annual Fertility Rate	Standardized Annual Fertility Rate
1	AGUASCALIENTES	39.30	40.58
2	BAJA CALIFORNIA	33.30	29.61
3	BAJA CALIFORNIA SUR	38.40	35.86
4	CAMPECHE	33.20	36.61
5	COAHUILA	39.10	43.81
6	COLIMA	34.60	34.81
7	CHIAPAS	35.10	33.35
8	CHIHUAHUA	31.70	31.27
9	DISTRITO FEDERAL	31.80	25.26
10	DURANGO	42.40	47.54
11	GUANAJUATO	37.50	38.48
12	GUERRERO	46.50	46.79
13	HIDALGO	42.30	45.75
14	JALISCO	38.00	38.25
15	MEXICO	27.00	25.70
16	MICHOACAN	43.50	43.19
17	MORELOS	41.00	40.60
18	NAYARIT	35.20	37.85
19	NUEVO LEON	31.00	30.06
20	OAXACA	44.40	46.55
21	PUEBLA	46.20	51.29
22	QUERETARO	40.00	43.82
23	QUINTANA ROO	35.30	35.79
24	SAN LUIS POTOSI	40.50	42.97
25	SINALOA	41.30	40.63
26	SONORA	33.70	33.16
27	TABASCO	45.60	42.56
28	TAMAULIPAS	34.50	33.50
29	TLAXCALA	33.00	35.13
30	VERACRUZ	36.90	37.39
31	YUCATAN	36.20	37.47
32	ZACATECAS	39.10	41.07
	Mean	37.74	38.33
	S.D.	4.77	6.21
	C.V.	12.63	16.19
	Minimum	27.00	25.26
	Maximum	46.50	51.29

DEFINITION: Crude fertility rate 1979 is the ratio of births for the year 1979 to the population in 1980, multiplied by 1,000. Standardized fertility rate 1979 is calculated from the crude fertility rate 1979 indirect standardization, based on a state's population age structure in 1980 and a standard population (see text for further explanation).

SOURCE: Births: 1981 Anuario Estadistico, Population: 1980 Mexican Census of Population.

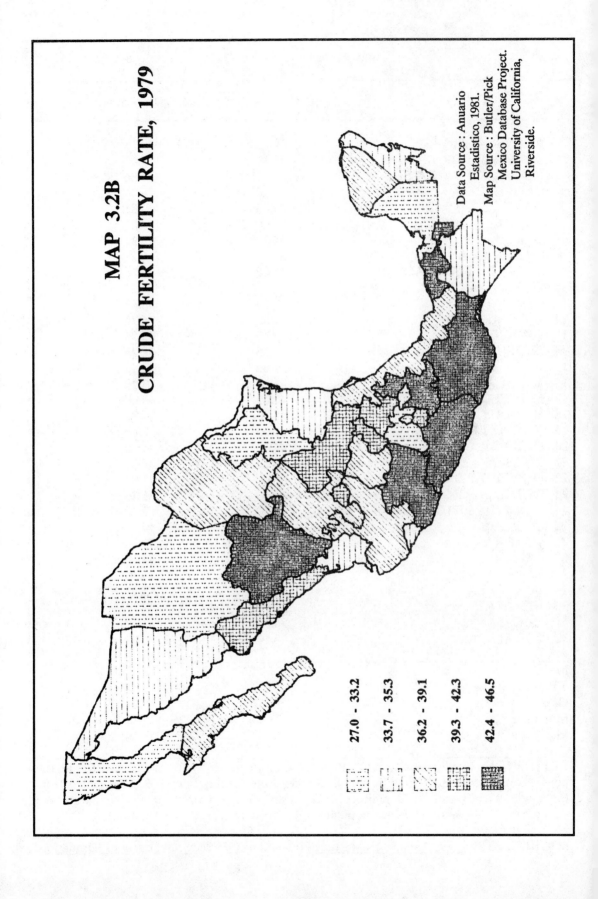

MAP 3.2B

CRUDE FERTILITY RATE, 1979

27.0 - 33.2

33.7 - 35.3

36.2 - 39.1

39.3 - 42.3

42.4 - 46.5

Data Source : Anuario
Estadistico, 1981.

Map Source : Butler/Pick
Mexico Database Project.
University of California,
Riverside.

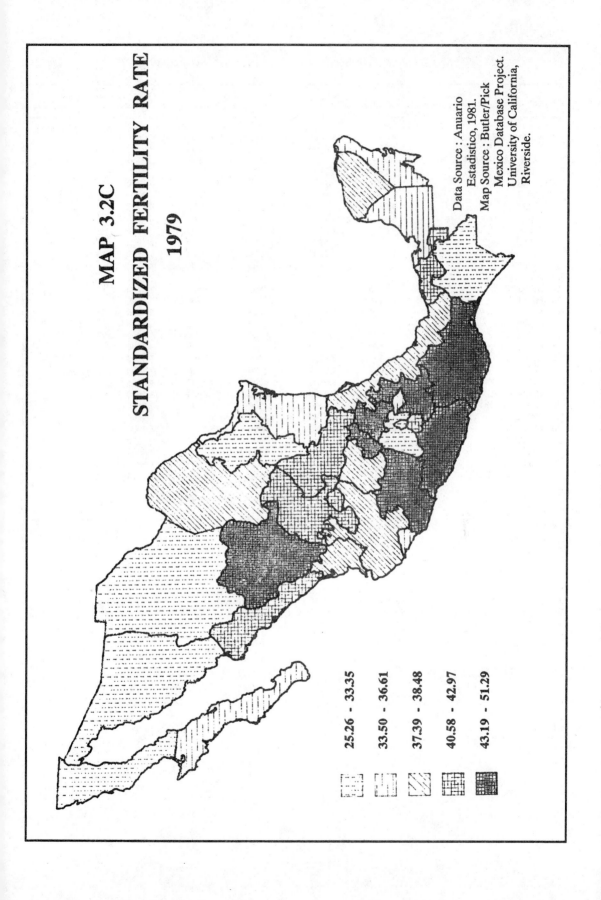

MAP 3.2C

STANDARDIZED FERTILITY RATE

1979

25.26 - 33.35

33.50 - 36.61

37.39 - 38.48

40.58 - 42.97

43.19 - 51.29

Data Source : Anuario
    Estadistico, 1981.
Map Source : Butler/Pick
Mexico Database Project.
University of California,
Riverside.

Table 3.8 Cumulative Fertility to Ever Married Women, 1976-77

No.	State	All Ages	Age < 25	Age 25 - 34	Age 35 - 44	Age 45+
1	AGUASCALIENTES	4.8824	1.5000	4.2500	7.1800	4.0000
2	BAJA CALIFORNIA	4.9597	1.9600	4.2600	6.8300	7.9000
3	BAJA CALIFORNIA SUR	ND	ND	ND	ND	ND
4	CAMPECHE	ND	ND	ND	ND	ND
5	COAHUILA	4.9091	1.7800	5.0600	7.8400	7.5800
6	COLIMA	ND	ND	ND	ND	ND
7	CHIAPAS	4.7210	1.6600	4.8000	7.0700	6.4700
8	CHIHUAHUA	4.4057	1.7300	3.3800	6.1300	6.4300
9	DISTRITO FEDERAL	3.6324	1.3600	3.2500	4.9500	5.6400
10	DURANGO	4.4969	1.6700	4.3200	7.3300	6.8000
11	GUANAJUATO	5.2803	1.5100	4.8300	7.6800	9.3500
12	GUERRERO	4.7429	1.8100	3.9100	6.7200	8.3100
13	HIDALGO	5.3110	1.8900	4.8000	7.3900	7.3500
14	JALISCO	5.0343	1.8600	4.4800	7.0600	7.3200
15	MEXICO	4.6496	1.7800	4.0300	7.2800	7.6100
16	MICHOACAN	5.4474	1.8500	4.7500	8.4100	8.3300
17	MORELOS	4.0882	1.4800	3.7600	6.5300	6.6700
18	NAYARIT	4.3038	2.0000	5.0000	6.0000	5.0000
19	NUEVO LEON	4.1530	1.6500	4.0500	5.7400	4.8800
20	OAXACA	4.9665	2.0700	4.2400	7.2200	7.5500
21	PUEBLA	4.7093	1.8100	4.1700	7.0500	7.5400
22	QUERETARO	5.4196	1.9800	5.0800	7.8900	9.0500
23	QUINTANA ROO	4.5484	2.0000	3.8000	7.3600	11.4000
24	SAN LUIS POTOSI	4.6029	1.8000	4.4900	5.9700	7.9500
25	SINALOA	4.5990	1.5700	4.3600	7.6500	5.9500
26	SONORA	4.5234	1.9500	3.7900	6.5100	6.5800
27	TABASCO	4.6481	1.8200	4.2700	6.5600	7.7300
28	TAMAULIPAS	4.8314	1.7900	3.9000	6.1100	8.6500
29	TLAXCALA	ND	ND	ND	ND	ND
30	VERACRUZ	3.8725	1.5300	3.9500	5.7200	6.6500
31	YUCATAN	3.8750	1.8600	3.7100	5.2300	3.3300
32	ZACATECAS	4.5000	1.5900	4.9300	7.0000	10.0000
	Mean	4.6469	1.7593	4.2721	6.8004	7.2150
	S.D.	0.4569	0.1836	0.5019	0.8333	1.7399
	C.V.	9.83	10.44	11.75	12.25	24.12
	Minimum	3.6324	1.3600	3.2500	4.9500	3.3300
	Maximum	5.4474	2.0700	5.0800	8.4100	11.400

DEFINITION: Numbers represent the average number of children born to respondents in each age group. The values for all ages are the ratio of the total number of children born for the age groups shown and the total number of ever married respondents.

NOTE: ND = no data.

SOURCE: 1976-77 World Fertility Survey (1978).

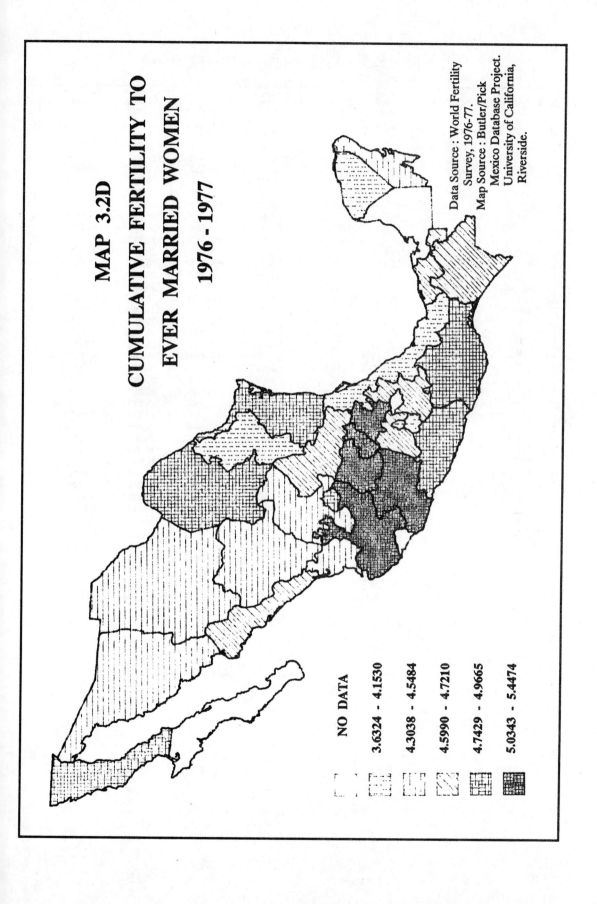

MAP 3.2D

CUMULATIVE FERTILITY TO

EVER MARRIED WOMEN

1976 - 1977

Data Source : World Fertility
Survey, 1976-77.

Map Source : Butler/Pick
Mexico Database Project.
University of California,
Riverside.

NO DATA

3.6324 - 4.1530

4.3038 - 4.5484

4.5990 - 4.7210

4.7429 - 4.9665

5.0343 - 5.4474

Table 3.9 Cumulative Fertility to Women, 1980

No.	State	Births to Women Ages 20-29	Total Women Ages 20-29	Cumulative Fertility Ages 20-29	Births to Women Ages 45-49	Total Women Ages 45-49	Cumulative Fertiltiy Ages 45-49
1	AGUASCALIENTES	71,218	42,858	1.6617	62,966	8,465	7.4384
2	BAJA CALIFORNIA	158,516	107,668	1.4723	138,884	21,978	6.3192
3	BAJA CALIFORNIA SUR	31,743	18,871	1.6821	21,,247	3,226	6.5862
4	CAMPECHE	69,855	36,040	1.9383	40,106	6,867	5.8404
5	COAHUILA	216,977	129,128	1.6803	174,403	27,071	6.4424
6	COLIMA	47,690	28,603	1.6673	43,609	5,518	7.9030
7	CHIAPAS	354,601	174,155	2.0361	181,655	31,995	5.6776
8	CHIHUAHUA	264,841	167,127	1.5847	236,290	36,759	6.4281
9	DISTRITO FEDERAL	1,125,829	918,556	1.2257	897,195	174,373	5.1453
10	DURANGO	167,663	86,591	1.9363	152,090	20,547	7.4021
11	GUANAJUATO	428,204	240,268	1.7822	376,315	50,133	7.5063
12	GUERRERO	331,962	159,376	2.0829	231,456	38,167	6.0643
13	HIDALGO	238,188	118,930	2.0028	171,978	26,863	6.4020
14	JALISCO	570,861	362,440	1.5750	514,433	72,805	7.0659
15	MEXICO	1,167,725	662,480	1.7627	794,897	121,582	6.5379
16	MICHOACAN	394,986	223,104	1.7704	354,647	50,557	7.0148
17	MORELOS	137,148	79,077	1.7344	108,723	18,142	5.9929
18	NAYARIT	102,970	53,696	1.9176	88,242	12,012	7.3462
19	NUEVO LEON	318,616	218,963	1.4551	266,043	42,965	6.1921
20	OAXACA	330,632	179,783	1.8391	248,884	46,524	5.3496
21	PUEBLA	484,608	265,628	1.8244	381,578	62,099	6.1447
22	QUERETARO	109,747	59,127	1.8561	88,795	12,001	7.3990
23	QUINTANA ROO	42,298	20,802	2.0334	19,362	2,918	6.6354
24	SAN LUIS POTOSI	230,192	124,746	1.8453	202,214	30,337	6.6656
25	SINALOA	274,379	148,105	1.8526	200,549	28,067	7.1454
26	SONORA	202,101	129,332	1.5627	169,765	25,849	6.5676
27	TABASCO	188,862	90,110	2.0959	107,739	16,352	6.5887
28	TAMAULIPAS	252,129	162,325	1.5532	218,626	36,713	5.9550
29	TLAXCALA	79,845	42,283	1.8883	66,513	9,940	6.6914
30	VERACRUZ	789,588	445,247	1.7734	570,908	100,816	5.6629
31	YUCATAN	144,589	87,296	1.6563	108,422	20,235	5.3581
32	ZACATECAS	154,133	78,970	1.9518	156,717	19,064	8.2206
	National Total	9,482,696	5,661,685	56.7004	7,395,251	1,180,940	209.6891
	Mean	296,334	176,928	1.7719	231,102	36,904	6.5528
	S.D.	273,542	187,428	0.1976	205,756	36,162	0.7388
	C.V.	92.31	105.93	11.15	89.03	97.99	11.27
	Minimum	31,743	18,871	1.2257	19,362	2,918	5.1453
	Maximum	1,167,725	918,556	2.0959	897,195	174,373	8.2206

DEFINITION: Cumulative fertility is defined as thew number of childern ever born to women in that age group to the total number of women in that age group.

SOURCE: 1980 Mexican Census of Population, Volume 1, Table 13.

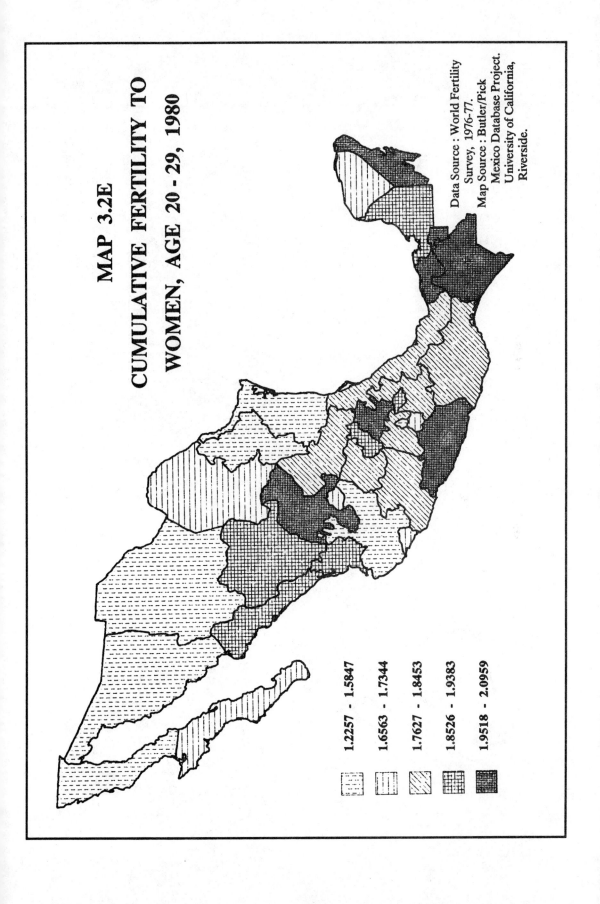

MAP 3.2E
CUMULATIVE FERTILITY TO
WOMEN, AGE 20 - 29, 1980

Data Source : World Fertility
Survey, 1976-77.
Map Source : Butler/Pick
Mexico Database Project.
University of California,
Riverside.

1.2257 - 1.5847

1.6563 - 1.7344

1.7627 - 1.8453

1.8526 - 1.9383

1.9518 - 2.0959

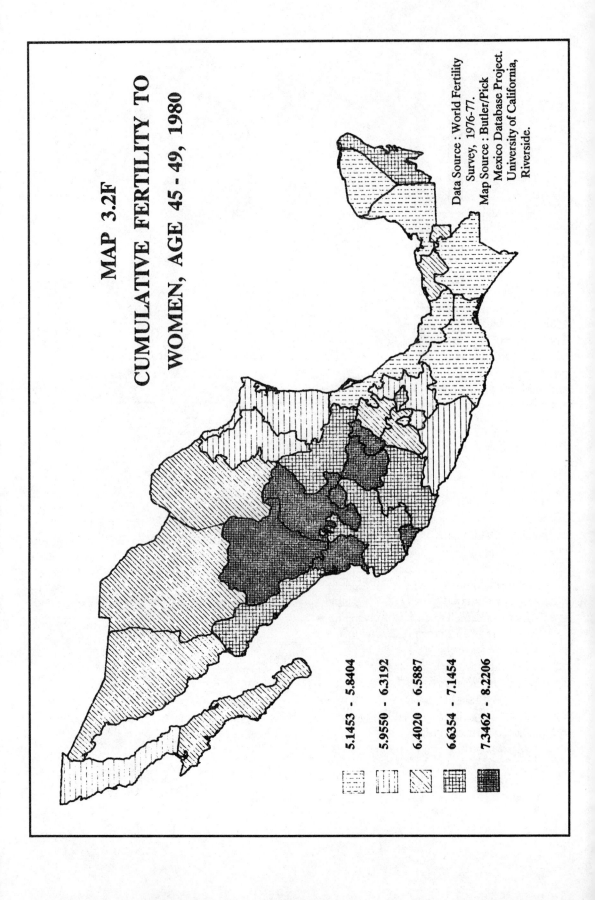

MAP 3.2F
CUMULATIVE FERTILITY TO
WOMEN, AGE 45 - 49, 1980

Data Source : World Fertility
Survey, 1976-77.
Map Source : Butler/Pick
Mexico Database Project.
University of California,
Riverside.

5.1453 - 5.8404

5.9550 - 6.3192

6.4020 - 6.5887

6.6354 - 7.1454

7.3462 - 8.2206

Family Planning

Wasted Pregnancies, 1976-77

The variable for wasted pregnancies measures the ratio of total lifetime wasted pregnancies to total lifetime fertile pregnancies. Wasted pregnancies include miscarriages, still births, and induced abortions. This non-conventional measure is intended to indicate the geographic distribution of ratios of pregnancy success or failure in Mexico. On average, the ratio of pregnancy failures to successes is 0.10. There is moderate variation in this ratio among states (Table 3.10).

As seen in Map 3.3A, the regional distribution for wasted pregnancies shows correspondence with that of 1980 urbanization (Map 2.6A). This is seen by the high ratios of wasted pregnancies in the states containing the three primary cities. The central metropolitan zone has a very high ratio, with the Federal District having the second highest state ratio of 0.14. Jalisco state, containing the Guadalajara metropolitan region, has the highest state ratio of 0.15. Nuevo Leon, containing Monterrey, has a high rate at 0.12, as do the highly urbanized Baja California is also high at 0.13. The southeast region states of Quintana Roo and Yucatan are also very high. High rates may indicate inadequacies in health and medical care related to childbearing, or they may be the result of other unknown factors. States low in wasted pregnancies include the rural states of Hidalgo, Oaxaca, and Tabasco, as well as more urbanized Queretaro and Aguascalientes. The only applicable standard regions are the central metropolitan zone, northeast, and southeast, all having high level of wasted pregnancies.

Induced Abortions, 1976-77

Induced abortions is the ratio of induced abortions to wasted pregnancies. It distinguishes induced abortions from other types of wasted pregnancies, including spontaneous abortions, i.e. miscarriages, and still births. The product of the induced abortions ratio and the wasted pregnancies ratio equals the ratio of induced abortions to pregnancies shown in Table 3.11. In Mexico there is a low rate of abortion, as indicated by a mean induced abortion ratio of 0.05. This is further shown by the ratio of abortions to fertile pregnancies, which is only 0.006 for the nation as a whole. This ratio is much lower than that in most advanced nations. For example, in the United States, the same ratio was 0.40 in 1977 and 0.43 in 1980 (U.S. Bureau of the Census, 1984).

Map 3.3B indicates considerable geographic variation in the induced abortion ratio, which may reflect differences in the legal and social environment for abortion among states. The reader should be cautioned regarding this variable, due to presence of random error from the small numbers of abortions in the World Fertility Survey sample.

The largest area of high values for the abortion ratio is in the northeast region plus the neighboring states of Coahuila, San Luis Potosi, and Queretaro. In addition the Federal District, Morelia, and Guerrero form a contiguous region having a high abortion ratio. States with having no induced abortions indicated by WFS respondents include Aguacalientes, Chihuahua, Hidalgo, Michoacan, Nayarit, and Zacatecas.

Women Knowing An Efficient Birth Control Method, 1976-77

This variable represents the ratio of women knowing an efficient birth control method to all respondents. It had a mean by state of 88 percent in 1976-77. This figure reflects the large strides in birth control in Mexico achieved by the late 70s. This was reflected in the nation's declining standardized birth rate during the 70s (Rubin-Kurtzman, 1987). There is relatively low state variation in birth control knowledge, with extremes varying from a low of only 63.2 percent in Oaxaca to levels of 95 percent in ten states (see Table 3.12). The standard deviation is 0.10, with a low coefficient of variation of only 11.5. This contrasts with a C.V. for standardized fertility rate of 16.

Map 3.3C reveals a very distinctive regional pattern of variation. The northwest region and Aguascalientes have the highest ratios, greater than 97 percent for all states. The populous, urbanized states of the Federal District, Jalisco, and Nuevo Leon also have high ratios. On the other hand, Oaxaca, Veracruz, Puebla, Hildalgo, and Queretaro are very low in birth control knowledge. In the southeast region, birth control knowledge is high in urbanized Yucatan (96 percent), and high also in less urban Quintana Roo (95 percent), possibly a result of its high inmigration in the 70s from other states (see Map 4.3C). For the country as a whole, there is a consistent contoured pattern ranging from high values in the northwest to low values in the gulf and south, with the southeast showing aberrant values.

There is an inverse relationship of knowledge of birth control with standardized fertility rate (Map 3.2C). This tends to confirm the inverse relationship between birth control and fertility reported elsewhere (Garcia y Garma, 1979). There also is a significant relationship between contraceptive knowledge and 1980 urbanization, as revealed by a highly significant correlation. This relationship has also been found in a number of studies. It also shows a strong relationship to secondary education. Since it is so highly correlated with fertility, birth control knowledge is a crucial variable in understanding the nation's overall population growth and in setting future population policies.

Birth Control Pill Use, 1976-77

Birth control pill use measures the ratio, in percent, of birth control pill users to users of all efficent birth control methods. As seen below, the birth control pill was the leading contraceptive technique in Mexico in 1976-77, as well as in subsequent surveys in 1978 and 1982.

Percentage Distribution of Contraceptive Use for Exposed Respondents

Method	WFS*,1976-77	ENPUA**,1978	END***,1982
Birth Control Pill	35.8	35.4	29.7
Intrauterine Device(IUD)	18.8	16.1	13.8
Sterilization (female)	8.9	17.8	28.1
Other modern methods	13.9	13.7	15.2
Modern Methods---Total	77.4	83.0	86.8
Traditional Methods---Total	22.6	17.0	13.2
TOTAL	100.0	100.0	100.0

* World Fertility Survey (SPP, 1978, 1979a,b).
** Encuesta Nacional de Prevalencia en el Uso de Metodos Anticonceptivos (CPNPF, 1980).
*** Encuesta Nacional Demografica (CONAPO, 1982).

The statewide results for use of birth control methods are shown in Table 3.13. The statewide mean for birth control pill use by state was 38.5 percent, with moderate variation. The range of pill use from a low of 15.4 percent in Oaxaca to a high of 65.1 percent in Sinaloa. There is clear geographic gradation from north to south in levels of pill use (see Map 3.3D). The north, encompassing the northwest, north, and northeast regions, has high levels of pill use, with the exception of Nuevo Leon, while the central flank of Mexico has low to moderate levels of use. The Federal District and state of Mexico have low values, 28.6 percent and 22.3 percent respectively. The pacific south region has a low average value of 27.1 percent. This north-south axis may in part reflect the affordability of this contraceptive method, since income declines in Mexico from north to south (see Map 8.4A and 8.4B). Exceptions to these similar north-south differentials are the Federal District and state of Mexico, which have high income but low birth control pill use. The contraceptive support systems in those states may favor alternative modern birth control methods of IUD and sterilization.

Besides income, birth control pill use has a similar geographic pattern to literacy and education, again with the exception of the Federal District. Greater literacy and education may enhance recognition of the availability of the methods, as well as improve effectiveness of use. The patterns of contraceptive pill use and women knowing an efficient birth control method are similar in declining from north to south. This correspondence may indicate the presence of north-south educational and economic differentials influencing both contraceptive variables.

Female Sterilization, 1976-77

Female sterilization was third in importance as a contraceptive method in Mexico in 1976-77 (see text table on contraceptive use). However, subsequently this method has been Mexico's most rapidly growing contraceptive method. In 1982, it nearly equalled pill use at 28.1 percent of users versus 29.7 percent for the pill. It is expected that by now it is the leading contraceptive method in Mexico.

Since it is an irreversible method, it tends to be adopted by older women, whereas the birth control pill is characteristically adopted by younger women (Bronfman, Lopez, and Tuiran, 1986).

In 1976-77, the state average for female sterilization was 10.3 percent, with a moderate coefficient of variation of 49. The regional distribution must be cautiously appraised, due to the small number of survey respondents. Regions of higher female sterilization were the northeast region plus Coahuila; the gulf region plus Puebla, Mexico, and Oaxaca; and the adjoining two-state area of Jalisco and Zacatecas. States with low levels of female sterilization, Sinaloa, San Luis Potosi, Morelos, Guerrero, and Chiapas, were scattered throughout the country.

The geographic pattern in Map 3.3E is not readily explained, and does not seem to match many other atlas dimensions. In addition to random variation, it may be that regional differences in government and private health entities providing sterilization services may have influenced this unusual geographic distribution.

Table 3.10 Wasted Pregnancies, 1976-77

No.	State	Ratio
1	AGUASCALIENTES	0.0345
2	BAJA CALIFORNIA	0.1311
3	BAJA CALIFORNIA SUR	ND
4	CAMPECHE	ND
5	COAHUILA	0.1397
6	COLIMA	ND
7	CHIAPAS	0.0676
8	CHIHUAHUA	0.0882
9	DISTRITO FEDERAL	0.1436
10	DURANGO	0.1275
11	GUANAJUATO	0.1059
12	GUERRERO	0.1158
13	HIDALGO	0.0552
14	JALISCO	0.1537
15	MEXICO	0.1088
16	MICHOACAN	0.1019
17	MORELOS	0.0957
18	NAYARIT	0.1051
19	NUEVO LEON	0.1182
20	OAXACA	0.0525
21	PUEBLA	0.0804
22	QUERETARO	0.0477
23	QUINTANA ROO	0.1376
24	SAN LUIS POTOSI	0.0722
25	SINALOA	0.1066
26	SONORA	0.1056
27	TABASCO	0.0546
28	TAMAULIPAS	0.1081
29	TLAXCALA	ND
30	VERACRUZ	0.0697
31	YUCATAN	0.1410
32	ZACATECAS	0.0901
	Mean	0.0985
	S.D.	0.0326
	C.V.	33.10
	Minimum	0.0345
	Maximum	0.1537

DEFINITION: Ratio is the number of lifetime wasted pregnancies to the number of lifetime fertile pregnancies reported by respondents.

NOTE: ND = no data.

SOURCE: 1976-77 World Fertility Survey.

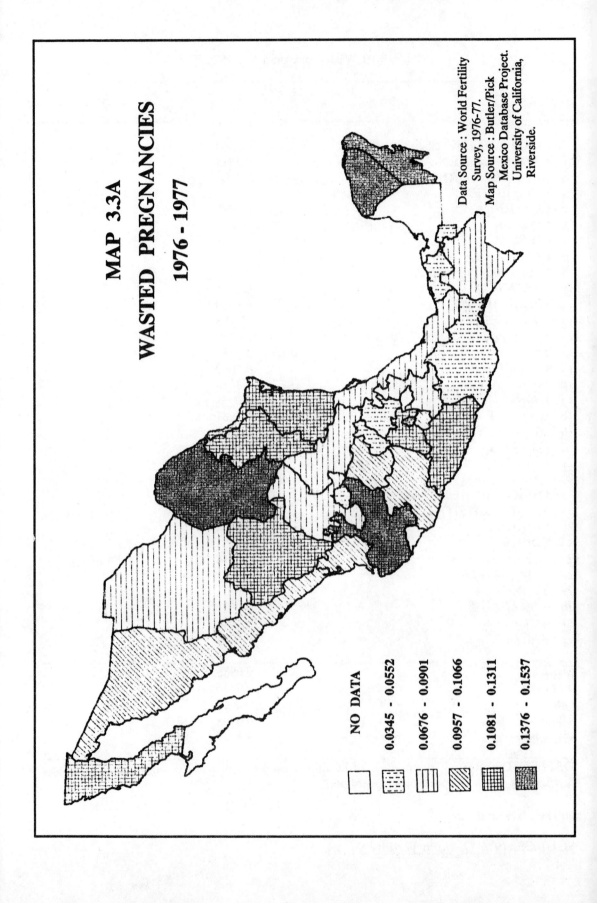

MAP 3.3A
WASTED PREGNANCIES
1976 - 1977

Data Source : World Fertility
Survey, 1976-77.

Map Source : Butler/Pick
Mexico Database Project.
University of California,
Riverside.

NO DATA

0.0345 - 0.0552

0.0676 - 0.0901

0.0957 - 0.1066

0.1081 - 0.1311

0.1376 - 0.1537

Table 3.11 Induced Abortions, 1976-77

No.	State	Ratio
1	AGUASCALIENTES	0.0000
2	BAJA CALIFORNIA	0.0741
3	BAJA CALIFORNIA SUR	ND
4	CAMPECHE	ND
5	COAHUILA	0.0833
6	COLIMA	ND
7	CHIAPAS	0.0395
8	CHIHUAHUA	0.0000
9	DISTRITO FEDERAL	0.0938
10	DURANGO	0.0104
11	GUANAJUATO	0.0265
12	GUERRERO	0.0769
13	HIDALGO	0.0000
14	JALISCO	0.0109
15	MEXICO	0.0467
16	MICHOACAN	0.0000
17	MORELOS	0.1111
18	NAYARIT	0.0000
19	NUEVO LEON	0.0672
20	OAXACA	0.0625
21	PUEBLA	0.0411
22	QUERETARO	0.0678
23	QUINTANA ROO	0.0500
24	SAN LUIS POTOSI	0.0652
25	SINALOA	0.0490
26	SONORA	0.0323
27	TABASCO	0.1071
28	TAMAULIPAS	0.1087
29	TLAXCALA	ND
30	VERACRUZ	0.0602
31	YUCATAN	0.0909
32	ZACATECAS	0.0000
Mean		0.0491
S.D.		0.0369
C.V.		75.15
Minimum		0.0000
Maximum		0.1111

DEFINITION: Ratio is the number of induced abortions to wasted pregnancies reported by respondents.

NOTE: ND = no data.

SOURCE: 1976-77 World Fertility Survey.

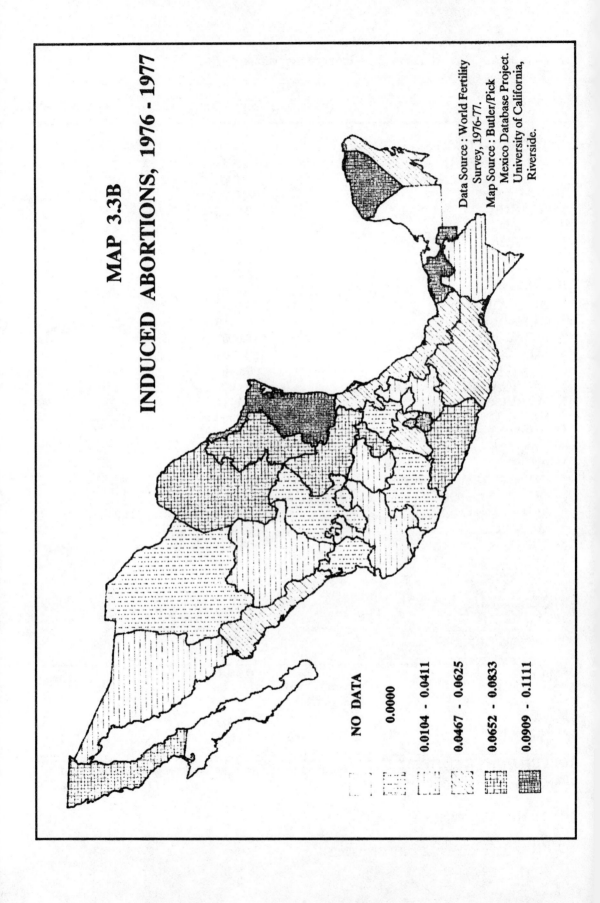

MAP 3.3B

INDUCED ABORTIONS, 1976 - 1977

NO DATA

0.0000

0.0104 - 0.0411

0.0467 - 0.0625

0.0652 - 0.0833

0.0909 - 0.1111

Data Source : World Fertility
Survey, 1976-77.

Map Source : Butler/Pick
Mexico Database Project.
University of California,
Riverside.

Table 3.12 Knowledge of Efficient Birth Control Method, 1976-77

No.	State	Knowledgability Ratio
1	AGUASCALIENTES	ND
2	BAJA CALIFORNIA	0.9860
3	BAJA CALIFORNIA SUR	ND
4	CAMPECHE	ND
5	COAHUILA	0.9600
6	COLIMA	ND
7	CHIAPAS	0.8310
8	CHIHUAHUA	0.9610
9	DISTRITO FEDERAL	0.9660
10	DURANGO	0.9730
11	GUANAJUATO	0.8810
12	GUERRERO	0.8540
13	HIDALGO	0.7530
14	JALISCO	0.9640
15	MEXICO	0.9010
16	MICHOACAN	0.8980
17	MORELOS	0.8400
18	NAYARIT	ND
19	NUEVO LEON	0.9300
20	OAXACA	0.6320
21	PUEBLA	0.7370
22	QUERETARO	0.7410
23	QUINTANA ROO	0.9490
24	SAN LUIS POTOSI	0.9180
25	SINALOA	0.9780
26	SONORA	0.9740
27	TABASCO	0.8210
28	TAMAULIPAS	0.9420
29	TLAXCALA	ND
30	VERACRUZ	0.6990
31	YUCATAN	0.9650
32	ZACATECAS	0.7800
	Mean	0.8782
	S.D.	0.0989
	C.V.	11.26
	Minimum	0.6320
	Maximum	0.9860

DEFINITION: Ratio is the number of respondents knowing an efficient birth control method to total number of respondents.

NOTE: ND = no data.

SOURCE: 1976-77 World Fertility Survey.

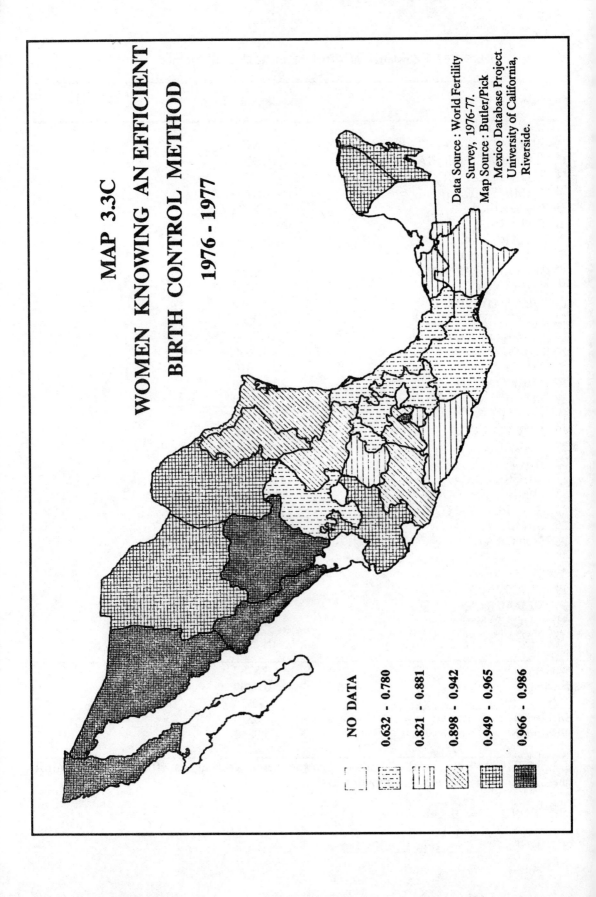

MAP 3.3C

WOMEN KNOWING AN EFFICIENT
BIRTH CONTROL METHOD

1976 - 1977

Data Source : World Fertility
Survey, 1976-77.

Map Source : Butler/Pick
Mexico Database Project.
University of California,
Riverside.

NO DATA

0.632 - 0.780

0.821 - 0.881

0.898 - 0.942

0.949 - 0.965

0.966 - 0.986

Table 3.13 Use of Birth Control Methods, 1976-77

No.	State	Current Birth Control Users	Ratio of Birth Control Pill Use	Ratio of Sterilization Use	Ratio of I.U.D. Use
1	AGUASCALIENTES	ND	ND	ND	ND
2	BAJA CALIFORNIA	58	0.5690	0.0862	0.0862
3	BAJA CALIFORNIA SUR	ND	ND	ND	ND
4	CAMPECHE	ND	ND	ND	ND
5	COAHUILA	44	0.5909	0.1136	0.1364
6	COLIMA	1	1.0000	1.0000	1.0000
7	CHIAPAS	34	0.2647	0.0294	0.1765
8	CHIHUAHUA	93	0.4624	0.0968	0.1935
9	DISTRITO FEDERAL	409	0.2861	0.0929	0.2812
10	DURANGO	44	0.5455	0.0682	0.1136
11	GUANAJUATO	42	0.2857	0.0714	0.2619
12	GUERRERO	45	0.3111	0.0444	0.0667
13	HIDALGO	26	0.3846	0.0769	0.1154
14	JALISCO	108	0.3611	0.1667	0.0833
15	MEXICO	197	0.2234	0.1675	0.2538
16	MICHOACAN	54	0.2778	0.0741	0.1852
17	MORELOS	36	0.2222	0.0278	0.2778
18	NAYARIT	25	0.5600	0.0800	0.0400
19	NUEVO LEON	82	0.3415	0.2073	0.1585
20	OAXACA	13	0.1538	0.1538	0.1538
21	PUEBLA	49	0.1837	0.1429	0.1429
22	QUERETARO	27	0.2963	0.0741	0.4074
23	QUINTANA ROO	34	0.4118	0.1471	0.0588
24	SAN LUIS POTOSI	34	0.6176	0.0294	0.0882
25	SINALOA	66	0.6515	0.0606	0.0455
26	SONORA	49	0.4286	0.1020	0.0612
27	TABASCO	21	0.2857	0.1429	0.0476
28	TAMAULIPAS	51	0.4314	0.1373	0.1176
29	TLAXCALA	ND	ND	ND	ND
30	VERACRUZ	59	0.3390	0.1186	0.1525
31	YUCATAN	16	0.3125	0.0625	0.3125
32	ZACATECAS	5	0.6000	0.2000	0.2000
	Mean	64	0.3851	0.1028	0.1562
	S.D.	77	0.1441	0.0506	0.0936
	C.V.	120.88	37.42	49.22	59.92
	Minimum	5	0.1538	0.0278	0.0400
	Maximum	409	0.6515	0.2073	0.4074

DEFINITION: Ratios are based on the number of respondents currently using an effective birth control method (column 1) and the method currently being used at the time of the survey.

NOTE: ND = no data.

SOURCE: 1976-77 World Fertility Survey.

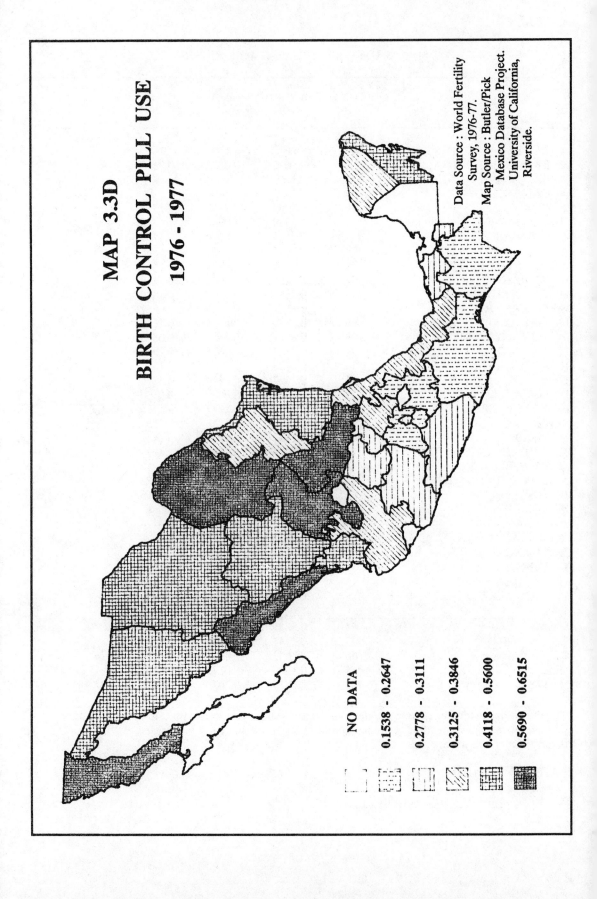

MAP 3.3D
BIRTH CONTROL PILL USE
1976 - 1977

Data Source : World Fertility
Survey, 1976-77.
Map Source : Butler/Pick
Mexico Database Project.
University of California,
Riverside.

NO DATA

0.1538 - 0.2647

0.2778 - 0.3111

0.3125 - 0.3846

0.4118 - 0.5600

0.5690 - 0.6515

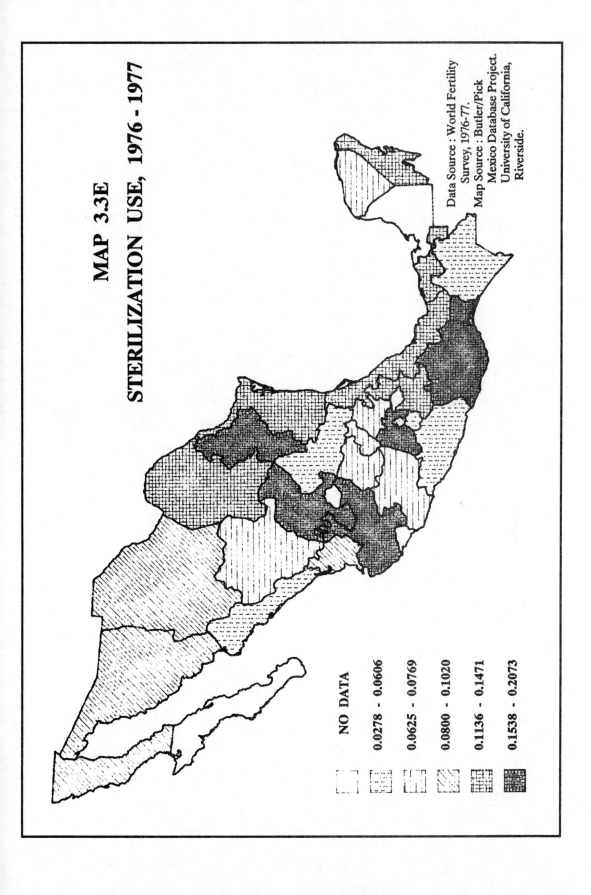

MAP 3.3E

STERILIZATION USE, 1976 - 1977

Data Source : World Fertility
Survey, 1976-77.
Map Source : Butler/Pick
Mexico Database Project.
University of California,
Riverside.

NO DATA

0.0278 - 0.0606

0.0625 - 0.0769

0.0800 - 0.1020

0.1136 - 0.1471

0.1538 - 0.2073

4

MIGRATION

Introduction

This chapter focuses on migration patterns as determined from various analyses of the 1980 Mexican census. While the information is from the 1980 census, the data are such that an analysis of the population native to state indicates to what extent there has been historical population movement among various Mexican states. In contrast, an analysis also is presented comparing migration streams between 1979 and 1980. Other information is presented on lifetime inmigrants and outmigrants and inmigrants and outmigrants for the previous year, e.g., 1979 - 1980. Net migration for the time period of 1979 - 1980 also is shown. Finally, inmigration for the 272 municipios for the six Mexican states along the U.S. border is presented. As in previous chapters, the information described is only a small part of that available.

Population Native to State, 1980

Population native to state in 1980 measures the stability/mobility of the population. For an individual, it measures stability from time of birth. Table 4.1 shows the mean value for population native to state in 1980 to be 82 percent. This implies a surprising amount of geographic stability given Mexico's rapid population growth in the twentieth century. There was small variation, as reflected in a coefficient of variation of 15.

States with the smallest percent native population are Quintana Roo (45 percent), Baja California (54 percent), and Mexico (60 percent). The native population of Quintana Roo was reduced by a large inmigration due in part to the planned expansion of the tourist sector. Mexico, surrounding the Federal District, grew as a result of the expansion of Mexico City. In these two states, native populations were reduced by extensive inmigration during 70s, while the same effect occurred in Baja in the 50s and 60s (Butler et al., 1987a). The highest proportions native are in Yucatan (94 percent), Oaxaca (93 percent), Zacatecas (93 percent), and Guerrero (93 percent). One explanation is the rural nature of the latter three, which is associated with lower rates of inmigration (see Maps 4.3.A and 4.3.C). Yucatan, however, although highly urbanized in 1980 (73 percent), has a very low rate of inmigration.

By region, rates of native population are low in the central zone, adjacent Morelos, the growth states of Baja California Sur and Quintana Roo, and slow-growing Tamaulipas (see Map 4.1). On the other hand, the ratios are highest in the pacific south and high in the west, gulf, and southern north regions. Ignoring the inconsistent southeast region and the central zone, rates are higher in areas south of the central east-west axis. A consequence is that the central zone is encircled by 13 states with much higher proportion native. This reflects in part the major migration streams of the 70s from many of the encircling states into the central zone (Fukurai, Pick, and Butler, 1987b). Similar streams from the encirling states into the Federal District for lifetime migration in 1950 had been noted by Whetten and Burnight (1956).

Generally, there is a north-south division with northern states having a lower proportion of native born than southern states. The major exceptions to this generalization are the Federal District and its two surrounding states and the developing tourist state of Quintana Roo on the Yucatan peninsula.

One explanation of the differences in proportions native to state is that massive rural-to-urban migration in the twentienth century left rural states with high proportions native, while inmigrants to urban states decreased the proportion native. This conclusion is supported by the strong negative correlation of -0.60 between population native to state and 1980 urbanization. An implication is that urban areas have served as "melting pots" of inmigrants, while rural areas are more stable. From an economic standpoint, a related relationship is the inverse one between population native to state and gross state revenue, reflected in a significant correlation of 0.48. In sum, this variable reflects Mexico's historical patterns of interstate and interregional migration.

Table 4.1 Population Native to State, 1980

No.	State	Population Native To State	Total Population	Ratio
1	AGUASCALIENTES	426,276	519,439	0.8206
2	BAJA CALIFORNIA	632,525	1,177,886	0.5370
3	BAJA CALIFORNIA SUR	152,975	215,139	0.7111
4	CAMPECHE	337,422	420,553	0.8023
5	COAHUILA	1,302,100	1,557,265	0.8361
6	COLIMA	260,331	346,293	0.7518
7	CHIAPAS	1,919,510	2,084,717	0.9208
8	CHIHUAHUA	1,720,241	2,005,477	0.8578
9	DISTRITO FEDERAL	6,165,883	8,831,079	0.6982
10	DURANGO	1,050,237	1,182,320	0.8883
11	GUANAJUATO	2,732,569	3,006,110	0.9090
12	GUERRERO	1,960,449	2,109,513	0.9293
13	HIDALGO	1,405,807	1,547,493	0.9084
14	JALISCO	3,715,199	4,371,998	0.8498
15	MEXICO	4,559,256	7,564,335	0.6027
16	MICHOACAN	2,658,472	2,868,824	0.9267
17	MORELOS	676,972	947,089	0.7148
18	NAYARIT	628,339	726,120	0.8653
19	NUEVO LEON	1,864,286	2,513,044	0.7418
20	OAXACA	2,209,121	2,369,076	0.9325
21	PUEBLA	3,029,721	3,347,685	0.9050
22	QUERETARO	644,852	739,605	0.8719
23	QUINTANA ROO	100,701	225,985	0.4456
24	SAN LUIS POTOSI	1,514,408	1,673,893	0.9047
25	SINALOA	1,604,571	1,849,879	0.8674
26	SONORA	1,247,653	1,513,731	0.8242
27	TABASCO	957,862	1,062,961	0.9011
28	TAMAULIPAS	1,424,569	1,924,484	0.7402
29	TLAXCALA	497,851	556,597	0.8945
30	VERACRUZ	4,790,161	5,387,680	0.8891
31	YUCATAN	995,746	1,063,733	0.9361
32	ZACATECAS	1,057,467	1,136,830	0.9302
Mean		1,695,110		0.8223
S.D.		1,422,266		0.1212
C.V.		83.90		14.74
Minimum		100,701		0.4456
Maximum		6,165,883		0.9361

DEFINITION: Ratio is the population native to state to the total population.

SOURCE: 1980 Mexican Census of Population, Volume 1, Table 11.

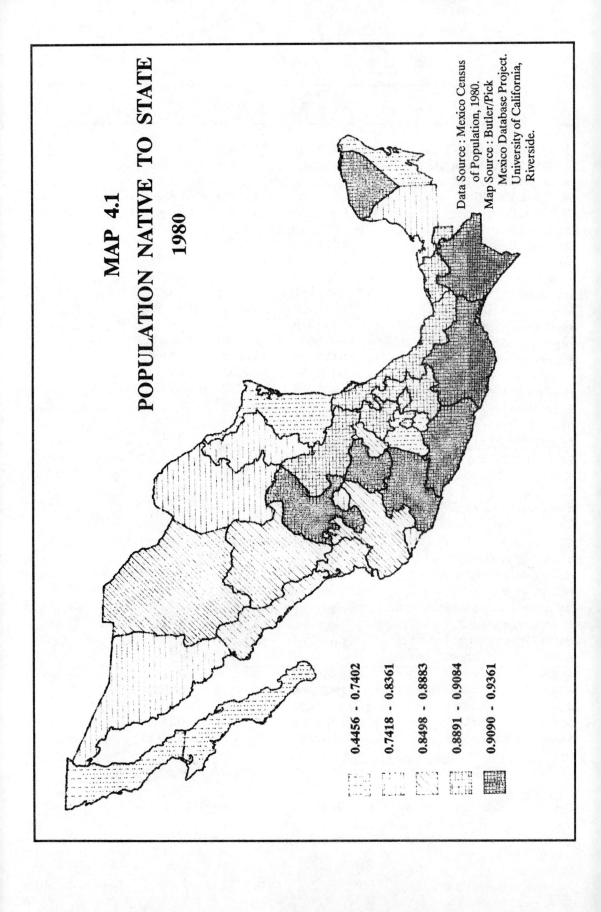

MAP 4.1

POPULATION NATIVE TO STATE

1980

Data Source : Mexico Census
of Population, 1980.
Map Source : Butler/Pick
Mexico Database Project.
University of California,
Riverside.

0.4456 - 0.7402

0.7418 - 0.8361

0.8498 - 0.8883

0.8891 - 0.9084

0.9090 - 0.9361

Lifetime Migration

Inmigrants per Capita, Lifetime, 1980

Lifetime inmigrants measures the number of residents of a state who inmigrated to that state from another state in Mexico at any time point during a resident's lifetime. This variable, as well as lifetime outmigration, 1979-80 inmigration, and 1979-80 outmigration, exclude foreign migration, but include all unspecified population which can be associated with a destination state for inmigration or an origin state for outmigration. Since a respondent indicating migration, but not specifying origin or destination, can only be identified by destination, i.e. his/her 1980 state of residence, the total number of inmigrants by state is higher than the total number of outmigrants by state (see Table 4.2).

In 1980, there were 8,456,914 lifetime inmigrants from other Mexican states. The larger states accounted for a high proportion of these. In particular, the Federal District, Mexico, Jalisco, Veracruz, and Nuevo Leon had received 56 percent of all lifetime inmigrants, while they accounted for 43 percent of 1980 population. The large numbers of historical inmigrants to the states reflects largely the substantial stream of migrants from rural areas to the three largest metropolitan areas, located in four of the states (Unikel, 1977).

Lifetime inmigrants are shown on Map 4.2A on a per capita basis, that is the number of lifetime inmigrants divided by the 1980 population of the receiving state. This approach adjusts for the effect of state population size, thus allowing a comparison of inmigration to states of highly different sizes. The lifetime inmigration and outmigration data are shown in Table 4.2. The mean lifetime inmigration rate is 12.8 percent, indicating that, on the average, one out of eight 1980 residents of states migrated into the state at some point in their lifetime. There is moderate statewide variation in this rate. Quintana Roo has the highest rate of 41 percent, implying that over a third of 1980 residents had inmigrated. Since Quintana Roo was Mexico's leading percentage growth state in the 70s, many migrants entered in that decade. Other high inmigration states on a per capita basis are Baja California, Baja California Sur, Mexico, and the Federal District. Baja California experienced high inmigration in the 50s, 60s, and 70s (Butler et al., 1987a) due, among other things, to its proximity to the United States and its prosperous economy. Baja California Sur was also a high growth state in the 1970s. The Federal District and Mexico have been receiving states for the large flow from rural areas into the Mexican City metropolitan area over many decades (Unikel, 1977). States with the lowest percent inmigration rates are the poorer income states of Oaxaca, Yucatan, and Puebla.

On a regional basis, the border region has moderate to high lifetime inmigration, with the central state of Chihuahua having the lowest rate. In the west and central regions, there is an inconsistent pattern, with the highest rates in the major metropolitan states. The gulf has had low lifetime percent inmigration, even though Veracruz is large in total numbers of lifetime inmigrants. The pacific south has the lowest inmigration rate of all regions. Reasons include its weak economy, as reflected by low level of income (see Maps 8.4A-B), and its rural nature, since Mexico's major internal migration streams in this century have tended to be rural to urban, rather than the reverse (Unikel, 1977). The southeast region is inconsistent, with Quintana Roo and Campeche, growth states in the 70s, showing high inmigration, but Yucatan with a low lifetime inmigration rate of only six percent.

Outmigrants per Capita, Lifetime, 1980

Lifetime outmigrants in 1980 totalled 7,254,633. The major sending states in number of outmigrants were the Federal District, with 1.2 million outmigrants; the state of Mexico, with 0.57 million; and Veracruz, Jalisco, Michoacan, Guanajuato, and Puebla, with 0.34 to 0.45 million apiece. These states tend to be among the more populous, and in the top third of inmigration states in volume (see Table 4.2).

On a per capita basis, that is, lifetime outmigrants divided by the population of the sending state, there are smaller differences among states, since the effect of population size is controlled. The average for the states percent lifetime outmigration for states is 11.4 percent, which implies there is one lifetime outmigrant for every nine 1980 residents of the state. The highest outmigration rates, exceeding 14 percent, are for the states of Durango, Hidalgo, Morelos, and San Luis Potosi. At the other extreme are the states of Chiapas, Nuevo Leon, and Chihuahua, with under seven percent outmigration.

By region, the highest lifetime outmigrant states tend to be located in the interior of the country, especially in the southern north region and in the central region(see Map 4.2B). In the central metropolitan zone, there is high outmigration from the Federal District, but low outmigration from the state of Mexico. This reflects in part the inability of the dense and overcrowded Federal District to retain its huge population which built up historically. The border region has much variation, with Baja California and Tamaulipas relatively high and Chihuahua and Nuevo Leon low. The gulf region is the lowest region in terms of lifetime outmigrants, averaging only six percent. This low outmigration may be due to the older, more settled nature of this region. The southeast is also rather low. The pacific south has moderate outmigration, with Oaxaca the highest, followed by Guerrero and Chiapas with low outmigration.

Table 4.2 Lifetime Migration, 1980

No.	State	Number of Lifetime Inmigrants	Per Capita Lifetime Inmigrants	Number of Lifetime Outmigrants	Per Capita Lifetime Outmigrants	Number of Lifetime Net Migrants	Per Capita Lifetime Net Migrants
1	AGUASCALIENTES	75,519	0.1454	61,344	0.1181	14,175	0.0273
2	BAJA CALIFORNIA	325,519	0.2764	155,618	0.1321	169,901	0.1442
3	BAJA CALIFORNIA SUR	50,563	0.2350	22,834	0.1061	27,729	0.1289
4	CAMPECHE	62,841	0.1494	39,800	0.0946	23,041	0.0548
5	COAHUILA	187,645	0.1205	184,626	0.1186	3,019	0.0019
6	COLIMA	66,047	0.1907	45,614	0.1317	20,433	0.0590
7	CHIAPAS	78,269	0.0375	110,389	0.0530	-32,120	-0.0154
8	CHIHUAHUA	187,694	0.0936	139,187	0.0694	48,507	0.0242
9	DISTRITO FEDERAL	1,785,473	0.2022	1,226,301	0.1389	559,172	0.0633
10	DURANGO	107,799	0.0912	181,020	0.1531	-73,221	-0.0619
11	GUANAJUATO	225,650	0.0751	361,716	0.1203	-136,066	-0.0453
12	GUERRERO	115,175	0.0546	247,733	0.1174	-132,558	-0.0628
13	HIDALGO	121,938	0.0788	231,120	0.1494	-109,182	-0.0706
14	JALISCO	514,221	0.1176	417,180	0.0954	97,041	0.0222
15	MEXICO	1,632,107	0.2158	572,833	0.0757	1,059,274	0.1400
16	MICHOACAN	207,346	0.0723	390,623	0.1362	-183,277	-0.0639
17	MORELOS	175,769	0.1856	138,739	0.1465	37,030	0.0391
18	NAYARIT	83,470	0.1150	93,362	0.1286	-9,892	-0.0136
19	NUEVO LEON	398,777	0.1587	156,077	0.0621	242,700	0.0966
20	OAXACA	120,257	0.0508	299,533	0.1264	-179,276	-0.0757
21	PUEBLA	233,500	0.0697	344,013	0.1028	-110,513	-0.0330
22	QUERETARO	85,043	0.1150	82,613	0.1117	2,430	0.0033
23	QUINTANA ROO	93,364	0.4131	20,858	0.0923	72,506	0.3208
24	SAN LUIS POTOSI	128,554	0.0768	244,100	0.1458	-115,546	-0.0690
25	SINALOA	206,944	0.1119	186,987	0.1011	19,957	0.0108
26	SONORA	192,784	0.1274	144,014	0.0951	48,770	0.0322
27	TABASCO	89,926	0.0846	83,053	0.0781	6,873	0.0065
28	TAMAULIPAS	279,889	0.1454	232,615	0.1209	47,274	0.0246
29	TLAXCALA	46,935	0.0843	73,367	0.1318	-26,432	-0.0475
30	VERACRUZ	428,569	0.0795	429,236	0.0797	-667	-0.0001
31	YUCATAN	66,042	0.0621	97,093	0.0913	-31,051	-0.0292
32	ZACATECAS	83,285	0.0733	241,035	0.2120	-157,750	-0.1388
	National Total	8,456,914		7,254,633		1,202,281	
	Mean	264,279	0.1284	226,707	0.1136	37,571	0.0148
	S.D.	390,345	0.0766	222,991	0.0315	228,792	0.0850
	C.V.	147.70	59.67	98.36	27.74	608.95	575.17
	Minimum	46,935	0.0375	20,858	0.0530	-183,277	-0.1388
	Maximum	1,785,473	0.4131	1,226,301	0.2120	1,059,274	0.3208

DEFINITION: Lifetime inmigrants is the number of migrants into a state for the lifetimes of current residents. Lifetime outmigrants is the number of migrants out of a state for the lifetimes of current residents. Foreign migration is excluded from all migration variables, but unspecified population is included. As explained in the text, the total number of unspecified migrants is higher for inmigrants than for outmigrants. As a result, the sum of net lifetime migrants is positive for the nation.

SOURCE: 1980 Mexican Census of Population, Resumen General, Volume 2, Table 39.

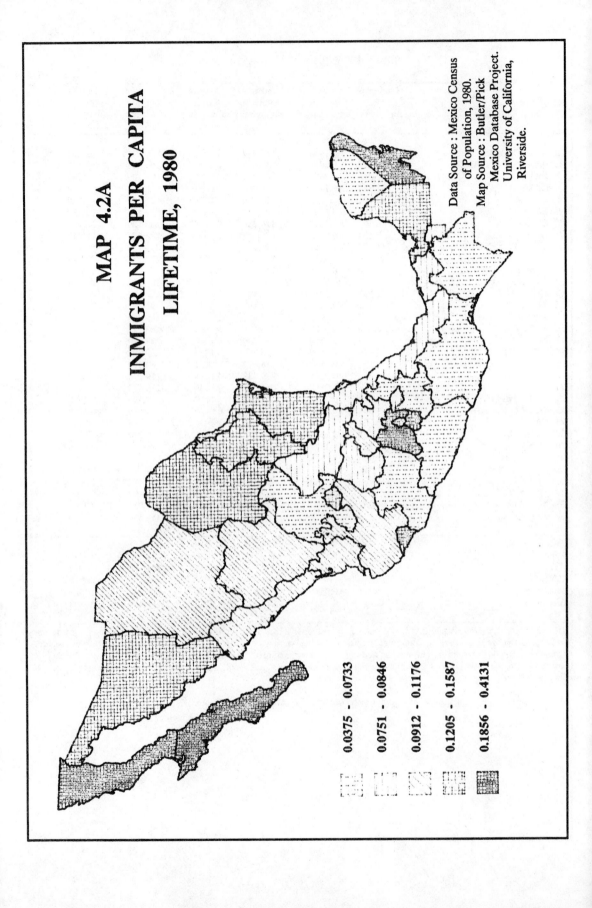

MAP 4.2A
INMIGRANTS PER CAPITA
LIFETIME, 1980

Data Source : Mexico Census
of Population, 1980.
Map Source : Butler/Pick
Mexico Database Project.
University of California,
Riverside.

0.0375 - 0.0733
0.0751 - 0.0846
0.0912 - 0.1176
0.1205 - 0.1587
0.1856 - 0.4131

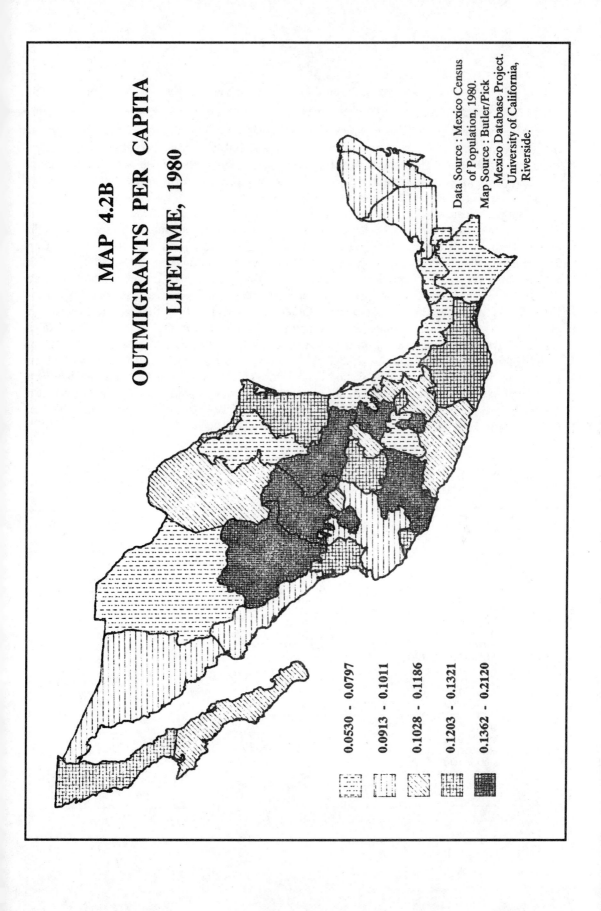

MAP 4.2B

OUTMIGRANTS PER CAPITA

LIFETIME, 1980

Data Source : Mexico Census
of Population, 1980.
Map Source : Butler/Pick
Mexico Database Project.
University of California,
Riverside.

0.0530 - 0.0797

0.0913 - 0.1011

0.1028 - 0.1186

0.1203 - 0.1321

0.1362 - 0.2120

Migration Streams in Previous Year, 1980

Map 4.3A shows the eighteen largest interstate migration streams for the period 1979-80 (Fukurai, et al., 1987b). These eighteen streams comprise only about two percent of the country's 992 interstate streams. The data exclude foreign in- and outmigrants, as well as 1979-80 migrants who did not specify states of migration origin and destination. Since unspecified respondents are excluded, the data are identical to those utilized for net migration (see Table 4.3 and text table below).

The largest stream of 65,913 is from the Federal District to the state of Mexico. This stream is of great importance, representing 9.9 percent of all 1979-80 interstate migrants who specified origin and destination. It reflects a continuing overspilling of population from the Mexico City metropolitan region and from the Federal District into the state of Mexico (Van Arsdol et al., 1976; Schteingart, 1988). At the same time, the second largest stream of 13,208 is a reverse one, i.e. from the state of Mexico to the Federal District. It partly reflects migration from remaining rural parts of the state of Mexico into the Federal District. Other major streams are from origin states with high outmigration rates, including Guanajuato, Veracruz, Guerrero, and Oaxaca. The latter three states are below average in urbanization, so that these streams may reflect in part a long-term historical pattern of rural-to-urban migration (Unikel, 1977). Also present are major streams from the Federal District and state of Mexico to Jalisco and Michoacan. The Mexico City-to-Jalisco stream has been postulated to be historically important, not only as a source of inmigrants to Guadalajara, but also as a major intermediate stop for continuing migration from Jalisco to the northwest, especially Baja California (Butler et al., 1987a).

Migration Streams-Previous Year, 1980

Rank	Origin	Destination	Stream Size
1	DISTRITO FEDERAL	MEXICO	65,913
2	MEXICO	DISTRITO FEDERAL	13,208
3	VERACRUZ	DISTRITO FEDERAL	9,476
4	PUEBLA	DISTRITO FEDERAL	9,050
5	OAXACA	DISTRITO FEDERAL	8,311
6	PUEBLA	MEXICO	7,811
7	VERACRUZ	MEXICO	6,933
8	MICHOACAN	MEXICO	6,917
9	GUERRERO	MEXICO	6,537
10	OAXACA	MEXICO	6,474
11	HIDALGO	DISTRITO FEDERAL	6,274
12	DISTRITO FEDERAL	VERACRUZ	6,103
13	TAMAULIPAS	NUEVO LEON	6,090
14	DISTRITO FEDERAL	JALISCO	6,046
15	HIDALGO	MEXICO	5,588
16	GUANAJUATO	MEXICO	5,290
17	DISTRITO FEDERAL	MICHOACAN	5,135
18	MEXICO	MICHOACAN	5,108
	MEXICO	VERACRUZ	4,935
	MEXICO	PUEBLA	4,925
	DISTRITO FEDERAL	PUEBLA	4,716
	DISTRITO FEDERRAL	GUANAJUATO	4,206
	GUANAJUATO	DESTRITO FEDERAL	4,159

SOURCE: <u>1980 Mexican Census of Population</u>, Resumen General, Volume 2.

The major 1979-80 migration streams are concentrated along Mexico's central flank and south. This is not surprising since these areas are among the country's most populous (see Table 2.1B). The only exception to this concentration is the major stream from Tamaulipas to Nuevo Leon.

Major internal migration streams were analyzed by Whetten and Burnight (1956), based on the 1950 Census. Comparison with the present streams is somewhat hampered by the 1950 streams being lifetime streams, for non-continguous states. Nevertheless, a rough comparison shows that in 1950 there was a relatively greater volume of inmigration to the Federal District, a greatly reduced role for the state of Mexico, and greater prevalence of streams in the northern regions.

Inmigrants and Outmigrants Per Capita, Previous Year, 1980

In the year prior to the census of 1980, there were roughly 3/4 million domestic internal migrants in Mexico, with the exact number depending on the treatment of unspecified categories. This gives a one-year national migration rate of about one percent. For both 1979-80 inmigration and out-migration, there is close correspondence in geographic distribution to patterns already discussed for lifetime inmigration and outmigration. Similar close correspondence was noted between recent and lifetime migration patterns in a cluster-analysis study, based on information on all 992 internal streams (Fukurai et al., 1988). This analysis discusses recent migration patterns, focussing on differences from lifetime in- and outmigration patterns. The data are presented in Table 4.3.

Inmigration, 1979-80. As seen in Table 4.3, the statewide mean for 1979-80 inmigration rate is 1.4 percent, with a moderate coefficient of variation among states, about equal to variation for lifetime inmigration rate. One year inmigration rates varied from highs in the range of 3.0 to 4.3 percent for the 70s growth states of Quintana Roo and Baja California Sur to values of 0.4 to 0.7 percent for Chiapas, Oaxaca, and Guerrero.

There are several major differences from the geographic pattern for lifetime inmigration rate (see Map 4.3B). One is that the Federal District has about an average value, in contrast to its very high value for lifetime inmigration. This indicates a slowing of migration in the late 70s into the Federal District. However, the growth rate for the state of Mexico continues to be very high, implying that inflow into the Mexico City metropolitan region continues, but is directed to the outlying parts of the metropolis. Another difference is the substantially higher inmigration into the state of Zacatecas, relative to its historically low inmigration rate. On the other hand, inmigration 1979-80 into the northeast region slowed relative to lifetime rates. This reflects a reversal in historical migration flows to this part of the border (see Margulis and Tuiran, 1984).

Outmigration, 1979-80. The mean state outmigration rate, 1979-80, was 1.0 percent, with a moderate coefficient of variation of 27. Map 4.3C reveals fairly close correspondence with the pattern of lifetime outmigration, with the following differences. The 1970-80 growth states of Baja California, Quintana Roo, Mexico, and Campeche have relatively greater outmigration rates in 1979-80, versus their lifetime rates. This may be due in part to return migration of some of the population inmigrating in the 70s or to other unknown reasons. Several states show reduced relative outmigration in 1979-80, versus lifetime rates. These include Michoacan, Jalisco, and Yucatan. The Federal District has among the highest one-year outmigration rates of 1.5 percent, and due to its size, accounts for 19 percent of outmigrants from all states.

Net Inmigrants per Capita, Previous Year, 1980

Net inmigration rate for a state measures the difference between 1979-80 inmigrants to a state and 1979-80 outmigrants, divided by the 1980 population of the state. It represents the increment or decrement in population growth rate due to migration over the one year period. The remainder of a state's growth rate is determined by natural increase, i.e. fertility minus mortality. In the case of this variable, foreign inmigrants are excluded, and unlike the previous four migration variables, the unspecified population is excluded. The reason for varying from our normal policy of including unspecified categories is that inclusion of unspecified would imply a divergence between total inmigrants and total outmigrants, i.e. net migration would not sum to zero. This is because the number of unspecified differs for inmigrants versus outmigrants, as explained at the start of the chapter.

The net inmigration rate varies between a low of -0.7 percent for Guerrero to a high of 2.3 percent for Quintana Roo (see Table 4.3 and Map 4.3D). By region, the pacific south has the lowest rate, with a net regional migration loss of 31,985 persons, or -0.5 percent. The southern north region, consisting of Zacatecas and San Luis Potosi, also has a high net outmigration rate (see Map 4.3C).

The Federal District has a low rate of -0.4 percent. In gross terms, this rate represents 114,944 inmigrants and 129,847 outmigrants. It is important to note that this net outmigration varies from a historical pattern in the twentieth century until the 70s of net inmigration (Unikel, 1977). By contrast, the state of Mexico has a net inmigration rate of 0.9 percent. Also, the other major metropolitan states of Jalisco and Nuevo Leon have net inmigration rates of 0.4 and 0.1 percent respectively. Queretaro's high net inmigration rate of 0.6 percent is due to lower than average outmigration and higher than average inmigration, some of which may be due to metropolitan overspill from Mexico City. Although the entire border region has a positive net inmigration rate of 0.03 percent, Nuevo Leon's rate of 0.4 percent is much higher than the other border states'. The low net inmigration rate of 0.03 percent in Baja California likely reflects its role as the major temporary stop for migrants continuing on to the United States.

The pattern of net migration is opposite to that for fertility (see Map 3.2C). One major exception to this inverse relationship is the Federal District, which has low values for both fertility and migration. Overall, the relationship implies that high fertility regions of Mexico are largely less attractive ones for inmigration.

Table 4.3 Migration in Previous Year, 1980

No.	State	Number of Previous Yr. Inmigrants	Per Capita Previous Yr. Inmigrants	Number of Previous Yr. Outmigrants	Per Capita Previous Yr. Outmigrants	Number of Previous Yr. Net Inmigrants	Per Capita Previous Yr. Net Inmigrants
1	AGUASCALIENTES	7,407	0.0143	4,639	0.0089	1,918	0.0037
2	BAJA CALIFORNIA	22,641	0.0192	19,304	0.0164	412	0.0003
3	BAJA CALIFORNIA SUR	6,433	0.0299	3,252	0.0151	2,613	0.0121
4	CAMPECHE	9,255	0.0220	4,276	0.0102	4,084	0.0097
5	COAHUILA	18,142	0.0116	15,069	0.0097	713	0.0005
6	COLIMA	8,323	0.0240	5,044	0.0146	2,729	0.0079
7	CHIAPAS	9,421	0.0045	11,989	0.0058	-4,694	-0.0023
8	CHIHUAHUA	16,300	0.0081	12,745	0.0064	933	0.0005
9	DISTRITO FEDERAL	114,944	0.0130	129,847	0.0147	-37,385	-0.0042
10	DURANGO	13,556	0.0115	13,860	0.0117	-2,727	-0.0023
11	GUANAJUATO	24,215	0.0081	23,776	0.0079	-4,118	-0.0014
12	GUERRERO	13,656	0.0065	24,594	0.0117	-14,308	-0.0068
13	HIDALGO	15,497	0.0100	16,542	0.0107	-3,835	-0.0025
14	JALISCO	46,997	0.0107	34,291	0.0078	4,879	0.0011
15	MEXICO	153,912	0.0203	63,810	0.0084	66,178	0.0087
16	MICHOACAN	28,289	0.0099	27,888	0.0097	-3,908	-0.0014
17	MORELOS	16,588	0.0175	11,773	0.0124	2,808	0.0030
18	NAYARIT	9,974	0.0137	8,597	0.0118	625	0.0009
19	NUEVO LEON	30,892	0.0123	17,120	0.0068	19,297	0.0041
20	OAXACA	17,105	0.0072	26,896	0.0114	-12,983	-0.0055
21	PUEBLA	27,606	0.0082	28,582	0.0085	-5,389	-0.0016
22	QUERETARO	11,579	0.0157	6,280	0.0085	4,363	0.0059
23	QUINTANA ROO	9,832	0.0435	3,792	0.0168	5,083	0.0225
24	SAN LUIS POTOSI	15,689	0.0094	17,301	0.0103	-4,141	-0.0025
25	SINALOA	20,105	0.0109	20,159	0.0109	-2,535	-0.0014
26	SONORA	19,669	0.0130	14,445	0.0095	2,726	0.0018
27	TABASCO	10,510	0.0099	10,099	0.0095	-1,360	-0.0013
28	TAMAULIPAS	24,526	0.0127	20,238	0.0105	1,048	0.0005
29	TLAXCALA	5,359	0.0096	4,970	0.0089	-396	-0.0006
30	VERACRUZ	42,558	0.0079	43,776	0.0081	-9,297	-0.0017
31	YUCATAN	7,730	0.0073	8,402	0.0079	-1,627	-0.0015
32	ZACATECAS	13,974	0.0123	15,419	0.0136	-2,776	-0.0024
	National Total	792,684		668,775			
	Mean	24,771	0.0136	20,899	0.0105		
	S.D.	30,299	0.0077	23,252	0.0028		
	C.V.	122.31	56.33	111.26	26.64		
	Minimum	5,359	0.0045	3,352	0.0058	-37,385	-0.0068
	Maximum	153,912	0.0435	129,847	0.0168	66,178	0.0225

DEFINITION: Inmigrants in previous year are the number of migrants into a state in the previous year. Outmigrants in previous year are the number of migrants out of a state in the previous year. Foreign migration is excluded from all migration variables. For in- and outmigrants, unspecified population is included. However, the total number of unspecified migrants is higher for inmigrants than for outmigrants, as explained in the text. Net migrants is the difference of inmigrants minus outmigrants. In calculating net migrnats in previous year, the unspecified population is excluded, in order that net migrants sum to zero for the nation.

SOURCE: 1980 Mexican Census of Population, Resumen General, Volume 2, Table 39.

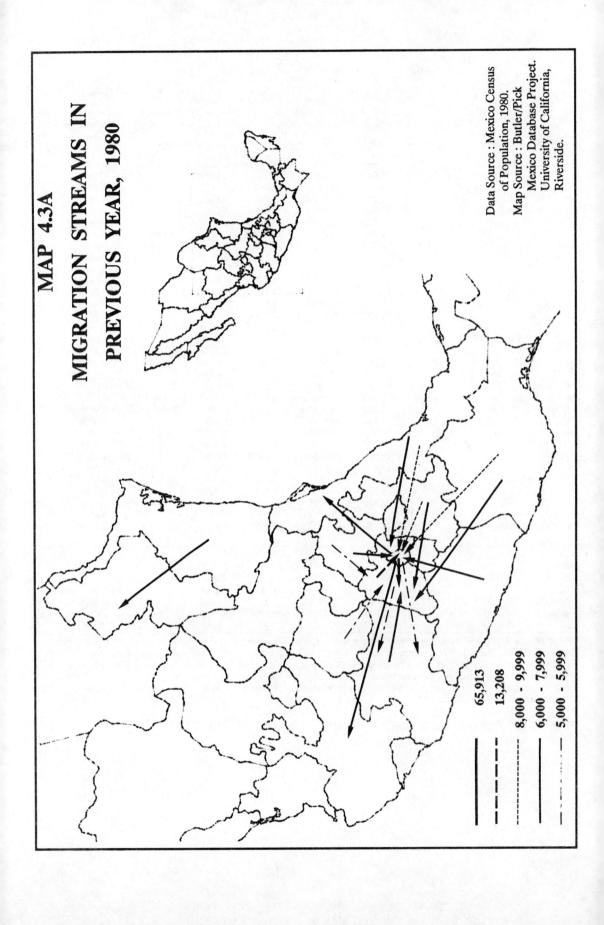

MAP 4.3A

MIGRATION STREAMS IN
PREVIOUS YEAR, 1980

Data Source : Mexico Census
of Population, 1980.
Map Source : Butler/Pick
Mexico Database Project.
University of California,
Riverside.

65,913

13,208

8,000 - 9,999

6,000 - 7,999

5,000 - 5,999

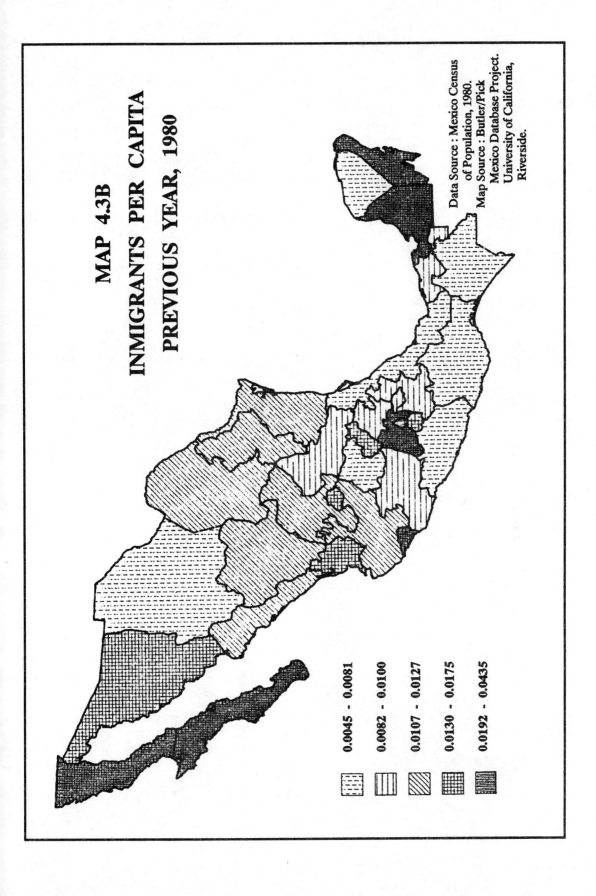

MAP 4.3B
INMIGRANTS PER CAPITA
PREVIOUS YEAR, 1980

Data Source : Mexico Census
of Population, 1980.

Map Source : Butler/Pick
Mexico Database Project.
University of California,
Riverside.

0.0045 - 0.0081

0.0082 - 0.0100

0.0107 - 0.0127

0.0130 - 0.0175

0.0192 - 0.0435

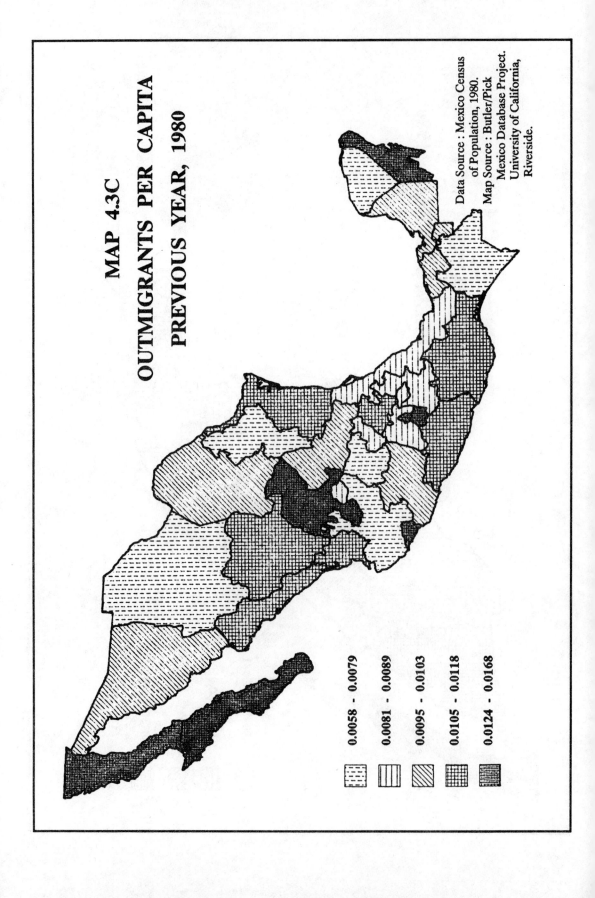

MAP 4.3C
OUTMIGRANTS PER CAPITA
PREVIOUS YEAR, 1980

Data Source : Mexico Census
of Population, 1980.

Map Source : Butler/Pick
Mexico Database Project.
University of California,
Riverside.

0.0058 - 0.0079

0.0081 - 0.0089

0.0095 - 0.0103

0.0105 - 0.0118

0.0124 - 0.0168

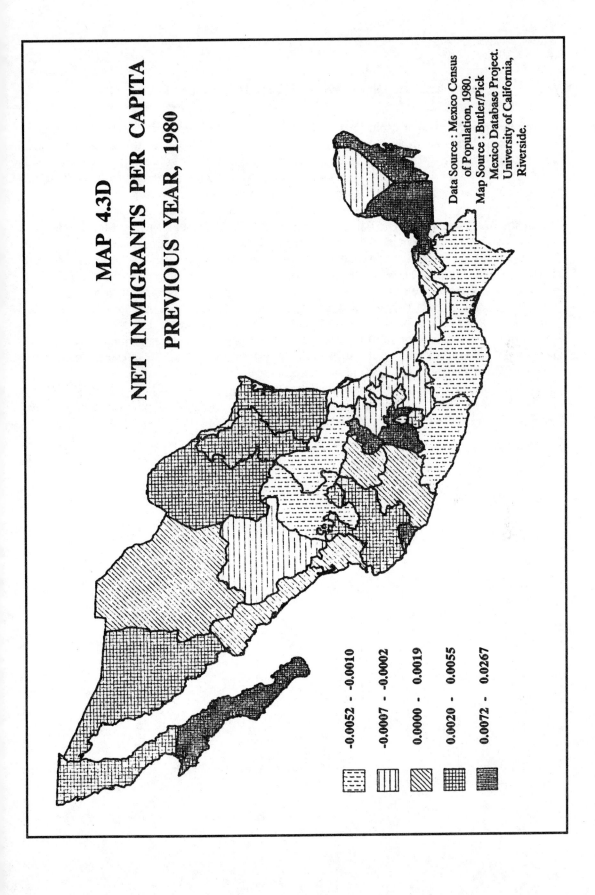

MAP 4.3D

NET INMIGRANTS PER CAPITA
PREVIOUS YEAR, 1980

Data Source : Mexico Census
of Population, 1980.
Map Source : Butler/Pick
Mexico Database Project.
University of California,
Riverside.

-0.0052 - -0.0010

-0.0007 - -0.0002

0.0000 - 0.0019

0.0020 - 0.0055

0.0072 - 0.0267

Inmigrants per Capita, Previous Year, Borderlands Region, 1980

The inmigration rate per capita averaged 1.2 percent for the municipios in the border region. There was moderate variation, with a coefficient of variation of 87. By state, the average municipio inmigration varied from 2.5 percent in Baja California to 9.9 percent in Chihuahua (compare with state results in Map 4.4). Five of the ten municipios with the highest inmigration levels are located in Nuevo Leon, while four of the ten municipios with lowest inmigration levels are in Sonora.

There are three major zones of inmigration, two neighboring the border and another in the extreme south of Tamaulipas. The Baja/Northwest Sonora zone includes Tijuana, Mexicali, and Tecate in Baja, and six Sonoran municipios. It consists of 30,472 inmigrants, with an inmigration rate of 2.25 percent. In addition, to the south and contiguous to the Baja/Northwest Sonora zone, there is a twelve municipio zone of somewhat lower rates, which extends to Guaymas in the south and then northwards halfway up the state towards Nogales. The second large inmigration zone in northern Neuvo Leon and parts of Coahuila and Tamaulipas includes 27 municipios over the entire urban-to-rural range from the large border cities of Nuevo Laredo to rural areas. This zone has 11,181 inmigrants, with an inmigration rate of 1.8 percent. One explanation of the high inmigration to both major inmigration zones involves the attraction of urban portions of the U.S.-Mexican border strip, an attraction extending southwards into the borderlands.

A third inmigration zone is the metropolitan area of Ciudad Madero and Tampico, which has a population of 400,401. These two municipios encompass a very small geographical area, and account for 8,007 inmigrants, with an inmigration rate of 2.0 percent.

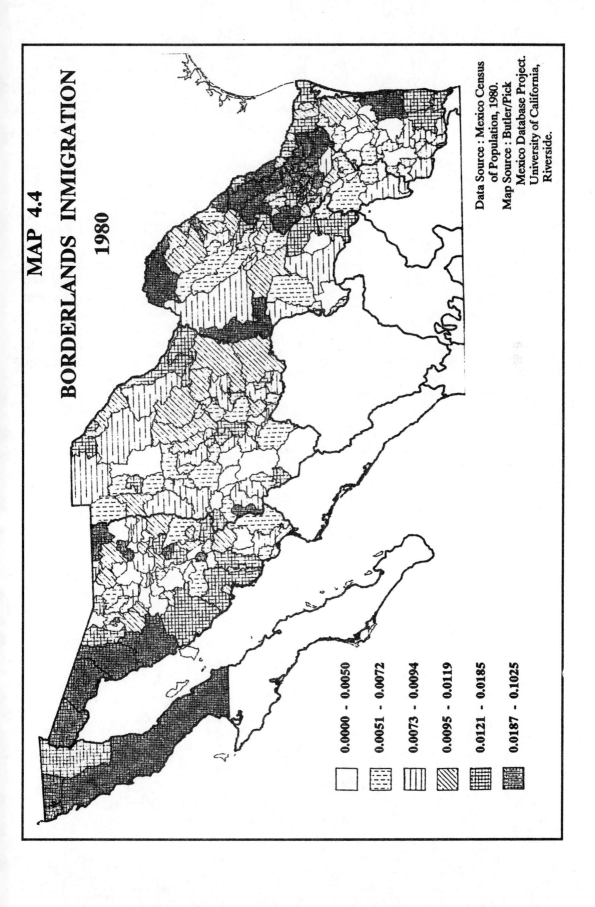

MAP 4.4

BORDERLANDS INMIGRATION

1980

Data Source : Mexico Census
of Population, 1980.
Map Source : Butler/Pick
Mexico Database Project.
University of California,
Riverside.

0.0000 - 0.0050

0.0051 - 0.0072

0.0073 - 0.0094

0.0095 - 0.0119

0.0121 - 0.0185

0.0187 - 0.1025

5

MORTALITY AND HEALTH

Introduction

Chapter 5 examines mortality and health in Mexico using data obtained from the 1980 Mexican census and from various anuarios. Mortality data are for 1979 while health data are for 1980. The seven measures of mortality presented include the crude infant mortality rate (that is, the ratio, for one year, of infant deaths to 1,000 live births), the total annual mortality rate (that is, deaths per 1,000 population), and a standardized annual mortality which in essence controls for varying age structures among the states. Standardized mortality rates also are presented for the four major causes of death in Mexico: (1) cardiovascular, (2) respiratory, (3) infectious diseases, and (4) trauma.

Two maps are presented regarding health. The first one illustrates the availability of hospitals and clinics among the states; the second one presents information on the extent to which children in the various states do not have weekly meat or eggs in their diet.

Mortality

Infant Mortality Rate, 1980

The infant mortality rate is a measure of mortality to infants in the first year of life. It is defined as the ratio, for a one year period, of deaths to persons under one year of age to 1,000 live births. In 1988, Mexico's infant mortality rate is estimated at 50 (Population Reference Bureau, 1988). The infant mortality rate tends to be related to health and medical care conditions, and more generally to economic development levels, in a nation or other geographic unit (Rabell et al., 1986). By comparison, in 1988 the infant mortality rate of Latin America is estimated at 57, and the rates for the United States and Japan are estimated at 10.0 and 5.2 respectively (Population Reference Bureau, 1988).

In Mexico, there are severe inadequacies in information on infant mortality. Data from the vital statistics system, which registers births and deaths, are incomplete, so that the data tend to underestimate infant mortality (Bruch et al., 1980; Rabell et al., 1986). Although the 1980 census data on infant deaths possibly are somewhat inaccurate, the infant mortality rate can be indirectly estimated from census data, based on the number of children born living and the survivorship of children after birth. The infant mortality rates presented on Map 5.1A and Table 5.1 were estimated using an indirect method (Rabell et al. 1988). The mean infant mortality rate in 1980 by state is 73.1. This may be compared to the historical national aggregate rates shown below.

Historical Infant Mortality Rates for Mexico

Year	Infant Mortality Rate Range of Variation
1940	170-230
1950	130-170
1960	80-110
1970	65- 95
1980	74

SOURCE : 1940-70 data, Aguirre and Camposortega, 1982; 1980 data, Rabell, 1986.

There is very small variation among states. The highest rates, in the range of 80-89, are for Durango, Zacatecas, Tlaxcala, Puebla, Tabasco, Chiapas, and Oaxaca. On the other hand, the lowest rates are in Yucatan, Quintana Roo, and Baja California. By region, the pacific south has the highest rates, followed by the north, central, and gulf regions. The border region is low, except for Chihuahua, as is the southeast.

As suggested by Rabell (1986), infant mortality shows a close correspondence with indicators of economic underdevelopment, such as low income (Map 8.4A), and to indicators of poor health, such as children receiving no weekly meat or eggs (Map 5.2B). However, it does not have an inverse relationship with hospitals and clinics per 10,000 population (Map 5.2A), but, rather, hospitals and clinics are positively related to infant mortality. The reason may be that Mexican health planning has placed hospitals in areas of greater infant morbidity and mortality. Another reason may be that beginning in 1972, infant deaths have been registered at place of the death, rather than place of residence (Partida, 1982). Therefore, moribund infants may have been treated, and registered, in states with better availability of hospitals.

In Mexico in 1980, infectious and parasitic disease was the leading cause of death for infants (Rabell, 1986). Thus, there is a substantial correspondence between geographic patterns of infant mortality and standardized mortality rate from infections (Map 5.1F).

Crude and Standardized Mortality Rates, 1979

The crude mortality rate is the ratio of deaths to total population for a one year period. It is useful as an indicator of the current extent of mortality in a population. However, it is has a weakness of being dependent on the age structure of a population. For instance, for a very young population with a low crude mortality rate, the crude rate may reflect young age, rather than favorable mortality. Age standardization of the crude rate adjusts the rate for the relative youth of its age structure. In the atlas, standardized mortality rates are calculated by indirect standardization (see Shryock and Siegel, 1976, for a more complete explanation). This method adjusts the crude mortality rate for a given population, in this case Mexico, by reference to a standard population. For the indirect standardizations performed in this chapter of the atlas, the standard population selected is England and Wales, 1964 (Preston, Keyfitz, and Schoen, 1972). The method adjusts the crude death rate of the standard population by a factor which is the ratio of the number of deaths in the given population divided by the number of deaths based on the mortality rates of the standard population and the age structure of the given population. Later in the chapter, the same method is applied to cause-specific death rates, such as the crude mortality rate for heart diseases.

Among the states of Mexico, there are not large differences in age structure. This is seen by the low coefficients of variation for the age structure variables in Table 2.2. As a result, indirect standardization has only slight effects on mortality patterns, and the Maps 5.1B and 5.1C for crude mortality rate and standardized mortality are very similar (also see Table 5.2). Thus, the rest of the discussion, which focuses on the standardized mortality rate, applies also to crude mortality rate, with exceptions noted.

The national crude mortality rate in 1979 was 6.3. As seen in the following table, the crude mortality rate in Mexico has dropped greatly in the twentieth century, and life expectancy at birth has improved.

Mexican Crude Mortality Rate, 1930-1988

Year	Crude Mortality Rate	Life Expectancy
1930	26.6	37
1940	23.4	41
1950	16.1	49
1960	11.5	59
1970	10.1	62
1979	6.3	66
1988	6.0	66

SOURCE : Martinez, 1982; Rabell, 1986; Population Reference Bureau, 1988.

In 1979, states had an average standardized mortality rate of 6.3. Variation among states was low, but higher than for standardized fertility rate. The highest standardized mortality rates are in the states of Puebla, Oaxaca, and Hidalgo. These states are also among the highest in infant mortality rates and are among Mexico's poorest states (see Table 8.11). At the other extreme are the states of Quintana Roo, Nayarit, Nuevo Leon, Sinaloa, and Durango being average to low in infant mortality but having moderate to high incomes. By region, the northwest and northeast have low standardized mortality. These regions benefit in the health of their popululations by relative economic prosperity, proximity to the United States, and a prevalence of hospitals in the northwest. The west and central regions have generally high standardized mortality, with the notable exception of the Federal District. Mortality in these regions is elevated by especially high death rates from respiratory diseases, which may be due in part to the effects of air pollution and altitude. The Federal District, with a standardized mortality rate of only 5.0, has very high income level and relatively advanced health care services. In the southern and southeastern regions, standardized mortality rates show great variation from state to state.

Standardized Mortality Rate from Cardiovascular Diseases, 1979

This and subsequent analyses describe standardized mortality rates by four leading causes of death -- cardiovascular, respiratory, infectious and parasitic diseases, and trauma. The geographic patterns of mortality rates for the four leading causes are very different. When the four patterns are added together, they largely account for the overall pattern of standardized mortality rate. The following table presents the mortality from nine leading causes of death in Mexico in 1979.

Mortality in Mexico by Cause of Death, 1979

Cause of Death	Number of Deaths	Percent of Total
Cardiovascular Diseases	69,327	16.2
Trauma	63,641	14.9
Infectious and Parasitic Diseases	61,138	14.3
Respiratory Diseases	59,475	13.9
Digestive Diseases	29,938	7.0
Undefined Diseases	29,658	6.9
Cancer	27,865	6.5
Diseases of Infancy	26,941	6.3
Nutritional, Metabolic, Endocrine and Immunity Diseases	24,033	5.6
Others	36,201	8.4
Total	428,217	100.0

SOURCE : Anuario Estadastico, 1984.

Thus the four leading causes of death accounted for three fifths of all deaths in 1979. As shown in Table 5.3 and Map 5.1D, the mean statewide standardized mortality rate from cardiovascular diseases in 1980 was 0.87, with low variation among states. Cardiovascular disease was the leading cause of death in 1979 for both men and women. Its heaviest effects were in the age ranges of 40 years and older for both sexes (Rabell et al., 1986).

There is generally a decreasing level of standardized cardiovascular mortality rate from north to south. In the north, Chihuahua has the highest rate in all of Mexico at 1.17, with other border states, except Baja California also having very high rates. Other states with high rates include Durango, Hidalgo, and Colima. The central flank of the country has, on average, moderate rates. The Federal District and state of Mexico are somewhat below average. The pacific south region has very low rates. Four of the five Mexican states with the lowest standardized heart mortality rates are located in a region located just south of the Federal District, and including the states of Puebla, Chiapas, Oaxaca, and Guerrero. The southeast region varies from very low in Quintana Roo to average in Campeche and Yucatan.

Standardized cardiovascular mortality is highly correlated with urbanization (Map 2.6A). This may be related, among other reasons, to increased physical and mental stress and adverse diets in urban areas. The Federal District and Mexico are exceptions to this relationship, since they are among the most urbanized states, while having below average cardiovascular mortality rates. It may be that in these states a superior health care system for cardiovascular diseases offsets the potential detrimental stress and diet effects.

Standardized Mortality Rate from Respiratory Diseases, 1979

Mortality from respiratory diseases was the fourth leading cause of death in Mexico in 1979. The mean statewide standardized mortality rate for respiratory diseases is 0.78 (see Table 5.3). Variation in this mortality rate is the highest among cause-specific rates for the four major causes examined in this atlas.

Map 5.1E shows that the central region, excepting the Federal District and Morelos, has a concentration of states with very high rates. This area includes states with the three highest respiratory mortality rates : Puebla -- 1.73, Tlaxcala -- 1.67, and Guanajuato -- 1.39. The area's high rates are likely related to the detrimental environmental influences of air pollution produced by the Mexico City and Puebla metropolitan areas and to other unknown causes. The below average respiratory mortality in the Federal District is surprising given the often extreme air pollution and high altitude of the District. In fact, air pollution in the Federal District area is considered among the world's worst (Schteingart, 1988). However, these adverse factors may be offset by a more advanced health care system. The west region is also high in respiratory mortality. The border and south regions are moderate to low, while the gulf region is low. The southeast region varies, with Quintana Roo and Campeche low and more urbanized Yucatan having average rates.

Standardized Mortality Rate from Infectious and Parasitic Diseases, 1979

Mortality from infectious and parasitic diseases was the third largest cause of death in Mexico in 1979. As shown in the following table, mortality from these diseases showed a remarkable decline from 1930 to 1975.

Mortality Rates for Infectious and Parasitic Diseases, Mexico, 1930-75

	1930	1950	1970	1975
Diarrea and Enteritis	0.460	0278	0.141	0.084
Pneumonia and Influenza	0.269	0.266	0.170	0.087
Malaria	0.164	0.089	0.000	0.000
Whooping cough	0.112	0.046	0.100	NA
Smallpox	0.105	0.000	0.000	0.000
Measles	0.902	0.209	0.024	NA

NA = not available.

SOURCE : Coplamar, 1979.

The remarkable drop was largely due to the implementation of public health measures, including vaccination, widespread use of antibiotics, and improved sanitation. In 1979, these diseases took their greatest toll in the young age range of 0-14 years. They caused 60 percent of deaths in the first two years, but only 10 to 20 percent of deaths above age 20 (Rabell et al., 1986).

Table 5.3 indicates that the statewide mean standardized death rate for infectious/parasitic diseases in 1979 was 1.05, with moderate variation among states. There is generally a north-south differential, with the south having higher rates (see Map 5.1F). The pacific south region has an average rate of 1.80, versus a rate of 0.78 for the border region. The central flank of the country has rates varying from moderate to high. An exception is the Federal District, with a low standardized rate of 0.59, corresponding to its low standardized rates for the other major causes of death. Among other reasons, this is probably due to a relatively strong public health system. On the other hand, the state of Mexico is average in infectious/parasitic mortality. The southeast varies greatly, from a very low rate in Quintana Roo, to a low rate in Campeche, and a high rate in Yucatan.

There is a strong inverse relationship between the geographic distribution of infectious/parasitic diseases and urbanization. One reason is that the public health infrastructure necessary to control infectious/parasitic diseases is stronger and more effective in urban as opposed to rural areas. Exceptions to this relationship are Colima, Aguascalientes, and Yucatan, which have high infectious/parasitic mortality rates while being highly urbanized.

Standardized Mortality Rate from Trauma, 1979

Trauma, which includes accidents and violence, was Mexico's second leading cause of death in 1979. This cause of death is of less importance in nearly all of the world's other very large nations (Preston, Keyfitz, and Schoen, 1972). By sex, trauma is over twice as important for Mexican males than females (Rabell et al., 1986). For males, its occurrence is concentrated in the 10-45 age range, while for females in the 10-30 age range. For males of age 20 in 1975, trauma accounted for two thirds of all deaths, while it was responsible for 40 percent of deaths for males at age 40. The high level of trauma may be attributed partly to Mexican societal norms encouraging aggressiveness, especially in males. Also, the high rate of auto accidents may be encouraged by increasing urbanization, and by high alcohol consumption, concentrated in certain parts of the country.

The 1979 mean standardized mortality rate from trauma was 0.97 (see Table 5.3). The geographic distribution of trauma deaths shows little adherance to standard regions. Map 5.1G illustrates that there is a five state area of high trauma deaths, consisting of Colima, Michoacan, Guerrero, Morelos, and Puebla. Colima has the highest statewide for trauma mortality rate of 1.57. Another state with a very high rate is Tabasco. The country's lowest rates are located in Nuevo Leon, the Federal District, and Yucatan. In these urbanized states, the presence of major metropolitan areas may lead to better preventive control of trauma, as well as to improved care for victims. Standardized mortality from trauma has a signficant positive correlation with expenditures on alcoholic beverages (see Map 6.5B). Alcoholism may influence both accidents, including car accidents, and violence, such as homocides.

Table 5.1 Annual Infant Mortality Rate, Offical and Estimated, 1980

No. State	Official Infant Mortality Rate			Estimated Mortality Rate
	Infant Deaths 1980	Births 1980	Infant Mortality Rate	
1 AGUASCALIENTES	962	20,515	46.89	78.92
2 BAJA CALIFORNIA	1,202	38,697	31.06	56.89
3 BAJA CALIFORNIA SUR	328	8,659	37.88	59.02
4 CAMPECHE	519	14,295	36.31	59.12
5 COAHUILA	1,819	59,059	30.80	66.77
6 COLIMA	481	12,368	38.89	69.31
7 CHIAPAS	2,628	77,426	33.94	82.54
8 CHIHUAHUA	2,777	64,810	42.85	78.37
9 DISTRITO FEDERAL	10,783	291,372	37.01	NA
10 DURANGO	940	48,967	19.20	85.15
11 GUANAJUATO	6,852	99,640	68.77	79.32
12 GUERRERO	2,201	99,018	22.23	79.73
13 HIDALGO	2,779	65,030	42.73	80.55
14 JALISCO	6,539	165,855	39.43	75.72
15 MEXICO	13,385	202,002	66.26	78.98
16 MICHOACAN	3,789	126,401	29.98	77.25
17 MORELOS	762	36,545	20.85	67.03
18 NAYARIT	469	25,618	18.31	74.20
19 NUEVO LEON	2,417	81,278	29.74	58.62
20 OAXACA	4,104	104,670	39.21	82.43
21 PUEBLA	8,094	147,618	54.83	88.63
22 QUERETARO	1,650	28,943	57.01	72.97
23 QUINTANA ROO	311	8,765	35.48	54.56
24 SAN LUIS POTOSI	2,050	55,749	36.77	78.61
25 SINALOA	1,185	73,799	16.06	66.22
26 SONORA	1,740	49,739	34.98	62.37
27 TABASCO	1,850	53,788	34.39	83.94
28 TAMAULIPAS	1,719	65,263	26.34	65.00
29 TLAXCALA	1,169	14,717	79.43	85.15
30 VERACRUZ	5,223	197,852	26.40	78.57
31 YUCATAN	1,532	38,716	39.57	54.56
32 ZACATECAS	1,871	42,293	44.24	85.46
National Average			38.91	74.00
National Total	94,130	2,419,467		
Mean	2,942	75,608	38.06	73.10
S.D.	3,102	65,189	14.59	10.28
C.V.	105.45	86.22	38.33	14.06
Minimum	311	8,765	16.06	54.56
Maximum	13,385	291,372	79.43	88.63

DEFINITION: Official infant mortality rate equals 1,000 times the number of infant deaths divided by the number of births in 1980. The estimated infant mortality rate was indirectly determined by Rabell et al. from census data based on the number of children born living and the survivorship of children after birth (for full explanation, see Rabell et al., 1980).

NOTE: NA = not available.

SOURCE: Official rate: 1981 Annuario Estadistico, Tables 3.1.9 and 3.1.10; estimated rate: Rabell et al., 1980.

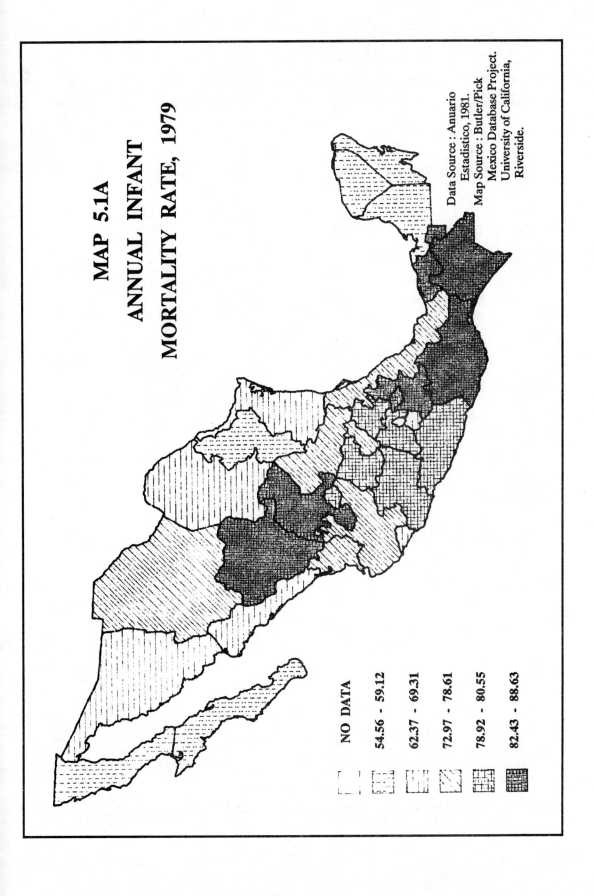

MAP 5.1A
ANNUAL INFANT
MORTALITY RATE, 1979

Data Source : Anuario
Estadistico, 1981.
Map Source : Butler/Pick
Mexico Database Project.
University of California,
Riverside.

NO DATA

54.56 - 59.12

62.37 - 69.31

72.97 - 78.61

78.92 - 80.55

82.43 - 88.63

Table 5.2 Annual Mortality Rates, 1979

No.	State	Number of Deaths 1979	Total Population 1980	Annual Mortality Rate 1979	Standardized Annual Mortality Rate 1979
1	AGUASCALIENTES	3,317	519,439	6.3857	6.17
2	BAJA CALIFORNIA	6,806	1,177,886	5.7781	5.67
3	BAJA CALIFORNIA SUR	1,179	215,139	5.4802	5.16
4	CAMPECHE	1,977	420,553	4.7010	5.33
5	COAHUILA	9,294	1,557,265	5.9682	6.00
6	COLIMA	2,459	346,293	7.1009	7.36
7	CHIAPAS	11,580	2,084,717	5.5547	5.54
8	CHIHUAHUA	12,838	2,005,477	6.4015	6.64
9	DISTRITO FEDERAL	48,421	8,831,079	5.4830	5.01
10	DURANGO	6,183	1,182,320	5.2295	5.27
11	GUANAJUATO	23,702	3,006,110	7.8846	7.31
12	GUERRERO	13,062	2,109,513	6.1920	5.76
13	HIDALGO	12,363	1,547,493	7.9891	7.53
14	JALISCO	28,765	4,371,998	6.5794	6.37
15	MEXICO	43,700	7,564,335	5.7771	6.47
16	MICHOACAN	20,241	2,868,824	7.0555	6.27
17	MORELOS	5,655	947,089	5.9709	6.12
18	NAYARIT	3,671	726,120	5.0556	4.68
19	NUEVO LEON	11,706	2,513,044	4.6581	4.71
20	OAXACA	23,676	2,369,076	9.9938	7.55
21	PUEBLA	31,697	3,347,685	9.4683	8.71
22	QUERETARO	5,025	739,605	6.7942	6.80
23	QUINTANA ROO	826	225,985	3.6551	4.35
24	SAN LUIS POTOSI	10,971	1,673,893	6.5542	5.98
25	SINALOA	8,887	1,849,879	4.8041	4.79
26	SONORA	9,289	1,513,731	6.1365	5.60
27	TABASCO	6,732	1,062,961	6.3333	6.27
28	TAMAULIPAS	10,504	1,924,484	5.4581	5.17
29	TLAXCALA	3,784	556,597	6.7985	6.57
30	VERACRUZ	32,317	5,387,680	5.9983	5.96
31	YUCATAN	7,981	1,063,733	7.5028	6.40
32	ZACATECAS	6,921	1,136,830	6.0880	5.53
	National Total	425,529	67,405,700		
	Mean	13,298		6.2759	0.0603
	S.D.	12,175		1.2877	0.0097
	C.V.	91.56		20.52	16.15
	Minimum	826		3.6551	0.0435
	Maximum	48,421		9.9938	0.0871

DEFINITION: Annual mortality rate is the ratio of deaths for the year 1979 to the population in 1980, multiplied by 1,000. Standardized mortality rate is calculated from the annual mortality rate 1979 by indirect standardizatio, based on a state's population age structure in 1980 and a standard population (see text for explanation).

SOURCE: Deaths: 1981 Annuario Estadistico, population: 1980 Mexican Census of Population.

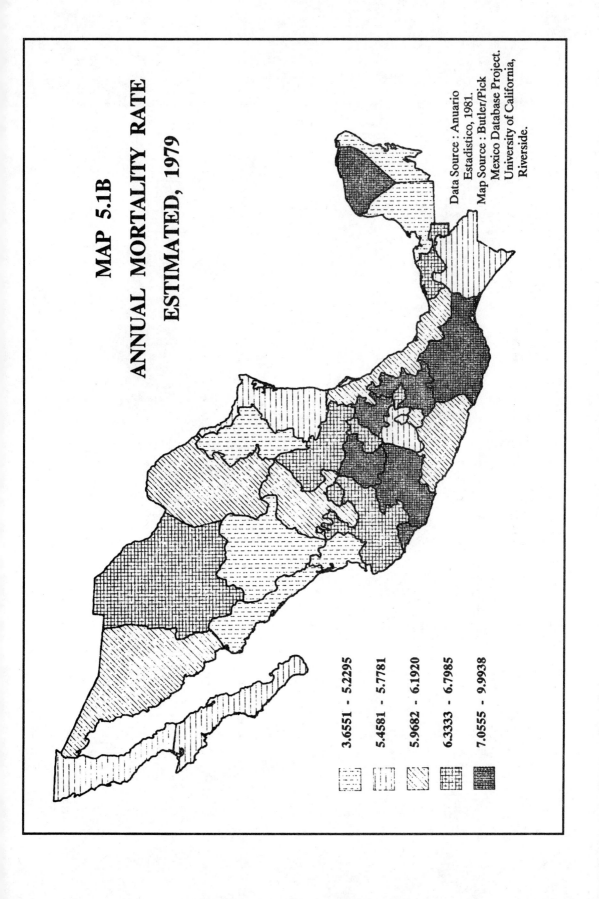

MAP 5.1B
ANNUAL MORTALITY RATE
ESTIMATED, 1979

Data Source : Anuario
Estadistico, 1981.
Map Source : Butler/Pick
Mexico Database Project.
University of California,
Riverside.

3.6551 - 5.2295

5.4581 - 5.7781

5.9682 - 6.1920

6.3333 - 6.7985

7.0555 - 9.9938

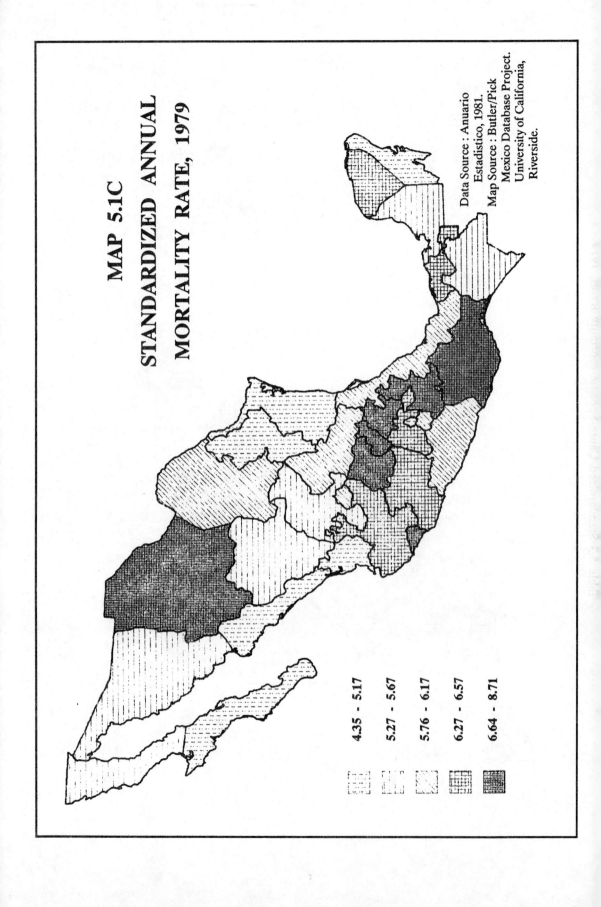

MAP 5.1C
STANDARDIZED ANNUAL
MORTALITY RATE, 1979

Data Source : Anuario
Estadistico, 1981.
Map Source : Butler/Pick
Mexico Database Project.
University of California,
Riverside.

4.35 - 5.17

5.27 - 5.67

5.76 - 6.17

6.27 - 6.57

6.64 - 8.71

Table 5.3 Standardized Cause-Specific Mortality Rates, 1979

No.	State	Cardiovascular		Respiratory		Infections		Trauma	
		Number of Deaths	Standardized Mortality Rate	Number of Deaths	Standardized Mortality Rate	Number of Deaths	Standardized Mortality Rate	Number of Deaths	Standardized Mortality Rate
1	AGUASCALIENTES	496	0.8100	508	0.9500	564	1.2400	399	0.8100
2	BAJA CALIFORNIA	1,212	0.8600	719	0.5400	777	0.8100	1,251	1.0200
3	BAJA CALIFORNIA SUR	175	0.6600	132	0.5400	165	0.9000	197	0.8400
4	CAMPECHE	316	0.8300	204	0.5300	276	0.7800	326	0.8500
5	COAHUILA	1,854	1.0800	1,145	0.6900	1,110	0.8300	1,163	0.7300
6	COLIMA	389	1.0500	216	0.6200	390	1.3700	524	1.5700
7	CHIAPAS	1,157	0.5100	1,107	0.5100	2,705	1.4600	1,559	0.7300
8	CHIHUAHUA	2,612	1.1700	1,570	0.7500	1,502	0.9800	1,784	0.9000
9	DISTRITO FEDERAL	9,500	0.8200	7,104	0.6700	4,347	0.5900	5,234	0.5300
10	DURANGO	1,407	1.0800	666	0.5600	467	0.4600	1,221	1.0700
11	GUANAJUATO	3,692	1.0100	4,413	1.3900	3,482	1.2600	2,902	0.9700
12	GUERRERO	1,561	0.6200	1,254	0.5500	2,574	1.3300	2,528	1.1600
13	HIDALGO	1,762	0.9500	2,122	1.3100	1,802	1.2900	1,774	1.1500
14	JALISCO	5,356	1.0200	3,931	0.8600	3,501	0.9400	3,944	0.9300
15	MEXICO	5,596	0.8200	8,697	1.1900	7,011	1.0700	6,468	0.8700
16	MICHOACAN	3,379	0.9100	2,461	0.7700	2,768	1.0300	4,098	1.3700
17	MORELOS	1,021	0.9500	522	0.5300	706	0.9500	1,254	1.3800
18	NAYARIT	701	0.7600	404	0.5100	463	0.7200	695	0.9500
19	NUEVO LEON	3,126	1.1100	1,864	0.7100	1,041	0.5000	1,157	0.4600
20	OAXACA	2,283	0.5800	1,930	0.6500	5,882	2.6000	2,938	1.1400
21	PUEBLA	3,355	0.7900	6,188	1.7300	5,242	1.7700	3,826	1.1700
22	QUERETARO	702	0.8700	882	1.1900	826	1.2400	665	0.9400
23	QUINTANA ROO	92	0.5000	68	0.3400	115	0.6100	244	1.1500
24	SAN LUIS POTOSI	1,688	0.7900	1,696	0.9200	1,560	1.0300	1,464	0.8600
25	SINALOA	1,840	0.9200	940	0.4800	929	0.5700	1,941	1.0000
26	SONORA	2,100	1.0500	1,139	0.6600	1,052	0.8300	1,498	0.9500
27	TABASCO	956	0.8900	643	0.5900	1,345	1.2700	1,540	1.3900
28	TAMAULIPAS	2,423	1.0300	1,049	0.4900	1,021	0.6300	1,739	0.8800
29	TLAXCALA	534	0.8300	985	1.6700	607	1.2300	314	0.5600
30	VERACRUZ	2,731	0.8400	2,340	0.4800	4,807	1.1000	5,708	1.0700
31	YUCATAN	1,319	0.8300	931	0.7400	1,140	1.2800	748	0.6700
32	ZACATECAS	1,104	0.7600	1,155	0.9500	892	0.8800	1,020	0.9000
	National Total	66,439		58,985		61,069		62,123	
	Mean	2,076	0.8656	1,843	0.7834	1,908	1.0484	1,941	0.9678
	S.D.	1,895	0.1671	2,036	0.3461	1,794	0.4130	1,625	0.2490
	C.V.	91.26	19.30	110.47	44.18	94.02	39.39	83.72	25.73
	Minimum	92	0.5000	68	0.3400	115	0.4600	197	0.4600
	Maximum	9,500	1.1700	8,697	1.7300	7,011	2.6000	6,468	1.5700

DEFINITION: Annual cause-specific mortality rate is the ratio of deaths in 1979 due to a specific cause to the population in 1980, multiplied by 1,000. The standardized cause-specific mortality rate is calculated from the annual cause-specific mortality rate 1979 by indirect standardization, based on a state's population age structure in 1980 and a standard population (see text for explanation).

SOURCE: Deaths by cause: 1984 Anuario Estadístico, population: 1980 Mexican Census of Population.

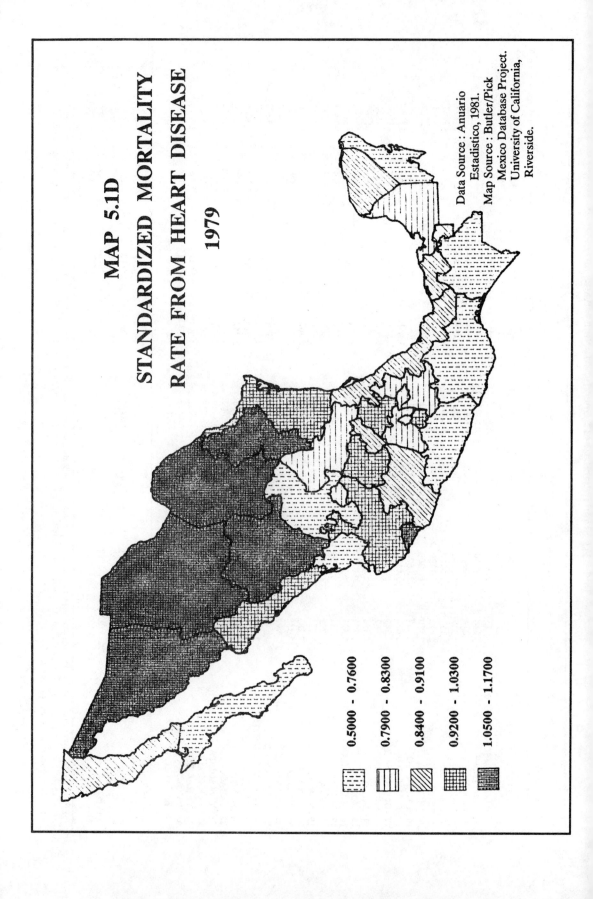

MAP 5.1D

STANDARDIZED MORTALITY

RATE FROM HEART DISEASE

1979

Data Source : Anuario
Estadistico, 1981.
Map Source : Butler/Pick
Mexico Database Project.
University of California,
Riverside.

0.5000 - 0.7600

0.7900 - 0.8300

0.8400 - 0.9100

0.9200 - 1.0300

1.0500 - 1.1700

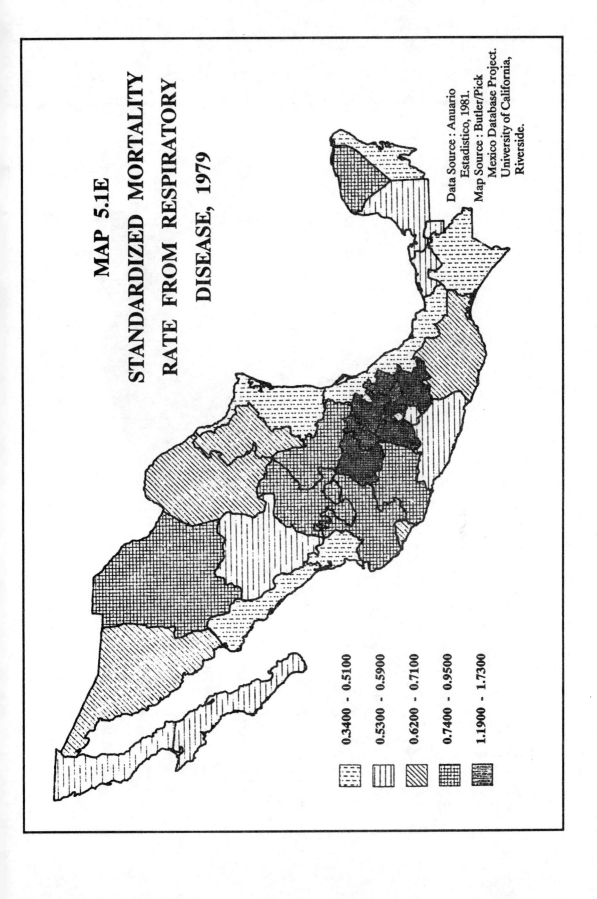

MAP 5.1E

STANDARDIZED MORTALITY

RATE FROM RESPIRATORY

DISEASE, 1979

Data Source : Anuario
Estadistico, 1981.
Map Source : Butler/Pick
Mexico Database Project.
University of California,
Riverside.

0.3400 - 0.5100

0.5300 - 0.5900

0.6200 - 0.7100

0.7400 - 0.9500

1.1900 - 1.7300

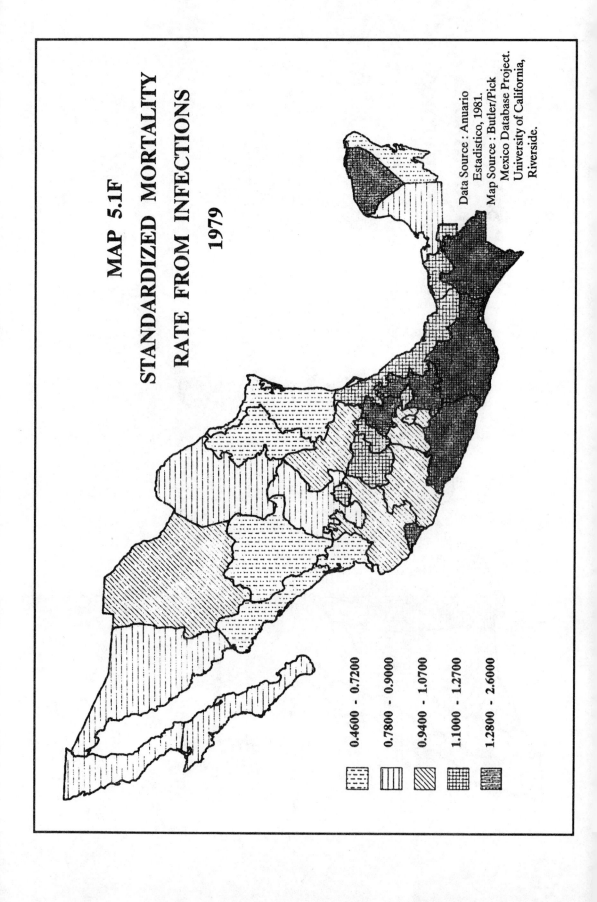

MAP 5.1F
STANDARDIZED MORTALITY
RATE FROM INFECTIONS
1979

Data Source : Anuario
Estadistico, 1981.
Map Source : Butler/Pick
Mexico Database Project.
University of California,
Riverside.

0.4600 - 0.7200
0.7800 - 0.9000
0.9400 - 1.0700
1.1000 - 1.2700
1.2800 - 2.6000

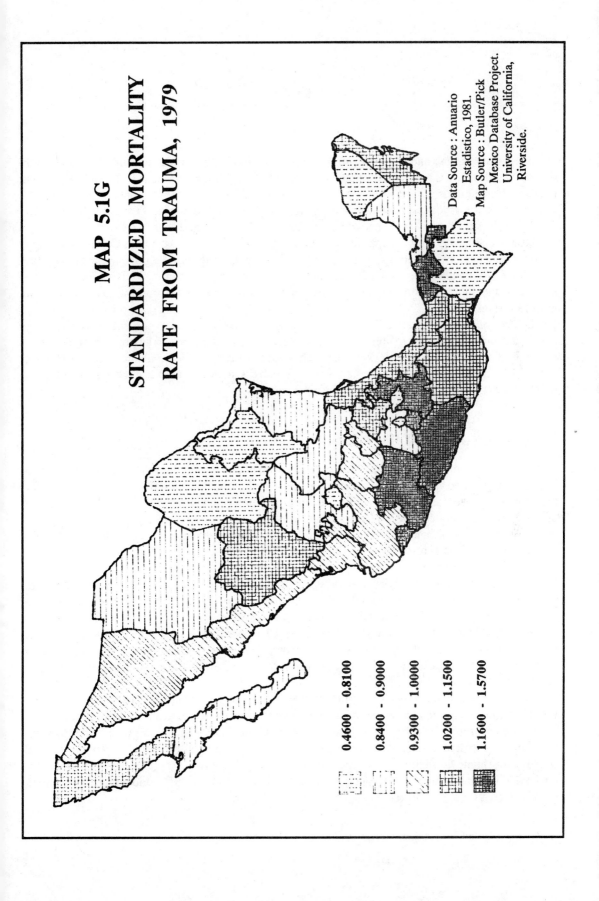

MAP 5.1G

STANDARDIZED MORTALITY

RATE FROM TRAUMA, 1979

Data Source : Anuario
Estadistico, 1981.
Map Source : Butler/Pick
Mexico Database Project.
University of California,
Riverside.

0.4600 - 0.8100

0.8400 - 0.9000

0.9300 - 1.0000

1.0200 - 1.1500

1.1600 - 1.5700

Health

Hospitals and Clinics, 1980

The rate of hospitals and clinics per 10,000 population in 1980 is a crude measure of the #IHealth serviceshealth services available to the general population. The mean rate is 0.15, while the mean number of hospitals is 53. The range is from a low of 0.10 in Campeche to a high of 0.89 in Quintana Roo. There is moderate variation among states, with a standard deviation about half the mean. Twenty of the states are in the range of 0.21 to 0.38 (see Table 5.4 and Map 5.2A).

Oaxaca, Queretaro, and Chiapas are in the upper ranges while Nuevo Leon, Colima, Durango, Michoacan, Zacatecas, Coahuila, and the Federal District have the lowest prevalence of hospitals and clinics. All pacific south states have a high rate of hospitals and clinics, while all other regions have substantial intra-regional variation. The Federal District and its surrounding area have low to moderate rates.

The distribution of the rate of hospital and clinics is inversely related to percent urban (see Map 2.6A). It is inversely related to literacy, primary education, and the urban indicator of potable water. It is related to population growth 1975-80, which tended to take place in urban and tourist areas (see Table 2.1A). It is also strongly related, on a per capita basis, to hotels, air passengers, and air flights, which also are associated with growth and tourism areas.

Children Receiving No Weekly Meat or Eggs, 1980

This variable measures the proportion of population of children under six who receive no weekly meat or eggs. The variable serves as an indicator of childhood undernourishment. The statewide mean of 10.7 percent indicates that a significant proportion of children in Mexico have a deficient diet. There is moderate variation in the variable. At the high extreme are Zacatecas, Guanajuato, and Queretaro, in which about a fifth of children receive no weekly meat or eggs. At the other extreme less than 5 percent of the children in Baja California and Baja California Sur are undernourished (see Table 5.5).

Map 5.2B shows that the entire northwest region has consistently low values. This is a region of high income combined with good availability of meat and diary products. The central metropolitan zone and state of Nuevo Leon have low values of 4.9 and 5.6 respectively. These values reflect the presence of urban centers with high income levels. There is a nine-state region with high values, which includes the rest of the central region, except Morelos, the southern north region, plus Guanajuato and Aguascalientes. The pacific south is also high, while the gulf and southeast regions are low to moderate.

The pattern of childern receiving no meat or eggs is strongly associated, in expected directions, with urbanization and related variables, as well as dependency ratio, education, and literacy. Comparing the geographic distributions for the present variable and urbanization (Map 2.6A), they appear opposite, with several minor differences. States in the southern north and central regions reveal consistently higher childhood undernourishment than the south, whereas the two areas are equivalent in urbanization. Also, Aguascalientes has a high extent of childhood undernourishment, even though it is very urbanized.

Table 5.4 Hospitals and Clinics per 10,000 Population, 1980

No.	State	Hospitals, Clinics, Etc.	Ratio
1	AGUASCALIENTES	19	0.3658
2	BAJA CALIFORNIA	32	0.2717
3	BAJA CALIFORNIA SUR	7	0.3254
4	CAMPECHE	4	0.0951
5	COAHUILA	29	0.1862
6	COLIMA	5	0.1444
7	CHIAPAS	92	0.4413
8	CHIHUAHUA	45	0.2244
9	DISTRITO FEDERAL	170	0.1925
10	DURANGO	18	0.1522
11	GUANAJUATO	92	0.3060
12	GUERRERO	81	0.3840
13	HIDALGO	47	0.3037
14	JALISCO	91	0.2081
15	MEXICO	183	0.2419
16	MICHOACAN	45	0.1569
17	MORELOS	20	0.2112
18	NAYARIT	22	0.3030
19	NUEVO LEON	29	0.1154
20	OAXACA	138	0.5825
21	PUEBLA	87	0.2599
22	QUERETARO	35	0.4732
23	QUINTANA ROO	20	0.8850
24	SAN LUIS POTOSI	40	0.2390
25	SINALOA	54	0.2919
26	SONORA	49	0.3237
27	TABASCO	32	0.3010
28	TAMAULIPAS	40	0.2078
29	TLAXCALA	17	0.3054
30	VERACRUZ	111	0.2060
31	YUCATAN	33	0.3102
32	ZACATECAS	20	0.1759
	Mean	53	0.2872
	S.D.	45	0.1514
	C.V.	84.88	52.72
	Minimum	4	0.0951
	Maximum	183	0.8850

DEFINITION: Ratio is the number of hospitals, clinics, etc. to total population multiplied by 0.0001.

SOURCE: 1980 Mexican Census of Population, Volume 1, Table 18.

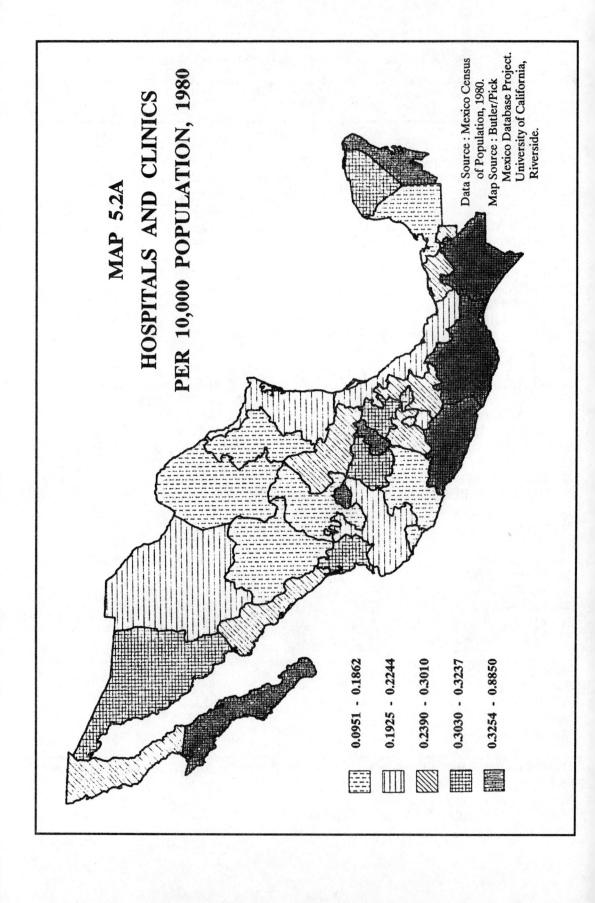

MAP 5.2A

HOSPITALS AND CLINICS

PER 10,000 POPULATION, 1980

Data Source : Mexico Census
of Population, 1980.

Map Source : Butler/Pick
Mexico Database Project.
University of California,
Riverside.

0.0951 - 0.1862

0.1925 - 0.2244

0.2390 - 0.3010

0.3030 - 0.3237

0.3254 - 0.8850

Table 5.5 Children Receiving No Weekly Meat or Eggs, 1980

No.	State	Population Receiving No Meat or Eggs	Total Population Age < 6	Ratio
1	AGUASCALIENTES	14,205	81,668	0.1739
2	BAJA CALIFORNIA	6,398	157,635	0.0406
3	BAJA CALIFORNIA SUR	1,585	32,143	0.0493
4	CAMPECHE	3,800	62,398	0.0609
5	COAHUILA	14,232	225,148	0.0632
6	COLIMA	5,067	54,166	0.0935
7	CHIAPAS	32,219	289,434	0.1113
8	CHIHUAHUA	23,371	271,103	0.0862
9	DISTRITO FEDERAL	40,038	1,190,698	0.0336
10	DURANGO	19,645	168,709	0.1164
11	GUANAJUATO	89,504	438,715	0.2040
12	GUERRERO	43,053	297,307	0.1448
13	HIDALGO	32,410	226,013	0.1434
14	JALISCO	69,144	621,972	0.1112
15	MEXICO	75,583	1,166,423	0.0648
16	MICHOACAN	59,618	414,085	0.1440
17	MORELOS	9,674	132,497	0.0730
18	NAYARIT	12,711	120,177	0.1058
19	NUEVO LEON	20,216	357,662	0.0565
20	OAXACA	43,206	305,736	0.1413
21	PUEBLA	77,977	476,210	0.1637
22	QUERETARO	26,233	130,517	0.2010
23	QUINTANA ROO	2,778	36,524	0.0761
24	SAN LUIS POTOSI	41,648	245,170	0.1699
25	SINALOA	17,039	275,583	0.0618
26	SONORA	11,440	216,222	0.0529
27	TABASCO	10,819	165,939	0.0652
28	TAMAULIPAS	16,779	267,300	0.0628
29	TLAXCALA	11,461	77,168	0.1485
30	VERACRUZ	70,619	713,803	0.0989
31	YUCATAN	10,160	129,846	0.0782
32	ZACATECAS	46,468	198,648	0.2339
Mean		29,972	298,332	0.1072
S.D.		24,698	276,612	0.0530
C.V.		82.40	92.72	49.44
Minimum		1,585	32,143	0.0336
Maximum		89,504	1,190,698	0.2339

DEFINITION: Ratio is the population specifying receiving no weekly meat or eggs age < 6 to the total population age < 6. Note that the population not providing a response to these questions are not included in the values shown.

SOURCE: 1980 Mexican Census of Population, Volume 1, Table 17.

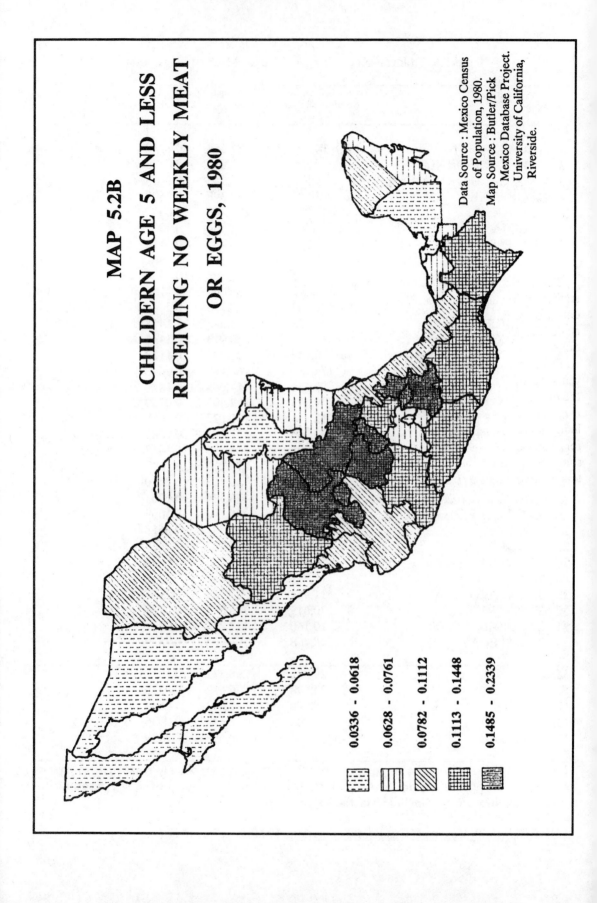

MAP 5.2B

CHILDERN AGE 5 AND LESS

RECEIVING NO WEEKLY MEAT

OR EGGS, 1980

Data Source : Mexico Census
of Population, 1980.
Map Source : Butler/Pick
Mexico Database Project.
University of California,
Riverside.

0.0336 - 0.0618

0.0628 - 0.0761

0.0782 - 0.1112

0.1113 - 0.1448

0.1485 - 0.2339

6

SOCIAL CHARACTERISTICS

Introduction

This section focuses on various social characteristics of the Mexican population, primarily at the state level, but also some material is presented at the municipio level. Also, for the state of Oaxaca, data are presented for the 571 municipios. Sources for the information included in this chapter include Mexican censuses, 1900 - 1980 anuarios, and several cited historical documents and publications.

First, an examination of literacy is undertaken. Unfortunately, comparisons for various census years is difficult because the Mexican census used changing years of age in the base for calculating the percent literate, e.g., 15 and over in 1980 as opposed to 6 and over in 1950. Second, a series of maps and information using a variety of educational measures for 1980 are shown. Third, a focus on indigenous language speakers utilizes data from 1900 through 1980. Fourth, non-Catholic religion for 1980 is illustrated for all Mexican states, and for the municipios in the oil region. Fifth, consumption of certain goods and services is examined for 1984 and 1985. Sixth, trials and penal sentences are examined. Finally, a number of housing characteristics are presented.

Literacy

Literacy, 1980

The percent literate population 15 years of age and over is shown for each state in 1980 and illustrated on Map 6.1A. The lowest rate of literacy in 1980 is in the state of Chiapas (62%) while the highest rate of literacy is in the Federal District (94%). With the exception of the Federal District, there is a substantial north to south gradient, with the north typically having a higher percent literate than southern states. The major exceptions to this north-south gradient are the already noted highest rate for the Federal District and relatively high rates for the states of Mexico, Colima, Jalisco, and Aguascalientes. The pacific south region has extremely low rates, while gulf and southeast regions have moderate to low rates. All northeast states, and most north states, had extremely high rates of literacy in 1980 (see Map 6.1A).

The mean literacy rate in 1980 is 82.5 percent. As seen in Table 6.1, variation in literacy decreased over the eighty year period to 1980, so that by 1980 literacy had a low coefficient of variation of only 11. This drop may imply more consistent national educational standards.

The geographic distribution pattern for literacy was consistent from 1930 to 1980, in spite of the approximate four-fold literacy increase (see Table 6.2). This is seen, for example, by high correlations of 1980 literacy with 1970 literacy of 0.98 and with 1950 literacy of 0.94. Such a stable pattern implies that the pattern of state differences in education has been maintained in this century.

The geographic distribution of literacy shows highly significant relationships with other socioeconomic distributions. Not surprisingly, it is strongly related to education at all levels. It also is related to urbanization, and urban-related variables including potable water and presence of electricity and television. In the area of economics, it is strongly associated with percent of workers in non-agricultural occupations and labor force, and to high income. In the opposite direction, literacy varies inversely with agricultural occupation and labor force and low income, as well as with proportions of indigenous language speaking and population native to state. Overall, literacy is a pivotal variable, which is strongly related to many other atlas variables.

Literacy, 1900

Map 6.1B illustrates literacy in 1900. Literacy in 1900, measured for the population aged 10 years and over, was extremely low, with only about one in five persons literate. However, the decreasing literacy from north to south, noted in all subsequent census years, regardless of the age criterion utilized, was already established by 1900. No data were reported in 1900 for Baja California Sur and Quintana Roo.

The states with the highest literacy were the six U.S. borderlands states, with average literacy of 34.8 percent, and the Federal District, with 49.5 percent literacy. The borderlands high literacy may be due to higher standards of living and proximity to the much more highly literate population of the United States. The Federal District's high literacy level was likely due to its strong economy and educational system. At the opposite extreme were the pacific southern states of Guerrero, Oaxaca, and Chiapas, with literacy levels of 8.9, 11.1, and 13.1 percent respectively. This very large gap of 3 to 5 times between the literacy extremes reveals a nation with great differences.

As seen below, the nation's literacy levels increased substantially from 1900 to 1980.

Literacy Levels in Mexico, 1900-1980

Year	National Percent Literate	Mean State Percent Literate
1900	22.3	24.3
1930	38.5	42.2
1950	56.8	58.7
1970	76.3	76.1
1980	83.0	82.5

NOTE: Definition corresponds to Table 6.1.

Literacy Change, 1930-1970

As Table 6.2 shows, state literacy levels increased, on average, by 33.4 percent between 1930 and 1970. At the high end, the state of Mexico increased by 46.8 percent. This increase is related to transformation of Mexico state during this period from a rural to an urban state, due to spillover growth of the Mexico City metropolitan area. Other states which experienced literacy increases of over 40 percent were Durango, San Luis Potosi, Zacatecas, and Tabasco. The first three are adjacent states in the southern north region, an area had only moderate urbanization increase from 1930-70. States which tended to increase the least in literacy over the period include Baja California and the Federal District. These states had the highest literacy in 1930, with about three quarters literate. Thus, in 1930 they had less potential for substantial increase. Besides the Federal District, two other major metropolitan states of Jalisco and Nuevo Leon experienced literacy increases near the national average. Overall, the pattern shows little resemblence to standard regions (see Map 6.1C).

One conclusion that can be drawn from the longitudinal picture of literacy in Mexico is that it is extremely difficult for a state to overcome its initial handicap in reducing literacy. While literacy definitely improved over the period of 1900 through 1980, states that started out in 1900 with low rates continued, for the most part, to have relatively lower rates of literacy 80 years later in 1980. From a policy perspective, additional resources and emphasis will be needed in certain states to bring their literacy rates up to the national norm.

Population Knows Alphabet, 1900-1980

Figure 6.1 presents information about the population knowing the alphabet (same as literacy) for the years 1900 through 1980. Figure 6.1 illustrates the national average and states with the highest and lowest population knowing the alphabet in 1980, the Federal District and Chiapas, respectively. In 1980, over 94 percent of the population in the Federal District reported knowing the alphabet whereas only 62 percent of the population in Chiapas did so. The initial discrepancy that existed as early as 1900 continued virtually the same during the 80 year time-span. While the population knowing the alphabet in both entities increased between 1900 and 1980, the increase was substantially the

142

same; thus the disparity between the two states remained much as the same in 1980 as it existed in 1900. The percentages below of the population knowing the alphabet illustrates the changes that have been taken place between 1900 and 1980.

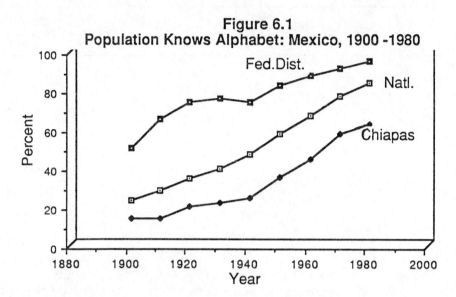

Figure 6.1
Population Knows Alphabet: Mexico, 1900 -1980

SOURCE: Estadisticas Historicas de Mexico, 1985, Table 2.3.

Population Knowing the Alphabet

Year	Nation	Chiapas	Federal District
1900	22.3	13.1	49.5
1910	22.7	13.4	64.6
1921	33.9	19.6	73.1
1930	38.5	21.0	75.1
1940	46.0	23.8	73.0
1950	56.8	34.6	81.7
1960	66.5	43.6	86.9
1970	76.3	56.7	90.9
1980	83.0	62.0	94.1

DEFINITION: Population 10 years of age and who know the alphabet. Same as literacy.

SOURCE: Estadisticas Historicas de Mexico, 1985, Table 2.3.

Table 8.1 Literacy, 1900-1980

No.	State	1900 Literate Pop. Age 10+	Ratio	1930 Literate Pop. Age 10+	Ratio	1950 Literate Pop. Age 6+	Ratio	1970 Literate Pop. Age 10+	Ratio	1980 Literate Pop. Age 15+	Ratio
1	AGUASCALIENTES	16,820	0.2141	45,161	0.4708	104,608	0.6903	189,808	0.8532	252,624	0.8914
2	BAJA CALIFORNIA	14,344	0.4116	27,580	0.7730	149,309	0.8125	513,750	0.8824	650,957	0.9338
3	BAJA CALIFORNIA SUR			21,003	0.6214	38,069	0.7732	74,526	0.8764	113,019	0.9248
4	CAMPECHE	15,909	0.2485	26,291	0.4393	61,398	0.6207	131,846	0.7718	195,442	0.8299
5	COAHUILA	74,265	0.3417	170,719	0.5448	428,459	0.7405	658,769	0.8759	815,426	0.9209
6	COLIMA	16,025	0.3252	24,694	0.5314	59,208	0.6673	128,521	0.8013	169,129	0.8714
7	CHIAPAS	32,046	0.1309	76,317	0.2105	245,591	0.3463	587,637	0.5673	700,369	0.6215
8	CHIHUAHUA	75,388	0.3143	194,797	0.5594	498,413	0.7285	938,465	0.8707	1,061,015	0.9115
9	DISTRITO FEDERAL	208,742	0.4948	702,459	0.7513	2,067,970	0.8174	4,417,195	0.9091	5,230,018	0.9412
10	DURANGO	58,688	0.2147	124,502	0.4365	346,924	0.6859	523,409	0.8567	570,757	0.9053
11	GUANAJUATO	129,467	0.1634	190,874	0.2747	466,282	0.4428	963,024	0.6470	1,240,307	0.7595
12	GUERRERO	29,244	0.0892	80,315	0.1804	233,976	0.3200	580,506	0.5540	738,840	0.6441
13	HIDALGO	90,936	0.2174	124,300	0.2652	271,039	0.4053	493,692	0.6213	596,005	0.7003
14	JALISCO	242,253	0.2821	396,106	0.4312	856,753	0.6118	1,775,358	0.8063	2,111,860	0.8675
15	MEXICO	124,621	0.1899	192,022	0.2826	532,035	0.4805	1,856,916	0.7506	3,609,060	0.8638
16	MICHOACAN	120,979	0.1770	223,220	0.3016	515,628	0.4571	1,012,136	0.6622	1,175,222	0.7477
17	MORELOS	30,849	0.2605	34,265	0.3685	129,267	0.5878	308,965	0.7462	449,977	0.8311
18	NAYARIT	25,807	0.2290	52,425	0.4221	141,018	0.6161	282,264	0.7854	329,245	0.8351
19	NUEVO LEON	78,871	0.3330	183,117	0.6045	473,758	0.7846	1,028,031	0.8934	1,353,941	0.9272
20	OAXACA	74,098	0.1108	154,979	0.2017	421,289	0.3705	791,099	0.5802	853,262	0.6407
21	PUEBLA	151,778	0.2088	242,569	0.2991	584,362	0.4490	1,131,943	0.6678	1,354,667	0.7323
22	QUERETARO	27,943	0.1642	37,552	0.2267	81,274	0.3619	196,385	0.6205	291,811	0.7389
23	QUINTANA ROO			4,011	0.5144	13,222	0.6289	43,289	0.7619	102,411	0.8313
24	SAN LUIS POTOSI	72,601	0.1738	121,009	0.3042	334,430	0.4873	602,932	0.7095	717,821	0.7836
25	SINALOA	53,824	0.2471	121,009	0.4204	297,308	0.5819	658,493	0.7874	875,528	0.8610
26	SONORA	59,263	0.3672	134,595	0.5865	301,443	0.7278	643,045	0.8644	801,485	0.9146
27	TABASCO	22,471	0.2094	48,059	0.3271	165,091	0.5774	375,882	0.7616	468,950	0.8201
28	TAMAULIPAS	51,153	0.3229	142,398	0.5795	434,910	0.7423	842,590	0.8567	1,010,799	0.9029
29	TLAXCALA	24,372	0.2005	54,533	0.3817	124,540	0.5499	213,999	0.7666	254,752	0.8322
30	VERACRUZ	139,167	0.2071	310,988	0.3248	801,184	0.4892	1,811,202	0.7056	2,366,283	0.7663
31	YUCATAN	51,397	0.2281	138,601	0.4853	266,295	0.6409	391,842	0.7378	515,538	0.8097
32	ZACATECAS	72,482	0.2096	123,914	0.3910	313,093	0.5915	490,140	0.8123	499,150	0.8506
	Mean	72,860	0.2429	141,108	0.4222	367,442	0.5871	770,552	0.7614	983,615	0.8254
	S.D.	56,429	0.0881	134,001	0.1522	369,117	0.1423	807,756	0.1013	1,046,138	0.0885
	C.V.	77.45	36.25	94.76	36.04	100.46	24.24	104.83	13.30	106.36	10.72
	Minimum	14,344	0.0892	4,011	0.1804	13,222	0.3200	43,289	0.5540	102,411	0.6215
	Maximum	242,253	0.4948	702,459	0.7730	2,067,970	0.8174	4,417,195	0.9091	5,230,018	0.9412

DEFINITION: The literacy ratios are the literate population to the total population of the specified age group for each year shown.

NOTE: For 1900, data for Baja Sur are included with Baja California and data for Quintana Roo are included with Yucatan.

SOURCE: 1900 Mexican Census of Population; 1930, 1930, 1950, 1970 Mexican Census of Population; 1980 Mexican Census of Population, Volume 1, Table 4; Estadisticas Historicas (1985).

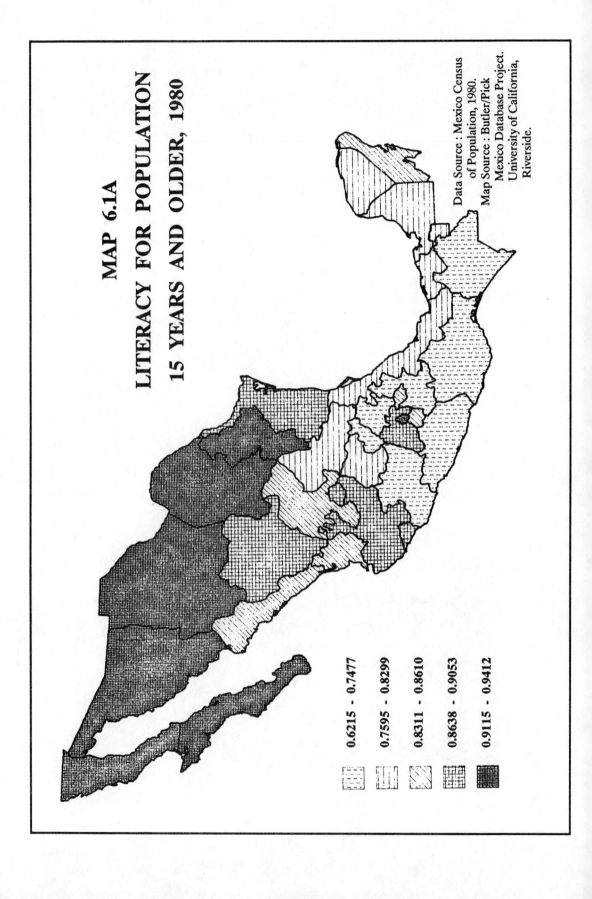

MAP 6.1A

LITERACY FOR POPULATION

15 YEARS AND OLDER, 1980

Data Source : Mexico Census
of Population, 1980.

Map Source : Butler/Pick
Mexico Database Project.
University of California,
Riverside.

0.6215 - 0.7477

0.7595 - 0.8299

0.8311 - 0.8610

0.8638 - 0.9053

0.9115 - 0.9412

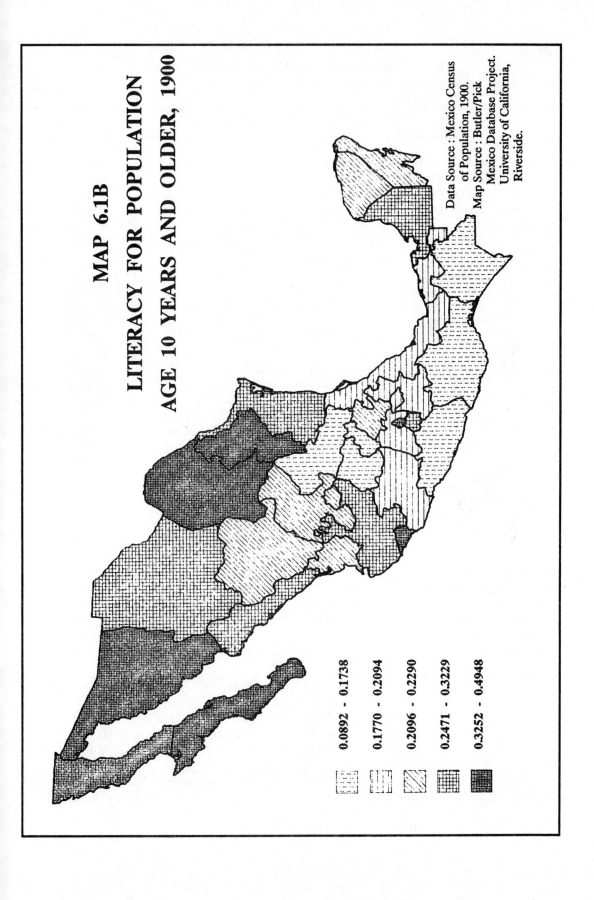

MAP 6.1B

LITERACY FOR POPULATION

AGE 10 YEARS AND OLDER, 1900

Data Source : Mexico Census
of Population, 1900.
Map Source : Butler/Pick
Mexico Database Project.
University of California,
Riverside.

0.0892 - 0.1738

0.1770 - 0.2094

0.2096 - 0.2290

0.2471 - 0.3229

0.3252 - 0.4948

Table 6.2 Literacy Change: 1930-1970

No. State	1930 Percent Literate	1970 Percent Literate	Change in Percent Literate 1930 - 1970
1 AGUASCALIENTES	0.4708	0.8532	0.3824
2 BAJA CALIFORNIA	0.7730	0.8824	0.1094
3 BAJA CALIFORNIA SUR	0.6214	0.8764	0.2550
4 CAMPECHE	0.4393	0.7718	0.3325
5 COAHUILA	0.5448	0.8759	0.3311
6 COLIMA	0.5314	0.8013	0.2699
7 CHIAPAS	0.2105	0.5673	0.3568
8 CHIHUAHUA	0.5594	0.8707	0.3113
9 DISTRITO FEDERAL	0.7513	0.9091	0.1578
10 DURANGO	0.4365	0.8567	0.4202
11 GUANAJUATO	0.2747	0.6470	0.3723
12 GUERRERO	0.1804	0.5540	0.3736
13 HIDALGO	0.2652	0.6213	0.3561
14 JALISCO	0.4312	0.8063	0.3751
15 MEXICO	0.2826	0.7506	0.4680
16 MICHOACAN	0.3016	0.6622	0.3606
17 MORELOS	0.3685	0.7462	0.3777
18 NAYARIT	0.4221	0.7854	0.3633
19 NUEVO LEON	0.6045	0.8934	0.2889
20 OAXACA	0.2017	0.5802	0.3785
21 PUEBLA	0.2991	0.6678	0.3687
22 QUERETARO	0.2267	0.6205	0.3938
23 QUINTANA ROO	0.5144	0.7619	0.2475
24 SAN LUIS POTOSI	0.3042	0.7095	0.4053
25 SINALOA	0.4204	0.7874	0.3670
26 SONORA	0.5865	0.8644	0.2779
27 TABASCO	0.3271	0.7616	0.4345
28 TAMAULIPAS	0.5795	0.8567	0.2772
29 TLAXCALA	0.3817	0.7666	0.3849
30 VERACRUZ	0.3248	0.7056	0.3809
31 YUCATAN	0.4853	0.7378	0.2525
32 ZACATECAS	0.3910	0.8123	0.4213
Mean	0.4222	0.7614	0.3391
S.D.	0.1546	0.1029	0.0776
C.V.	36.61	13.51	22.87
Minimum	0.1804	0.5540	0.1094
Maximum	0.7730	0.9091	0.4680

DEFINITION: Ratio is the difference between the percentage of population literate in 1970 and the percentage literate in 1930.

SOURCE: Estadisticas Historicas de Mexico, 1985.

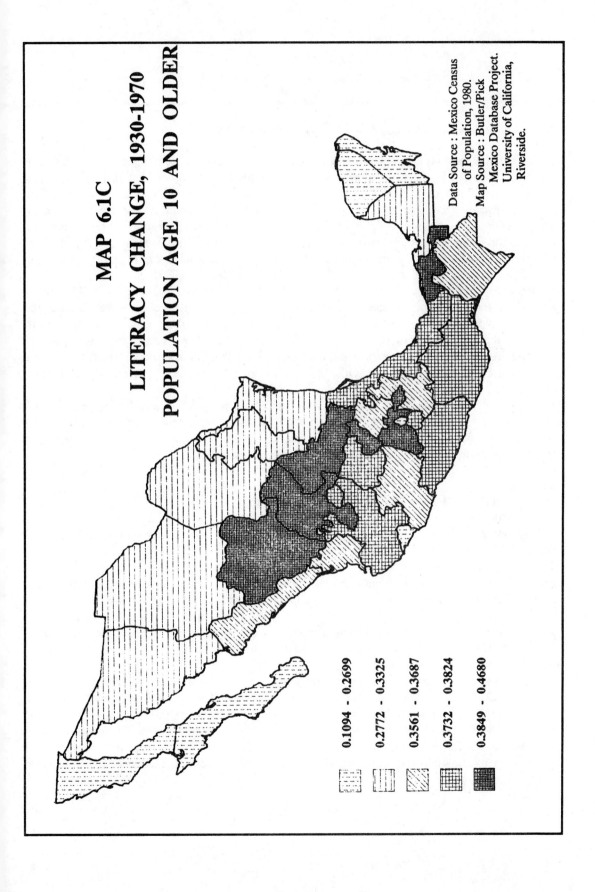

MAP 6.1C
LITERACY CHANGE, 1930-1970
POPULATION AGE 10 AND OLDER

Data Source : Mexico Census
of Population, 1980.
Map Source : Butler/Pick
Mexico Database Project.
University of California,
Riverside.

0.1094 - 0.2699

0.2772 - 0.3325

0.3561 - 0.3687

0.3732 - 0.3824

0.3849 - 0.4680

Education

Primary Education for Population 30 Years of Age and Older, 1980

This variable represents the proportion of population, 30 years and older in 1980, which had completed grade school, i.e. six years of primary education, but had not proceeded on to post-primary education (see Table 6.3). Map 6.2A, and the three following ones showing levels of education, should be examined together to give a multi-layered view of Mexican education in 1980. For the nation an average of 16.1 percent of population 30 years and older had a primary education as defined. By state, the mean value is 14.8 percent, with a moderate coefficient of variation of 33. By comparison, 7.8 percent of U.S. population, 25 years and older, had completed primary education, i.e. eight years in the U.S., but not proceeded on to high school (Bogue, 1985).

Similar to literacy data presented in the previous section, there is a north-south axis. The border region, plus Baja California Sur have high values, as do the central metropolitan zone, Tlaxcala, and the northern portion of the west region. The two "urban" states of the Federal District and Nuevo Leon had the highest rates of 26 percent and 24 percent respectively. The lowest primary education rates, as was true for literacy, are in the states of Guerrero, Oaxaca, and Chiapas in the south, having an average value of 7 percent. Other low states include Michoacan (9 percent) and Queretaro (10 percent).

The four education variables and literacy are highly interrelated. In fact, the only correlations between these five variables that are not significant are those between primary education for population age 15-29 and the secondary education and higher education variables. Nevertheless, there are fine distinctions in the geographic patterns which will be discussed.

Primary Education for Population 15-29 Years of Age, 1980

Primary education, 15-29 years of age, is defined as the proportion of population, 15-29 years of age in 1980, that had finished grade school, but had not proceeded on to post-primary education. The data presented here for this age level probably reflects more recent educational experiences and thus may present a better picture than the post-30 age level of the improvements made in the educational system during recent decades. The mean statewide percentage for Mexico in 1980 was 21.0, which represent a nearly half-fold increase over the value for these 30 years of age and older in 1980. The coefficient of variation was a low moderate 21. Rates for primary education for population 15-29 years of age show a somewhat different distribution than for the same variable for population 30 years and older(see Table 6.3).

The geographic pattern shows a north-south axis typical of education and literacy characteristics (see Map 6.2B). The highest rates are in Aguascalientes, Chihuahua, Coahuila, and Zacatecas in the north region, as well as in Tlaxcala. Zacatecas shows a major reversal to a high value for the present variable from a low value for the 30+ age level in the prior variable. The central zone is high, with values for the state of Mexico exceeding the Federal District. Regions with the lowest rates are the pacific south and southeast. Hidalgo, in the central region, has the nation's lowest rate at 12 percent.

Secondary Education for Population 14 Years of Age and Older, 1980

This variable is defined as the proportion of the population that has a third grade of secondary education but no higher education. The mean for this variable in Mexico in 1980 is 5.8 percent (see Table 6.4). The coefficient of variation is a moderate 32. By region, the highest levels of secondary education are in the border region and the central zone. As shown by Map 6.2C, the states with the highest levels are the major urban centers of the Federal District and Nuevo Leon, each with 10 percent. By contrast, the other major urban center, Jalisco, has only an average level of secondary education. Regions with low secondary education are the pacific south, and an area encompassing the southern north and eastern west regions. The nation's lowest levels are in Chiapas and Oaxaca, each only 3 percent.

Secondary education has a highly significant correlation of 0.84 with higher education. Thus both variables share common significant relationships with other characteristics. Both have strong relationships with urbanization (Map 2.6A) and urban-related variables including potable water, electricity, television, phones, and motor vehicles, all per capita. There are strong associations with admininstrative and service occupations and the economic variables of high income and value of corporations. On the other hand, both secondary and higher education are inversely related to dependency ratio, agricultural occupation, crowding, low income, and no meat and eggs.

Higher Education for Population 17 Years of Age and Older, 1980

Higher education is measured by the population 17 years and older listed in the census as having higher education ("con ensenanza superior"). It excludes persons having a subprofessional career. Table 6.4 shows that the mean state level of higher education was 4.8 percent. There was more variation than for lesser education; however, the coefficient of variation was a moderate 51. As with previous educational and literacy dimensions, the north-south gradient is clearly apparent (see Map 6.2D). In geographic distribution, there are very few differences from the pattern for secondary education. One difference is the high relative level for Jalisco at 5.8 percent, versus its average level for secondary education. This may be due partly to the presence of many institutions of higher education in Guadalajara. The highest rate was in the Federal District (14 percent), with Nuevo Leon being the only other state approximating this level, at 10 percent. The lowest rates were in the states of Chiapas and Oaxaca (under 2 percent), with very low rates also recorded for Zacatecas, Hidalgo, Guanajuato, and Guerrero (under 3 percent).

Table 6.3 Primary Education, 1980

No. State	Population Age 15-29			Population Age 30 +		
	With Primary Education	Total Population	Ratio	With Primary Education	Total Population	Ratio
1 AGUASCALIENTES	39,174	142,930	0.2741	26,790	140,484	0.1907
2 BAJA CALIFORNIA	70,484	349,370	0.2017	70,437	347,765	0.2025
3 BAJA CALIFORNIA SUR	13,532	62,718	0.2158	11,694	59,492	0.1966
4 CAMPECHE	20,833	115,873	0.1798	18,172	119,640	0.1519
5 COAHUILA	114,793	434,130	0.2644	98,280	451,355	0.2177
6 COLIMA	22,156	96,844	0.2288	16,714	97,240	0.1719
7 CHIAPAS	68,544	578,423	0.1185	38,394	549,550	0.0699
8 CHIHUAHUA	152,022	567,002	0.2681	122,342	596,984	0.2049
9 DISTRITO FEDERAL	618,072	2,797,464	0.2209	730,490	2,759,363	0.2647
10 DURANGO	75,438	305,700	0.2468	47,880	324,769	0.1474
11 GUANAJUATO	164,644	807,852	0.2038	86,991	825,216	0.1054
12 GUERRERO	84,284	545,285	0.1546	44,892	601,823	0.0746
13 HIDALGO	88,452	766,967	0.1153	47,090	449,197	0.1048
14 JALISCO	281,437	1,180,125	0.2385	199,384	1,254,284	0.1590
15 MEXICO	552,566	2,149,705	0.2570	370,821	2,028,653	0.1828
16 MICHOACAN	137,585	766,967	0.1794	75,712	804,899	0.0941
17 MORELOS	54,187	265,111	0.2044	39,483	276,131	0.1430
18 NAYARIT	36,239	188,105	0.1927	25,008	206,139	0.1213
19 NUEVO LEON	150,902	724,892	0.2082	173,005	735,336	0.2353
20 OAXACA	123,093	601,126	0.2048	52,567	730,636	0.0719
21 PUEBLA	198,612	873,524	0.2274	131,462	976,238	0.1347
22 QUERETARO	43,775	199,481	0.2194	20,322	195,455	0.1040
23 QUINTANA ROO	11,197	66,423	0.1686	7,294	56,768	0.1285
24 SAN LUIS POTOSI	86,828	428,385	0.2027	55,631	487,699	0.1141
25 SINALOA	100,850	506,003	0.1993	71,047	510,838	0.1391
26 SONORA	87,649	431,689	0.2030	84,987	444,618	0.1911
27 TABASCO	59,280	301,309	0.1967	33,092	270,482	0.1223
28 TAMAULIPAS	126,358	536,254	0.2356	111,332	583,214	0.1909
29 TLAXCALA	42,626	145,849	0.2923	25,466	160,458	0.1587
30 VERACRUZ	282,899	1,473,924	0.1919	208,224	1,613,911	0.1290
31 YUCATAN	38,763	289,870	0.1337	40,471	346,828	0.1167
32 ZACATECAS	73,974	280,303	0.2639	31,084	306,505	0.1014
Mean			0.2097			0.1482
S.D.			0.0429			0.4909
C.V.			20.45			33.14
Minimum			0.1153			0.0699
Maximum			0.2923			0.2647

DEFINITION: Ratios are the population within the age group passing sixth grade to the total population of that age group.

SOURCE: 1980 Mexican Census of Population, Volume 1, Table 5.

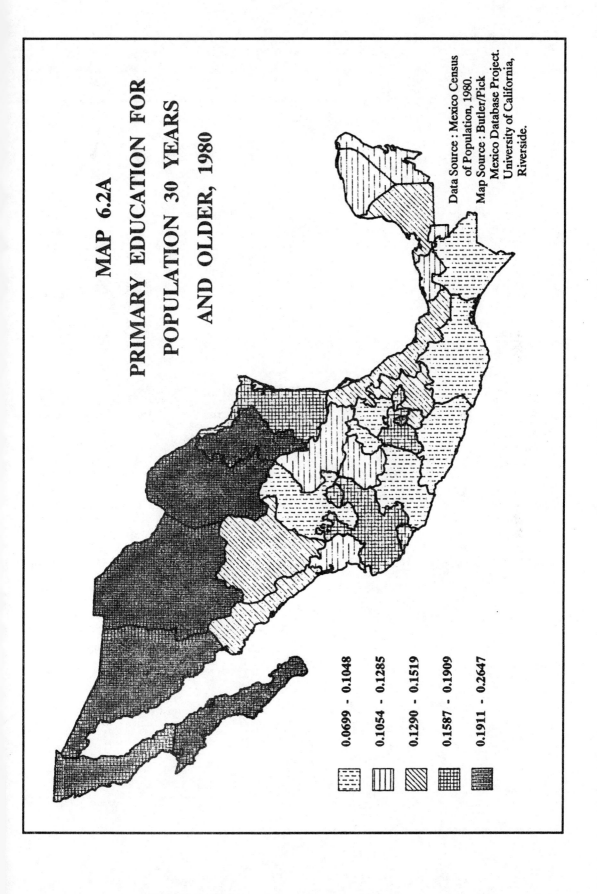

MAP 6.2A
PRIMARY EDUCATION FOR
POPULATION 30 YEARS
AND OLDER, 1980

Data Source : Mexico Census
of Population, 1980.
Map Source : Butler/Pick
Mexico Database Project.
University of California,
Riverside.

0.0699 - 0.1048

0.1054 - 0.1285

0.1290 - 0.1519

0.1587 - 0.1909

0.1911 - 0.2647

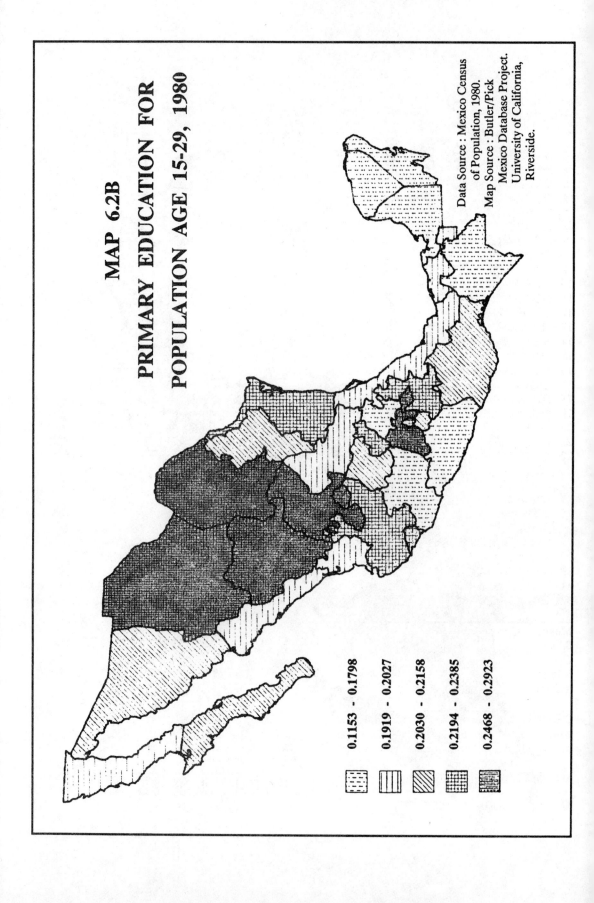

MAP 6.2B

PRIMARY EDUCATION FOR
POPULATION AGE 15-29, 1980

Data Source : Mexico Census
of Population, 1980.
Map Source : Butler/Pick
Mexico Database Project.
University of California,
Riverside.

0.1153 - 0.1798

0.1919 - 0.2027

0.2030 - 0.2158

0.2194 - 0.2385

0.2468 - 0.2923

Table 6.4 Secondary & Higher Education, 1980

No. State	Secondary Education			Higher Education		
	With Secondary Education	Population Age 14+	Ratio	With Higher Education	Population Age 17+	Ratio
1 AGUASCALIENTES	16,344	297,523	0.0549	11,873	257,469	0.0461
2 BAJA CALIFORNIA	64,100	728,428	0.0880	42,939	637,655	0.0673
3 BAJA CALIFORNIA SUR	9,826	127,725	0.0769	6,318	112,062	0.0564
4 CAMPECHE	14,181	246,184	0.0576	7,873	215,587	0.0365
5 COAHUILA	62,125	926,658	0.0670	53,966	809,577	0.0667
6 COLIMA	15,440	203,691	0.0758	8,674	176,602	0.0491
7 CHIAPAS	29,708	1,182,450	0.0251	19,430	1,030,106	0.0189
8 CHIHUAHUA	76,405	1,218,090	0.0627	52,607	1,061,423	0.0496
9 DISTRITO FEDERAL	592,387	5,761,842	0.1028	743,930	5,154,447	0.1443
10 DURANGO	32,651	664,556	0.0491	22,926	570,835	0.0402
11 GUANAJUATO	67,764	1,716,871	0.0395	41,164	1,482,945	0.0278
12 GUERRERO	53,483	1,205,616	0.0444	26,257	1,044,953	0.0251
13 HIDALGO	40,477	892,345	0.0454	21,750	778,620	0.0279
14 JALISCO	141,622	2,550,598	0.0555	128,541	2,221,936	0.0579
15 MEXICO	317,720	4,375,445	0.0726	241,267	3,821,452	0.0631
16 MICHOACAN	70,999	1,654,228	0.0429	53,100	1,423,879	0.0373
17 MORELOS	43,648	566,561	0.0770	27,796	496,194	0.0560
18 NAYARIT	28,777	414,438	0.0694	14,793	357,916	0.0413
19 NUEVO LEON	149,469	1,525,535	0.0980	135,535	1,341,740	0.1010
20 OAXACA	42,730	1,392,935	0.0307	20,498	1,222,446	0.0168
21 PUEBLA	86,148	1,963,466	0.0439	68,858	1,697,778	0.0406
22 QUERETARO	21,042	415,015	0.0507	15,227	359,643	0.0423
23 QUINTANA ROO	7,641	128,566	0.0594	4,633	113,297	0.0409
24 SAN LUIS POTOSI	40,069	961,262	0.0417	33,609	835,602	0.0402
25 SINALOA	59,444	1,067,008	0.0557	49,109	925,462	0.0531
26 SONORA	73,161	915,659	0.0799	40,472	803,779	0.0504
27 TABASCO	26,115	600,571	0.0435	18,018	520,672	0.0346
28 TAMAULIPAS	75,151	1,169,744	0.0642	63,136	1,026,106	0.0615
29 TLAXCALA	19,885	321,070	0.0619	9,027	278,954	0.0324
30 VERACRUZ	140,657	3,231,239	0.0435	109,259	2,830,347	0.0386
31 YUCATAN	33,163	662,856	0.0500	23,087	587,395	0.0393
32 ZACATECAS	20,134	620,933	0.0324	13,954	527,882	0.0264
Mean			0.0582			0.0478
S.D.			0.01836			0.02426
C.V.			32.40			50.76
Minimum			0.0251			0.0168
Maximum			0.1028			0.1443

DEFINITION: Secondary Education Ratio is the population age 14+ with third level secondary education to total population age 14+. Higher Education Ratio is the population age 17+ with higher education ("con ensenanza superior") to total population age 17+.

SOURCE: 1980 Mexican Census of Population, Volume 2, Table 7.

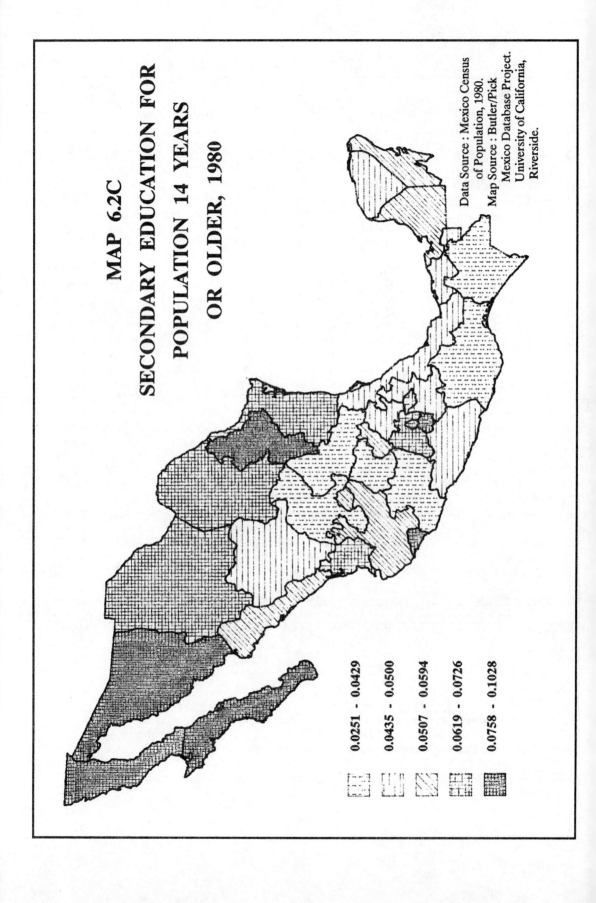

MAP 6.2C

SECONDARY EDUCATION FOR

POPULATION 14 YEARS

OR OLDER, 1980

0.0251 - 0.0429

0.0435 - 0.0500

0.0507 - 0.0594

0.0619 - 0.0726

0.0758 - 0.1028

Data Source : Mexico Census
of Population, 1980.
Map Source : Butler/Pick
Mexico Database Project.
University of California,
Riverside.

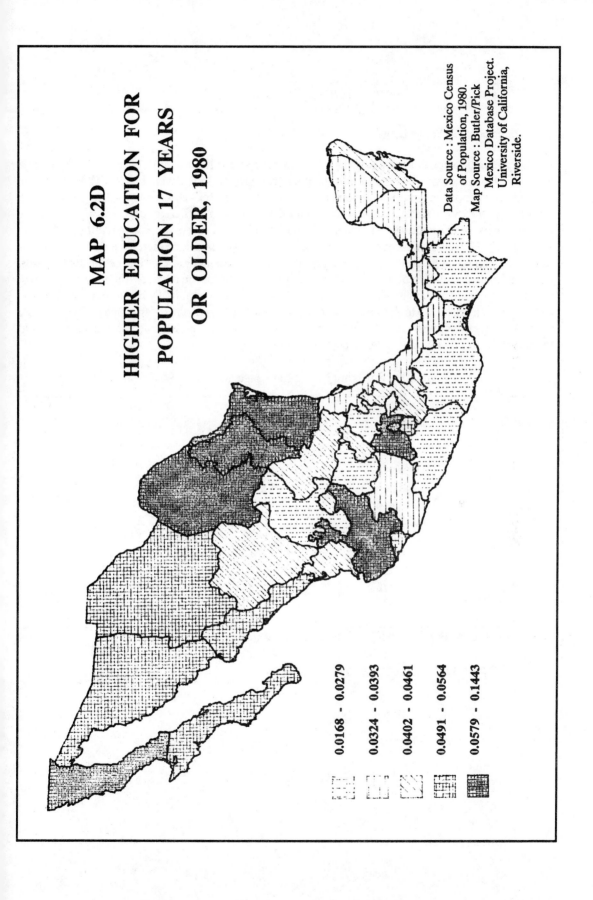

MAP 6.2D

HIGHER EDUCATION FOR
POPULATION 17 YEARS
OR OLDER, 1980

Data Source : Mexico Census
of Population, 1980.

Map Source : Butler/Pick
Mexico Database Project.
University of California,
Riverside.

0.0168 - 0.0279

0.0324 - 0.0393

0.0402 - 0.0461

0.0491 - 0.0564

0.0579 - 0.1443

Indigenous Language

Population Speaking Native Language, Mexico : 1900-1980

The population speaking a native language in Mexico for the various census years from 1900 through 1980 is shown in Figure 6.2 and the data are reported in the table below. The population speaking indigenous language in 1980 was measured by the Mexican census for the population 5 years of age and over. The percentage of population speaking a native language was highest during the early years of this century. The decline in native speakers, reached a low percent of 3.1 at the 1950 census. However, subsequently the percentage of native speakers increased during each census period. Thus, 7.8 percent of the population was a native speaker at the time of the 1980 census. Also, while the population of Mexico dramatically increased over the decades, the volume of native speakers varied, decreasing from 1900 through 1950 but increasing rapidly thereafter. At the time of the 1980 census, over 5 million persons reported that they were a native language speaker. While the percentage of native speakers in 1980 was only about half that in 1900, the volume had increased from slightly over 2 million in 1900 to over 5 million in 1980.

Population Speaking Native Language, Mexico : 1900-1980

Year	Native Language	Total Population	% Native Language
1900	2,078,914	13,607,259	15.3
1910	1,960,306	15,160,369	12.9
1921	1,820,844	14,334,780	12.7
1930	1,185,162	16,552,722	7.2
1940	1,237,018	19,653,552	6.3
1950	795,069	25,791,017	3.1
1960	1,104,955	34,923,129	3.2
1970	3,111,415	48,225,238	6.5
1980	5,181,038	66,846,833	7.8

DEFINITION : Population 5 years of age or more that speak a native language.

SOURCE: Estadisticas Historicas de Mexico, 1985.

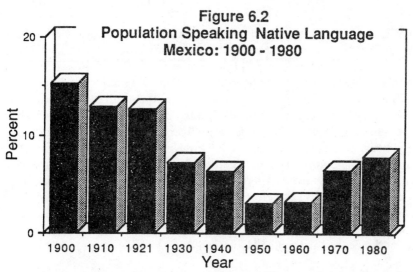

Figure 6.2
Population Speaking Native Language
Mexico: 1900 - 1980

DEFINITION: Population 5 years of age and more who speak a native language.

SOURCE: Estadisticas Historicas de Mexico, 1985.

Population Speaking an Indigenous Language, 1980

For the nation in 1980, there were 5.2 million native speakers. Of these, 23 percent did not speak Spanish. The major indigenous language groupings were as follows: Mexicano or Nahuatl (26.7 percent), Maya (12.9 percent), Zapoteco (8.2 percent), Mixteco (6.2 percent), Otomi (5.9 percent), Triqui (4.1 percent), other (31.0 percent), and unspecified (5.0 percent) (SPP, 1982-84). The state mean is 10.6 percent; however, the coefficient of variation is 130 which indicates that there is substantial variation among the states in population speaking an indigenous language (see Table 6.5). The state with the highest percentage of population speaking an indigenous language in 1980 was Yucatan (53.2 percent). Well over a third of the population in Oaxaca and Quintana Roo also spoke a native language in 1980, and over one out of every four persons in Chiapas and almost as many in Campeche were native speakers. San Luis Potosi, Veracruz, Guerrero, and Puebla all had slightly over 10 percent native speakers.

As illustrated on Map 6.3A, the most highly indigenous regions are the southeast, with about one third indigenous population, and the south, with about one fifth. Next in importance are the gulf region and the central region. However, in the central region, the Federal District has only two percent indigenous. The least indigenous region is the west, with only two percent indigenous. Generally the geographical distribution of the indigenous speaking population has not varied much over the years (Memorias, 1950; and various census documents).

Indigenous language speaking is strongly related to agricultural labor force and occupation, and low income. It is also strongly associated with hospitals and clinics per capita (see Map 5.2A) and non-Catholic religion (see Map 6.4A). It is inversely related to education and literacy.

Population Speaking Indigenous Language, 1900

The measure of population speaking an indigenous language in 1900 was based upon the total population of all ages; therefore any direct comparisons with 1980 are precluded. However, in 1900 a state mean of 13.7 percent of the population spoke an indigenous language, a level over twice that of 1980. The coefficient of variation was 125 which is not too different from the CV in 1980. Thus, the variation in distribution in native speaking population in 1900 and 1980 were quite similar. Typical of 1900, and all subsequent years up through 1980, there is a predominant north-south axis (see Map 6.3B). The only exceptions to this phenomenon are the north region state of Sonora, which had about twelve percent native speakers in 1900, and the gulf state of Tabasco, which had only nine percent native speakers. States with the lowest percentages of indigenous language speakers in 1900 were Aguascalientes, Coahuila, Colima, Jalisco, Nuevo Leon, Tamaulipas, and Zacatecas, all with less than one percent native speakers. States with a high percentage of native speakers in 1900 were Yucatan (69 percent), Oaxaca (52 percent), Campeche (42 percent), Chiapas (36 percent), and Puebla (32 percent), Guerrero (24 percent), and Veracruz (20 percent). In addition, five other states had more than ten percent indigenous speakers in 1900. These geographic patterns shown for 1900 carried almost exactly up through 1980. As with other variables for 1900, no information was available for the Federal District and Quintana Roo.

Population Speaking an Indigenous Language, State of Oaxaca , 1980

The population speaking an indigenous language in the state of Oaxaca in 1980 is shown for each of the 571 municipios on Map 6.3C. in Figures 6.3A, 6.3B, and the text table below. In 1980 the population of state of state of Oaxaca was 2,369,076, of whom 891,048, or 37.5 percent, reported speaking a native language. Of the 891,048 native language speakers, 225,632, or 9.5 percent of the total and 25.3 percent of the native speakers, spoke only a native language.

The municipio variation is substantial with some municipios comprising between 97 and 100 percent of the population being native speakers. Other municipios have less than four percent indigenous speakers. As Map 6.3C illustrates, there are multiple municipio concentrations of indigenous speaking populations. Traditionally there are 60 different languages spoken in Oaxaca (Anuario Estadistico de Oaxaca, 1985).

Population Speaking a Native Language, Oaxaca : 1980

| Native | Total Speaker | | Do Not Speak Spanish | |
Language	Number	Percent	Number	Percent
Chinanteco	66,811	7.5	17,439	26.1
Mazateco	107,757	12.1	45,122	41.9
Mixteco	206,411	23.2	52,653	25.5
Mixe	69,476	7.8	23,960	34.5
Zapoteco	347,006	38.9	62,165	17.9
All Others	93,587	10.5	24,293	30.0
Total	891,048	100.0	225,632	

SOURCE: 1980 Mexico Census of Population, State of Oaxaca volumes.

In 1980, there were five major native languages spoken in Oaxaca : Chinanteco, Mazateco, Mixteco, Mixe, and Zapoteco. In addition there were several other languages that are combined in the

Figures 6.3A, 6.3B and in the text table under the category of "All Others." As shown in the table, native speakers are categorized into those who only speak a native language. On the average, twenty five percent of the native speakers do not speak Spanish. The major native languages in Oaxaca in 1980 were Zapoteco and Mixteco. However, the greatest proportion of native speakers who did not speak Spanish were the Mazateco and Mixe. While Zapoteco was the largest native language group, they also had the lowest proportion of persons who only spoke their native language. As might be suspected from other data included in this Atlas, persons speaking various native languages clustered in certain areas of the state.

Population Speaking Indigenous Language, State of Oaxaca, 1940

In 1940 indigenous language was measured both by the population that spoke an indigenous language exclusively and by those who were bilingual, e.g., also spoke Spanish. The age used as a criterion measure in 1940 was for the population five of age and older. Overall in 1940, 34.4 percent of the population of Oaxaca spoke exclusively an indigenous language.

Variation among the thirty districts and 571 municipios within districts in Oaxaca in 1940 was extensive (Memorias, 1950:57-66). Another 25.1 percent of the population spoke a native language and Spanish. Thus, almost 60 percent of the Oaxaca population in 1940 spoke an indigenous language.

As shown below six of the thirty districts in 1940 had over 50 percent of its population exclusively speaking an indigenous language.

District	Percent
Mixe	79.06
Teotitlan	75.62
Villa Alta	70.64
Choapan	53.97
Juxtlahuaca	53.95
Tlaxiaco	52.19

In contrast, five districts had less than ten percent exclusively speaking an indigenous language.

District	Percent
Centro	0.90
Coixtlahuaca	1.88
Zaachila	4.04
Zimatlan	7.21
Teposcolula	7.82

The range of bilingualism, by district was from a low of 11.08 and 11.45 in the Districts of Etla and Ejutla, respectively to highs of 46.97 and 47.93 in the Districts of Tlacolula and Miahustlan, respectively. Within districts, the range was from those with no indigenous speakers to those with everyone exclusively speaking a native language. Similar to the state information for all of Mexico, the indigenous language geographical distribution pattern is similar at different time periods. While the percentage of native speakers has diminished, the distribution established during earlier periods remains.

160

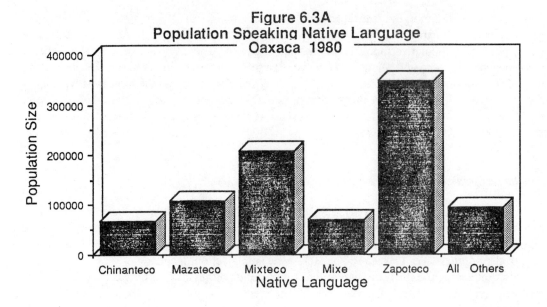

Figure 6.3A
Population Speaking Native Language
Oaxaca 1980

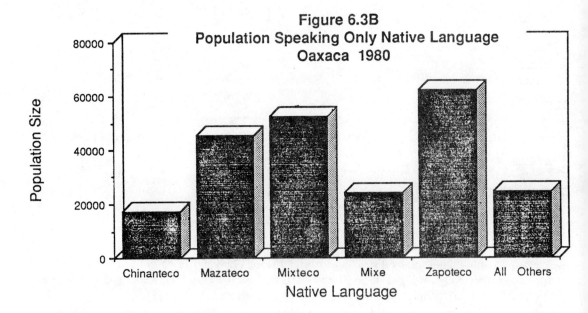

Figure 6.3B
Population Speaking Only Native Language
Oaxaca 1980

DEFINITION: Figure 6.3A--Population 5 years of age and older who speak a native language.
Figure 6.3B--Population 5 years of age and older who speak only a native language.
SOURCE: 1980 Mexican Census of Population: Oaxaca.

Table 6.5 Population Speaking Indigenous Language, 1900, 1980

No.	State	Indigenous Speaking Population	1900 Total Population	Ratio	Indigenous Speaking Population	Population Age 5+ 1980	Ratio
1	AGUASCALIENTES	0	102,416	0.0000	5,680	439,901	0.0129
2	BAJA CALIFORNIA	1,111	47,624	0.0233	21,429	1,028,937	0.0208
3	BAJA CALIFORNIA SUR				3,864	183,700	0.0210
4	CAMPECHE	35,977	86,542	0.4157	77,090	358,069	0.2153
5	COAHUILA	55	296,938	0.0002	19,369	1,340,017	0.0145
6	COLIMA	0	65,115	0.0000	3,971	297,506	0.0133
7	CHIAPAS	129,843	360,799	0.3599	492,700	1,728,756	0.2850
8	CHIHUAHUA	22,025	327,784	0.0672	68,504	1,748,449	0.0392
9	DISTRIO FEDERAL	9,494	541,516	0.0175	208,466	7,760,321	0.0269
10	DURANGO	3,847	370,294	0.0104	19,419	1,002,214	0.0194
11	GUANAJUATO	12,188	1,061,724	0.0115	35,181	2,553,762	0.0138
12	GUERRERO	117,735	479,205	0.2457	274,426	1,793,319	0.1530
13	HIDALGO	177,806	605,051	0.2939	304,085	1,314,391	0.2314
14	JALISCO	3,918	1,153,891	0.0034	64,760	3,720,186	0.0174
15	MEXICO	121,288	934,463	0.1298	360,402	6,442,042	0.0559
16	MICHOACAN	50,063	935,808	0.0535	113,299	2,455,900	0.0461
17	MORELOS	26,983	160,115	0.1685	31,443	816,209	0.0385
18	NAYARIT	4,166	150,098	0.0278	24,140	619,249	0.0390
19	NUEVO LEON	0	327,937	0.0000	29,865	2,171,959	0.0138
20	OAXACA	495,698	948,633	0.5225	891,048	2,024,527	0.4401
21	PUEBLA	325,124	1,021,133	0.3184	488,131	2,830,813	0.1724
22	QUERETARO	24,213	232,389	0.1042	22,436	620,366	0.0362
23	QUINTANA ROO				82,772	187,719	0.4409
24	SAN LIUS POTOSI	31,937	575,432	0.0555	193,247	1,422,179	0.1359
25	SINALOA	7,823	296,701	0.0264	37,993	1,578,542	0.0241
26	SONORA	25,894	221,682	0.1168	61,139	1,307,012	0.0468
27	TABASCO	14,292	159,834	0.0894	56,519	895,928	0.0631
28	TAMAULIPAS	0	218,948	0.0000	29,458	1,666,882	0.0177
29	TLAXCALA	26,774	172,315	0.1554	30,780	472,878	0.0651
30	VERACRUZ	196,466	981,030	0.2003	634,208	4,643,970	0.1366
31	YUCATAN	213,936	309,652	0.6909	489,958	921,780	0.5315
32	ZACATECAS	258	462,190	0.0006	5,256	958,233	0.0055
	National Total	2,078,914	13,607,259	4.1087	5,181,038	57,305,716	3.3931
	Mean	69,297	437,112	0.1370	161,907	1,790,804	0.1060
	S.D.	112,151	344,325	0.1725	217,019	1,699,682	0.1378
	C.V.	161.84	78.77	125.98	134.04	94.91	129.98
	Minimum	0	47,624	0.0000	3,864	183,700	0.0055
	Maximum	495,698	1,153,891	0.6909	891,048	7,760,321	0.5315

NOTE: For 1900, data for Baja Sur are included with Baja California and data for Quintana Roo are included with Yucatan.

DEFINITION: 1980 Ratio of population age 5+ speaking an indigenous language to population 5+. Those not specifying age are excluded, those speaking an indigenous language include those that do and those that do not speak Spanish also.

DEFINITION: 1900 Ratio of Population speaki8ng an indigenous language to total population. The 1900 Census does not specify whether these people also speak Spanish. Therefore, this numerator may include those exclusivly speaking an indigenous language or it may include all indigenous speakers regardless of proficiency in Spanish, as the 1980 variable does. No determination can be made from the data source.

SOURCE: 1900 Mexican Census of Population; 1980 Mexican of Population, Volume 2, Table 15.

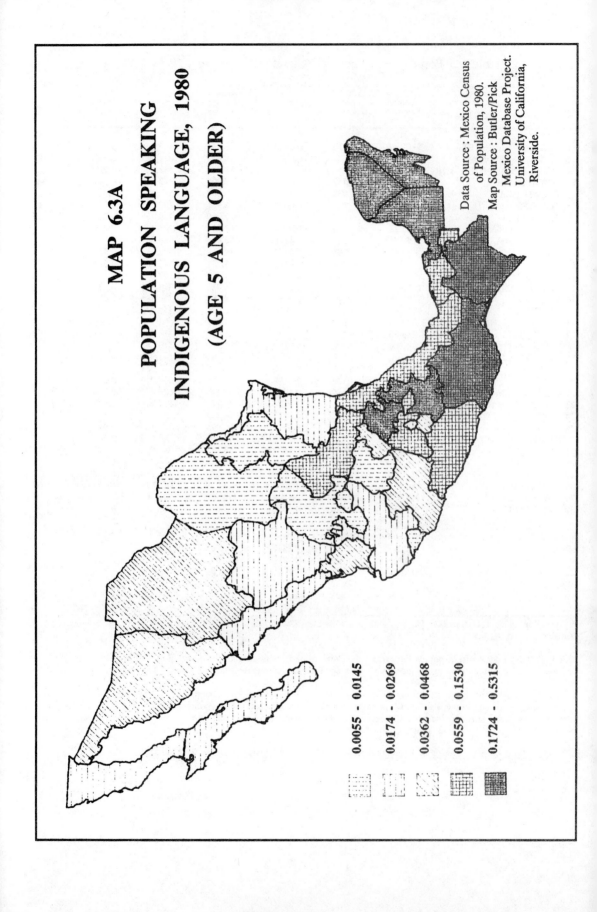

MAP 6.3A

POPULATION SPEAKING

INDIGENOUS LANGUAGE, 1980

(AGE 5 AND OLDER)

Data Source : Mexico Census
of Population, 1980.

Map Source : Butler/Pick
Mexico Database Project.
University of California,
Riverside.

0.0055 - 0.0145

0.0174 - 0.0269

0.0362 - 0.0468

0.0559 - 0.1530

0.1724 - 0.5315

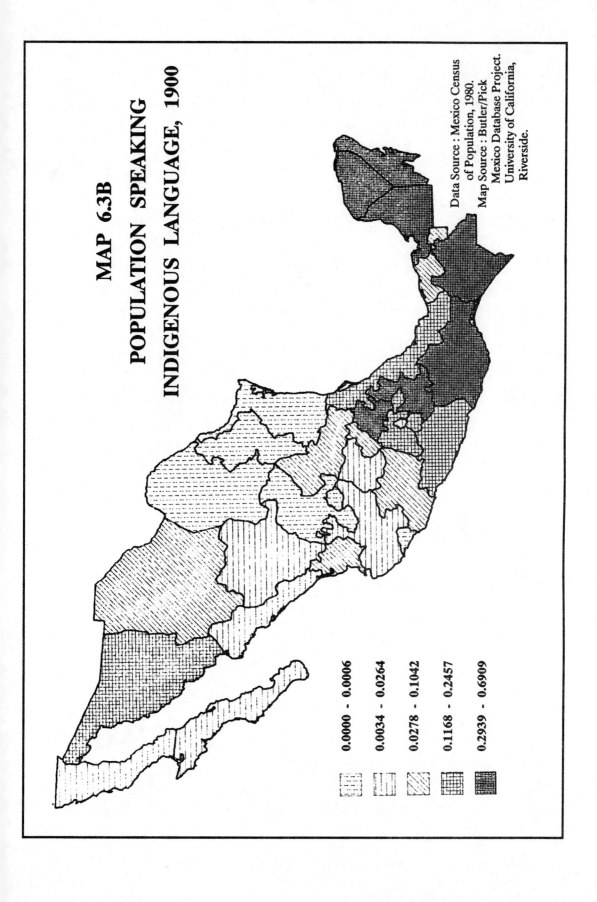

MAP 6.3B
POPULATION SPEAKING
INDIGENOUS LANGUAGE, 1900

Data Source : Mexico Census
of Population, 1980.
Map Source : Butler/Pick
Mexico Database Project.
University of California,
Riverside.

0.0000 - 0.0006

0.0034 - 0.0264

0.0278 - 0.1042

0.1168 - 0.2457

0.2939 - 0.6909

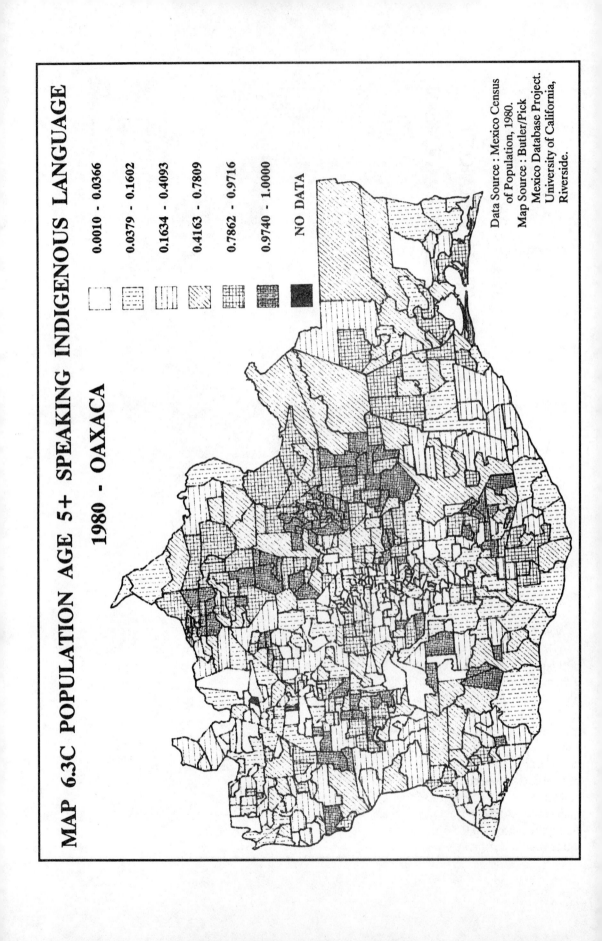

MAP 6.3C POPULATION AGE 5+ SPEAKING INDIGENOUS LANGUAGE
1980 - OAXACA

0.0010 - 0.0366
0.0379 - 0.1602
0.1634 - 0.4093
0.4163 - 0.7809
0.7862 - 0.9716
0.9740 - 1.0000
NO DATA

Data Source : Mexico Census
of Population, 1980.
Map Source : Butler/Pick
Mexico Database Project.
University of California,
Riverside.

Non-Catholic Religion

Unlike the U.S. census, Mexican census elicits information on religion. The material presented in this section examines the non-Catholic population in Mexico for 1980 as reported by the census. The non-Catholic category consists of several different religious orientations. They are combined here because any one of them is insufficient for analysis.

As seen in the following table, the non-Catholic population in Mexico for 1980 as reported by the Census consisted of non-Catholic religion population of several different orientations plus non-believing population ("no tiene religion").

Religious Groups in Mexico in 1980

Religious group	Population	Percent of Non-Catholic	Percent of Mexican Population
Catholic	61,916,757		92.6
Non-catholic	4,929,990		4.3
Protestant or Evangelist	2,201,609	77.5	3.3
Jewish	61,790	2.2	0.1
Other	578,138	20.3	0.9
No religion	2,088,453		3.1
TOTAL	66,846,747*	100.0	100.0

* NOTE: 86 persons did not specify religion.

SOURCE: 1980 Mexican Census of Population, Resumen General, Volume 2, Table 54.

Non-Catholic Religion Population, 1980

While most of the population of Mexico continues to identify themselves as Catholic, 4.3 percent of the population reports that they believe in a non-Catholic religion. The range among the states is from less than one percent to slightly over 15 percent non-Catholic religion (see Table 6.6). The highest percentage of non-Catholic religion is in the southeast region, with Chiapas and Tabasco having 15 percent non-Catholic religion and Quintana Roo (13 percent), Campeche (9 percent), Yucatan (8 Percent), and Morelos and Tamaulipas (7 percent) all having substantially more non-Catholic religion than other states in Mexico. The border states have relatively high percentages of non-Catholic religion, while rates are especially low in the west, a region of strong Catholicism. The central region and central zone have average percents non-Cathlic religion.

Map 6.4A shows that the geographic pattern of non-Catholic religion is not strongly related to many other characteristics in this atlas. There are significant relationships with indigenous language (compare with Map 6.3A) and oil and natural gas production in 1986 (see Maps 7.3A, 7.3B). The latter relationship may be due to the historical coincidence that oil production was located in the same southern and eastern parts of the country as was the non-Catholic population (Pick et al., 1987b). There is an opposite relationship between non-Catholic religion and elderly population (Map 2.3C).

Non-Catholic Religion Population, Oil Region, 1980

The oil region has a tropical climate and contains exceptional natural resources including petroleum. Oil development in the region over the past ten years has had diverse economic and population effects. Map 6.4B presents non-Catholic population for the oil region states of Veracruz, Tabasco, and Campeche. While the percentage of the non-Catholic population in the oil region is substantially similar to the national average, that is about six percent, variation among the three oil region states is substantial. Thus, Tabasco has 13.7 percent persons who are non-Catholic religious believers while Campeche is 8.9 percent non-Catholic, and 5.2 percent of Veracruz is non-Catholic. Within the oil region there are four zones of high non-Catholic concentration that also correspond quite closely to areas where the population professes to have no religion. However, there also is variation within these states in the percent of non-Catholic religion. In Veracruz, there is a general tendency for a higher percentage of non-Catholics in the south, corresponding to the overall higher percentage of non-Catholics in Tabasco and Campeche. For oil region municipios, there are correspondences between percent non-Catholic religion and both percent petroleum workers and fertility (Pick, 1987b).

Table 6.6 Non-Catholic Religion, 1980

No. State	Non-Catholic Population	Non-Catholic Ratio	No Religion Population	No Religion Ratio
1 AGUASCALIENTES	3,980	0.0077	4,804	0.0092
2 BAJA CALIFORNIA	72,951	0.0645	47,460	0.0403
3 BAJA CALIFORNIA SUR	5,683	0.0271	5,792	0.0269
4 CAMPECHE	37,779	0.0949	22,433	0.0533
5 COAHUILA	86,742	0.0571	39,294	0.0252
6 COLIMA	5,035	0.0148	5,164	0.0149
7 CHIAPAS	273,552	0.1458	208,571	0.1000
8 CHIHUAHUA	118,948	0.0614	69,752	0.0348
9 DISTRITO FEDERAL	325,490	0.0379	244,973	0.0277
10 DURANGO	34,300	0.0298	31,836	0.0269
11 GUANAJUATO	26,021	0.0088	47,543	0.0158
12 GUERRERO	67,797	0.0333	73,066	0.0346
13 HIDALGO	63,240	0.0419	39,671	0.0256
14 JALISCO	60,563	0.0140	39,744	0.0091
15 MEXICO	256,072	0.0344	129,915	0.0172
16 MICHOACAN	43,383	0.0155	70,240	0.0245
17 MORELOS	59,924	0.0653	29,899	0.0316
18 NAYARIT	18,189	0.0259	22,717	0.0313
19 NUEVO LEON	139,849	0.0568	49,757	0.0198
20 OAXACA	113,936	0.0499	84,325	0.0356
21 PUEBLA	123,432	0.0374	50,285	0.0150
22 QUERETARO	6,579	0.0090	6,124	0.0083
23 QUINTANA ROO	27,413	0.1279	11,641	0.0515
24 SAN LUIS POTOSI	61,088	0.0372	31,300	0.0187
25 SINALOA	47,005	0.0279	167,236	0.0904
26 SONORA	53,940	0.0370	55,807	0.0369
27 TABASCO	148,757	0.1505	74,560	0.0701
28 TAMAULIPAS	134,840	0.0724	63,063	0.0328
29 TLAXCALA	18,109	0.0328	5,247	0.0094
30 VERACRUZ	309,147	0.0608	303,246	0.0563
31 YUCATAN	79,993	0.0778	36,011	0.0339
32 ZACATECAS	17,887	0.0160	16,976	0.0149
Mean	88,801	0.0492	65,264	0.0326
S.D.	87,102	0.0372	70,468	0.0217
C.V.	98.09	75.72	107.97	66.54
Minimum	3,980	0.0077	4,804	0.0083
Maximum	325,490	0.1505	303,246	0.1000

DEFINITION: Non-Catholic Ratio is the population specifying a non-Catholic religion to the total population. No Religion Ratio is the population specifying no religion ("no tiene religion") to the total population 1980.

SOURCE: 1980 Mexican Census of Population, Volume 1, Table 16.

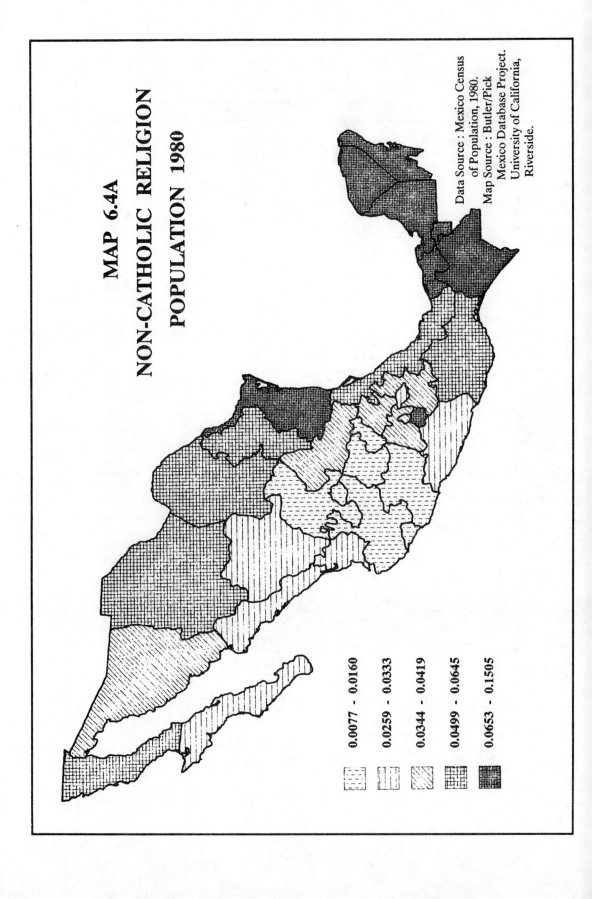

MAP 6.4A
NON-CATHOLIC RELIGION
POPULATION 1980

0.0077 - 0.0160

0.0259 - 0.0333

0.0344 - 0.0419

0.0499 - 0.0645

0.0653 - 0.1505

Data Source : Mexico Census
of Population, 1980.
Map Source : Butler/Pick
Mexico Database Project.
University of California,
Riverside.

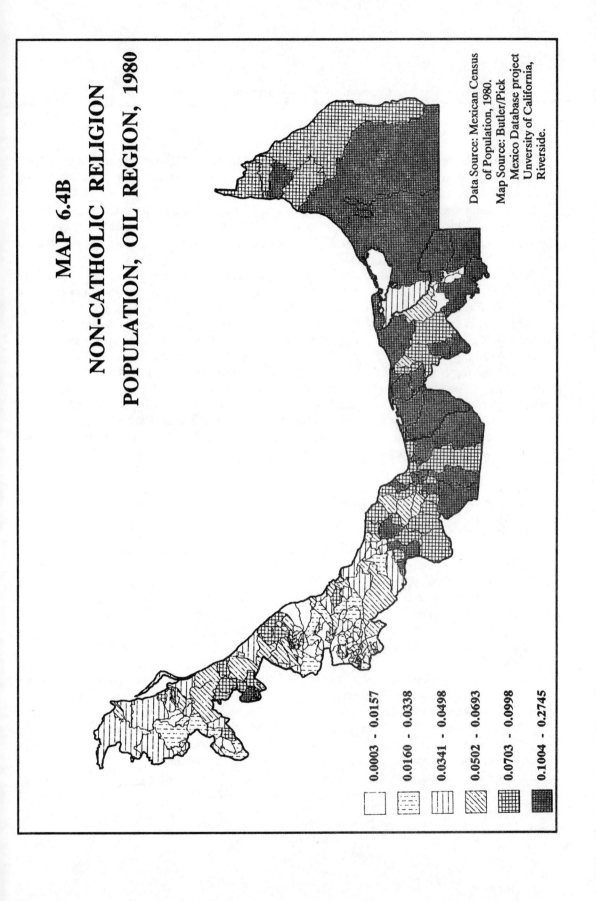

MAP 6.4B
NON-CATHOLIC RELIGION
POPULATION, OIL REGION, 1980

0.0003 - 0.0157
0.0160 - 0.0338
0.0341 - 0.0498
0.0502 - 0.0693
0.0703 - 0.0998
0.1004 - 0.2745

Data Source: Mexican Census
of Population, 1980.
Map Source: Butler/Pick
Mexico Database project
Unversity of California,
Riverside.

Consumption of Goods and Services

Gasoline, in Thousands of Liters Per Capita, 1985

The total consumption of gasoline in Mexico in 1985 was 18,633,720 (thousands of liters). On a national basis, there was a decline in gasoline consumption between 1982 and 1983 which then remained relatively constant for 1984 and 1985. While there was a general national decline, the greatest overall declines in gasoline consumption took place in Chihuahua, the Federal District, Durango, San Luis Potosi, Tamaulipas, Veracruz, and Yucatan. Only two states increased their gasoline consumption between 1982 and 1985--Guanajuato and Sinaloa, with Guanajuato having a substantial increase (Anuario Estadistico, 1986).

There was substantial variation among states in gasoline consumption with a very large coefficient of variation (see Table 6.7). By far the greatest gasoline consumption per capita in 1985 was in Baja California (0.77) and Baja California Sur (0.62). High rates also were recorded for the Federal District (0.50), Colima (0.50), and Nuevo Leon (0.47). The lowest rates were found for Mexico (0.05), Oaxaca (0.08), Coahuila (0.11) and Veracruz (0.12). The low rate for the state of Mexico may be due to some of the state's consumption being recorded in the Federal District. Generally the northwest, north, and northeast region states have the highest per capita consumption, although Nayarit is an exception with its low consumption rate. The gulf and south pacific region states have extremely low gasoline consumption on a per capita basis (see Map 6.5A).

Gasoline consumption is associated with education and literacy, urbanization and a strong state economy, as indicated by gross state revenues, high income, and number of corporations. It is also associated with number of vehicles and hotels/pensions.

Number of Establishments Selling Alcoholic Beverages, 1985

In 1985, there were almost 300,000 establishments selling alcoholic beverages (Anuario Estadistico, 1986). Map 6.5B and discussion in this section describe the number of establishments selling alcoholic beverages per 100 population in 1985 for each state (see Table 6.8). The state with the highest rate in 1985 was the tourist state of Quintana Roo (0.97). Other states with very high rates include Colima (0.84), and Oaxaca (0.83). States with relatively high rates compared to the remaining states are Aguascalientes, Baja California, Guerrero, Hidalgo, Morelos, Nayarit, and Puebla. States with extremely low rates are the Federal District and Sinaloa (0.11), Chiapas (0.22), and Jalisco (0.23). There is no discernable regional pattern insofar as the number of establishments selling alcoholic beverages per 100 population. On the other hand, there is some variation within states as to the kind of establishment that predominates in selling alcoholic beverages with some states having higher rates of "cantinas" while others have higher rates for "pulquerias." However, stores dominate in almost all states. There also is variation among states by urban and rural location of places selling alcoholic beverages. For example, in Quintana Roo, almost 80 percent of establishments selling alcoholic beverages are located in urban areas. In Durango, Hidalgo, and Morelos the establishments are more nearly equally distributed between urban and rural areas. On the other hand, in Queretaro and Zacatecas, a higher proportion of alcoholic selling establishments are located in the rural than urban areas (Anuario Estadistico, 1986).

Public Sports Events, 1984

Information on public sports events was obtained from 1986 the Anuario Estadistico. The information presented here does not include bullfights (taurinos) but does include all functions reported for the various states in 1984. No discernable regional pattern emerged insofar as public sports events are concerned. There was substantial variation among the states (see Map 6.5C).

Aguascalientes apparently is the most sports oriented state with a rate of 0.79. The next closest states are Campeche with a rate of 0.55, Zacatecas with a rate of 0.36, and Baja California Sur with a rate of 0.33. Other states with relatively high rates when compared to the remaining states in Mexico are Baja California, the Federal District, Guanajuato, Morelos, Nuevo Leon, Quintana Roo, and San Luis Potosi. As shown in Table 6.9, all of these latter states, however, have much lower rates than the former group.

Several states did not report any public sporting events taking place in the year 1984, Chiapas, Durango, Oaxaca, Puebla, and Yucatan. States with extremely low rates are Michoacan, Queretaro, and Tlaxcala. Most other states also had low rates but significantly higher rates than the former states.

In 1984, Mexico had 33 bullfight rings with the Federal District, Jalisco, and Michoacan each having four, while Zacatecas had three. All other states had fewer bullrings and half of the states did not have a bullring in 1984. The number of bullfights in 1984 ranged from 68 in Jalisco, 27 in the Federal District, 25 in Michoacan, 23 in Guerrero, 22 in Aguascalientes, to none in 16 states. As with sporting events, there is no discernable regional pattern to a state having a bullfight ring and/or the number of bullfights.

Films, 1984

In Mexico in 1984 there were 1,790 cinema theatres. The rate of films shown by state is illustrated on Map 6.5D, for each of the states. There was substantial variation among the states in rate of films shown in 1984 (see Table 6.10). The highest rate of films shown in 1984 was by far in the state of Quintana Roo, with virtually double the rate of the next highest states and a rate of 0.42 compared to the lowest rate of 0.32 in Chiapas. Other states with relatively high rates are Baja California Sur, Colima, the Federal District, Jalisco, Morelos, Nayarit, Nuevo Leon, and Tabasco. States with low rates are Baja California, Chiapas with the lowest rate in Mexico, Durango, Oaxaca, Sinaloa, Tlaxacala with a rate almost as low as Chiapas, and Veracruz. Except for the high rate of films in the west and generally low rates in the south and gulf, there is no regional consistency in states with high and low rates of films in 1984. The per capita rate of films is associated with population growth 1970-80, as well as with tourism related variables, including hotels, airports, and air passengers. It is also associated with service occupation, but has an opposite pattern to agricultural occupation.

Table 6.7 Gasoline Consumption in Thousands of Liters, 1985

No.	State	Gasoline Consumption	Ratio
1	AGUASCALIENTES	204,576	0.3479
2	BAJA CALIFORNIA	1,029,407	0.7669
3	BAJA CALIFORNIA SUR	153,907	0.6299
4	CAMPECHE	160,132	0.3356
5	COAHUILA	186,108	0.1052
6	COLIMA	195,861	0.4984
7	CHIAPAS	295,515	0.1250
8	CHIHUAHUA	758,835	0.3325
9	DISTRITO FEDERAL	5,069,065	0.5018
10	DURANGO	459,677	0.3437
11	GUANAJUATO	695,978	0.2045
12	GUERRERO	385,198	0.1613
13	HIDALGO	317,421	0.1811
14	JALISCO	1,201,982	0.2423
15	MEXICO	451,265	0.0526
16	MICHOACAN	447,687	0.1378
17	MORELOS	270,173	0.2512
18	NAYARIT	150,745	0.1834
19	NUEVO LEON	1,355,190	0.4741
20	OAXACA	205,315	0.0764
21	PUEBLA	611,258	0.1612
22	QUERETARO	249,838	0.2990
23	QUINTANA ROO	71,302	0.2787
24	SAN LUIS POTOSI	315,375	0.1665
25	SINALOA	602,650	0.2875
26	SONORA	626,929	0.3642
27	TABASCO	316,944	0.2636
28	TAMAULIPAS	590,651	0.2699
29	TLAXCALA	120,639	0.1915
30	VERACRUZ	728,129	0.1189
31	YUCATAN	232,972	0.1923
32	ZACATECAS	173,046	0.1349
Mean		582,305	0.2712
S.D.		863,768	0.1619
C.V.		148.34	59.70
Minimum		71,302	0.0526
Maximum		5,069,065	0.7669

DEFINITION: Ratio is 1985 gas consumption in thousands of liters to total population 1985.

SOURCE: 1986 Anuario Estadistico, Table 4.3.12.

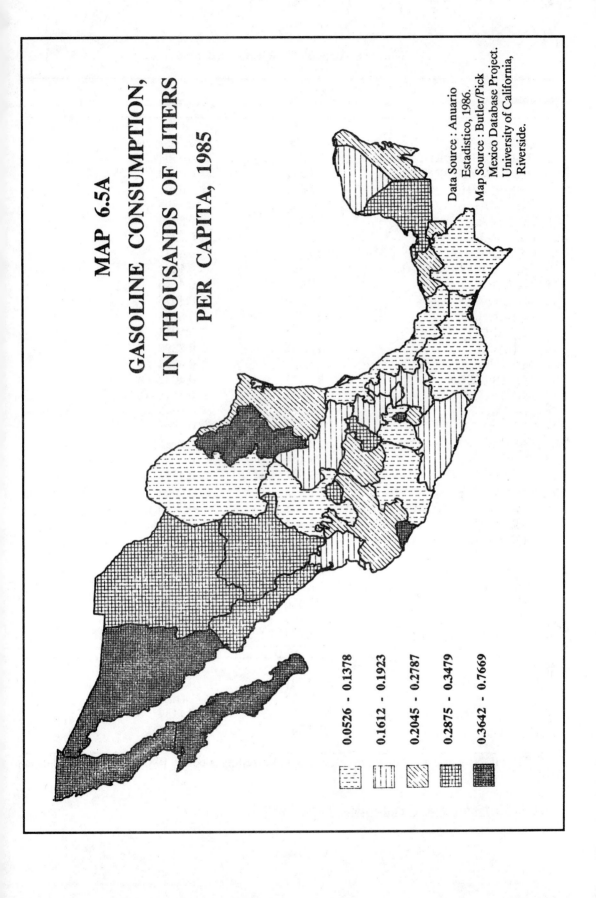

MAP 6.5A

GASOLINE CONSUMPTION,
IN THOUSANDS OF LITERS
PER CAPITA, 1985

Data Source : Anuario
Estadistico, 1986.

Map Source : Butler/Pick
Mexico Database Project.
Universite of California,
Riverside.

0.0526 - 0.1378

0.1612 - 0.1923

0.2045 - 0.2787

0.2875 - 0.3479

0.3642 - 0.7669

Table 6.8 Alcohol Establishments, 1985

No.	State	Alcohol Establishments	Ratio
1	AGUASCALIENTES	3,226	0.5487
2	BAJA CALIFORNIA	8,731	0.6504
3	BAJA CALIFORNIA SUR	1,212	0.4960
4	CAMPECHE	2,071	0.4341
5	COAHUILA	6,893	0.3898
6	COLIMA	3,300	0.8397
7	CHIAPAS	5,273	0.2231
8	CHIHUAHUA	10,353	0.4537
9	DISTRITO FEDERAL	11,525	0.1141
10	DURANGO	6,079	0.4546
11	GUANAJUATO	13,530	0.3976
12	GUERRERO	14,774	0.6185
13	HIDALGO	10,418	0.5944
14	JALISCO	11,361	0.2290
15	MEXICO	37,346	0.4354
16	MICHOACAN	13,135	0.4042
17	MORELOS	5,938	0.5521
18	NAYARIT	4,721	0.5745
19	NUEVO LEON	10,202	0.3569
20	OAXACA	22,266	0.8285
21	PUEBLA	23,100	0.6092
22	QUERETARO	3,841	0.4597
23	QUINTANA ROO	2,472	0.9664
24	SAN LUIS POTOSI	7,008	0.3700
25	SINALOA	2,384	0.1137
26	SONORA	5,016	0.2914
27	TABASCO	3,503	0.2913
28	TAMAULIPAS	8,468	0.3870
29	TLAXCALA	2,664	0.4229
30	VERACRUZ	22,326	0.3646
31	YUCATAN	5,446	0.4496
32	ZACATECAS	5,888	0.4591
	Mean	9,202	0.4619
	S.D.	7,701	0.1903
	C.V.	83.68	41.20
	Minimum	1,212	0.1137
	Maximum	37,346	0.9664

DEFINITION: Ratio is number of establishments selling alcohol 1985 to total population 1985.

SOURCE: 1986 Anuario Estadistico, Table 4.3.10.

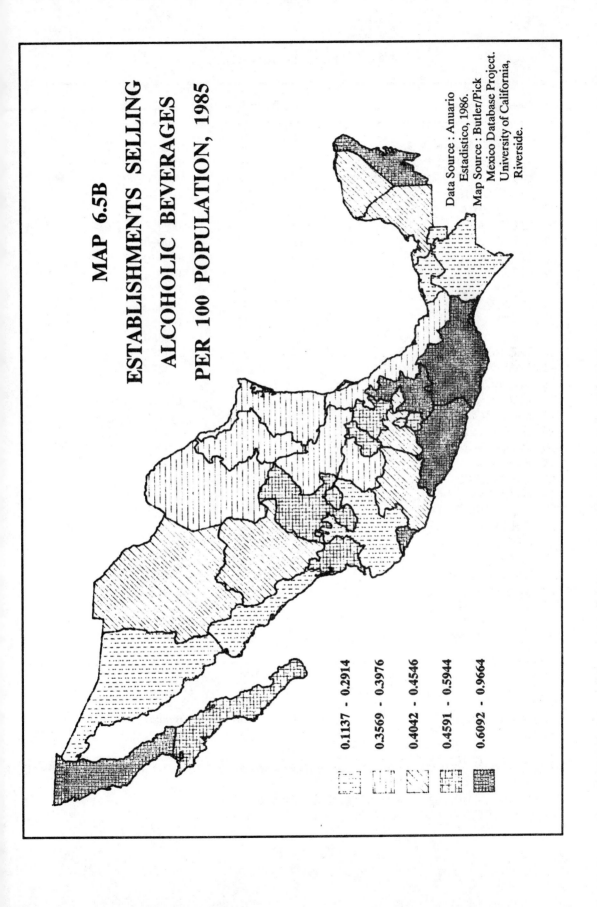

MAP 6.5B

ESTABLISHMENTS SELLING
ALCOHOLIC BEVERAGES
PER 100 POPULATION, 1985

Data Source : Anuario
Estadistico, 1986.

Map Source : Butler/Pick
Mexico Database Project.
University of California,
Riverside.

0.1137 - 0.2914

0.3569 - 0.3976

0.4042 - 0.4546

0.4591 - 0.5944

0.6092 - 0.9664

Table 6.9 Public Sports Events, 1984

No.	State	Sports Events	Ratio
1	AGUASCALIENTES	464	0.7892
2	BAJA CALIFORNIA	307	0.2287
3	BAJA CALIFORNIA SUR	82	0.3356
4	CAMPECHE	264	0.5533
5	COAHUILA	93	0.0526
6	COLIMA	18	0.0458
7	CHIAPAS	0	0.0000
8	CHIHUAHUA	100	0.0438
9	DISTRITO FEDERAL	1,368	0.1354
10	DURANGO	0	0.0000
11	GUANAJUATO	422	0.1240
12	GUERRERO	156	0.0653
13	HIDALGO	114	0.0650
14	JALISCO	425	0.0857
15	MEXICO	196	0.0228
16	MICHOACAN	13	0.0040
17	MORELOS	200	0.1860
18	NAYARIT	51	0.0621
19	NUEVO LEON	408	0.1427
20	OAXACA	0	0.0000
21	PUEBLA	0	0.0000
22	QUERETARO	8	0.0096
23	QUINTANA ROO	35	0.1368
24	SAN LUIS POTOSI	241	0.1272
25	SINALOA	44	0.0210
26	SONORA	30	0.0174
27	TABASCO	96	0.0798
28	TAMAULIPAS	23	0.0105
29	TLAXCALA	1	0.0016
30	VERACRUZ	303	0.0495
31	YUCATAN	0	0.0000
32	ZACATECAS	462	0.3602
	Mean	185	0.1174
	S.D.	266	0.1744
	C.V.	143.92	148.55
	Minimum	0	0.0000
	Maximum	1,368	0.7892

DEFINITION: Ratio is the number of public sports events 1984 to total population 1984.

SOURCE: 1986 Anuario Estadistico, Table 3.4.2.

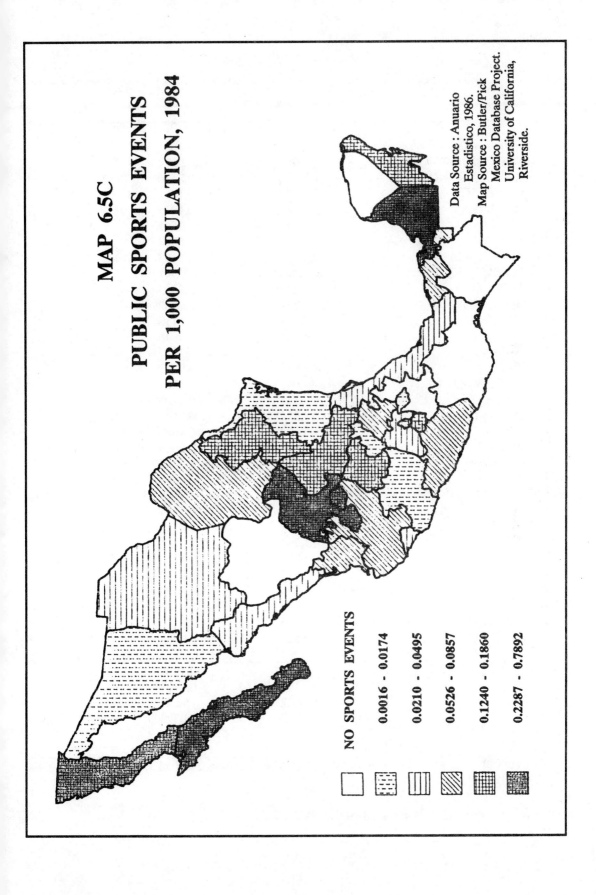

MAP 6.5C
PUBLIC SPORTS EVENTS
PER 1,000 POPULATION, 1984

NO SPORTS EVENTS

0.0016 - 0.0174

0.0210 - 0.0495

0.0526 - 0.0857

0.1240 - 0.1860

0.2287 - 0.7892

Data Source : Anuario
Estadistico, 1986.

Map Source : Butler/Pick
Mexico Database Project.
University of California,
Riverside.

Table 6.10 Films, 1984

No.	State	Public Films	Ratio
1	AGUASCALIENTES	9,883	0.1681
2	BAJA CALIFORNIA	9,045	0.0674
3	BAJA CALIFORNIA SUR	5,156	0.2110
4	CAMPECHE	6,871	0.1440
5	COAHUILA	22,555	0.1275
6	COLIMA	10,079	0.2565
7	CHIAPAS	7,637	0.0323
8	CHIHUAHUA	25,228	0.1105
9	DISTRITO FEDERAL	236,494	0.2341
10	DURANGO	7,287	0.0545
11	GUANAJUATO	29,329	0.0862
12	GUERRERO	26,693	0.1118
13	HIDALGO	14,855	0.0848
14	JALISCO	105,981	0.2137
15	MEXICO	64,482	0.0752
16	MICHOACAN	39,061	0.1202
17	MORELOS	18,333	0.1705
18	NAYARIT	14,621	0.1779
19	NUEVO LEON	46,499	0.1627
20	OAXACA	17,899	0.0666
21	PUEBLA	34,151	0.0901
22	QUERETARO	7,092	0.0849
23	QUINTANA ROO	10,740	0.4199
24	SAN LUIS POTOSI	13,016	0.0687
25	SINALOA	14,884	0.0710
26	SONORA	13,793	0.0801
27	TABASCO	19,050	0.1584
28	TAMAULIPAS	31,345	0.1432
29	TLAXCALA	3,058	0.0485
30	VERACRUZ	45,088	0.0736
31	YUCATAN	17,316	0.1429
32	ZACATECAS	12,422	0.0969
	Mean	29,373	0.1298
	S.D.	42,363	0.0778
	C.V.	144.22	59.94
	Minimum	3,058	0.0323
	Maximum	236,494	0.4199

DEFINITION: Ratio is the number of public film showings 1984 to total population 1984 multiplied by 0.1.

SOURCE: 1986 Anuario Estadistico, Table 3.4.2.

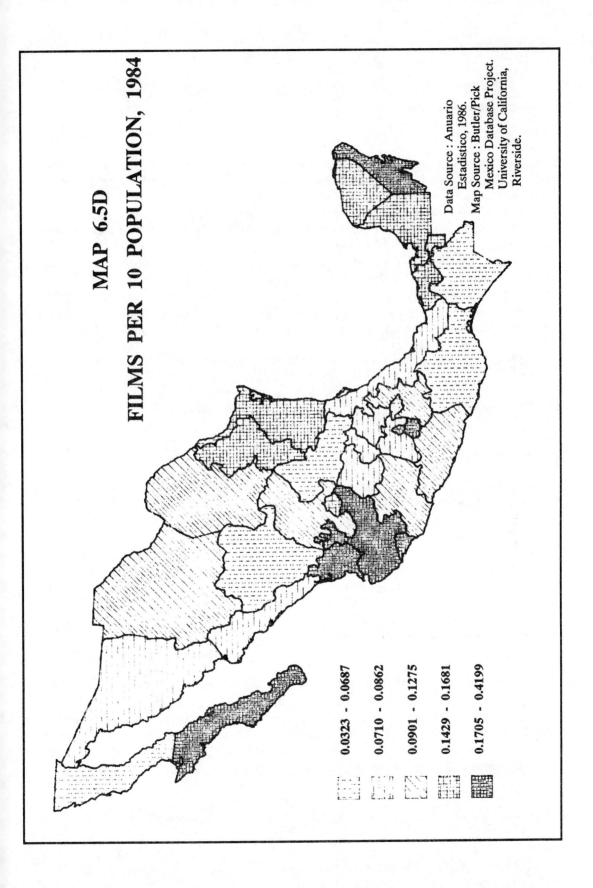

MAP 6.5D

FILMS PER 10 POPULATION, 1984

Data Source : Anuario
Estadistico, 1986.

Map Source : Butler/Pick
Mexico Database Project.
University of California,
Riverside.

0.0323 - 0.0687

0.0710 - 0.0862

0.0901 - 0.1275

0.1429 - 0.1681

0.1705 - 0.4199

Crime

Trials, 1979

Table 6.11 and Map 6.6A present information on the number of trials in Mexico by state. The ratio was caculated on the basis of number of trials in 1979 per 10 people utilizing 1980 population figures as the base. There were extreme differences in the rates of trials in 1979 with a substantial coefficient of variation of 151. Two states had extremely high rates--Nuevo Leon (0.1187) and Morelos (0.1082). Also Sinaloa (0.0516) and the Federal District (0.0538) had rates substantially higher than all other states. On the other hand, Aguascalientes, Guanajuato, Hidalgo, Michoacan, Quintana Roo, San Luis POtosi, and Zacatecas had extremely low rates of trials. Interestingly, several states with the lowest trial rates had the highest penal sentences in 1983 (see Table 6.12 and Map 6.6B). These unusual states regarding trials and penal sentences are Aguascalientes, Guanajuato, San Luis Potosi, and Zacatecas. Thus in these states being brought to trial apparently resulted in a higher rate of conviction. On the other hand, Hidalgo had both low rates of trials and sentences.

The north region general has low to medium rates while the northeast and northwest generally have mixed rates. The central region, with the exception of the Federal District and Morelos, has low rates as do two of the three states in the pacific south. Among the various regions, the greastest consistency in number of trials and sentences is for the border region.

Penal Sentences, 1983

Penal sentences in 1983 per 100 population for the states of Mexico were obtained from the Anuario Estadistico (1986). There were approximately 69,000 persons sentenced in 1983. There was somewhat substantial variation among the states in penal sentences with consistency being reported in the number of sentences by states in 1982 and 1983 (see Table 6.12).

States with the highest rates by far are Tabasco with Baja California and Baja California Sur having higher rates than all of the other remaining states. Other states with high rates are Aguascalientes, Colima, Chihuahua, Guanajuato, Queretaro, San Luis Potosi, Sonora, Tamaulipas, and Zacatecas. States with extreme low rates are Campeche, Coahuila, Durango, Hidalgo, and Yucatan. Other states with relatively low rates are Mexico, Morelos, Nuevo Leon, Oaxaca, and Tlaxcala. The regional variation shown on Map 6.6B is peculiar with the U.S.-Mexico border states typically having either extremely high or low rates. For the remainder of Mexico, there is no discernable regional pattern.

Overall in Mexico about 10 percent of crimes are at the Federal level and 90 percent at the local level. Major Federal crimes are those contrary to health (Contra la salud) and fraud. At the local level, major crimes are bodily injury and robbery, and more prevalent than the remaining types of crimes is burglary (Danos en propriedad ajena). There is variation among states in proportion of Federal and local crimes and by type of crime. There also is variation among states in arrests and sentences by type of crime (see Anuario, 1986).

Table 6.11 Trials, 1979

No.	State	Total Trials	Ratio
1	AGUASCALIENTES	412	0.0079
2	BAJA CALIFORNIA	3,734	0.0317
3	BAJA CALIFORNIA SUR	249	0.0116
4	CAMPECHE	1,419	0.0337
5	COAHUILA	3,796	0.0244
6	COLIMA	921	0.0266
7	CHIAPAS	2,320	0.0111
8	CHIHUAHUA	4,280	0.0213
9	DISTRITO FEDERAL	47,552	0.0538
10	DURANGO	2,550	0.0216
11	GUANAJUATO	2,235	0.0074
12	GUERRERO	9,915	0.0470
13	HIDALGO	1,307	0.0084
14	JALISCO	14,503	0.0332
15	MEXICO	9,956	0.0132
16	MICHOACAN	2,694	0.0094
17	MORELOS	10,250	0.1082
18	NAYARIT	1,390	0.0191
19	NUEVO LEON	29,839	0.1187
20	OAXACA	5,731	0.0242
21	PUEBLA	5,129	0.0153
22	QUERETARO	806	0.0109
23	QUINTANA ROO	138	0.0061
24	SAN LUIS POTOSI	1,179	0.0070
25	SINALOA	9,534	0.0516
26	SONORA	5,524	0.0365
27	TABASCO	3,365	0.0317
28	TAMAULIPAS	7,579	0.0394
29	TLAXCALA	947	0.0170
30	VERACRUZ	6,924	0.0129
31	YUCATAN	3,707	0.0348
32	ZACATECAS	908	0.0080
	Mean	6,277	0.0282
	S.D.	9,499	0.0258
	C.V.	151.37	91.20
	Minimum	138	0.0061
	Maximum	47,552	0.1187

DEFINITION: Ratio is the number of trials 1979 to total population 1980.

SOURCE: 1980 Anuario Estadistico, Table 3.6.2.

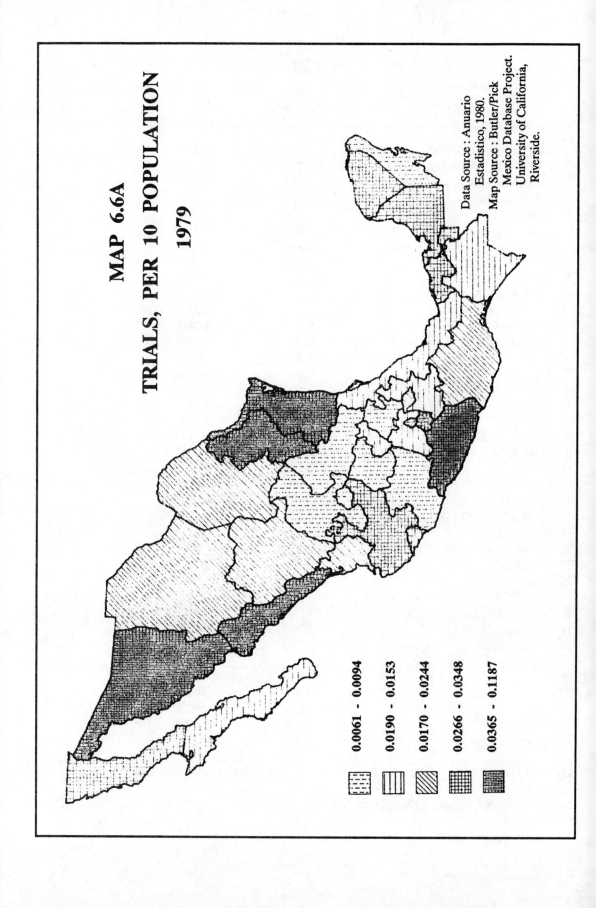

MAP 6.6A

TRIALS, PER 10 POPULATION

1979

0.0061 - 0.0094

0.0190 - 0.0153

0.0170 - 0.0244

0.0266 - 0.0348

0.0365 - 0.1187

Data Source : Anuario
Estadistico, 1980.
Map Source : Butler/Pick
Mexico Database Project.
University of California,
Riverside.

Table 6.12 Penal Sentences, 1983

No.	State	Persons Sentenced	Ratio
1	AGUASCALIENTES	810	0.1378
2	BAJA CALIFORNIA	3,098	0.2308
3	BAJA CALIFORNIA SUR	584	0.2390
4	CAMPECHE	151	0.0316
5	COAHUILA	607	0.0343
6	COLIMA	487	0.1239
7	CHIAPAS	1,943	0.0822
8	CHIHUAHUA	3,092	0.1355
9	DISTRITO FEDERAL	8,857	0.0877
10	DURANGO	518	0.0387
11	GUANAJUATO	4,266	0.1254
12	GUERRERO	1,712	0.0717
13	HIDALGO	572	0.0326
14	JALISCO	4,667	0.0941
15	MEXICO	5,392	0.0629
16	MICHOACAN	2,946	0.0907
17	MORELOS	617	0.0574
18	NAYARIT	672	0.0818
19	NUEVO LEON	1,651	0.0578
20	OAXACA	1,603	0.0596
21	PUEBLA	2,499	0.0659
22	QUERETARO	1,124	0.1345
23	QUINTANA ROO	239	0.0934
24	SAN LUIS POTOSI	2,010	0.1061
25	SINALOA	1,717	0.0819
26	SONORA	2,972	0.1727
27	TABASCO	3,661	0.3045
28	TAMAULIPAS	3,577	0.1635
29	TLAXCALA	346	0.0549
30	VERACRUZ	3,915	0.0639
31	YUCATAN	384	0.0317
32	ZACATECAS	1,623	0.1266
Mean		2,151	0.1023
S.D.		1,902	0.0644
C.V.		88.40	62.95
Minimum		151	0.0316
Maximum		8,857	0.3045

DEFINITION: Ratio is the number of persons sentenced 1983 to total population 1985 multiplied by 0.01.

SOURCE: 1983 Anuario Estadistico, Table 3.5.1.

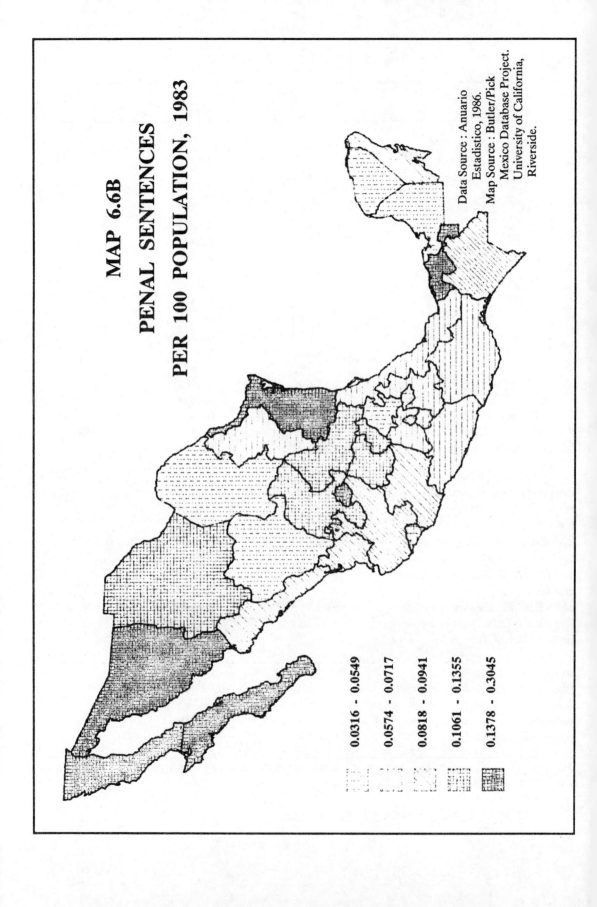

MAP 6.6B
PENAL SENTENCES
PER 100 POPULATION, 1983

0.0316 - 0.0549

0.0574 - 0.0717

0.0818 - 0.0941

0.1061 - 0.1355

0.1378 - 0.3045

Data Source : Anuario
Estadistico, 1986.

Map Source : Butler/Pick
Mexico Database Project.
University of California,
Riverside.

Housing

Number of Persons Per Housing Units, 1980

According to the 1980 Mexican census, the 66,365,920 population of Mexico lived in 12,074,609 housing units, or 5.50 persons per unit (Anuario, 1986). The number of housing units per capita in 1980 was established by dividing the number of housing units by the total population, as reported by the Mexican census. Slightly over two-thirds of these housing units were reported to be owned by their residents.

As shown in Table 6.13, states with the highest number of persons living in a housing unit were Aguascalientes (6.15), Guanajuato (6.28), Queretaro (6.10), and Zacatecas (6.15). Only Baja California at 4.89 had fewer than 5.0 persons per housing unit. Other states with a relatively low number of persons per housing unit in 1980 were Chihuahua (5.09), the Federal District (5.02), Quintana Roo (5.02), and Tamaaulipas (5.04). Map 6.7A illustrates that three of the six border states had a very low number of persons per housing unit, while the other three states had slightly below average rates. The Federal District had a low number of persons per housing unit; however, the state of Mexico and most other states in the greater central region had higher than average rates of persons per housing unit. Overall, however, the range of persons per housing unit in Mexico is not great. There is little apparent relationship between this variable and ecomic level of the state.

Crowding, 1980

Map 2.5 and accompanying discussion presented information on density of population, that is, the population per kilometer in each state. Here in Table 6.14 and Map 6.7B, focus is on density within dwelling units, crowding. Crowding is defined as the ratio of the number of dwellings with three or more rooms and six or more occupants to the number of dwellings with three or more rooms. The mean state value for crowding is 0.51. Patterns of crowding do not correspond to boundaries of standard regions. Crowding is highest in a large five state area encompassing the southern north and north central regions and in the state of Guanajuato in the west. Guanajuato has the highest crowding ratio for Mexico (59.5 percent). Other states with high crowding are Tlaxcala and Tabasco. These values are highly correlated with the dependency ratio, although not with the three major age categories. It is not surprising that crowding and dependency are highly correlated, since households with many dependents have difficulty in finding adequate housing.

Although not correlated with many economic indicators, crowding has high negative correlations with gross state product and the number and size of corporations (SACVs). This may reflect the influence of gross state economies on housing conditions. There is little association with cumulative fertility, but a high positive relationship with cumulative fertility as measured by the 1980 census to younger and older women. This is not surprising, since at the household level, more children often lead to crowded housing.

States with low crowding include Baja California, Chihuahua, Nuevo Leon, Tamaulipas, Yucatan, Quintana Roo, and surprisingly the Federal District. In fact, the Federal District has Mexico's lowest crowding ratio at 40.6 percent. These results, except for Quintana Roo, are substantially associated with dependency, i.e., percentage of children and older persons.

Crowding is significantly negatively associated with density. However, this negative relationship is not apparent in any discernable regional pattern. Thus density and crowding apparently are two quite different dimensions, at least at the state level.

Households with Potable Water, 1980

The distribution of households with potable water in 1980 is similar to many other dimensions by having a substantial north-south axis(see Table 6.15 and Map 6.7C). The primary exceptions are the Federal District with 93 percent of the households having potable water and the state of Mexico surrounding the Federal District having 82 percent potable water. Also, Colima (84 percent) and Aguascalientes (88 percent) have a high proportion of households with potable water. Nearly all of the northwest, north, and northeast regions have a high percent of households with potable water. The major exception in the northern part of Mexico is Tamaulipas with only 71 percent potable water. All states south of Mexico City have a low percentage of potable water. States with the least potable water, 51 percent or less, are Chiapas, Guerrero, Oaxaca, Tabasco, Veracruz, and Yucatan. This variable has a very high correlation of 0.81 with 1980 urbanization. Hence, it also is closely associated with many urban-related variables, and opposite to rural variables. It is also very strongly related to secondary and higher education.

Households Using Kitchen as a Bedroom, 1980

As shown in Table 6.15, an average of one in ten Mexican households in 1980 used the kitchen as a bedroom. However, there is substantial regional variation (see Map 6.7D). The southeast is the only region that has all states with high rates, Quintana Roo (20 percent), Campeche (18 percent), and Yucatan (11 percent). Other states with high rates are Oaxaca and Veracruz in the south and gulf regions, as well as Colima in the west region and the border state of Chihuahua. The largest area of a low rates for this variable consists of four states in the northern west and southern north regions, namely Durango, Zacatecas, Aguascalientes, and Jalisco. They all have less than six percent sharing the kitchen as a bedroom. The Federal District has a very low rate (5.3 percent), as does Tlaxcala (5.4 percent). The geographic pattern for this variable is similar to very few other variables. It is, however, positively associated with the indigenous language population, sex ratio, hotels and pensions, and air flights.

Households with Television, 1976-77

Households with televisions, 1976-77 was determined from households in the Mexico portion of the World Fertility Survey. As previously when WFS data are used, no information is available for Baja California Sur, Campeche, Colima, and Tlaxcala (see Table 6.16 and Map 6.7E). The mean state value was 45 percent, a rate well below the average household rate at the time in the U.S. The Federal District has the highest percentage of households with TVs (88 percent), while Baja California (87 percent), Yucatan (86 percent), and Chihuahua (77 percent) are also extremely high. Several states have less than 20 percent of households with TVs, Hidalgo, Chiapas, Oaxaca, Tabasco, and

Zacatecas. The border states have medium to high percentages of households with TVs. Since TV broadcasting in Mexico originates largely in cities, it is not surprising that percent households with TVs is strongly related to urbanization (Map 2.6A) and other urban-related characteristics.

Table 6.13 Occupants Per Housing Unit, 1980

No.	State	Occupants Per Housing Unit	Total Housing Untis	Ratio
1	AGUASCALIENTES	515,354	83,791	6.1505
2	BAJA CALIFORNIA	1,165,927	238,603	4.8865
3	BAJA CALIFORNIA SUR	212,868	39,671	5.3658
4	CAMPECHE	418,237	75,879	5.5119
5	COAHUILA	1,547,714	282,705	5.4747
6	COLIMA	342,258	64,270	5.3253
7	CHIAPAS	2,060,494	370,319	5.5641
8	CHIHUAHUA	1,994,357	391,464	5.0946
9	DISTRITO FEDERAL	8,773,395	1,747,102	5.0217
10	DURANGO	1,173,855	198,378	5.9173
11	GUANAJUATO	2,982,086	474,800	6.2807
12	GUERRERO	2,082,827	377,847	5.5124
13	HIDALGO	1,533,177	272,162	5.6333
14	JALISCO	4,343,792	776,809	5.5918
15	MEXICO	7,511,360	1,281,270	5.8624
16	MICHOACAN	2,851,256	494,638	5.7643
17	MORELOS	936,914	175,397	5.3417
18	NAYARIT	720,333	132,440	5.4389
19	NUEVO LEON	2,499,148	461,105	5.4199
20	OAXACA	2,355,580	448,665	5.2502
21	PUEBLA	3,325,681	589,485	5.6417
22	QUERETARO	735,259	120,503	6.1016
23	QUINTANA ROO	223,199	44,440	5.0225
24	SAN LUIS POTOSI	1,663,132	283,031	5.8761
25	SINALOA	1,833,487	319,834	5.7326
26	SONORA	1,501,184	276,848	5.4224
27	TABASCO	1,054,257	180,929	5.8269
28	TAMAULIPAS	1,912,069	379,476	5.0387
29	TLAXCALA	550,201	92,327	5.9593
30	VERACRUZ	5,356,637	1,015,323	5.2758
31	YUCATAN	1,057,388	200,966	5.2615
32	ZACATECAS	1,132,494	184,132	6.1504
	Mean	2,073,935	377,332	5.5537
	S.D.	1,950,003	366,104	0.3595
	C.V.	94.02	97.02	6.47
	Minimum	212,868	39,671	4.8865
	Maximum	8,773,395	1,747,102	6.2807

DEFINITION: Ratio is the number of housing occupants to the number of housing units 1980.

SOURCE: 1986 Anuario Estadistico, Table 2.3.1.

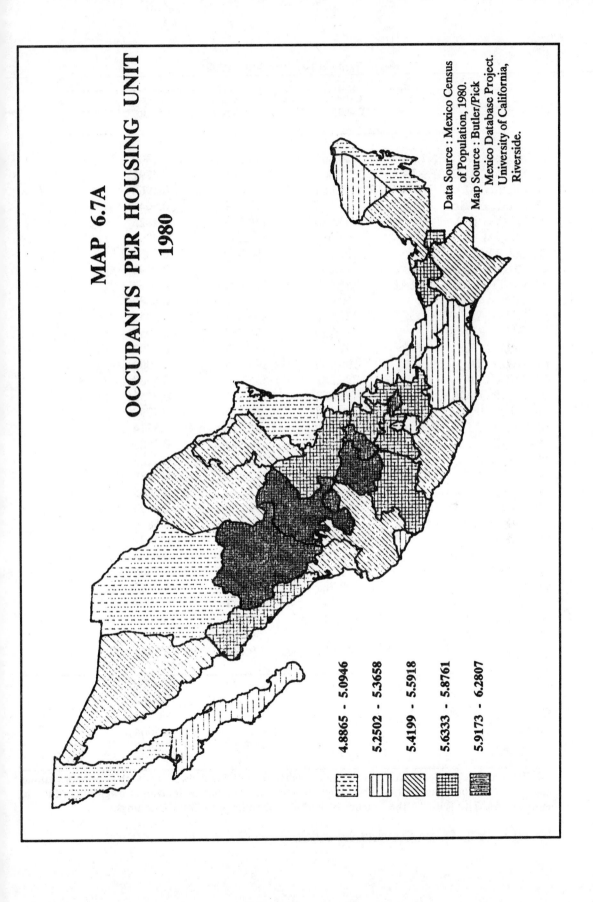

MAP 6.7A

OCCUPANTS PER HOUSING UNIT

1980

Data Source : Mexico Census
of Population, 1980.

Map Source : Butler/Pick
Mexico Database Project.
University of California,
Riverside.

4.8865 - 5.0946

5.2502 - 5.3658

5.4199 - 5.5918

5.6333 - 5.8761

5.9173 - 6.2807

Table 6.14 Crowding, 1980

No. State	Crowded Dwellings	Total Dwellings	Ratio
1 AGUASCALIENTES	24,361	45,961	0.5300
2 BAJA CALIFORNIA	52,480	122,296	0.4291
3 BAJA CALIFORNIA SUR	8,984	18,084	0.4968
4 CAMPECHE	10,756	21,339	0.5041
5 COAHUILA	63,086	130,759	0.4825
6 COLIMA	8,631	17,397	0.4961
7 CHIAPAS	31,734	58,340	0.5439
8 CHIHUAHUA	79,257	180,286	0.4396
9 DISTRITO FEDERAL	355,003	873,612	0.4064
10 DURANGO	50,673	90,345	0.5609
11 GUANAJUATO	122,062	205,091	0.5952
12 GUERRERO	27,739	54,857	0.5057
13 HIDALGO	42,906	78,120	0.5492
14 JALISCO	195,128	390,255	0.5000
15 MEXICO	299,281	555,316	0.5389
16 MICHOACAN	91,863	165,466	0.5552
17 MORELOS	28,012	58,379	0.4798
18 NAYARIT	18,609	35,021	0.5314
19 NUEVO LEON	101,453	219,542	0.4621
20 OAXACA	36,587	71,344	0.5128
21 PUEBLA	89,778	176,415	0.5089
22 QUERETARO	26,025	45,144	0.5765
23 QUINTANA ROO	4,099	9,330	0.4393
24 SAN LUIS POTOSI	57,917	103,074	0.5619
25 SINALOA	62,766	115,659	0.5427
26 SONORA	63,860	132,126	0.4833
27 TABASCO	23,178	39,924	0.5806
28 TAMAULIPAS	57,728	134,779	0.4283
29 TLAXCALA	16,649	28,717	0.5798
30 VERACRUZ	128,312	275,172	0.4663
31 YUCATAN	26,368	59,392	0.4440
32 ZACATECAS	46,891	79,711	0.5883

Mean			0.5100
SD.			0.5262
CV.			10.32
Minimum			0.4064
Maximum			0.5952

DEFINITION: Crowded Dwellings are the number of individual dwellings with 3 or more rooms and 6 or more occupants. Total Dwellings are the total number of individual dwellings with 3 or more rooms. The Ratio is the number of Crowded Dwellings to Total Dwellings.

SOURCE: 1980 Mexican Census of Population, Volume 2, Table 18.

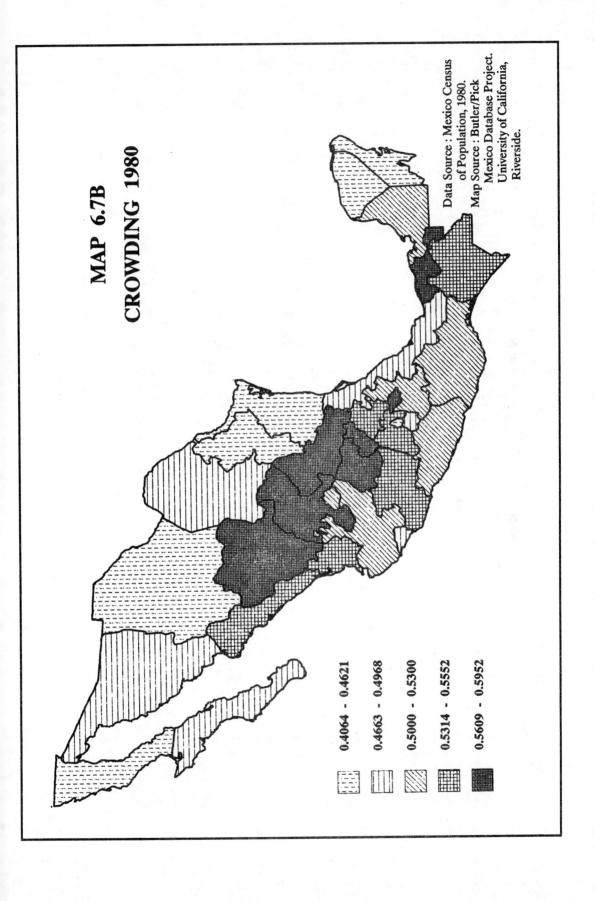

MAP 6.7B
CROWDING 1980

0.4064 - 0.4621

0.4663 - 0.4968

0.5000 - 0.5300

0.5314 - 0.5552

0.5609 - 0.5952

Data Source : Mexico Census
of Population, 1980.

Map Source : Butler/Pick
Mexico Database Project.
University of California,
Riverside.

Table 6.15 Household Characteristics, 1980

No.	State	Number of Households Total	Households Potable Water	Potable Water Ratio	Households Using Kitchen As Bedroom	Kitchen As Bedroom Ratio
1	AGUASCALIENTES	83,791	73,563	0.8779	4,985	0.0595
2	BAJA CALIFORNIA	238,603	186,328	0.7809	15,728	0.0659
3	BAJA CALIFORNIA SUR	39,671	30,597	0.7713	3,012	0.0759
4	CAMPECHE	75,879	45,350	0.5977	13,650	0.1799
5	COAHUILA	282,705	239,904	0.8486	26,996	0.0955
6	COLIMA	64,270	54,186	0.8431	8,117	0.1263
7	CHIAPAS	370,319	161,588	0.4363	33,655	0.0909
8	CHIHUAHUA	391,464	305,452	0.7803	45,918	0.1173
9	DISTRITO FEDERAL	1,747,102	1,628,415	0.9321	92,325	0.0528
10	DURANGO	198,378	145,348	0.7327	12,086	0.0609
11	GUANAJUATO	474,800	324,972	0.6844	33,926	0.0715
12	GUERRERO	377,847	179,927	0.4762	31,891	0.0844
13	HIDALGO	272,162	160,179	0.5885	29,420	0.1081
14	JALISCO	776,809	609,465	0.7846	36,346	0.0468
15	MEXICO	1,281,270	1,044,366	0.8151	94,512	0.0738
16	MICHOACAN	494,638	329,743	0.6666	33,045	0.0668
17	MORELOS	175,397	135,635	0.7733	13,472	0.0768
18	NAYARIT	132,440	94,513	0.7136	13,802	0.1042
19	NUEVO LEON	461,105	403,453	0.8750	41,971	0.0910
20	OAXACA	448,665	198,276	0.4419	51,054	0.1138
21	PUEBLA	589,485	354,411	0.6012	55,924	0.0949
22	QUERETARO	120,503	79,197	0.6572	12,062	0.1001
23	QUINTANA ROO	44,440	25,765	0.5798	8,753	0.1970
24	SAN LUIS POTOSI	283,031	142,118	0.5021	27,827	0.0983
25	SINALOA	319,834	214,237	0.6698	33,037	0.1033
26	SONORA	276,848	229,644	0.8295	27,714	0.1001
27	TABASCO	180,929	75,559	0.4176	13,483	0.0745
28	TAMAULIPAS	379,476	272,143	0.7172	36,956	0.0974
29	TLAXCALA	92,327	65,808	0.7128	4,977	0.0539
30	VERACRUZ	1,015,323	514,507	0.5067	133,329	0.1313
31	YUCATAN	200,966	100,861	0.5019	22,674	0.1128
32	ZACATECAS	184,132	106,654	0.5792	8,290	0.0450
	Mean	377,332	266,630	0.6780	31,904	0.0928
	S.D.	366,104	316,555	0.6812	28,304	0.0944
	C.V.	97.02	118.72	21.07	88.71	36.10
	Minimum	39,671	25,765	0.4176	3,012	0.0450
	Maximum	1,747,102	1,628,415	0.9321	133,329	0.1970

DEFINITION: Potable Water Ratio is the number of households with potable water to the number of households. Kitchen As Bedroom Ratio is the number of households where the kitchen is used as a bedroom to the total number of households. Total household is the number of owned houses.

SOURCE: 1980 Mexican Census of Population, Volume 1, Tables 21 & 22.

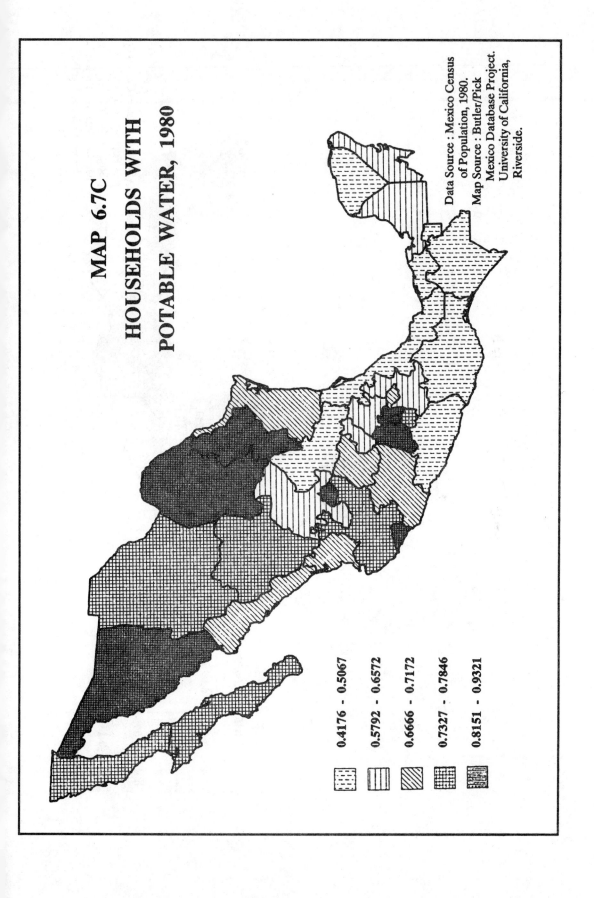

MAP 6.7C

HOUSEHOLDS WITH

POTABLE WATER, 1980

Data Source : Mexico Census
of Population, 1980.

Map Source : Butler/Pick
Mexico Database Project.
University of California,
Riverside.

0.4176 - 0.5067

0.5792 - 0.6572

0.6666 - 0.7172

0.7327 - 0.7846

0.8151 - 0.9321

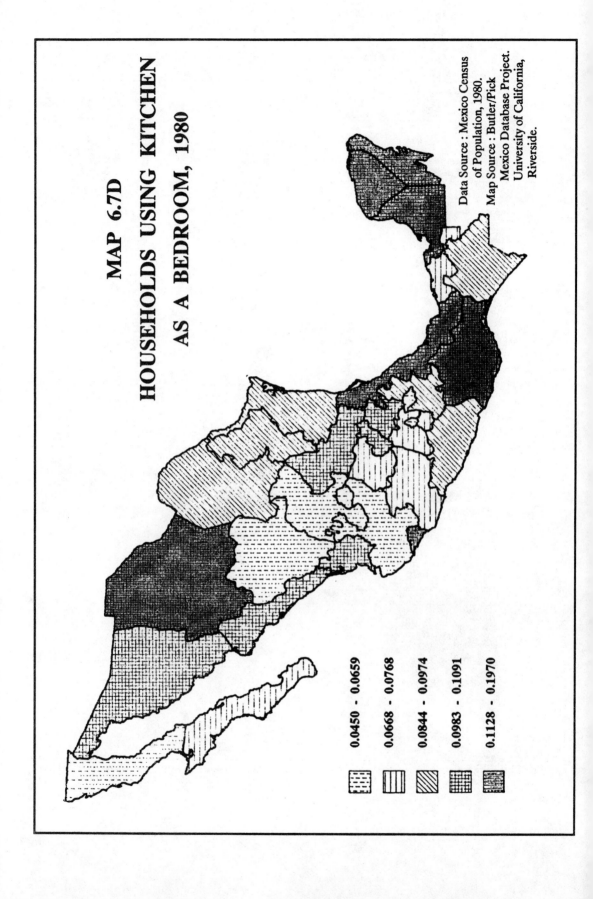

MAP 6.7D

HOUSEHOLDS USING KITCHEN

AS A BEDROOM, 1980

0.0450 - 0.0659

0.0668 - 0.0768

0.0844 - 0.0974

0.0983 - 0.1091

0.1128 - 0.1970

Data Source : Mexico Census
of Population, 1980.
Map Source : Butler/Pick
Mexico Database Project.
University of California,
Riverside.

Table 6.16 Households With Television, 1976-77

No.	State	Ratio
1	AGUASCALIENTES	70.7
2	BAJA CALIFORNIA	86.7
3	BAJA CALIFORNIA SUR	ND
4	CAMPECHE	ND
5	COAHUILA	56.3
6	COLIMA	ND
7	CHIAPAS	14.0
8	CHIHUAHUA	77.5
9	DISTRITO FEDERAL	87.8
10	DURANGO	51.6
11	GUANAJUATO	43.3
12	GUERRERO	31.8
13	HIDALGO	16.5
14	JALISCO	62.8
15	MEXICO	63.9
16	MICHOACAN	22.3
17	MORELOS	33.3
18	NAYARIT	25.6
19	NUEVO LEON	63.5
20	OAXACA	9.5
21	PUEBLA	32.6
22	QUERETARO	38.5
23	QUINTANA ROO	42.9
24	SAN LUIS POTOSI	44.9
25	SINALOA	48.4
26	SONORA	54.5
27	TABASCO	12.8
28	TAMAULIPAS	47.1
29	TLAXCALA	ND
30	VERACRUZ	36.0
31	YUCATAN	86.0
32	ZACATECAS	7.7

Mean	45.30
S.D.	23.73
C.V.	52.39
Minimum	7.70
Maximum	87.80

DEFINITION: Ratio is the survey respondents with television to all survey respondents.

NOTE: ND = no data.

SOURCE: 1976-77 World Fertility Survey.

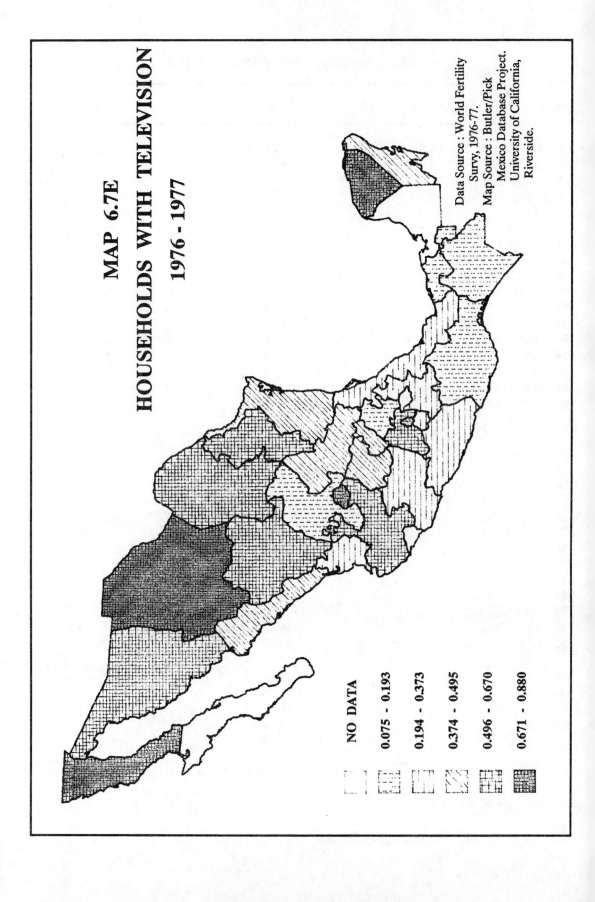

MAP 6.7E

HOUSEHOLDS WITH TELEVISION

1976 - 1977

Data Source : World Fertility
Survy, 1976-77.

Map Source : Butler/Pick
Mexico Database Project.
University of California,
Riverside.

NO DATA

0.075 - 0.193

0.194 - 0.373

0.374 - 0.495

0.496 - 0.670

0.671 - 0.880

7

THE ECONOMY

Introduction

There are extensive data available reflecting various aspects of the Mexican economy. This chapter presents some of the information available from a variety of sources, including the Mexican census, anuarios, and miscellaneous government reports. The first section of the chapter examines the value of the peso vs. the U.S. dollar between 1960 and 1986. Then, an examination of the labor force by industry in 1980 is presented. Natural resource production, agricultural production, and energy production are explored in detail. Also included in this chapter are indicators of economic development, the labor force, and various types of production. Again it should be noted that while the information presented generally covers the 1980s, longitudinal data are discussed and available from many sources.

Currency

The value of the Mexican peso, relative to the U.S. dollar, is shown in Figures 7.1A and 7.1B for the period 1937 to 1988. Figure 7.1A presents the data using the logarithmic scale. Statistics were drawn from the International Monetary Fund, and refer to period average exchange rates (IMF, 1948-88). The Mexican peso was relatively stable for the period 1937 to 1948, increasing by only 54 percent. However, in the single year of 1948-49, it underwent devaluation and gained by 44 percent. It was again stable at around eight until 1954, when it increased by 50 percent to 12.50. That rate lasted for over twenty years until 1975. The value of the peso stood at 23 in 1980. Over the 1982-1988 term of the De La Madrid administration, a drop in oil price and large loans from major United States banks reflected a debt crisis and general financial crisis in Mexico. The peso lost much of its value, relative to the dollar, during this period, rising from 56 in 1982 to 2,281 in July, 1988, a 41 fold relative devaluation. This drop in the peso value is shown below.

Value of Peso in U.S. Dollars, 1979-1988

Year	Peso Value
1979	22.805
1980	22.951
1981	24.515
1982	56.402
1983	120.094
1984	167.828
1985	256.872
1986	611.773
1987	1,378.200
1988*	2,281.000

NOTE: the series refers to period averages of exchange rates for countries quoting rates in U.S. dollars per unit of national currency.
SOURCE: IMF, International Financial Statistics, 1979-88.
*July

In the case of two characteristics discussed in this chapter, value of corporations and gross state revenues, 1985 figures are presented both in unadjusted pesos and in pesos adjusted to earlier years. The purpose of this is to control for the large devaluation and help in comparisons over time in Tables 7.17 and 7.19. The 1985 value of corporations is given in terms of constant 1980 pesos, whereas the 1985 value of gross state revenues is given in terms of constant 1979 pesos. The adjustment is accomplished by multiplying an unadjusted figure for the later year by the ratio, peso value in the earlier year/peso value in the later year. For instance, to adjust to 1980 for value of corporations, each 1985 value is multiplied by the ratio, 1980 peso value/1985 peso value. The maps for these two variables are based on adjusted pesos.

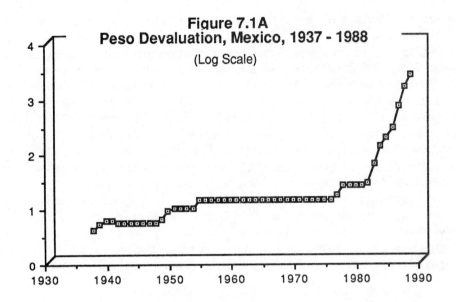

Figure 7.1A
Peso Devaluation, Mexico, 1937 - 1988
(Log Scale)

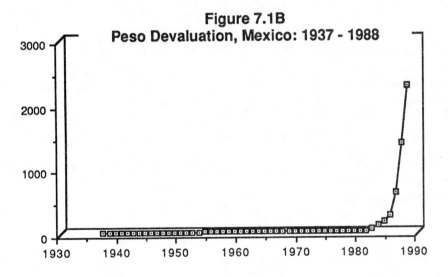

Figure 7.1B
Peso Devaluation, Mexico: 1937 - 1988

Labor Force by Industry, 1980

Information on the labor force by industry, 1980, is presented in five industry maps (Maps 7.2A-7.2E). The historical growth of labor force indicates a rise from 5.2 million economically active workers in 1930 to 21.9 million in 1980, an increase nearly proportional to the increase in national population. From 1940 to 1980, the labor force grew at a compound rate of 3.3 percent per year. Accompanying this growth was a shift in labor force composition, especially a decline in agriculture, from 70 percent in 1930 to 39 percent in 1970 and 30 percent in 1980 (37 percent in 1980, excluding population not specifying industry). This major reduction in agricultural labor force parallels declines in other nations, both developing and advanced. For instance, in the U.S., the proportion of the employed civilian labor force in agriculture declined from 23 percent in 1930 to 4.4 percent in 1970 and 3.4 percent in 1980 (Bogue, 1985). Another important change in Mexico has been the growth in personal service industries, including government, from 4.0 percent in 1930 to 20 percent in 1970 and 18 percent in 1980, excluding population not specifying industry. In the U.S., by comparison, service industry and government increased from 22 percent of the labor force in 1930 to 38 percent in 1980.

In the following discussion, the industry unspecified population is excluded. The table in Appendix A allows an adjustment for the data for the unspecified component.

Agriculture

The mean state percent in agricultural industry in 1980 was 29.2, with moderate variation among states. At the high end are the southern states of Chiapas and Oaxaca, with 57.4 and 55.3 percent of the labor force in agriculture. At the opposite extremes are the urbanized states of the Federal District, Nuevo Leon, and Baja California, with 6.1, 8.4, and 9.5 percent in agriculture (Table 7.1).

Since the Mexican census classifies agricultural industry and agricultural occupation nearly identically, the detailed discussion of geographic distribution of agriculture is deferred to agricultural occupation (see discussion accompanying Map 8.2D). The geographic distribution reveals areas of high agricultural labor force in the southern and southeastern part of Mexico, with less agricultural labor force in the northern part of the country. The only general exception to this north-south pattern are the heavily agricultural states of Zacatecas and Nayarit and heavily urbanized states of Mexico and Federal District.

Commerce

As shown in Table 7.2, the commerce industry labor force constituted on average 8.5 percent of the labor force in 1980, with a pattern generally opposite to that of the agricultural workforce. There are high levels of commerce in the border states plus Baja California Sur and low levels in the pacific south and gulf regions. The high commerce level of 10.5 percent in the northern border tier is due to the heavily urbanized border and to the large amount of commerce and trade with the neighboring United States. In general, the geographic pattern for the commerce industry corresponds very closely to that for urbanization (see Map 2.6A). An important exception is the completely urbanized Federal District, which has a below average commerce sector at 7.3 percent. Some of the Federal District's international commerce may in fact be displaced to the border region, in proximity to the

U.S., Mexico's foremost commercial partner. In the southeast region, Quintana Roo has very high percent in commerce (12.5 percent), even though it has only medium urbanization.

Construction

The construction sector comprises an average of 6.2 percent of the labor force, with lower variation than for sectors already discussed. Given the growth of the capital city, it is not surprising that the size of the Federal District's construction sector is 9.7 percent. Likewise Nuevo Leon with the major city of Monterrey has a large contruction sector at 7.3 percent. The smaller states of Baja California Sur and Colima also have high construction sectors, which may reflect their population growth and building related to tourism. In the pacific south, Michoacan, and the eastern central region, there is a low level of construction industry. Puebla's low percentage (3.7 percent), in spite of the presence of a major city, is likely due to the more traditional and settled nature of that city. The southeast has a moderate to high construction sector, which reflects in part its growth in population, and oil industry in the case of Campeche (see Table 7.3).

Manufacturing

Table 7.4 illustrates that there is an average of 10.3 percent of the labor force in Mexico in manufacturing. States with the highest manufacturing sectors are Nuevo Leon (24.6 percent) and Mexico (21.0 percent). Metropolitan areas in these states contain a diversity of major industrial companies and plants. The Federal District has much lower manufacturing sector (12.4 percent), but a significant amount of greater Mexico City's manufacturing has been located on the metropolitan periphery, which extends into the state of Mexico. The smallest manufacturing sector is located in the pacific south region, with a level of only 4.4 percent. This area lacks the energy capacity (see Map 7.5) as well as the distribution and transportation networks to support manufacturing. The geographic distribution pattern for manufacturing resembles that for commerce, with the following important exceptions: (1) Puebla is more significant for manufacturing than for commerce, (2) the northwest region is less important for manufacturing relative to commerce, (3) in the southeast, Yucatan is more important than Quintana Roo for manufacturing, a reversal of the pattern for commerce.

Personal Service

The average value for the personal service industry in 1980 was 9.2 percent, a proportion which is likely to grow based on historical trends. Variation among states is the least among the industries (see Table 7.5). There are high values for states with significant exposure to foreign commerce and tourism, including Baja California, Baja California Sur, Nuevo Leon, Tamaulipas, Colima, Guerrero, and Quintana Roo. Among the lowest states in level of the service industry are the Federal District and Guanajuato. However, states surrounding the Federal District, i.e. Mexico and Morelia, have high service sectors.

Table 7.1 Agricultural Industry Labor Force, 1980

No.	State	Agricultural Industry Workers	Economically Active Population	Ratio
1	AGUASCALIENTES	28,615	159,943	0.1789
2	BAJA CALIFORNIA	38,180	403,279	0.0947
3	BAJA CALIFORNIA SUR	13,538	69,954	0.1935
4	CAMPECHE	42,836	134,423	0.3187
5	COAHUILA	76,343	483,898	0.1578
6	COLIMA	30,291	108,754	0.2785
7	CHIAPAS	421,561	734,047	0.5743
8	CHIHUAHUA	137,909	664,707	0.2075
9	DISTRITO FEDERAL	202,336	3,312,581	0.0611
10	DURANGO	110,311	357,163	0.3089
11	GUANAJUATO	187,495	978,013	0.1917
12	GUERRERO	318,424	719,154	0.4428
13	HIDALGO	187,043	505,091	0.3703
14	JALISCO	267,824	1,413,854	0.1894
15	MEXICO	367,888	2,410,236	0.1526
16	MICHOACAN	344,325	872,775	0.3945
17	MORELOS	76,303	303,838	0.2511
18	NAYARIT	84,819	210,188	0.4035
19	NUEVO LEON	67,308	803,764	0.0837
20	OAXACA	474,793	858,283	0.5532
21	PUEBLA	447,439	1,081,573	0.4137
22	QUERETARO	65,035	224,435	0.2898
23	QUINTANA ROO	23,136	79,341	0.2916
24	SAN LUIS POTOSI	181,346	532,115	0.3408
25	SINALOA	156,542	568,427	0.2754
26	SONORA	100,765	484,277	0.2081
27	TABASCO	127,459	327,502	0.3892
28	TAMAULIPAS	112,362	624,497	0.1799
29	TLAXCALA	65,906	174,965	0.3767
30	VERACRUZ	678,029	1,796,219	0.3775
31	YUCATAN	115,336	367,825	0.3136
32	ZACATECAS	148,474	300,963	0.4933

Mean			0.292338
S.D.			0.130492
C.V.			44.63
Minimum			0.061100
Maximum			0.574300

DEFINITION: Ratio is the population in agricultural industries to the economically active population age 12+.

SOURCE: 1980 Mexican Census of Population, Volume 1, Tables 6 & 7.

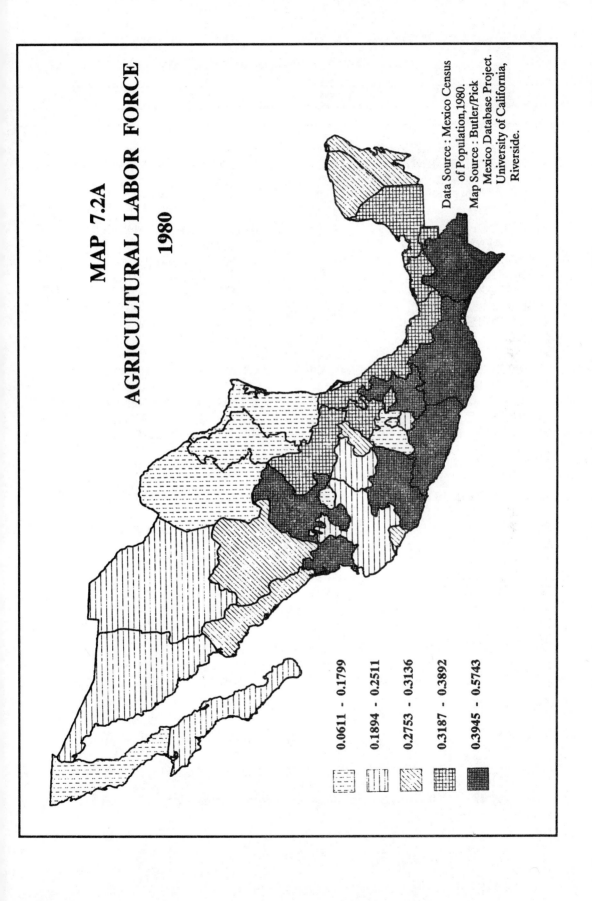

MAP 7.2A

AGRICULTURAL LABOR FORCE

1980

Data Source : Mexico Census
    of Population, 1980.
Map Source : Butler/Pick
    Mexico Database Project.
    University of California,
    Riverside.

0.0611 - 0.1799

0.1894 - 0.2511

0.2753 - 0.3136

0.3187 - 0.3892

0.3945 - 0.5743

Table 7.2 Commerce Industry Labor Force

No.	State	Commerce Industry Workers	Economically Active Population	Ratio
1	AGUASCALIENTES	16,566	159,943	0.1036
2	BAJA CALIFORNIA	55,454	403,279	0.1375
3	BAJA CALIFORNIA SUR	8,289	69,954	0.1185
4	CAMPECHE	10,821	134,423	0.0805
5	COAHUILA	49,163	483,898	0.1016
6	COLIMA	11,381	108,754	0.1046
7	CHIAPAS	34,139	734,047	0.0465
8	CHIHUAHUA	67,457	664,707	0.1015
9	DISTRITO FEDERAL	134,858	3,312,581	0.0407
10	DURANGO	25,920	357,163	0.0726
11	GUANAJUATO	49,464	978,013	0.0506
12	GUERRERO	49,978	719,154	0.0695
13	HIDALGO	27,197	505,091	0.0538
14	JALISCO	157,843	1,413,854	0.1116
15	MEXICO	245,000	2,410,236	0.1016
16	MICHOACAN	70,661	872,775	0.0810
17	MORELOS	29,159	303,838	0.0960
18	NAYARIT	19,169	210,188	0.0912
19	NUEVO LEON	89,990	803,764	0.1120
20	OAXACA	34,393	858,283	0.0401
21	PUEBLA	82,621	1,081,573	0.0764
22	QUERETARO	18,171	224,435	0.0810
23	QUINTANA ROO	9,934	79,341	0.1252
24	SAN LUIS POTOSI	39,957	532,115	0.0751
25	SINALOA	51,912	568,427	0.0913
26	SONORA	51,286	484,277	0.1059
27	TABASCO	20,608	327,502	0.0629
28	TAMAULIPAS	70,613	624,497	0.1131
29	TLAXCALA	9,740	174,965	0.0557
30	VERACRUZ	134,702	1,796,219	0.0750
31	YUCATAN	33,621	367,825	0.0914
32	ZACATECAS	19,229	300,963	0.0639

National Total				2.7319
Mean				0.0854
S.D.				0.0250
C.V.				29.34
Minimum				0.0401
Maximum				0.1375

DEFINITION: Ratio is the population in commerce industries to population economically active age 12+. This category includes the census designations, commerce and loging services.

SOURCE: <u>1980 Mexican Census of Population</u>, Volume 1, Tables 6 & 7.

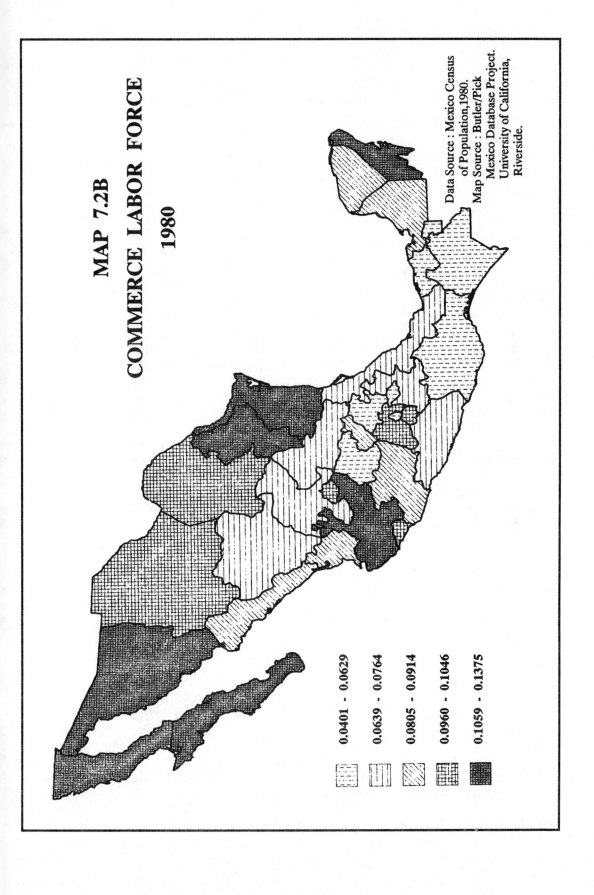

MAP 7.2B

COMMERCE LABOR FORCE

1980

Data Source : Mexico Census
of Population, 1980.

Map Source : Butler/Pick
Mexico Database Project.
University of California,
Riverside.

0.0401 - 0.0629

0.0639 - 0.0764

0.0805 - 0.0914

0.0960 - 0.1046

0.1059 - 0.1375

Table 7.3 Construction Industry Labor Force, 1980

No.	State	Construction Industry Workers	Economcally Active Population	Ratio
1	AGUASCALIENTES	10,625	159,943	0.0664
2	BAJA CALIFORNIA	25,010	403,279	0.0620
3	BAJA CALIFORNIA SUR	4,876	69,954	0.0697
4	CAMPECHE	8,681	134,423	0.0646
5	COAHUILA	31,698	483,898	0.0655
6	COLIMA	7,310	108,754	0.0672
7	CHIAPAS	18,929	734,047	0.0258
8	CHIHUAHUA	41,285	664,707	0.0621
9	DISTRITO FEDERAL	321,627	3,312,581	0.0971
10	DURANGO	16,763	357,163	0.0469
11	GUANAJUATO	62,693	978,013	0.0641
12	GUERRERO	22,552	719,154	0.0314
13	HIDALGO	17,939	505,091	0.0355
14	JALISCO	80,092	1,413,854	0.0566
15	MEXICO	138,731	2,410,236	0.0576
16	MICHOACAN	38,135	872,775	0.0437
17	MORELOS	22,131	303,838	0.0728
18	NAYARIT	11,263	210,188	0.0536
19	NUEVO LEON	58,712	803,764	0.0730
20	OAXACA	18,370	858,283	0.0214
21	PUEBLA	39,961	1,081,573	0.0369
22	QUERETARO	16,296	224,435	0.0726
23	QUINTANA ROO	4,562	79,341	0.0575
24	SAN LUIS POTOSI	26,191	532,115	0.0492
25	SINALOA	30,211	568,427	0.0531
26	SONORA	29,206	484,277	0.0603
27	TABASCO	16,365	327,502	0.0500
28	TAMAULIPAS	45,234	624,497	0.0724
29	TLAXCALA	7,599	174,965	0.0434
30	VERACRUZ	82,113	1,796,219	0.0457
31	YUCATAN	22,433	367,825	0.0610
32	ZACATECAS	18,744	300,963	0.0623

National total	1.8014
Mean	0.0563
S.D.	0.0155
C.V.	27.57
Minimum	0.0214
Maximum	0.0971

DEFINITION: Ratio is the population in construction industries to the economically active population age 12+.

SOURCE: 1980 Mexican Census of Population, Volume 1, Tables 6 & 7.

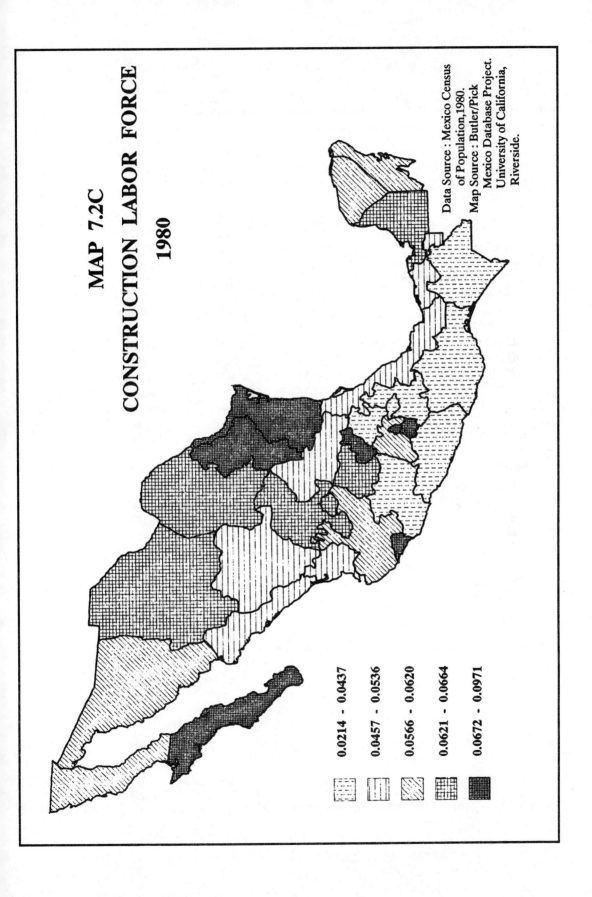

MAP 7.2C

CONSTRUCTION LABOR FORCE

1980

Data Source : Mexico Census
of Population, 1980.
Map Source : Butler/Pick
Mexico Database Project.
University of California,
Riverside.

0.0214 - 0.0437
0.0457 - 0.0536
0.0566 - 0.0620
0.0621 - 0.0664
0.0672 - 0.0971

Table 7.4 Manufacturing Industry Labor Force, 1980

No.	State	Manufacturing Industry Workers	Economically Active Population	Ratio
1	AGUASCALIENTES	23,323	159,943	0.1458
2	BAJA CALIFORNIA	54,698	403,279	0.1356
3	BAJA CALIFORNIA SUR	5,226	69,954	0.0747
4	CAMPECHE	9,925	134,423	0.0738
5	COAHUILA	69,841	483,898	0.1443
6	COLIMA	8,155	108,754	0.0750
7	CHIAPAS	25,576	734,047	0.0348
8	CHIHUAHUA	82,286	664,707	0.1238
9	DISTRITO FEDERAL	407,001	3,312,581	0.1229
10	DURANGO	27,151	357,163	0.0760
11	GUANAJUATO	80,307	978,013	0.0821
12	GUERRERO	35,859	719,154	0.0499
13	HIDALGO	42,452	505,091	0.0840
14	JALISCO	229,277	1,413,854	0.1622
15	MEXICO	505,855	2,410,236	0.2099
16	MICHOACAN	69,745	872,775	0.0799
17	MORELOS	29,078	303,838	0.0957
18	NAYARIT	16,241	210,188	0.0773
19	NUEVO LEON	197,791	803,764	0.2461
20	OAXACA	40,283	858,283	0.0469
21	PUEBLA	120,031	1,081,573	0.1110
22	QUERETARO	39,381	224,435	0.1755
23	QUINTANA ROO	4,554	79,341	0.0574
24	SAN LUIS POTOSI	47,484	532,115	0.0892
25	SINALOA	40,197	568,427	0.0707
26	SONORA	46,493	484,277	0.0960
27	TABASCO	22,266	327,502	0.0680
28	TAMAULIPAS	74,481	624,497	0.1193
29	TLAXCALA	25,575	174,965	0.1462
30	VERACRUZ	144,494	1,796,219	0.0804
31	YUCATAN	35,671	367,825	0.0970
32	ZACATECAS	14,427	300,963	0.0479

National Total			3.2993
Mean			0.1031
S.D.			0.0475
C.V.			46.10
Minimum			0.0348
Maximum			0.2461

DEFINITION: Ratio is the population in manufacturing industries to economically active population. This category includes the census designations manufacturing (transformation) and refining of petroleum.

SOURCE: 1980 Mexican Census of Population, Volume 1, Tables 6 & 7.

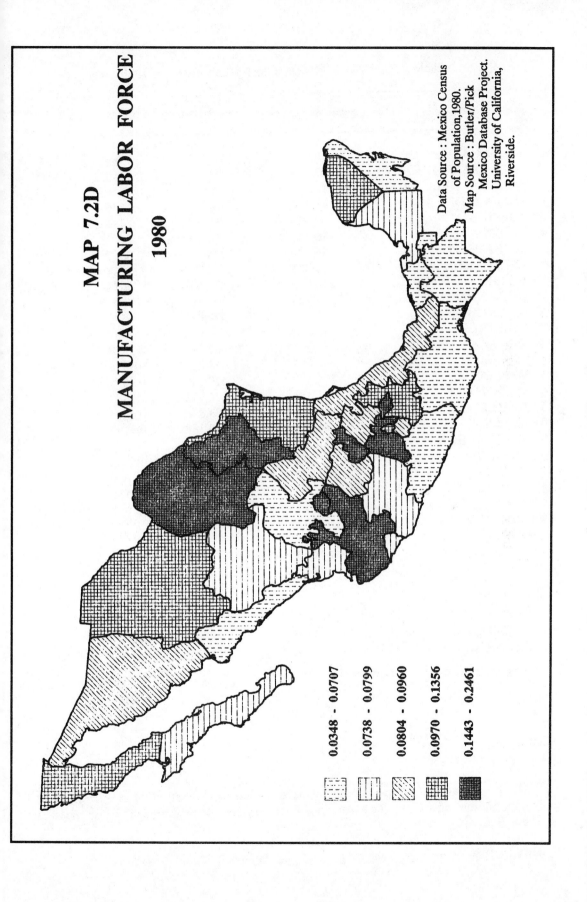

MAP 7.2D

MANUFACTURING LABOR FORCE

1980

Data Source : Mexico Census
of Population, 1980.
Map Source : Butler/Pick
Mexico Database Project.
University of California,
Riverside.

0.0348 - 0.0707

0.0738 - 0.0799

0.0804 - 0.0960

0.0970 - 0.1356

0.1443 - 0.2461

Table 7.5 Personal Service Industry Labor Force, 1980

No.	State	Personal Service Industry Workers	Economically Active Population	Ratio
1	AGUASCALIENTES	20,514	159,943	0.1283
2	BAJA CALIFORNIA	67,323	403,279	0.1669
3	BAJA CALIFORNIA SUR	12,143	69,954	0.1736
4	CAMPECHE	18,266	134,423	0.1359
5	COAHUILA	69,510	483,898	0.1436
6	COLIMA	16,413	108,754	0.1509
7	CHIAPAS	48,196	734,047	0.0657
8	CHIHUAHUA	85,323	664,707	0.1284
9	DISTRITO FEDERAL	222,606	3,312,581	0.0672
10	DURANGO	39,126	357,163	0.1095
11	GUANAJUATO	51,065	978,013	0.0522
12	GUERRERO	97,606	719,154	0.1357
13	HIDALGO	51,945	505,091	0.1028
14	JALISCO	180,655	1,413,854	0.1278
15	MEXICO	332,344	2,410,236	0.1379
16	MICHOACAN	77,073	872,775	0.0883
17	MORELOS	43,829	303,838	0.1443
18	NAYARIT	24,846	210,188	0.1182
19	NUEVO LEON	131,095	803,764	0.1631
20	OAXACA	67,961	858,283	0.0792
21	PUEBLA	109,276	1,081,573	0.1010
22	QUERETARO	26,589	224,435	0.1185
23	QUINTANA ROO	12,828	79,341	0.1617
24	SAN LUIS POTOSI	61,032	532,115	0.1147
25	SINALOA	65,999	568,427	0.1161
26	SONORA	64,843	484,277	0.1339
27	TABASCO	30,681	327,502	0.0937
28	TAMAULIPAS	98,428	624,497	0.1576
29	TLAXCALA	17,295	174,965	0.0988
30	VERACRUZ	194,176	1,796,219	0.1081
31	YUCATAN	51,499	367,825	0.1400
32	ZACATECAS	27,629	300,963	0.0918

National Total	3.8554
Mean	0.1205
S.D.	0.0305
C.V.	25.28
Minimum	0.0522
Maximum	0.1736

DEFINITION: Ratio is the population in personal service industries to the economically active population, age 12+. This category includes the census designations, services and government.

SOURCE: 1980 Mexican Census of Population, Volume 1, Tables 6 & 7.

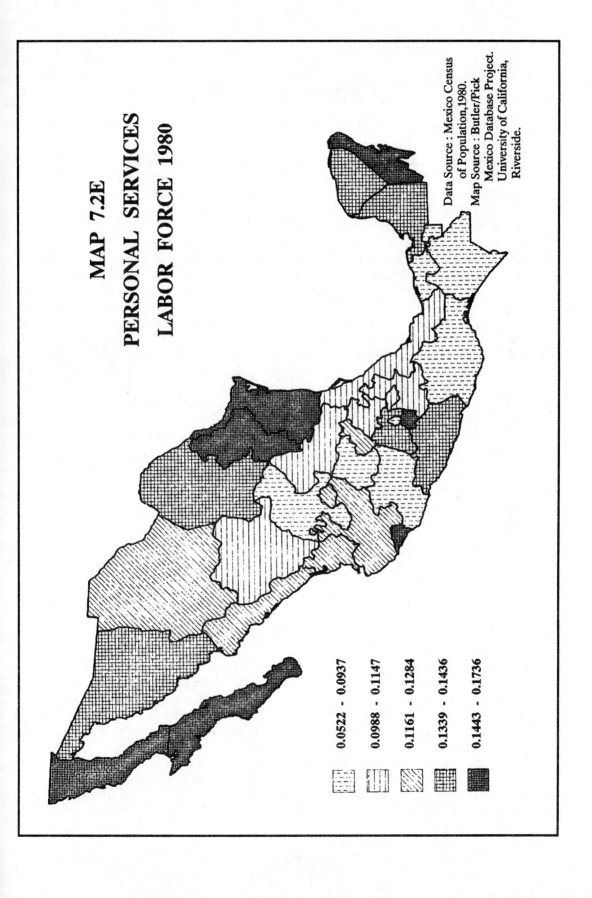

MAP 7.2E
PERSONAL SERVICES
LABOR FORCE 1980

Data Source : Mexico Census
    of Population,1980.
Map Source : Butler/Pick
    Mexico Database Project.
    University of California,
    Riverside.

0.0522 - 0.0937

0.0988 - 0.1147

0.1161 - 0.1284

0.1339 - 0.1436

0.1443 - 0.1736

Natural Resource Production

Crude Oil Production, 1986

In 1986, Mexico produced 912.6 million barrels of crude oil. As seen in Figure 7.2A, there was rapid growth in crude oil production in the period 1970-82, resulting in a six-fold increase. This increase was the result of the discovery and development of a major oil field in the gulf region in the mid 1970s. In the mid 1980s the rate of increase slowed in the period 1938-70, there was a slow rate of production increase, averaging 4.4 percent annually.

As a result of its major oil field, Mexico is one of the world's leading nations in petroleum resources. Mexico's proven crude oil reserves at the end of 1986 were 54.9 billion barrels, an amount estimated at 45.6 percent of the Western Hemisphere's and 7.9 percent of the world's proven reserves (PEMEX, 1986). By comparison, at the end of 1976, Mexico's proven oil reserves were only 6.3 billion barrels (Tamayo, 1985).

The most important state in crude oil production is Campeche, with entirely offshore production accounting for about two thirds of the nation's production (see Map 7.3A). Next in importance is Tabasco, with about a quarter of the country's production. Other important states are Veracruz and Chiapas, with 3.7 and 4.7 percent of production capacity respectively. Although Tabasco is second in oil production, among the oil states it has the most important onshore presence of oil industry, as indicated by a large number of petroleum workers, a large port for oil shipments at Coatzacoalcos, and refining capabilities (Pick et al., 1987b).

Another indicator of oil production, presented in Table 7.6 is the number of wells. Nuevo Leon and Tamaulipas have a large amount of drilling activity, although so far it has resulted in only minor production. By region, crude oil production is centered in the gulf region, and single states in the pacific south (Chiapas) and southeast (Campeche). The northeast has very minor production, and all other regions are essentially non-productive.

Natural Gas Production, 1986

Mexico has major natural gas production and reserves. In 1986, Mexico's natural gas production was 35.5 billion cubic meters. This represented 1.97 percent of the world's production (PEMEX, 1986). The country's estimated natural gas reserves in 1986 totalled 2.15 trillion cubic meters, equivalent to 16.0 percent of the Western Hemisphere's proven reserves and 2.1 percent of the world's proven reserves (see Table 7.6).

As shown in Map 7.3B, nearly half of Mexico's natural gas production is onshore in the state of Tabasco. Other important states are Campeche offshore and Chiapas onshore, accounting for a quarter and an eighth of production respectively. In addition, Tamaulipas, Veracruz, and Nuevo Leon together account for about an eighth of production. Natural gas production, centered in the south, supplies northern states through gas pipelines, the most important of which is a major pipeline connecting Cactus, Chiapas, to Monterrey, Nuevo Leon.

Natural gas production is centered in the three adjacent southern states of Tabasco, Campeche, and Chiapas, which do not form a standard region. The gulf and northeast regions are the most coherent as standard regions, since all states within them are natural gas producers. The oil producing and gas producing states are identical, with the exception of San Luis Potosi, which only produces oil. Figure 7.2B illustrates the growth in natural gas production between 1939 and 1986.

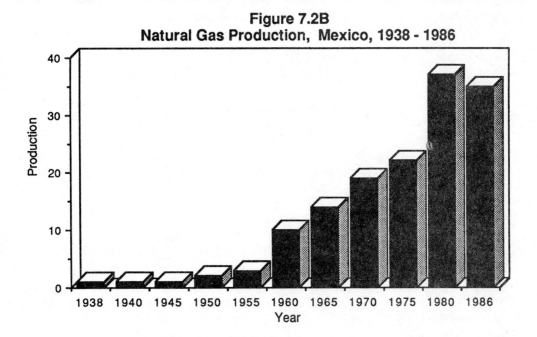

Figure 7.2B
Natural Gas Production, Mexico, 1938 - 1986

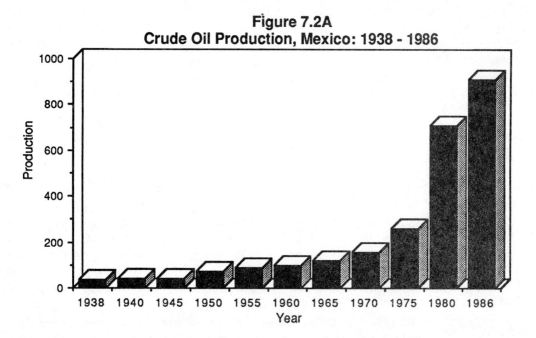

Figure 7.2A
Crude Oil Production, Mexico: 1938 - 1986

SOURCE: 1986 PEMEX Anuario Estaditico.

Copper Production, 1985

Copper is one of the major minerals mined in Mexico. In 1985 the nation produced 184,474 tons of copper, accounting for 2.3 percent of the world's production (U.S. Department of the Interior, 1986). The following table indicates that Mexico's annual copper production fluctuated over the decade prior to 1985.

Annual Copper Production in Mexico, 1976-1985

Year	Annual Copper Production (tons)
1976	88,970
1978	87,186
1980	175,399
1982	229,178
1984	192,385
1985	184,474

SOURCE: <u>Anuarios Estadisticos</u>, 1980, 1986.

There is a strong concentration of copper production in three states in the north and northwest (see Table 7.7). Sonora is the foremost copper producer, with 84.4 percent of the national production. Its production can be further pinpointed principally to three mining sites of Nacazari, Cananea, and La Caridad (Tamayo, 1985). States next in importance are Zacatecas and Chihuahua, together producing 11.8 percent of the national total. Other less important states are Guerrero, Queretaro, Durango, Baja California Sur, and Michoacan.

The geographic distribution of copper production has been fairly steady over the decade 1976-85. However, one change has been the reduction in importance of several states. From 1979 to 1985, Baja California Sur, Michoacan, Agauascalientes, and Queretaro lost 1,628, 1,225, 1,090, and 709 tons of production respectively. Map 7.3C shows the geographic distribution of copper production.

Gold Production, 1985

From pre-Hispanic times, gold has been an important mineral in Mexico. In 1985, Mexican gold production totalled 7,791 kilograms. This is somewhat higher than the 1978-80 average annual national production of 6,097 kilograms. Gold production shows great variation among states (see Map 7.3D). Sixteen states have less than 5 kilograms of annual production, while seven states, Guanajuato, Durango, Zacatecas, Jalisco, Chihuahua, Sonora, and Hidalgo, account for 88 percent of the gold production (see Table 7.8). The leading states are Guanajuato and Durango, with 2,565 and 1,867 kilograms of production respectively. These states consistently led in production over the 1976-85 period.

By region, gold production is high in the northwest, north, and west, moderate in the central and pacific south, and low in the northeast, gulf, and southeast regions. However, in the northwest, there is only slight production on the Baja Peninsula. This pattern corresponds to that for silver production, with some differences (compare with Map 7.3E). The reason is that the two minerals are often located in the same deposits and ususally gold and silver are extracted from the same centers of production (Sanchez, 1973).

Silver Production, 1985

Mexico has produced silver for centuries, and is currently one of the world's leading producers, with 1985 production of 2.24 million kilograms of silver. This amount is 47 percent higher than the 1978-80 annual average of 1.47 million kilograms. Production is heavily weighted towards several states. The leading state is Zacatecas, with 0.71 million kilograms of silver production. Other important states are Chihuahua, Durango, Guanajuato, Hidalgo, and Sonora. Together, the six leading states produce 79 percent of the nation's silver (see Table 7.9).

Topographically, the major silver production is located in the Sierra Madre Occidental mountain range; in the mountainous areas of Zacatecas; and in the Cordillera Neovolcanica, a volcanic mountain range extending east-west across the central flank of the country (Tamayo, 1985). Although parts of this area are reachable by railroad or mountain roads, potential production is constrained by difficulty in access. Generally, the regional pattern shown on Map 7.3E resembles that for gold (see Map 7.3D). The most important production region by far is in the north region. The northwest, west, and pacific south regions have moderate production, while the northeast, gulf and southeast have low or non-existent production.

Timber Products, 1984

Mexico has important forest products, of which timber constituted 93 percent in value in 1984. In that year, total timber production value was 52.8 billion pesos. Non-timber production of such products as resins, gums, and waxes had a value of 4.2 billion pesos. As seen below, Mexican timber production has been steady, while production value in unadjusted pesos increased substantially for the first half of the 1980s.

Mexican Timber Production Volume and Values, 1980-1984

Year	Volume (in cubic meters)	Value (in millions of pesos)
1980	9,048,381	9,651
1981	8,954,393	12,394
1982	8,997,512	NA
1983	8,747,648	22,204
1984	9,448,521	52,798

SOURCE: Anuarios Estadisticos, 1985, 1986.

The leading species of timber produced is pine, which in 1984, has a production value of 44,509 million pesos (see Table 7.10). Other important timber species are tropical species, with production value of 2,341 millions pesos, and oak, valued at 2,034 million pesos.

Map 7.3F shows the regional distribution of timber products, dominated by pine. By topography, timber products are concentrated in the mountain ranges of Sierra Madre Occidental and Cordillera Neovolcanica. This includes timber in the states of Chihuahua, Durango, Jalisco, and Michoacan, which amounts to 73 percent of the nation's production. In the south, the states of Guerrero, Oaxaca, Chiapas, Campeche, and Quintana Roo have timber production, which consists partly of tropical species, totalling 6,991 million pesos. Other states of moderate production are Puebla and Tamaulipas. Among the least productive timber states are Baja California and Baja California Sur, and several of the smaller states along the central flank of the nation. By region, the most important are the north, west, and pacific south. This regional pattern has been stable, changing only slightly since 1980.

Table 7.6 Oil and Natural Gas Production, 1986

No. State	Number of Wells	Crude Oil Production		Natural Gas Production	
		Volume	Percent of Nation	Volume	Percent of Nation
ONSHORE					
4 CAMPECHE	3			38	0.11
5 COAHUILA	20			196	0.47
7 CHIAPAS	93	34,010	3.73	4,496	12.68
19 NUEVO LEON	317	57	0.01	930	2.62
21 PUEBLA	9	118	0.01	5	0.01
24 SAN LUIS POTOSI	19	17	0.00		
27 TABASCO	841	239,679	26.26	16,617	46.86
28 TAMAULIPAS	774	5,323	0.58	1,940	5.47
30 VERACRUZ	2,360	43,286	4.74	1,830	5.16
OFFSHORE					
4 CAMPECHE	146	584,371	64.03	8,968	25.29
28 TAMAULIPAS	18	3,117	0.34	198	0.56
30 VERACRUZ	43	2,661	0.29	245	0.69
National Total	4,643	912,639		35,463	
Mean	516	114,080		4,433	
S.D.	734	193,055		5,362	
C.V.	142.24	169.23		120.96	
Minimum	9	17		5	
Maximum	2,403	584,371		16,617	

DEFINITION: Crude oil production is production in 1986 of crude oil and condensate in thousands of barrels. Natural gas production is the production in 1986 of natural gas in millions of cubic meters.

NOTE: In calculating the statistics for this table, the sample includes only the states that produced crude oil or natural gas in 1986. The onshore and offshore production is combined for each state.

SOURCE: 1986 PEMEX Anuario Estadistico.

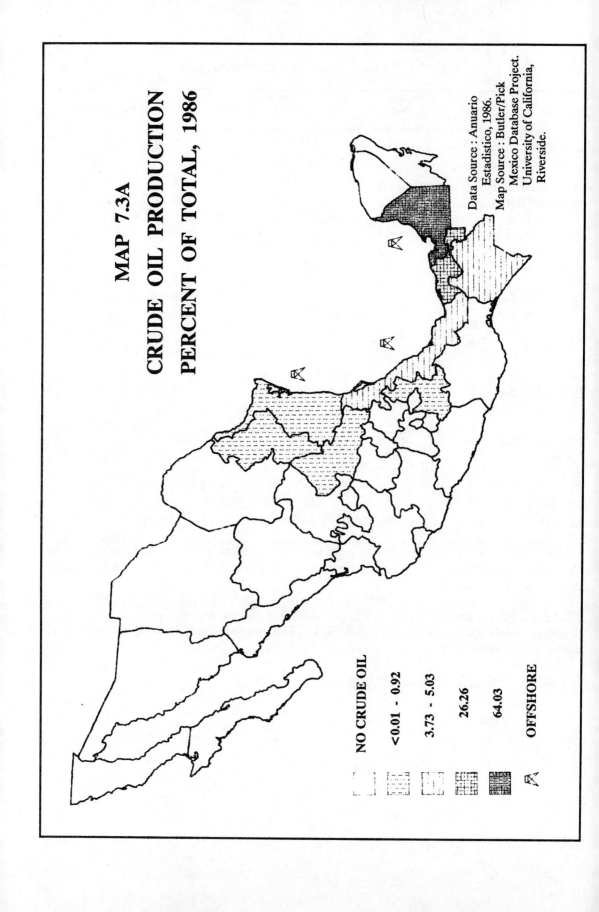

MAP 7.3A
CRUDE OIL PRODUCTION
PERCENT OF TOTAL, 1986

Data Source : Anuario
    Estadístico, 1986.
Map Source : Butler/Pick
    Mexico Database Project.
    University of California,
    Riverside.

NO CRUDE OIL

<0.01 - 0.92

3.73 - 5.03

26.26

64.03

OFFSHORE

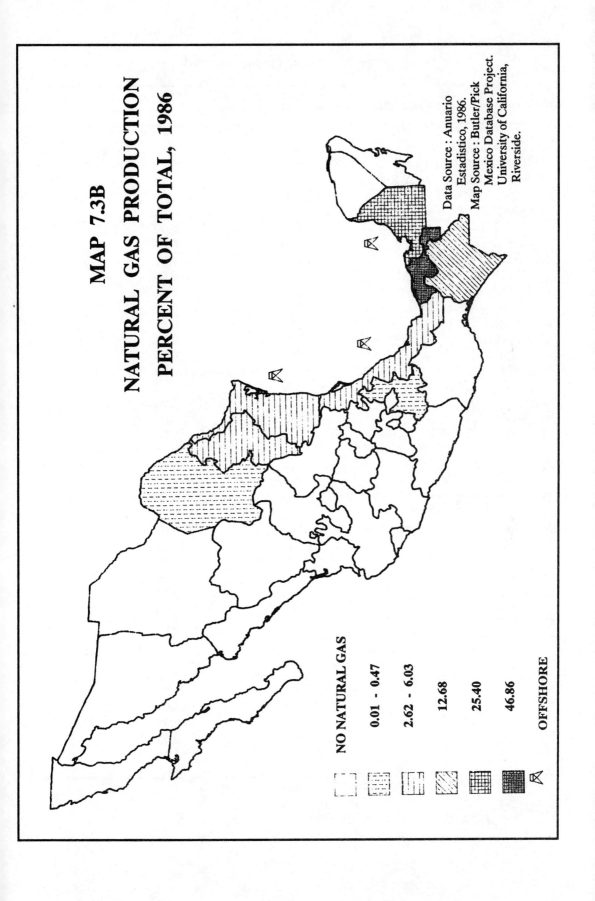

MAP 7.3B
NATURAL GAS PRODUCTION
PERCENT OF TOTAL, 1986

Data Source : Anuario
Estadistico, 1986.

Map Source : Butler/Pick
Mexico Database Project.
University of California,
Riverside.

NO NATURAL GAS

0.01 - 0.47

2.62 - 6.03

12.68

25.40

46.86

OFFSHORE

Table 7.7 Copper Production, 1985

No.	State	Tons of Copper Production	Percent of Nation
1	AGUASCALIENTES	0	0.00
2	BAJA CALIFORNIA	0	0.00
3	BAJA CALIFORNIA SUR	407	0.22
4	CAMPECHE	0	0.00
5	COAHUILA	1	0.00
6	COLIMA	0	0.00
7	CHIAPAS	0	0.00
8	CHIHUAHUA	9,094	4.93
9	DISTRITO FEDERAL	0	0.00
10	DURANGO	537	0.29
11	GUANAJUATO	101	0.06
12	GUERRERO	877	0.48
13	HIDALGO	1,508	0.82
14	JALISCO	456	0.25
15	MEXICO	1	0.00
16	MICHOACAN	280	0.15
17	MORELOS	6	0.00
18	NAYARIT	13	0.01
19	NUEVO LEON	0	0.00
20	OAXACA	12	0.01
21	PUEBLA	2	0.00
22	QUERETARO	550	0.30
23	QUINTANA ROO	0	0.00
24	SAN LUIS POTOSI	2,023	1.10
25	SINALOA	131	0.07
26	SONORA	155,688	84.40
27	TABASCO	0	0.00
28	TAMAULIPAS	0	0.00
29	TLAXCALA	0	0.00
30	VERACRUZ	0	0.00
31	YUCATAN	0	0.00
32	ZACATECAS	12,787	6.93

Total National Production		184,474	
Mean		5,765	3.12
S.D.		27,059	14.67
C.V.		469.38	469.38
Minimum		0	0.00
Maximum		155,688	84.40

DEFINITION: 1985 copper production figures are shown in tons.

SOURCE: 1986 Anuario Estadistico, Table 4.2.7.

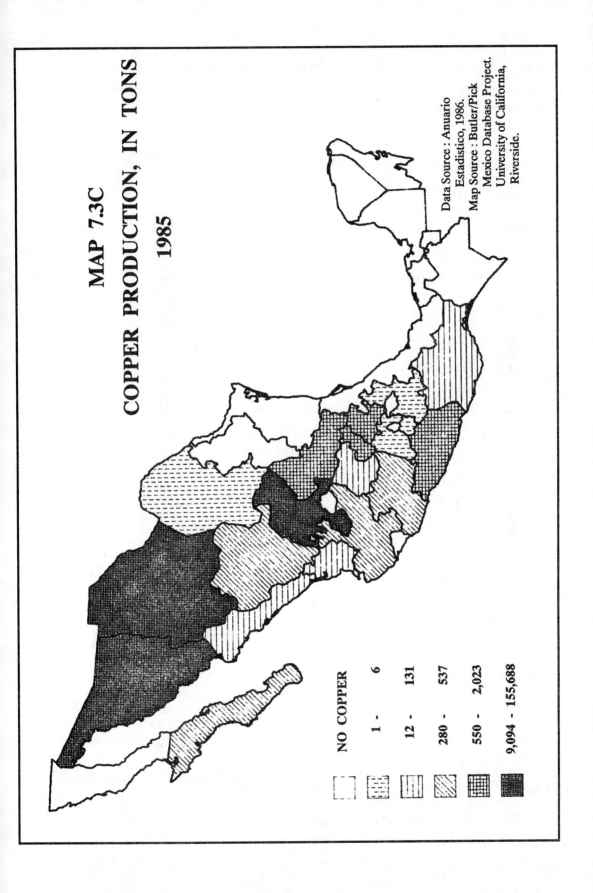

MAP 7.3C

COPPER PRODUCTION, IN TONS

1985

Data Source : Anuario
Estadistico, 1986.
Map Source : Butler/Pick
Mexico Database Project.
University of California,
Riverside.

NO COPPER

1 -   6

12 -   131

280 -   537

550 - 2,023

9,094 - 155,688

Table 7.8 Gold Production, in Kilograms, 1985

No.	State	Kilograms of Gold Production	Percent of Nation
1	AGUASCALIENTES	0	0.00
2	BAJA CALIFORNIA	0	0.00
3	BAJA CALIFORNIA SUR	26	0.33
4	CAMPECHE	0	0.00
5	COAHUILA	4	0.05
6	COLIMA	0	0.00
7	CHIAPAS	0	0.00
8	CHIHUAHUA	482	6.19
9	DISTRITO FEDERAL	0	0.00
10	DURANGO	1,867	23.96
11	GUANAJUATO	2,565	32.92
12	GUERRERO	150	1.93
13	HIDALGO	426	5.47
14	JALISCO	493	6.33
15	MEXICO	14	0.18
16	MICHOACAN	42	0.54
17	MORELOS	2	0.03
18	NAYARIT	50	0.64
19	NUEVO LEON	0	0.00
20	OAXACA	174	2.23
21	PUEBLA	2	0.03
22	QUERETARO	34	0.44
23	QUINTANA ROO	0	0.00
24	SAN LUIS POTOSI	209	2.68
25	SINALOA	244	3.13
26	SONORA	450	5.78
27	TABASCO	0	0.00
28	TAMAULIPAS	0	0.00
29	TLAXCALA	0	0.00
30	VERACRUZ	0	0.00
31	YUCATAN	0	0.00
32	ZACATECAS	557	7.15

Total National Production		7,791	
Mean		244	3.12
S.D.		545	6.99
C.V.		223.79	223.79
Minimum		0	0.00
Maximum		2,565	32.92

DEFINITION: 1985 gold production figures are shown in kilograms.

SOURCE: <u>1986 Anuario Estadistico</u>, Table 4.2.7.

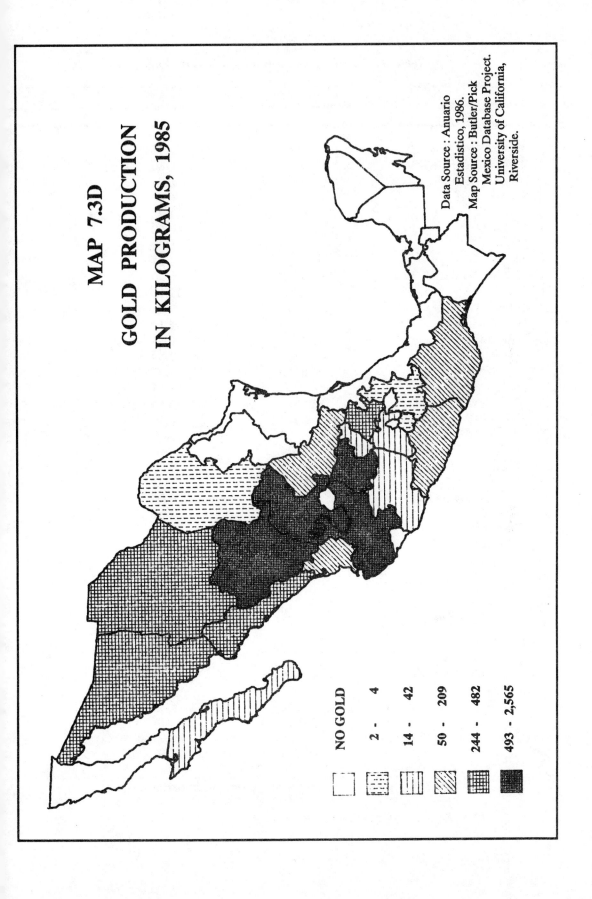

MAP 7.3D

GOLD PRODUCTION
IN KILOGRAMS, 1985

Data Source : Anuario
            Estadistico, 1986.
Map Source : Butler/Pick
            Mexico Database Project.
            University of California,
            Riverside.

NO GOLD

2 - 4

14 - 42

50 - 209

244 - 482

493 - 2,565

Table 7.9 Silver Production, in Kilograms, 1985

No.	State	Kilograms of Silver Production	Percent of Nation
1	AGUASCALIENTES	7,960	0.36
2	BAJA CALIFORNIA	0	0.00
3	BAJA CALIFORNIA SUR	919	0.04
4	CAMPECHE	0	0.00
5	COAHUILA	38,476	1.72
6	COLIMA	0	0.00
7	CHIAPAS	0	0.00
8	CHIHUAHUA	387,025	17.27
9	DISTRITO FEDERAL	0	0.00
10	DURANGO	250,587	11.18
11	GUANAJUATO	164,172	7.32
12	GUERRERO	93,099	4.15
13	HIDALGO	141,783	6.33
14	JALISCO	73,669	3.29
15	MEXICO	21,822	0.97
16	MICHOACAN	36,772	1.64
17	MORELOS	11,064	0.49
18	NAYARIT	10,717	0.48
19	NUEVO LEON	5	0.00
20	OAXACA	9,024	0.40
21	PUEBLA	26	0.00
22	QUERETARO	41,472	1.85
23	QUINTANA ROO	0	0.00
24	SAN LUIS POTOSI	96,257	4.29
25	SINALOA	28,068	1.25
26	SONORA	120,557	5.38
27	TABASCO	0	0.00
28	TAMAULIPAS	68	0.00
29	TLAXCALA	0	0.00
30	VERACRUZ	0	0.00
31	YUCATAN	0	0.00
32	ZACATECAS	708,124	31.59

Total National Production		2,241,666	
Mean		70,052	3.13
S.D.		142,318	6.35
C.V.		203.16	203.16
Minimum		0	0.00
Maximum		708,124	31.59

DEFINITION: 1985 silver production figures are shown in kilograms.

SOURCE: 1986 Anuario Estadistico, Table 4.2.7.

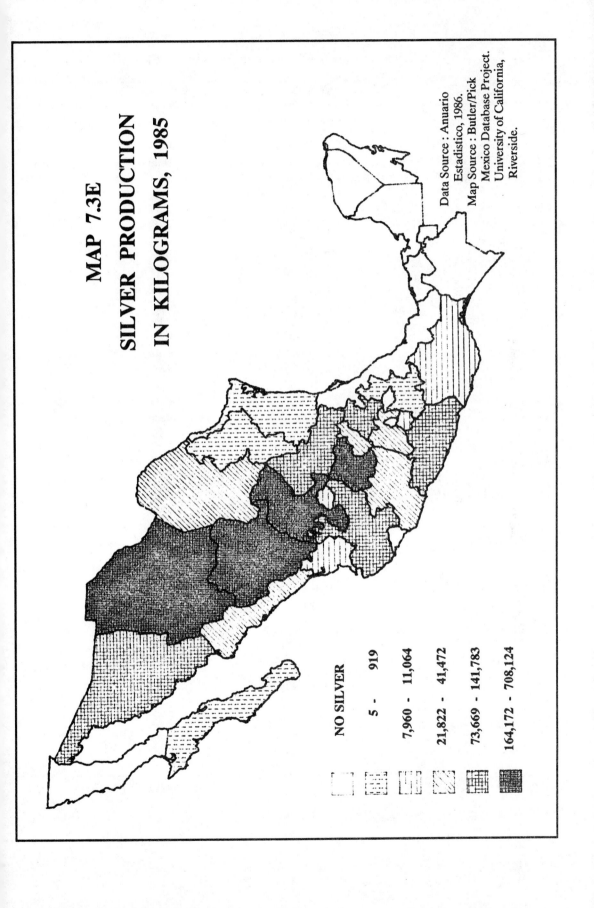

MAP 7.3E
SILVER PRODUCTION
IN KILOGRAMS, 1985

Data Source : Anuario
Estadistico, 1986.
Map Source : Butler/Pick
Mexico Database Project.
University of California,
Riverside.

NO SILVER

5 -   919

7,960 - 11,064

21,822 - 41,472

73,669 - 141,783

164,172 - 708,124

Table 7.10 Timber Production, in Pesos, 1984

No.	State	Value of Forestry Production	Percent of Nation
1	AGUASCALIENTES	23,201	0.04
2	BAJA CALIFORNIA	33,233	0.06
3	BAJA CALIFORNIA SUR	20,983	0.04
4	CAMPECHE	844,954	1.60
5	COAHUILA	71,882	0.14
6	COLIMA	11,913	0.02
7	CHIAPAS	2,428,313	4.60
8	CHIHUAHUA	12,062,927	22.85
9	DISTRITO FEDERAL	85,764	0.16
10	DURANGO	16,677,890	31.59
11	GUANAJUATO	90,541	0.17
12	GUERRERO	1,098,979	2.08
13	HIDALGO	495,170	0.94
14	JALISCO	4,179,762	7.92
15	MEXICO	2,607,079	4.94
16	MICHOACAN	5,541,842	10.50
17	MORELOS	6,573	0.01
18	NAYARIT	227,245	0.43
19	NUEVO LEON	306,471	0.58
20	OAXACA	1,793,789	3.40
21	PUEBLA	899,276	1.70
22	QUERETARO	42,832	0.08
23	QUINTANA ROO	824,638	1.56
24	SAN LUIS POTOSI	295,983	0.56
25	SINALOA	290,270	0.55
26	SONORA	457,719	0.87
27	TABASCO	85,642	0.16
28	TAMAULIPAS	556,836	1.06
29	TLAXCALA	252,503	0.48
30	VERACRUZ	383,108	0.73
31	YUCATAN	55,219	0.11
32	ZACATECAS	45,209	0.09

	Value	Percent
Total National Production	52,797,746	
Mean	1,649,930	3.13
S.D.	3,559,265	6.74
C.V.	215.72	215.72
Minimum	6,573	0.01
Maximum	16,677,890	31.59

DEFINITION: 1984 forestry production figures are shown in thousands of pesos.

SOURCE: 1986 Anuario Estadistico, Table 4.2.3.

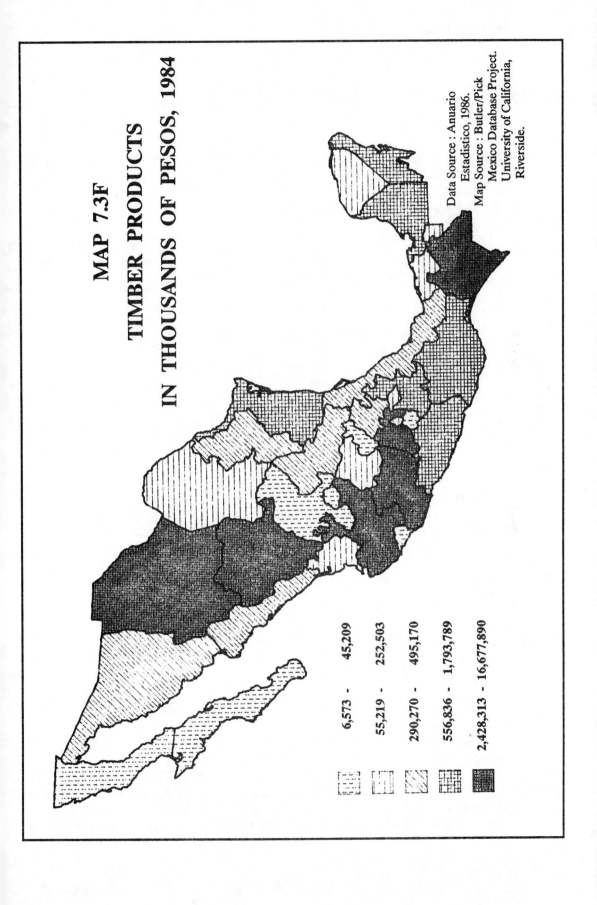

MAP 7.3F

TIMBER PRODUCTS
IN THOUSANDS OF PESOS, 1984

Data Source : Anuario
Estadistico, 1986.
Map Source : Butler/Pick
Mexico Database Project.
University of California,
Riverside.

6,573   -   45,209

55,219   -   252,503

290,270   -   495,170

556,836   -   1,793,789

2,428,313   -   16,677,890

Agricultural Production

Maize (Corn) Production, 1983

In 1983, Mexico produced 15.9 million tons of maize, with a value of 272.8 billion pesos, including unspecified. Maize is Mexico's leading agricultural product, constituting 30 percent of the nation's production of cultivated crops and fruits in 1983. As seen below, the production value and amount, cultivated area, and yield of maize increased from 1975 to 1983.

Mexican Corn Production, 1975-1983

Year	Value (millions of Pesos)	Production (tons)	Area (hectares)	Yield (ton/hectare)
1975	15,738	8,44 8,708	6,694,267	0.79
1979	30,031	8,448,795	5,568,831	0.83
1983	272,795	15,918,225	7,420,623	2.15

SOURCE:Anuarios Estadisticos, 1980 and 1986.

Mexico has consistently ranked among the top five nations in the world in maize production. On a state basis, the mean 1983 value of maize production is 8.5 billion pesos, with very large differences among states. Three states, Mexico, Jalisco, and Chiapas, accounted for 44 percent of maize production (see Table 7.11). Map 7.4A shows that maize production is highest in the west, central, and pacific south regions, plus Veracruz. These areas have the climate, especially necessary heat and humidity, and soils, favorable to corn production. Another important factor is the presence of high indigenous language population in the leading maize producing states, except in the west. The indigenous population, concentrated in the southern states (see Map 6.4A) has traditionally emphasized growing of corn, some of which has been marketed and other portions consumed domestically. Some of the domestically-consumed part is not included in federal statistics, so the southern states may be even more important as maize producers (Tamayo, 1985).

The southeast region has Mexico's lowest corn production. Even though it has high indigenous population, its climate and soil have been resistant to corn production. The northern states have generally lower, but inconsistent, maize production, compared to the south. Of these states, the north region has the greatest production, while the mostly arid Baja Peninsula has the least.

Frijol (Bean) Production, 1983

In 1983, the Mexican production of frijoles, or kidney beans, was 4.8 million tons. In monetary value, this constituted 4.0 percent of the national production of cultivated crops and fruits. Frijol is a major constituent of the Mexican diet. Many varieties are produced in Mexico. Although frijol is produced in nearly all states, tropical or temperate rainy climates favor production. The following table shows the national statistics on frijol production from 1975 to 1983.

The average state frijol production in 1983 is 1,241 million pesos, with a very high coefficient of variation of 183 (Table 7.12). The major frijol producing area consists of the states of Chihuahua, Durango, Zacatecas, Sinaloa, Nayarit, and Jalisco, which accounts for about two thirds of the nation's production. Other significant production is located in the remainder of the west region, the central region minus the Federal District and Tlaxcala, and the pacific south. The southeast has minor production, as does the borderlands, except for Coahuila (see Map 7.4B).

There is general correspondence in the geographic patterns of frijol production and maize production, except that frijol production is centered more to the north. The correspondence is explained partly by their similar climatic requirements and the fact that some Mexican frijol species grow in association with maize. There is not good correspondence between the distribution of frijol production and that of agricultural occupations (Map 8.2D). The reason is that the most important agricultural product, corn, and many other farm products are concentrated in the southern half of the nation.

Mexican Frijol Production, 1975-1983

Year	Value (million of Pesos)	Production (tons)	Cultivated Area (hectares)	Yield (ton/hectare)
1975	5,404	1,027,303	1,752,632	0.59
1979	6,054	641,287	1,040,910	0.62
1983	39,704	1,281,706	1,996,408	0.64

SOURCE: Anuarios Estadisticos, 1980 and 1986.

Fish Products, 1984

The amount of fish unloaded in tons measures fish production in a state, rather than consumption. The amount of fish produced varies from year to year depending on world and domestic markets, the fishing industry, and biological supply factors. The volume and value of fish products increased from 1975 to 1984, as seen in the following table.

Volume and Value of Fish Products, 1975-1984

Year	Value (millions of Pesos)	Production (tons)
1975	2,367	451,330
1980	20,299	1,058,566
1982	54,200	1,285,539
1984		992,704

SOURCE: Anuarios Estadisticos, 1980 and 1985.

The potential for future growth is great, as Mexico is endowed with vast potential for fishing, due to favorable ocean currents and broad continental shelves. Not surprisingly, fish production is concentrated in coastal states. Table 7.13 shows that three states, Baja California, Sonora, and Veracruz, stand out in importance, accounting for 55.4 percent of national production. Other important states are Baja California Sur, Sinaloa, and Campeche. By region, the northwest is the most important, having 55.5 percent of national production (see Map 7.4C). It is favored by abundant species, major presence of fish processing industries, and proximity to the U.S., for markets and investment (Tamayo, 1985). The second major area consists of most states bordering the Gulf of Mexico, especially Veracruz, Campeche, and Tamaulipas. This area is favored by the Gulf stream current and a wide continental shelf. The pacific south region has moderate fishing production. The interior of the nation has a small freshwater fish production.

Beef Production, in Thousands of Pesos, Average of 1976-80

Beef production is registered at the location of beef processing, and represents the concentration of the beef processing industry in Mexico, rather than beef grazing areas. For 1976-80, the average annual national value of beef production was 17.4 billion pesos. Beef production is one of the leading agricultural products of Mexico, although lower in value than maize production. By states beef production averaged 545 million pesos, with large differences among states (see Table 7.14). The most important beef production states are among the most populous, including the Federal District and Mexico, Jalisco, Nuevo Leon, and Veracruz. In addition, the border region, except Baja California, has moderate to high values, which is related to proximity to the United States, a major consumer of Mexican beef exports. The west and gulf regions also are major beef production regions. The southeast has a tropical climate largely unsuitable to beef production, and lack of population centers to attract beef processing plant, while the pacific south has low to moderate production.

The geographic pattern of beef production (Map 7.4D) compares substantially to that of total population in 1980 (Map 2.1A), except for the heightened beef production in the border region. This is due to the historical tendencies to locate beef processing plants near Mexican centers of population as well as in proxmity to the large U.S. market.

Table 7.11 Maize (Corn) Production, in Pesos, 1983

No.	State	Value of Maize Production	Percent of Nation
1	AGUASCALIENTES	1,437,181	0.53
2	BAJA CALIFORNIA	509,945	0.19
3	BAJA CALIFORNIA SUR	82,611	0.03
4	CAMPECHE	674,962	0.25
5	COAHUILA	898,980	0.33
6	COLIMA	1,716,273	0.63
7	CHIAPAS	35,151,220	12.98
8	CHIHUAHUA	6,768,288	2.50
9	DISTRITO FEDERAL	750,450	0.28
10	DURANGO	4,956,307	1.83
11	GUANAJUATO	13,812,698	5.10
12	GUERRERO	13,876,680	5.13
13	HIDALGO	9,303,157	3.44
14	JALISCO	43,746,482	16.16
15	MEXICO	39,497,622	14.59
16	MICHOACAN	18,844,544	6.96
17	MORELOS	1,122,452	0.42
18	NAYARIT	2,891,737	1.07
19	NUEVO LEON	1,991,472	0.74
20	OAXACA	8,453,583	3.12
21	PUEBLA	11,449,808	4.23
22	QUERETARO	3,334,232	1.23
23	QUINTANA ROO	392,640	0.15
24	SAN LUIS POTOSI	3,361,622	1.24
25	SINALOA	2,267,636	0.84
26	SONORA	1,580,887	0.58
27	TABASCO	1,674,870	0.62
28	TAMAULIPAS	11,848,657	4.38
29	TLAXCALA	3,390,816	1.25
30	VERACRUZ	13,577,860	5.01
31	YUCATAN	2,604,987	0.96
32	ZACATECAS	8,822,266	3.26

Total National Production	270,792,925	
Mean	8,462,279	3.12
S.D.	11,166,958	4.12
C.V.	131.96	131.96
Minimum	82,611	0.03
Maximum	43,746,482	16.16

DEFINITION: 1983 Maize production figures are shown in thousands of pesos. Maize for grain and feed are included.

SOURCE: 1986 Anuario Estadistico, Table 4.2.1.

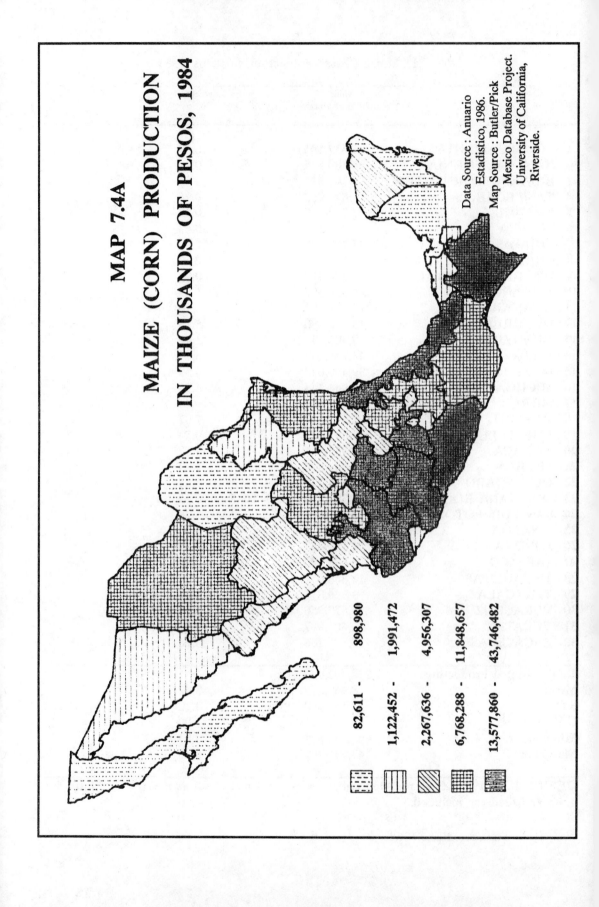

MAP 7.4A

MAIZE (CORN) PRODUCTION

IN THOUSANDS OF PESOS, 1984

Data Source : Anuario
Estadistico, 1986.

Map Source : Butler/Pick
Mexico Database Project.
University of California,
Riverside.

82,611 - 898,980

1,122,452 - 1,991,472

2,267,636 - 4,956,307

6,768,288 - 11,848,657

13,577,860 - 43,746,482

Table 7.12 Frijol (Bean) Production, in Pesos, 1983

No.	State	Value of Frijol Production	Percent of Nation
1	AGUASCALIENTES	244,157	0.62
2	BAJA CALIFORNIA	0	0.00
3	BAJA CALIFORNIA SUR	71,723	0.18
4	CAMPECHE	16,873	0.04
5	COAHUILA	165,284	0.42
6	COLIMA	0	0.00
7	CHIAPAS	1,654,626	4.17
8	CHIHUAHUA	2,196,777	5.53
9	DISTRITO FEDERAL	3,840	0.01
10	DURANGO	5,796,294	14.60
11	GUANAJUATO	2,155,688	5.43
12	GUERRERO	237,531	0.60
13	HIDALGO	1,389,801	3.50
14	JALISCO	1,892,265	4.77
15	MEXICO	740,914	1.87
16	MICHOACAN	607,360	1.53
17	MORELOS	172,995	0.44
18	NAYARIT	2,207,727	5.56
19	NUEVO LEON	141,577	0.36
20	OAXACA	584,584	1.47
21	PUEBLA	989,914	2.49
22	QUERETARO	524,725	1.32
23	QUINTANA ROO	105,097	0.27
24	SAN LUIS POTOSI	1,374,420	3.46
25	SINALOA	3,015,315	7.60
26	SONORA	0	0.00
27	TABASCO	0	0.00
28	TAMAULIPAS	563,559	1.42
29	TLAXCALA	0	0.00
30	VERACRUZ	630,629	1.59
31	YUCATAN	215,229	0.54
32	ZACATECAS	12,005,268	30.24

	Value of Frijol Production	Percent of Nation
Total National Production	39,704,172	
Mean	1,240,755	3.13
S.D.	2,274,345	5.73
C.V.	183.30	183.30
Minimum	0	0.00
Maximum	12,005,268	30.24

DEFINITION: 1983 frijol production figures are shown in thousands of pesos.

SOURCE: 1986 Anuario Estadistico, Table 4.2.1.

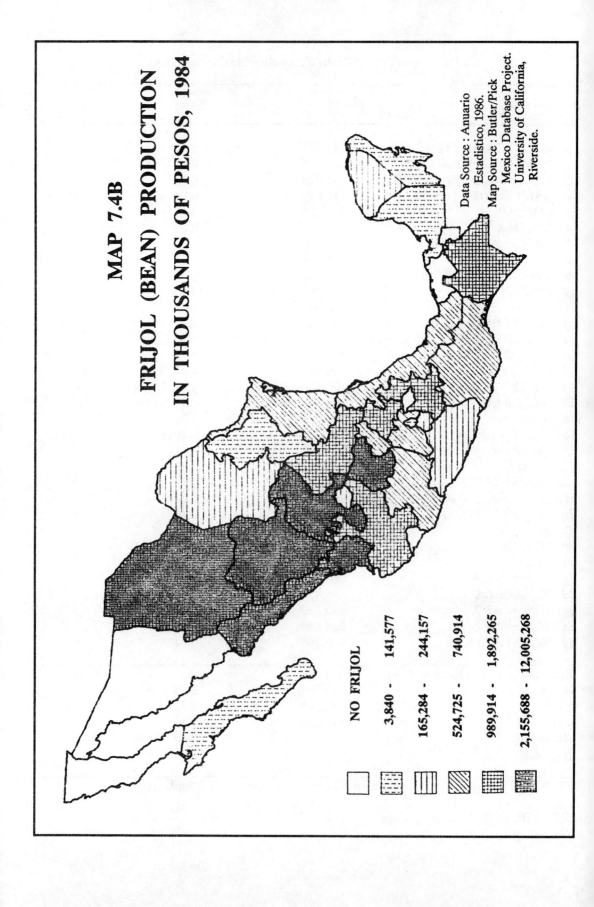

MAP 7.4B
FRIJOL (BEAN) PRODUCTION
IN THOUSANDS OF PESOS, 1984

Data Source : Anuario
Estadistico, 1986.

Map Source : Butler/Pick
Mexico Database Project.
University of California,
Riverside.

NO FRIJOL

3,840 - 141,577

165,284 - 244,157

524,725 - 740,914

989,914 - 1,892,265

2,155,688 - 12,005,268

Table 7.13 Fish Production, in Tons, 1984

No.	State	Tons of Fish Production	Percent of Nation
1	AGUASCALIENTES	1,015	0.10
2	BAJA CALIFORNIA	188,498	18.99
3	BAJA CALIFORNIA SUR	39,772	4.01
4	CAMPECHE	79,801	8.04
5	COAHUILA	1,627	0.16
6	COLIMA	7,055	0.71
7	CHIAPAS	19,095	1.92
8	CHIHUAHUA	587	0.06
9	DISTRITO FEDERAL	0	0.00
10	DURANGO	2,687	0.27
11	GUANAJUATO	2,502	0.25
12	GUERRERO	11,953	1.20
13	HIDALGO	3,777	0.38
14	JALISCO	17,099	1.72
15	MEXICO	4,955	0.50
16	MICHOACAN	25,005	2.52
17	MORELOS	773	0.08
18	NAYARIT	12,025	1.21
19	NUEVO LEON	501	0.05
20	OAXACA	11,471	1.16
21	PUEBLA	1,763	0.18
22	QUERETARO	339	0.03
23	QUINTANA ROO	3,118	0.31
24	SAN LUIS POTOSI	1,429	0.14
25	SINALOA	89,640	9.03
26	SONORA	221,002	22.26
27	TABASCO	31,635	3.19
28	TAMAULIPAS	40,102	4.04
29	TLAXCALA	572	0.06
30	VERACRUZ	140,712	14.18
31	YUCATAN	31,862	3.21
32	ZACATECAS	322	0.03
	Total National Production	992,694	
	Mean	31,022	3.13
	S.D.	54,432	5.48
	C.V.	175.46	175.46
	Minimum	0	0.00
	Maximum	221,002	22.26

DEFINITION: 1984 fish production figures are shown in tons. The figures refer to fish unloaded ashore.

SOURCE: 1986 Anuario Estadistico, Table 4.2.5.

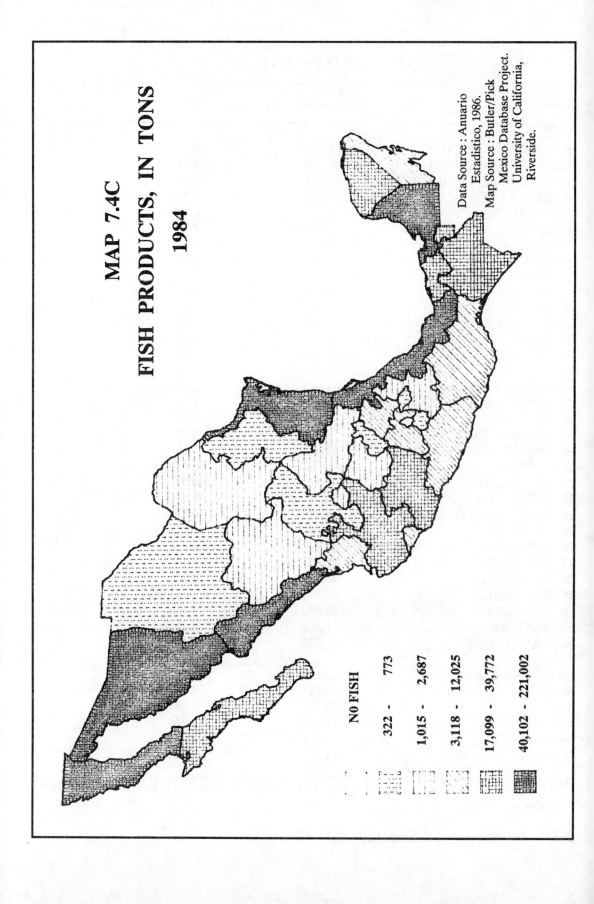

MAP 7.4C

FISH PRODUCTS, IN TONS

1984

Data Source : Anuario
Estadistico, 1986.

Map Source : Butler/Pick
Mexico Database Project.
University of California,
Riverside.

NO FISH

322 - 773

1,015 - 2,687

3,118 - 12,025

17,099 - 39,772

40,102 - 221,002

Table 7.14 Beef Production, in Pesos, Average of 1976-80

No.	State	Average Value of Beef Production	Percent of Nation
1	AGUASCALIENTES	204,718	1.17
2	BAJA CALIFORNIA	483,127	2.77
3	BAJA CALIFORNIA SUR	117,856	0.68
4	CAMPECHE	125,146	0.72
5	COAHUILA	612,952	3.52
6	COLIMA	147,558	0.85
7	CHIAPAS	508,730	2.92
8	CHIHUAHUA	774,525	4.44
9	DISTRITO FEDERAL	1,298,304	7.45
10	DURANGO	364,484	2.09
11	GUANAJUATO	739,369	4.24
12	GUERRERO	403,656	2.32
13	HIDALGO	280,827	1.61
14	JALISCO	1,301,314	7.46
15	MEXICO	2,416,572	13.86
16	MICHOACAN	609,170	3.49
17	MORELOS	171,455	0.98
18	NAYARIT	216,499	1.24
19	NUEVO LEON	908,729	5.21
20	OAXACA	245,993	1.41
21	PUEBLA	431,078	2.47
22	QUERETARO	141,526	0.81
23	QUINTANA ROO	48,012	0.28
24	SAN LUIS POTOSI	318,378	1.83
25	SINALOA	671,600	3.85
26	SONORA	726,940	4.17
27	TABASCO	608,981	3.49
28	TAMAULIPAS	804,076	4.61
29	TLAXCALA	49,793	0.29
30	VERACRUZ	1,269,349	7.28
31	YUCATAN	294,566	1.69
32	ZACATECAS	141,228	0.81

National Total		17,436,511	
Mean		544,891	3.13
S.D.		486,079	2.79
C.V.		89.21	89.19
Minimum		48,012	0.28
Maximum		2,416,572	13.86

DEFINITION: The average value of beef production from 1976 to 1980 in thousands of pesos.

SOURCE: 1980 Anuario Estadistico, Table 4.2.1.

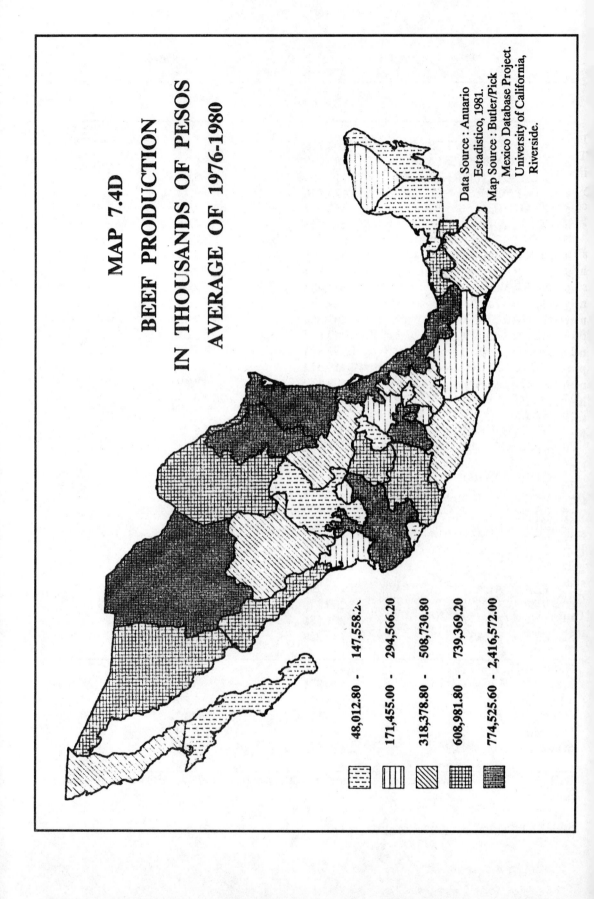

MAP 7.4D
BEEF PRODUCTION
IN THOUSANDS OF PESOS
AVERAGE OF 1976-1980

Data Source : Anuario
Estadistico, 1981.
Map Source : Butler/Pick
Mexico Database Project.
University of California,
Riverside.

48,012.80 - 147,558.20
171,455.00 - 294,566.20
318,378.80 - 508,730.80
608,981.80 - 739,369.20
774,525.60 - 2,416,572.00

Energy Production, 1985

Installed electrical energy capacity is measured in megawatts, or millions of watts. As seen in Figure 7.3 and Table 7.15, national energy capacity has grown very rapidly over the past three decades. This is shown by the growth of Mexico's installed electrical generation capacity from 3,048 megawatts in 1960 to 20,794 megawatts in 1985, which implies an compounded growth rate of 7.7 percent per year. Current capacity is one third hydroelectric and two thirds thermoelectric, including internal combustion, gas, and geothermal plants. Present electricity is almost entirely produced by the Federal Electrical Commission (La Comision Federal de Electricidad).

Average state energy capacity is 646 megawatts, but there are very large state differences. Three states account for about a third of the nation's capacity: Chiapas, with 3,509 megawatts of hydroelectric capacity, and Hidalgo and Mexico, which are largely thermoelectric. The latter two states are the most important suppliers of energy to Mexico City. The border region accounts for nearly another third of the national capacity, with each border state having about a thousand megawatts of capacity. This large capacity serves the needs of the highly urbanized and manufacturing-oriented border region (see Maps 2.6A and 7.2D). It should be noted that the Baja California capacity is over half geothermal. Its geothermal plants constitute the second largest geothermal producing site in North America and one of the largest worldwide (Butler and Pick, 1982). Other major energy producing states are Colima, with a 1,200 megawatt thermal capacity, and Guerrero, having 1,094 megawatts of almost entirely hyroelectric capacity. The Colima capacity is a major source of energy for the large city of Guadalajara in neighboring Jalisco, as well as for Colima's rapidly growing population and tourism industry.

In the first half of the 80s, growth in Mexican energy capacity was most rapid in Colima, and the border states of Baja California, Coahuila and Baja California Sur excluding the minor capacity of Zacatecas. States with significant existing production which experienced no capacity growth include Chiapas, Mexico, Guanajuato, Puebla, and Veracruz.

In 1985, per capita energy capacity for the nation was 0.28 kilowatts of installed capacity per person. This is much lower than the comparable 1985 figure of 3.00 for the United States (C.I.A., 1987; Population Reference Bureau, 1987). As seen in Table 7.16, states with the highest per capita energy capacity were Chiapas and Colima, both of which grid most of their production out of state. Other states with high per capita capacity include the four border states of Baja California, Sonora, Coahuila, and Tamaulipas, as well as Sinaloa and Aguascalientes. At the low extreme are the Federal District and Jalisco, with 0.01 and 0.04 kilowatts of capacity per person (see Map 7.5). These major metropolitan states are dependent on neighboring states for energy supply.

240

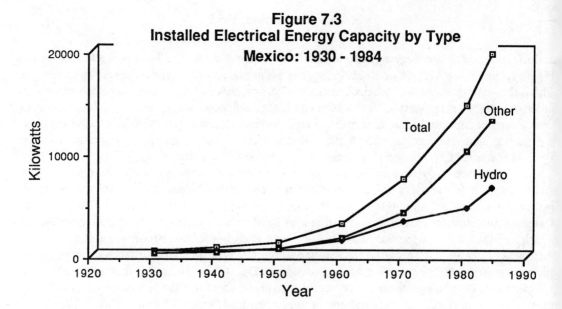

Figure 7.3
Installed Electrical Energy Capacity by Type
Mexico: 1930 - 1984

SOURCE: Estadisticas Historicas (1986).

Table 7.15 Installed Electrical Energy Capacity, by Type, 1930-1984, in Kilowatts

Total Capacity	Public	Class of Service Private	Mixed	Type of Plant Hydro	Other	Number of Plants
18,000				14,000	4,000	
35,000				30,000	5,000	
99,000				99,000		
192,000				192,000		
411,000				304,000	107,000	
681,000	479,000	148,000	54,000	389,000	292,000	
720,000	519,000	146,000	55,000	428,000	292,000	
1,234,000	916,000	223,000	46,000	607,000	628,000	
1,929,527	1,458,478	364,913	106,136	922,252	1,007,275	2,321
2,069,411	1,571,227	395,467	102,717	978,808	1,090,603	2,319
2,270,192	1,726,713	442,076	101,403	1,117,740	1,152,452	2,384
2,560,253	1,953,357	501,805	105,091	1,183,689	1,376,564	2,724
2,879,069	2,192,718	576,129	110,220	1,332,547	1,596,520	2,752
3,048,113	2,320,911	561,865	175,337	1,357,038	1,691,075	2,766
3,251,648	2,419,052	674,650	157,946	1,370,059	1,881,589	2,776
3,704,428	2,761,024	752,724	190,680	1,576,527	2,127,901	1,279
4,305,019	2,399,632	831,007	174,380	1,598,421	2,706,598	1,355
4,815,430	3,793,818	845,482	176,130	1,865,261	2,950,169	1,436
5,238,188	4,174,717	887,341	176,130	2,214,322	3,023,866	1,493
5,613,976	4,537,824	900,022	176,130	2,541,480	3,072,496	1,551
5,796,312	4,655,543	962,639	176,130	2,562,409	3,231,903	1,786
6,071,134	4,863,939	1,031,765	176,130	2,612,848	3,458,286	2,194
6,987,246	5,704,593	1,107,223	175,430	3,333,159	3,654,087	2,373
7,413,618	6,028,511	1,209,677	175,430	3,326,518	4,087,100	2,487
7,873,793	6,468,519	1,235,344	169,930	3,320,227	4,553,566	2,577
8,501,935	6,927,298	1,460,382	114,255	3,321,882	5,180,053	2,665
9,365,383	7,643,534	1,607,594	114,255	3,601,467	5,763,916	2,556
9,647,480	8,269,402	1,215,813	162,265	3,600,830	6,046,650	2,544
11,326,204	9,946,695	1,217,226	162,283	4,120,262	7,205,942	2,643
12,259,842	10,742,414	1,355,163	162,265	4,108,627	8,151,215	2,870
13,954,183	12,281,364	1,545,007	127,812	4,796,471	9,157,712	3,446
16,541,961	14,501,639	1,917,262	123,060	5,297,661	11,244,300	3,753
16,968,182	14,885,772	1,959,350	123,060	5,291,033	11,677,149	3,928
14,625,000	14,625,000			4,541,000	10,084,000	
17,396,000	17,396,000			4,723,000	12,673,000	
18,390,000	18,390,000			5,225,000	13,165,000	
19,004,000	19,004,000			6,532,000	12,472,000	
19,694,000	19,694,000			6,532,000	13,162,000	

TE: The "other" catagory includes thermal and other generating plants including "plantas de
ɔr" (1955-1966), "plantas de combustion interna" (1965-1976), and from 1965-1976 "plantas de
y geotermica."

JRCE: Estadisticas Historicas (1986).

Table 7.16 Installed Electrical Energy Capacity, in Megawatts

No.	State	1979 Installed Electrical Energy Capacity	1985 Installed Electrical Energy Capacity				
			Thermo-electric	Hydro-electric	Total Capacity	Percent of Nation	Per Capita
1	AGUASCALIENTES	2					
2	BAJA CALIFORNIA	617	938	0	938	5.00	0.0007
3	BAJA CALIFORNIA SUR	114	192	0	192	1.00	0.0008
4	CAMPECHE	273	181	0	181	1.00	0.0004
5	COAHUILA	394	1,066	0	1,066	5.00	0.0006
6	COLIMA	33	1,200	0	1,200	6.00	0.0031
7	CHIAPAS	2,051	0	3,509	3,509	17.00	0.0015
8	CHIHUAHUA	388	954	0	954	5.00	0.0004
9	DISTRITO FEDERAL	369	148	0	148	1.00	0.0000
10	DURANGO	559	415	0	415	2.00	0.0003
11	GUANAJUATO	1,015	907	0	907	4.00	0.0003
12	GUERRERO	1,124	56	1,038	1,094	5.00	0.0005
13	HIDALGO	1,226	1,782	4	1,786	9.00	0.0010
14	JALISCO	334	63	154	217	1.00	0.0000
15	MEXICO	1,807	1,180	317	1,497	7.00	0.0002
16	MICHOACAN	582	25	457	482	2.00	0.0001
17	MORELOS	22	0	0	0	0.00	0.0000
18	NAYARIT	12	2	2	4	0.00	0.0000
19	NUEVO LEON	1,072	1,078	0	1,078	5.00	0.0004
20	OAXACA	275	0	156	156	1.00	0.0001
21	PUEBLA	552	38	422	460	2.00	0.0001
22	QUERETARO	20	77	2	79	0.00	0.0001
23	QUINTANA ROO	66	29	0	29	0.00	0.0001
24	SAN LUIS POTOSI	88	801	20	821	4.00	0.0004
25	SINALOA	629	1,030	163	1,193	6.00	0.0006
26	SONORA	680	0	164	164	1.00	0.0001
27	TABASCO	17	0	0	0	0.00	0.0000
28	TAMAULIPAS	1,148	1,196	31	1,227	6.00	0.0006
29	TLAXCALA	5	0	0	0	0.00	0.0000
30	VERACRUZ	1,355	497	91	588	3.00	0.0001
31	YUCATAN	90	261	0	261	1.00	0.0002
32	ZACATECAS	32	15	2	17	0.00	0.0000
	National Total	16,951	14,131	6,532	20,663		
	Mean	530	442	204	646	3.13	0.0005
	S.D.	546	513	629	724	3.50	0.0006
	C.V.	103.01	116.07	308.09	112.14	99.68	135.20
	Minimum	2	0	0	4	0.00	0.0000
	Maximum	2051	1782	3509	3509	17.00	0.0031

DEFINITION: Electraical energy capacity values are shown in megawatts. The per capita column is the ratio of the total megawattage in 1985 to total population 1985.

NOTE: National totals exclude mobile plants.

SOURCE: 1980 Anuario Estadistico, Table 2.2.5; 1986 Anuario Estadistico, Table 2.2.5.

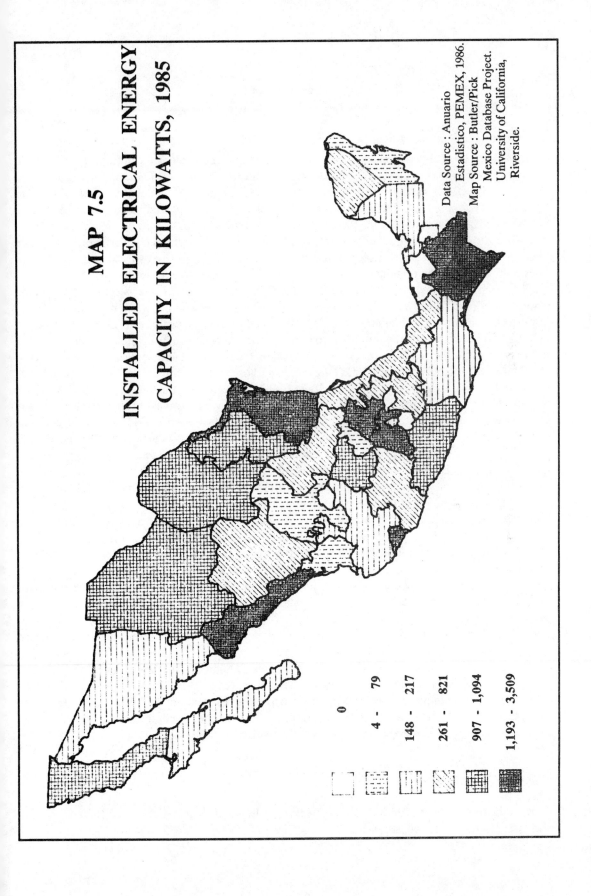

MAP 7.5

INSTALLED ELECTRICAL ENERGY

CAPACITY IN KILOWATTS, 1985

Data Source : Anuario
Estadistico, PEMEX, 1986.
Map Source : Butler/Pick
Mexico Database Project.
University of California,
Riverside.

0

4 - 79

148 - 217

261 - 821

907 - 1,094

1,193 - 3,509

Corporations

Value of S.A.C.V.s, 1985

In Mexico, the U.S. concept of a corporation is roughly equivalent to an S.A.C.V. (Sociedad Anonima Constituida). The value of S.A.C.V.s was adjusted for the devaluation of the peso versus the U.S. dollar, which is shown for the period 1937-1988 in Figure 7.1. Values are expressed in terms of constant 1980 pesos (see discussion at start of this chapter). The total adjusted value of S.A.C.V.s in 1985 was 81.6 billion pesos, while the unadjusted value was 913.3 billion pesos. While these values may appear low relative to the United States, in Mexico there is substantial government ownership of enterprises in certain industries, and there are other forms of private ownership in Mexico besides S.A.C.V.s. For the remainder of this discussion, values refer to adjusted values.

The mean state value of S.A.C.V.s in 1985 was 2.55 billion pesos. There is very large variation among states (see Table 7.17). There is concentration of private capital in a few urban centers. For instance, 61 percent of the value of S.A.C.V.s is located in three states, Nuevo Leon, Mexico, and Federal District, reflecting the dominant role in finance and big business of the metropolitan areas of Monterrey and Mexico City. In terms of total value, the next most important states are Coahuila, Baja California, and Chihuahua. Like Nuevo Leon, these states are prosperous ones, adjacent to the large U.S. marketplace and economy. Baja California contains Tijuana and Mexicali, Mexico's ninth and fourteenth largest cities in 1980. Tijuana especially is a business center in trade with the U.S. All three of these states are important in manufacturing (see Map 7.2D). Chihuahua and Baja California are the most important states for the maquiladora industry, accounting for nearly two thirds of maquila employment in 1986 (Stoddard, 1987). A portion of the ownership of the maquiladora industry is represented by Mexican S.A.C.V.'s. Map 7.6A portrays the per capita value of S.A.C.V.s in adjusted pesos. Scaling for projected 1985 population, the mean value for the nation implies an average of 962 pesos in S.A.C.V. value per person. By state, by far the most important is Nuevo Leon, with a per capita value of 10,941 pesos. Next in importance are Baja California and Coahuila, indicating the impact of border location on businesses engaged in manufacturing and trade with the U.S. These are followed by Mexico and Chihuahua, for reasons alluded to earlier, as well as Yucatan and Quintana Roo. Yucatan's population is nearly half in Merida, Mexico's 11th largest city and the major business center in the southeast. On the other hand, Quintana Roo is a small, rapid-growth state, with increasing business opportunities, especially tourism. The region with the lowest per capita corporate value is the pacific south. This is Mexico's most agricultural and lowest income region. The central flank of the country is generally low to moderate in value, with the exceptions of Mexico, Aguascalientes, and Queretaro.

There is a very close relationship between the value and number of corporations (see Map 7.6B). In comparing the value of corporations with gross state revenue (Map 7.7A), there are substantial differences. For example, Jalisco, and the southern states of Oaxaca and Chiapas are much higher in gross state revenue than in value of corporations. On the other hand, the border region is more important for corporate value than for gross state revenue.

Number of S.A.C.V. s, 1985

In 1985, there were 11,731 S.A.C.V.s in Mexico. The number of S.A.C.V.s per 1000 population varies somewhat in Mexico, as revealed by a coefficient of variation of 75. The average value is 0.17, which implies one corporation for every six thousand persons. The highest number of S.A.C.V.s/1,000 in the Federal District is not surprising given the capital's leadership in industry and commerce (see Table 7.18). Other states with high values for this variable are Nuevo Leon, containing the large metropolis of Monterrey; Baja California, with the cities of Tijuana and Mexicali; Baja California Sur, an economic growth area in the 80s; and Aguascalientes. The state lowest in S.A.C.V.s/1,000 is Chiapas, with a value of 0.019, which indicates one corporation per 54,000 persons. This is expected from a poor, rural state. The next lowest state, Tamaulipas, with a value of 0.028, is surprising, since it is a border state of medium urbanization and income. Other low states include Veracruz, Michoacan, Tlaxcala, and Oaxaca, the latter two rural states with among the lowest income levels in Mexico.

Map 7.6B illustrates that the number of S.A.C.V.s does not have a coherent regional pattern. Among major regions, only the northwest is consistent, with high values. This is due in part to its urbanization and its nearness to international trade and commerce with the U.S. The metropolitan nature of S.A.C.V.s is reflected in a highly significant and positive correlation with 1980 urbanization. Likewise, there are highly significant relationships with urban-related variables, such as higher education, telephones/capita, and the percentage of the labor force in agriculture. The variable has significant direct relationships with other economic variables such as gross state product per capita. The variable rarely has been utilized in academic studies on Mexico.

Table 7.17 Value of Corporations, Per Capita, 1985

No.	State	Corporation Value 1980	Corporation Value Per Capita 1980	Unadjusted Corporation Value 1985	Unadjusted Corporation Value Per Capita 1985	Adjusted Corporation Value 1985	Adjusted Corporation Value Per Capita 1985
1	AGUASCALIENTES	287,189	0.5529	627,126	1.0666	56,033	0.0953
2	BAJA CALIFORNIA	875,472	0.7433	3,373,868	2.5134	301,455	0.2246
3	BAJA CALIFORNIA SUR	133,700	0.6215	240,342	0.9837	21,474	0.0879
4	CAMPECHE	107,100	0.2547	221,319	0.4639	19,774	0.0414
5	COAHUILA	857,679	0.5508	3,841,416	2.1721	343,230	0.1941
6	COLIMA	130,788	0.3777	188,268	0.4791	16,821	0.0428
7	CHIAPAS	703,526	0.3375	212,686	0.0900	19,003	0.0080
8	CHIHUAHUA	471,084	0.2349	2,657,447	1.1645	237,442	0.1040
9	DISTRITO FEDERAL	11,141,300	1.2616	6,990,097	0.6920	624,565	0.0618
10	DURANGO	396,958	0.3357	770,774	0.5764	68,868	0.0515
11	GUANAJUATO	1,140,907	0.3795	2,516,478	0.7396	224,847	0.0661
12	GUERRERO	193,620	0.0918	225,671	0.0945	20,163	0.0084
13	HIDALGO	259,380	0.1676	460,003	0.2625	41,101	0.0235
14	JALISCO	2,242,716	0.5130	2,338,312	0.4714	208,928	0.0421
15	MEXICO	1,312,140	0.1735	11,354,094	1.3236	1,014,488	0.1183
16	MICHOACAN	165,890	0.0578	460,882	0.1418	41,179	0.0127
17	MORELOS	177,495	0.1874	815,136	0.7579	72,832	0.0677
18	NAYARIT	81,250	0.1119	434,225	0.5284	38,798	0.0472
19	NUEVO LEON	7,080,474	2.8175	31,276,533	10.9413	2,794,558	0.9776
20	OAXACA	900,995	0.3803	467,314	0.1739	41,754	0.0155
21	PUEBLA	883,483	0.2639	1,529,994	0.4035	136,704	0.0361
22	QUERETARO	405,934	0.5489	914,725	1.0947	81,730	0.0978
23	QUINTANA ROO	76,050	0.3365	309,929	1.2116	27,692	0.1083
24	SAN LUIS POTOSI	301,179	0.1799	1,178,829	0.6223	105,328	0.0556
25	SINALOA	554,600	0.2998	1,751,448	0.8355	156,491	0.0746
26	SONORA	681,660	0.4503	1,688,730	0.9811	150,888	0.0877
27	TABASCO	433,205	0.4075	795,285	0.6614	71,058	0.0591
28	TAMAULIPAS	92,285	0.0480	296,586	0.1355	26,499	0.0121
29	TLAXCALA	39,600	0.0711	4,000	0.0063	357	0.0006
30	VERACRUZ	1,303,523	0.2419	1,577,195	0.2576	140,922	0.0230
31	YUCATAN	1,801,109	1.6932	1,732,366	1.4300	154,786	0.1278
32	ZACATECAS	244,511	0.2151	382,728	0.2984	34,196	0.0267
	National Total	35,476,802		81,633,806		7,293,964	
	Mean	1,108,650	0.4658	2,551,056	1.0492	227,936	0.0937
	S.D.	21,190,076	0.5375	5,624,742	1.8648	502,571	0.1666
	C.V.	197.54	115.39	220.49	177.74	220.49	177.74
	Minimum	39,600	0.0480	4,000	0.0063	357	0.0006
	Maximum	11,141,300	2.8175	31,276,533	10.9413	2,794,558	0.9776

DEFINITION: Values shown are in thousands of Pesos. The ratios are the total value of corporations to the total population of the corresponding year.

SOURCE: 1980 Anuario Estadistico, Table 4.5.1; 1986 Anuario Estadistico, Table 4.7.1.

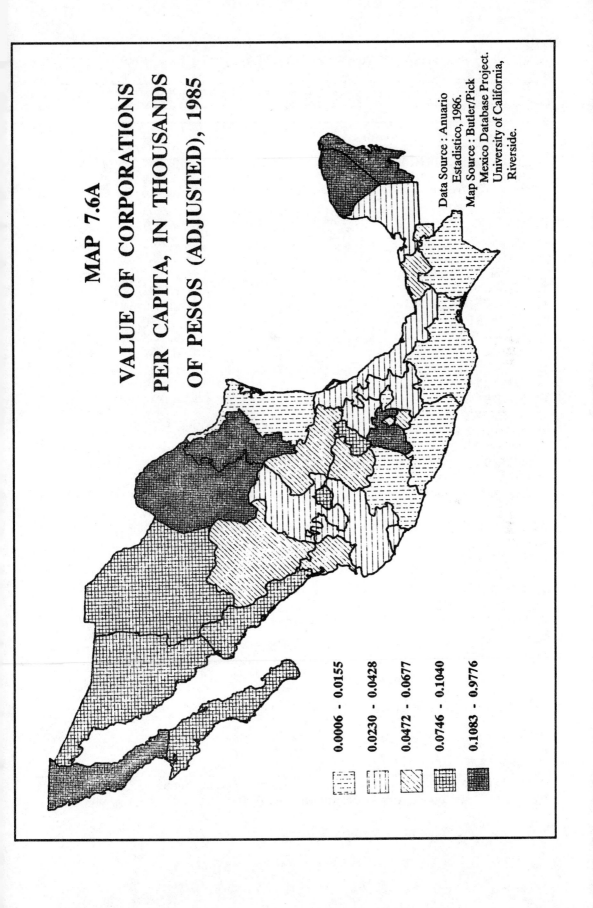

MAP 7.6A
VALUE OF CORPORATIONS
PER CAPITA, IN THOUSANDS
OF PESOS (ADJUSTED), 1985

Data Source : Anuario
Estadistico, 1986.
Map Source : Butler/Pick
Mexico Database Project.
University of California,
Riverside.

0.0006 - 0.0155
0.0230 - 0.0428
0.0472 - 0.0677
0.0746 - 0.1040
0.1083 - 0.9776

Table 7.18 Number of Corporations, Per Capita, 1985

No.	State	Number of Corporations	Number of Corporations Per 1,000 Persons
1	AGUASCALIENTES	200	0.3402
2	BAJA CALIFORNIA	758	0.5647
3	BAJA CALIFORNIA SUR	84	0.3438
4	CAMPECHE	41	0.0859
5	COAHUILA	425	0.2403
6	COLIMA	71	0.1807
7	CHIAPAS	44	0.0186
8	CHIHUAHUA	453	0.1985
9	DISTRITO FEDERAL	2,089	0.2068
10	DURANGO	158	0.1181
11	GUANAJUATO	684	0.2010
12	GUERRERO	117	0.0490
13	HIDALGO	99	0.0565
14	JALISCO	813	0.1639
15	MEXICO	1,222	0.1425
16	MICHOACAN	134	0.0412
17	MORELOS	165	0.1534
18	NAYARIT	60	0.0730
19	NUEVO LEON	1,256	0.4394
20	OAXACA	122	0.0454
21	PUEBLA	538	0.1419
22	QUERETARO	225	0.2693
23	QUINTANA ROO	42	0.1642
24	SAN LUIS POTOSI	261	0.1378
25	SINALOA	340	0.1622
26	SONORA	455	0.2643
27	TABASCO	181	0.1505
28	TAMAULIPAS	62	0.0283
29	TLAXCALA	34	0.0540
30	VERACRUZ	261	0.0426
31	YUCATAN	275	0.2270
32	ZACATECAS	62	0.0483
	National Total	11,731	
	Mean	367	0.1673
	S.D.	444	0.1234
	C.V.	121.12	73.76
	Minimum	34	0.0186
	Maximum	2,089	0.5647

DEFINITION: The number of corporations per capita is the number of S.A.C.V.s registered 1985 to the total population 1985 multiplied by 0.001.

SOURCE: 1986 Anuario Estadistico, Table 4.7.1.

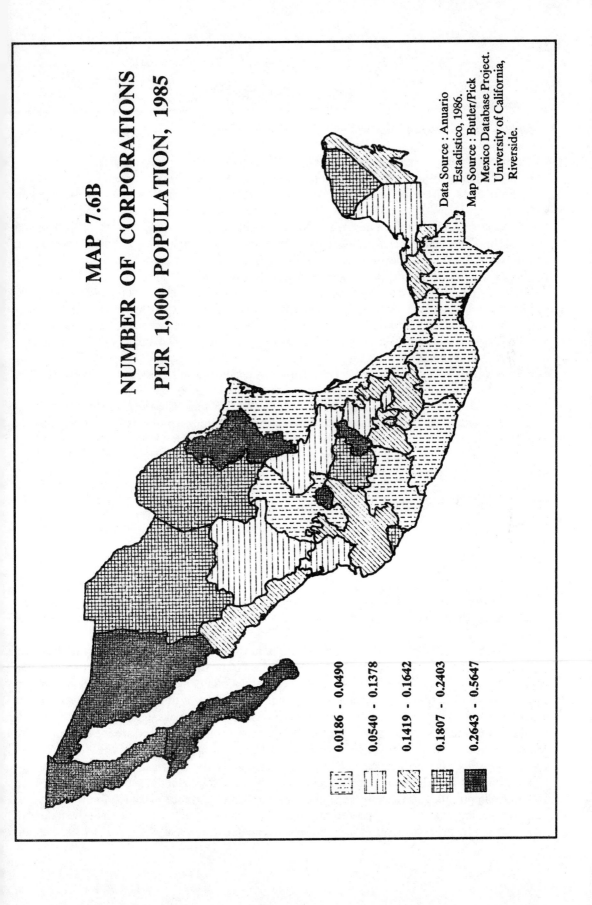

MAP 7.6B

NUMBER OF CORPORATIONS

PER 1,000 POPULATION, 1985

Data Source : Anuario
Estadistico, 1986.

Map Source : Butler/Pick
Mexico Database Project.
University of California,
Riverside.

0.0186 - 0.0490

0.0540 - 0.1378

0.1419 - 0.1642

0.1807 - 0.2403

0.2643 - 0.5647

Economic Development

Gross State Revenue, Per Capita, 1984

The total revenues for state governments in 1984 was 1.7 trillion current pesos. This amount grew from 248 billion pesos in 1980. The state revenues in 1984 represent 6.0 percent of the gross national product of 28.4 trillion pesos. The average gross state revenue in 1984 was 54.6 billion pesos, with a very large variation among states. States with revenues over 100 billion pesos included the Federal District with 427 billion pesos, and Nuevo Leon, Mexico, and Jalisco, with 140-170 billion pesos each. These states include the country's three major metropolitan areas and are among the most urbanized. At the low extreme in gross state revenue are Baja California Sur, Quintana Roo, and Nayarit, which are among the least populous states (see Table 7.19).

Shown on the Map 7.7A is gross state revenue per capita, adjusted in constant 1980 pesos as explained in the chapter introduction. The mean adjusted value is 3.14, with a high coefficient of variation of 67. There is a six-fold difference between the highest gross state revenue per capita in Tabasco and the lowest in Hidalgo. The extremely high level for Tabasco may be due to state revenue from direct and indirect benefits of the oil development centered in Tabasco (Lezama, 1987). On a per capita basis, high values are present in the prosperous northwestern states of Baja California, Baja California Sur and Sonora, in the large urban states of Nuevo Leon, Jalisco, and the Federal District, and in the southern and southeastern states of Oaxaca, Chiapas, Tabasco, Campeche, and Quintana Roo. High values in the southern states indicate that state governments are sizeable relative to population, even though personal income in the southern states tends to be very low (see Map 8.4A). Campeche's high value for gross state revenues per capita is due to its highly urban nature and above average per capita income, as well as to governmental revenues from oil development. States with the lowest state revenues per capita are located in various regions and include Hidalgo, Michoacan, San Luis Potosi, and Puebla. These states were slowly growing ones in percentage terms in the 1970s.

Total Value of New Mortgages, 1980

In 1980, the total value of new mortgages issued nationally was 72.3 billion pesos. This was equal to 1.7 percent of the 1980 gross national product of 4.28 trillion pesos. The state average value of mortgages was 2.3 billion pesos, with wide differences among states. Table 7.20 shows that the Federal District and Jalisco had the largest values of mortgages issued, in the range of 9-10 million pesos each. These were followed by Sonora, Nuevo Leon, and the state of Mexico, with 5-7 million pesos each. Altogether, these five states account for about half of mortgages issued. Sonora's high value is due to its position as an urban, high income state, adjacent to the U.S. Its housing values are more based on the value of the dollar than further south. It also has significant tourism and investment from the U.S. Among the lowest states in value of mortgages issued are the less populated central and southern states of Quintana Roo, Tlaxcala, and Campeche.

There is some correspondence with other economic variables. Mortgage values correspond to higher gross state revenues in the urban populous states and low values in smaller states (see Map 7.7B). An important difference is that Jalisco is second in importance in value of new mortgages, but fourth in importance for gross state revenues. This may be due to differences in the nature of major cities. Guadalajara in Jalisco has a more residential nature, versus the more industrial nature of Monterrey in Nuevo Leon and sections of the greater Mexico City metropolitan area in the state of Mexico.

Taxes and Duties in Relation to Revenues, 1984

This variable measures the ratio of taxes and duties (impuestos and derechos) to state revenues. In 1984, national state revenues were 1.7 trillion pesos, with 55 percent represented by taxes and duties. This percentage amount has shown modest fluctuation since 1980, when the proportion was 52 percent. By comparison, 1984 national municipio revenues were 121 billion pesos, with 75 percent in taxes and duties.

Map 7.7C demonstrates that the pattern of reliance on taxes/duties does not follow the standard regions. For instance, both the border and pacific south regions contain states from both extreme values. By state, the mean value is 62.7 percent (see Table 7.21). The highest value is for Chihuahua, for which 96 percent of state revenues were taxes and duties. This is followed by Hidalgo (92 percent) and Yucatan (83 percent). At the low extreme is Oaxaca, where taxes and duties accounted for only 16 percent of state revenues, followed by Nuevo Leon (27 percent).

In total value of taxes and duties collected, the Federal District is the leader, with 231 billion pesos collected in taxes and duties, even though these account for only 54 percent of revenues. The neighboring state of Mexico is second with 101 billion pesos collected in taxes and duties. Altogether, the central metropolitan zone accounts for a third of all taxes and duties collected at the state level in the nation.

Table 7.19 Gross State Revenue, Per Capita, 1984

No.	State	Gross State Revenue 1979	Gross State Revenue Per Capita 1979	Unadjusted Gross State Revenue 1984	Unadjusted Gross State Revenue Per Capita 1984	Adjusted Gross State Revenue 1984	Adjusted Gross State Revenue Per Capita 1984
1	AGUASCALIENTES	813,436	1.5660	12,036,025	20.4706	1,635,455	2.7815
2	BAJA CALIFORNIA	7,392,203	6.2758	62,683,858	46.6968	8,517,482	6.3452
3	BAJA CALIFORNIA SUR	619,798	2.8809	6,594,893	26.9912	896,114	3.6676
4	CAMPECHE	420,293	0.9994	16,589,104	34.7701	2,254,127	4.7246
5	COAHUILA	2,574,888	1.6535	26,945,328	15.2358	3,661,331	2.0702
6	COLIMA	427,040	1.2332	12,858,955	32.7199	1,747,274	4.4460
7	CHIAPAS	3,034,781	1.4557	69,984,000	29.6113	9,509,425	4.0236
8	CHIHUAHUA	2,361,326	1.1774	26,347,117	11.5449	3,580,046	1.5687
9	DISTRITO FEDERAL	95,677,667	10.8342	426,539,911	42.2251	57,958,243	5.7375
10	DURANGO	1,356,583	1.1474	16,453,283	12.3034	2,235,672	1.6718
11	GUANAJUATO	2,087,612	0.6945	43,045,728	12.6510	5,849,053	1.7190
12	GUERRERO	1,339,729	0.6351	26,437,944	11.0687	3,592,387	1.5040
13	HIDALGO	831,324	0.5372	12,069,529	6.8867	1,640,007	0.9358
14	JALISCO	10,359,306	2.3695	141,411,495	28.5089	19,214,993	3.8738
15	MEXICO	19,711,426	2.6058	143,708,598	16.7534	19,527,124	2.2764
16	MICHOACAN	1,940,493	0.6764	26,751,285	8.2320	3,634,964	1.1186
17	MORELOS	1,063,694	1.1231	22,003,448	20.4584	2,989,828	2.7799
18	NAYARIT	666,810	0.9183	9,811,670	11.9401	1,333,209	1.6224
19	NUEVO LEON	11,821,982	4.7042	168,390,792	58.9072	22,880,940	8.0043
20	OAXACA	4,556,809	1.9235	75,068,471	27.9324	10,200,303	3.7955
21	PUEBLA	2,270,981	0.6784	36,634,357	9.6611	4,977,876	1.3128
22	QUERETARO	1,529,404	2.0679	15,517,984	18.5716	2,108,583	2.5235
23	QUINTANA ROO	718,435	3.1791	9,137,800	35.7223	1,241,644	4.8539
24	SAN LUIS POTOSI	1,605,684	0.9593	17,466,052	9.2207	2,373,287	1.2529
25	SINALOA	3,268,576	1.7669	35,018,082	16.7041	4,758,256	2.2697
26	SONORA	2,912,012	1.9237	41,058,947	23.8546	5,579,089	3.2414
27	TABASCO	3,215,083	3.0246	92,565,955	76.9846	12,577,861	10.4607
28	TAMAULIPAS	2,877,603	1.4953	37,832,736	17.2882	5,140,712	2.3491
29	TLAXCALA	479,037	0.8607	12,411,493	19.7029	1,686,432	2.6772
30	VERACRUZ	6,528,947	1.2118	73,379,286	11.9843	9,970,777	1.6284
31	YUCATAN	1,205,579	1.1333	14,918,170	12.3147	2,027,080	1.6733
32	ZACATECAS	787,969	0.6931	15,039,703	11.7272	2,043,594	1.5935
	National Total	196,456,510		1,746,711,699		237,343,168	
	Mean	6,139,266	2.0127	54,584,741	23.1139	7,416,974	3.1407
	S.D.	16,573,030	1.9991	78,510,292	15.4967	10,667,979	2.1057
	C.V.	270	99.32	144	67.05	143.83	67.05
	Minimum	420,293	0.5372	6,594,893	6.8867	896,114	0.9358
	Maximum	95,677,667	10.8342	426,539,911	76.9846	57,958,243	10.4607

DEFINITION: Values shown are in thousands of pesos. The ratios are the state income to the total population of the corresponding year.

SOURCE: <u>1980 Anuario Estadistico</u>, Table 4.6.1; <u>1986 Anuario Estadistico</u>, Table 4.9.9.

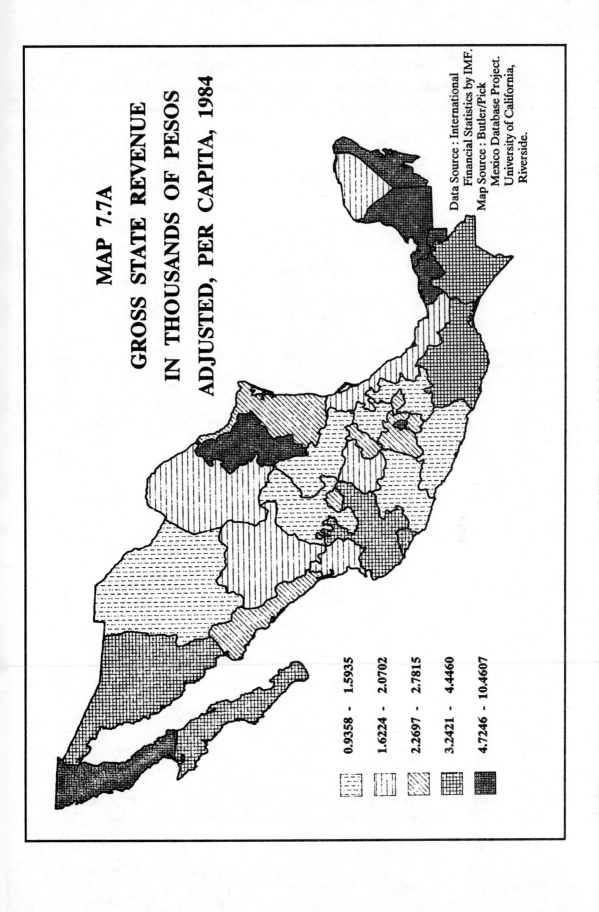

MAP 7.7A

GROSS STATE REVENUE

IN THOUSANDS OF PESOS

ADJUSTED, PER CAPITA, 1984

Data Source : International
Financial Statistics by IMF.

Map Source : Butler/Pick
Mexico Database Project.
University of California,
Riverside.

0.9358 - 1.5935

1.6224 - 2.0702

2.2697 - 2.7815

3.2421 - 4.4460

4.7246 - 10.4607

Table 7.20 Total Value of New Mortgages, 1980

No. State	Total Value of New Mortgages in Thousands of Pesos	Total Value of New Mortgages Per Capita
1 AGUASCALIENTES	1,283,704	2.47
2 BAJA CALIFORNIA	1,530,691	1.30
3 BAJA CALIFORNIA SUR	401,436	1.87
4 CAMPECHE	296,216	0.70
5 COAHUILA	1,135,216	0.73
6 COLIMA	950,431	2.75
7 CHIAPAS	1,253,586	0.60
8 CHIHUAHUA	2,762,539	1.38
9 DISTRITO FEDERAL	9,752,423	1.10
10 DURANGO	1,652,202	1.40
11 GUANAJUATO	2,692,849	0.90
12 GUERRERO	935,765	0.44
13 HIDALGO	546,071	0.35
14 JALISCO	9,182,779	2.10
15 MEXICO	5,476,402	0.72
16 MICHOACAN	1,239,035	0.43
17 MORELOS	659,225	0.70
18 NAYARIT	610,955	0.84
19 NUEVO LEON	6,962,391	2.77
20 OAXACA	648,732	0.27
21 PUEBLA	1,828,028	0.55
22 QUERETARO	1,215,196	1.64
23 QUINTANA ROO	149,916	0.66
24 SAN LUIS POTOSI	1,104,678	0.66
25 SINALOA	3,165,175	1.71
26 SONORA	7,252,343	4.79
27 TABASCO	431,578	0.41
28 TAMAULIPAS	2,264,286	1.18
29 TLAXCALA	227,890	0.41
30 VERACRUZ	2,419,751	0.45
31 YUCATAN	930,044	0.87
32 ZACATECAS	1,369,332	1.21
National Total	72,330,865	
Mean	2,260,340	1.20
S.D.	2,540,897	0.94
C.V.	112.41	78.54
Minimum	149,916	0.27
Maximum	9,752,423	4.79

DEFINITION: The total value of new mortgages per capita is the total value of new mortgages 1980 in thousands of pesos to the total population 1980.

SOURCE: 1980 Anuario Estadistico, Table 4.6.1.

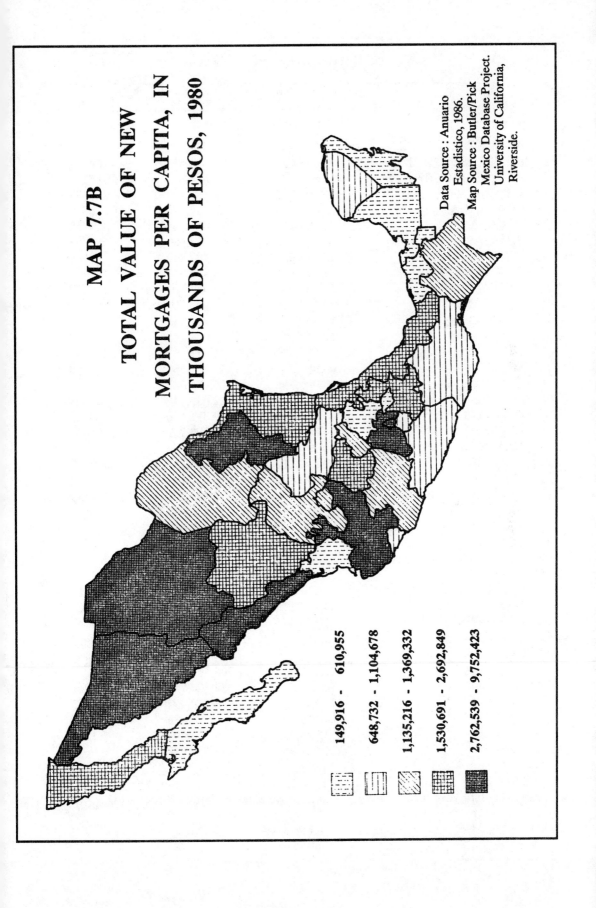

MAP 7.7B

TOTAL VALUE OF NEW
MORTGAGES PER CAPITA, IN
THOUSANDS OF PESOS, 1980

149,916 - 610,955

648,732 - 1,104,678

1,135,216 - 1,369,332

1,530,691 - 2,692,849

2,762,539 - 9,752,423

Data Source : Anuario
Estadistico, 1986.
Map Source : Butler/Pick
Mexico Database Project.
University of California,
Riverside.

Table 7.21 Taxes and Duties Collected, 1984

No.	State	Taxes & Duties Collected	Gross State Revenues	Ratio
1	AGUASCALIENTES	7,107,208	12,036,025	0.5905
2	BAJA CALIFORNIA	26,030,615	62,683,858	0.4153
3	BAJA CALIFORNIA SUR	4,821,990	6,594,893	0.7312
4	CAMPECHE	10,505,945	16,589,104	0.6333
5	COAHUILA	23,843,856	26,945,328	0.8849
6	COLIMA	6,044,113	12,858,955	0.4700
7	CHIAPAS	34,347,400	69,984,000	0.4908
8	CHIHUAHUA	25,388,035	26,347,117	0.9636
9	DISTRITO FEDERAL	231,041,852	426,539,911	0.5417
10	DURANGO	10,491,486	16,453,283	0.6377
11	GUANAJUATO	24,880,520	43,045,728	0.5780
12	GUERRERO	15,769,998	26,437,944	0.5965
13	HIDALGO	11,164,248	12,069,529	0.9250
14	JALISCO	57,537,452	141,411,495	0.4069
15	MEXICO	100,885,507	143,708,598	0.7020
16	MICHOACAN	18,906,308	26,751,285	0.7067
17	MORELOS	10,954,705	22,003,448	0.4979
18	NAYARIT	8,366,696	9,811,670	0.8527
19	NUEVO LEON	44,881,638	168,390,792	0.2665
20	OAXACA	11,760,698	75,068,471	0.1567
21	PUEBLA	24,800,117	36,634,357	0.6770
22	QUERETARO	10,090,896	15,517,984	0.6503
23	QUINTANA ROO	3,828,000	9,137,800	0.4189
24	SAN LUIS POTOSI	11,237,636	17,466,052	0.6434
25	SINALOA	23,146,848	35,018,082	0.6610
26	SONORA	31,135,044	41,058,947	0.7583
27	TABASCO	68,182,080	92,565,955	0.7366
28	TAMAULIPAS	26,993,021	37,832,736	0.7135
29	TLAXCALA	6,536,838	12,411,493	0.5267
30	VERACRUZ	54,917,175	73,379,286	0.7484
31	YUCATAN	12,324,075	14,918,170	0.8261
32	ZACATECAS	9,664,422	15,039,703	0.6426
	National Total	967,586,422	1,746,711,699	
	Mean	30,237,076	54,584,741	0.6266
	S.D.	41,739,433	78,510,292	0.1775
	C.V.	138.04	143.83	28.32
	Minimum	3,828,000	6,594,893	0.1567
	Maximum	231,041,852	426,539,911	0.9636

DEFINITION: Ratio is the peso value of state taxes and duties collected in 1984 to the gross state revenues in 1984. Values shown are in thousands of pesos.

SOURCE: 1986 Anuario Estadistico, Table 4.9.9.

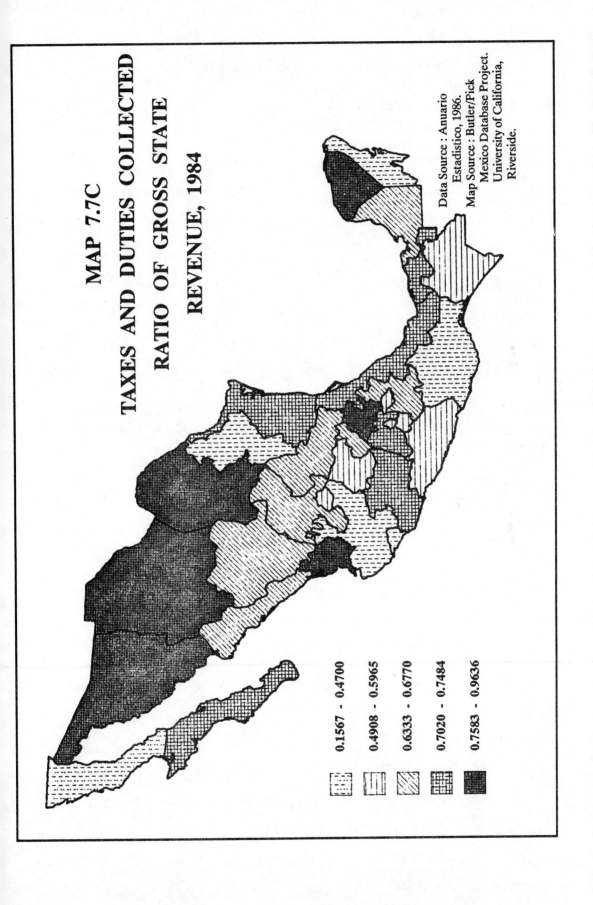

MAP 7.7C
TAXES AND DUTIES COLLECTED
RATIO OF GROSS STATE
REVENUE, 1984

Data Source : Anuario
Estadistico, 1986.
Map Source : Butler/Pick
Mexico Database Project.
University of California,
Riverside.

0.1567 - 0.4700

0.4908 - 0.5965

0.6333 - 0.6770

0.7020 - 0.7484

0.7583 - 0.9636

8

POPULATION ECONOMICS

Introduction

Chapter 8 expands upon the information presented in Chapter 7. The four major divisions in this chapter examine several components of the economically active population, occupational distribution, employment, and income. The information included in this chapter is primarily from the Mexican census. Most presentations are the state level; however, the extent of petroleum/mining workers in the municipios of the oil region also is shown. The overall economically active population, as well as its male and female components, are examined. Occupations are divided into professional and technical, administrative and managerial, agricultural, and others, except as noted above for the oil region municipios. Employment, or more accurately, unemployment and underemployment, are presented for the Mexican states, as measured by the 1980 Mexican census. Finally, three different levels of income are shown and discussed. As with all of the other information presented in the atlas, this chapter includes only a few of the dimensions available for 1980 and subsequent years as well as prior years.

Economically Active Population

Economically Active Population, 1980

The economically active population was determined by an analysis of 1980 Mexican census data. The census figures are for the economically active population of persons 12 years of age and older. Rates discussed here are determined by dividing the economically active population into the population 12 years of age and over. Variations described in this section are relatively minor compared to the many other differences reported for Mexico. The mean percentage of economically active population is 50.3 percent. The range in economically active population by state is from a high of 0.57 in Quintana Roo to a low of 0.43 in Zacatecas; as a consequence the measure of covariation is extremely low.

As shown on Table 8.1 and illustrated on Map 8.1A, overall the highest percentages of the economically active population by region is reported for the pacific south, with the states of Chiapas, Oaxaca, and Guerrero all having extremely high rates (0.54+); also Quintana Roo has an extremely high rate of an economically active population. States with a high rate (0.50+) are Baja California, the state on the U.S.-Mexico border with the highest rate, Chihuahua, Baja California Sur, and several states in the north-center, including Guanajuato, as well most of the remaining states surrounding the Federal District, and the southern states not already mentioned. States with the lowest rate of economically active population are located primarily in the southern part of the north, e.g., the states of Zacatecas, Sinaloa, Nayarit, Durango, and the border state of Coahuila.

There are relatively few close correspondences to other atlas characteristics. The geographic pattern for economic activity closely resembles those for number of hospitals and indigenous language, while it is opposite to that for literacy. Both of the former have high levels in the south, gulf, and southeast regions, similar to economic activity. There is relatively little correspondence between the economically active population and standard regions, except for the pacific south.

Economically Active Males, 1980

When proportion of the economically active population that is male is examined, that is for population 12 years of age and over, a completely different picture emerges from that of the overall economically active population. The mean male economically active population, according to the 1980 Mexican census, was 74.2 percent. This, of course, indicates that most of the economically active labor force in Mexico is male. By comparison, in the U.S. in 1980, the related measure of percent male in the civilian labor force was 57.5 percent (Bogue, 1985). For Mexico, the range in male economically active is from a high of 83.0 percent in Zacatecas to a low of 63.7 percent in the Federal District. As with the total economically active population, this range is not very large with a resulting very low coefficient of variation.

Table 8.2 presents the male economically active population and Map 8.1B illustrates its distribution by state. States in the pacific south, that have an overall high rate of economically active population, have an extremely low proportion of male economically active population, other states which follow this pattern are the urbanized states of the Federal District, Jalisco, and Baja California. In contrast, several states with a very low overall rate of economically active population have relatively high proportions of a male economically active population; among these states are the U.S.-Mexico border states of Coahuila and Baja California Sur. Other northeastern states which fall into this pattern are : Sonora, Sinaloa, and Nayarit.

One implication of the substantial difference between the overall economically active population and the male economically active population by state is that it is misleading to discuss the economically active population in Mexico in general terms; there is too large of a variation between the overall rate of economic activity and the proportion male economically active to rely on generalizations based on total figures at the state level. Generalizations about Mexico's economically active population should take into account male-female distribution differences.

Economically Active Females, 1980

The proportion of economically active females in 1980 was measured in the same manner as for males, the data are reported in Table 8.3 and illustrated on Map 8.1C.. The proportions male and female economically active sum to 1.0, and are thus exact inverses. Hence, the explanations given for proportion male economically active apply, in reverse, to the female proportion. The map for the female proportion is also included to emphasize the increasing importance of female economic activity. As seen below, both the volume and proportion of economically active females have expanded greatly since 1940.

Female Economic Activity in Mexico, 1940-80

Year	1940	1950	1960	1970	1980
Females Economically Active*	432	1,127	2,018	2,466	6,141
Total Economically Active*	5,858	8,272	11,253	12,955	22,066
Proportion Female	7.4	13.6	17.9	19.0	27.8

* in thousands
SOURCE : Estadisticas Historicas de Mexico, 1985.

As with the general and male economically active population, variation among states is relatively minor, although slightly somewhat greater than for the former. The mean female economically active population in 1980 was 25.8 percent. Variation ranged from an extreme high of 36.3 percent in the Federal District to an extreme low of 17.0 percent in Zacatecas.

The maquiladora industry possibly could have influenced the economically active male-female distribution in the states along the U.S. border since the vast majority of workers in the maquila industry are female. However, only Baja California has an extremely high rate of females in the labor force (31 percent), with Chihuahua (27 percent) and Tamaulipas (27 percent) also having a relatively high rate. On the other hand, Sonora (25 percent) and Coahuila (24 percent) have relatively low rates. In addition to the Federal District's extremely high rate, other states with high rates of economically active females include Baja California, Jalisco, Guanajuato, and the Pacific south states. Generally, the pacific south has high rates of female economically active population while there is little regional consistency in low rates.

Table 8.1 Economically Active Population, 1980

No.	State	Economically Active Population	Total Population	Ratio
1	AGUASCALIENTES	159,943	327,066	0.4890
2	BAJA CALIFORNIA	403,279	791,768	0.5093
3	BAJA CALIFORNIA SUR	69,954	139,149	0.5027
4	CAMPECHE	134,423	268,631	0.5004
5	COAHUILA	483,898	1,012,033	0.4781
6	COLIMA	108,754	223,221	0.4872
7	CHIAPAS	734,047	1,296,570	0.5661
8	CHIHUAHUA	664,707	1,332,389	0.4989
9	DISTRITO FEDERAL	3,312,581	6,173,145	0.5366
10	DURANGO	357,163	735,915	0.4853
11	GUANAJUATO	978,013	1,892,772	0.5167
12	GUERRERO	719,154	1,330,144	0.5407
13	HIDALGO	505,091	979,800	0.5155
14	JALISCO	1,413,854	2,794,678	0.5059
15	MEXICO	2,410,236	4,791,930	0.5030
16	MICHOACAN	872,775	1,825,979	0.4780
17	MORELOS	303,838	618,776	0.4910
18	NAYARIT	210,188	457,008	0.4599
19	NUEVO LEON	803,764	1,658,901	0.4845
20	OAXACA	858,283	1,525,124	0.5628
21	PUEBLA	1,081,573	2,120,202	0.5101
22	QUERETARO	224,435	456,864	0.4913
23	QUINTANA ROO	79,341	139,974	0.5668
24	SAN LUIS POTOSI	532,115	1,057,768	0.5031
25	SINALOA	568,427	1,171,692	0.4851
26	SONORA	484,277	996,841	0.4858
27	TABASCO	327,502	661,306	0.4952
28	TAMAULIPAS	624,497	1,273,958	0.4902
29	TLAXCALA	174,965	352,836	0.4959
30	VERACRUZ	1,796,219	3,530,802	0.5087
31	YUCATAN	367,825	716,300	0.5135
32	ZACATECAS	300,963	693,451	0.4340

Mean		689,565		0.5029
S.D.		688,928		0.0284
C.V.		99.91		5.64
Minimum		69,954		0.4340
Maximum		3,312,581		0.5668

DEFINITION: Ratio is the population economically active age 12+ to total population age 12+.

SOURCE: 1980 Mexican Census of Population, Volume 1, Table 6.

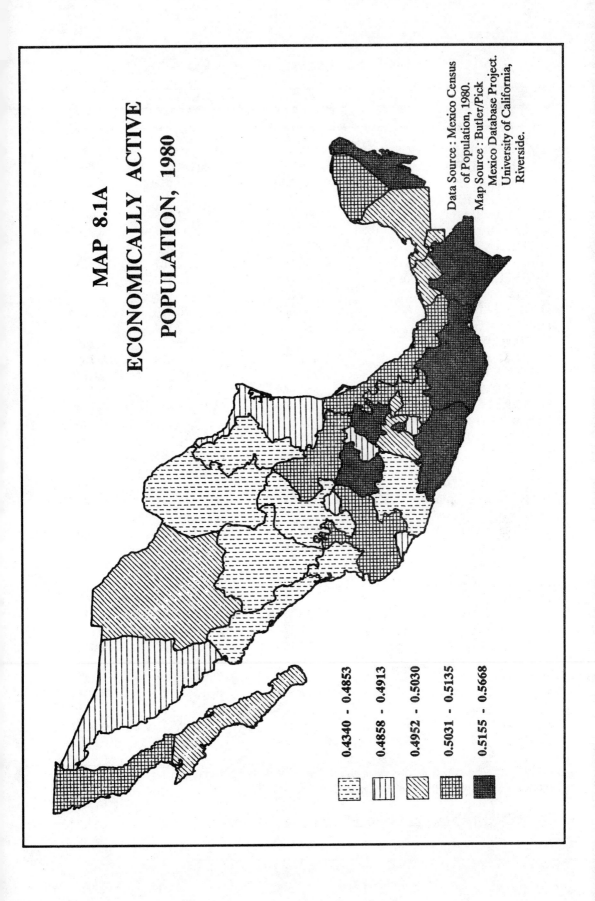

MAP 8.1A
ECONOMICALLY ACTIVE
POPULATION, 1980

Data Source : Mexico Census
of Population, 1980.
Map Source : Butler/Pick
Mexico Database Project.
University of California,
Riverside.

0.4340 – 0.4853

0.4858 – 0.4913

0.4952 – 0.5030

0.5031 – 0.5135

0.5155 – 0.5668

Table 8.2 Economically Active Males, 1980

No. State	Economically Active Male Population	Total Economically Active Population	Ratio
1 AGUASCALIENTES	117,362	159,943	0.7338
2 BAJA CALIFORNIA	282,646	403,279	0.7009
3 BAJA CALIFORNIA SUR	53,900	69,954	0.7705
4 CAMPECHE	102,403	134,423	0.7618
5 COAHUILA	368,174	483,898	0.7609
6 COLIMA	81,669	108,754	0.7510
7 CHIAPAS	532,708	734,047	0.7257
8 CHIHUAHUA	484,112	664,707	0.7283
9 DISTRITO FEDERAL	2,110,685	3,312,581	0.6372
10 DURANGO	267,668	357,163	0.7494
11 GUANAJUATO	708,608	978,013	0.7245
12 GUERRERO	493,054	719,154	0.6856
13 HIDALGO	377,014	505,091	0.7464
14 JALISCO	1,011,201	1,413,854	0.7152
15 MEXICO	1,751,363	2,410,236	0.7266
16 MICHOACAN	656,969	872,775	0.7527
17 MORELOS	220,796	303,838	0.7267
18 NAYARIT	167,136	210,188	0.7952
19 NUEVO LEON	594,972	803,764	0.7402
20 OAXACA	603,298	858,283	0.7029
21 PUEBLA	796,751	1,081,573	0.7367
22 QUERETARO	173,221	224,435	0.7718
23 QUINTANA ROO	59,282	79,341	0.7472
24 SAN LUIS POTOSI	400,460	532,115	0.7526
25 SINALOA	430,238	568,427	0.7569
26 SONORA	365,697	484,277	0.7551
27 TABASCO	255,889	327,502	0.7813
28 TAMAULIPAS	457,095	624,497	0.7319
29 TLAXCALA	129,513	174,965	0.7402
30 VERACRUZ	1,346,785	1,796,219	0.7498
31 YUCATAN	274,270	367,825	0.7457
32 ZACATECAS	249,867	300,963	0.8302
Mean	497,650	689,565	0.7417
S.D.	466,460	688,928	0.0331
C.V.	93.73	99.91	4.46
Minimum	53,900	69,954	0.6372
Maximum	2,110,685	3,312,581	0.8302

DEFINITION: Ratio is the economically active male population age 12+ to total economically active population, age 12+.

SOURCE: 1980 Mexican Census of Population, Volume 2, Table 12.

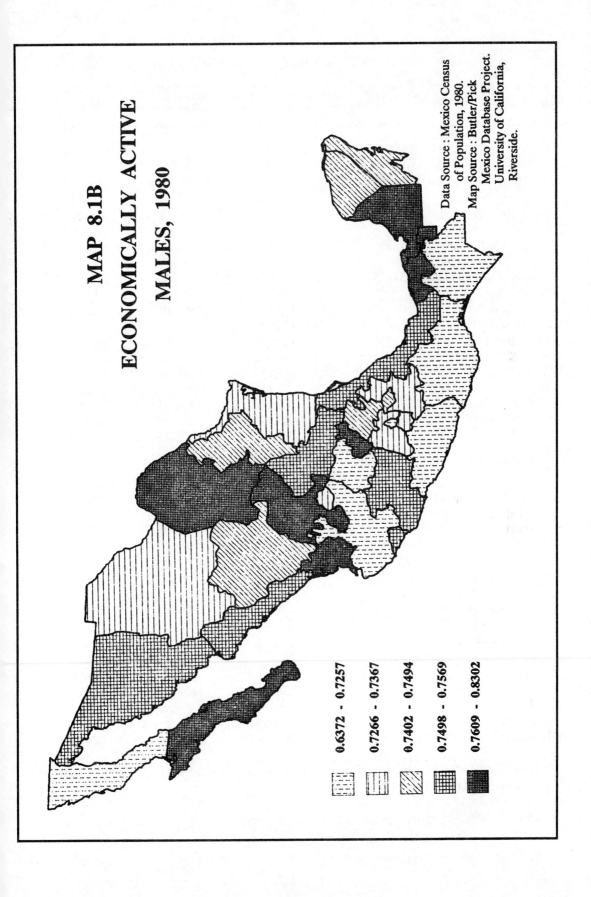

MAP 8.1B
ECONOMICALLY ACTIVE
MALES, 1980

Data Source : Mexico Census
of Population, 1980.
Map Source : Butler/Pick
Mexico Database Project.
University of California,
Riverside.

0.6372 - 0.7257
0.7266 - 0.7367
0.7402 - 0.7494
0.7498 - 0.7569
0.7609 - 0.8302

Table 8.3 Economically Active Females, 1980

No.	State	Economically Active Female Population	Total Economically Active Population	Ratio
1	AGUASCALIENTES	42,581	159,943	0.2662
2	BAJA CALIFORNIA	120,633	403,279	0.2991
3	BAJA CALIFORNIA SUR	16,054	69,954	0.2295
4	CAMPECHE	32,020	134,423	0.2382
5	COAHUILA	115,724	483,898	0.2391
6	COLIMA	27,085	108,754	0.2490
7	CHIAPAS	201,339	734,047	0.2743
8	CHIHUAHUA	180,595	664,707	0.2717
9	DISTRITO FEDERAL	1,201,896	3,312,581	0.3628
10	DURANGO	89,495	357,163	0.2506
11	GUANAJUATO	269,405	978,013	0.2755
12	GUERRERO	226,100	719,154	0.3144
13	HIDALGO	128,077	505,091	0.2536
14	JALISCO	402,653	1,413,854	0.2848
15	MEXICO	658,873	2,410,236	0.2734
16	MICHOACAN	215,806	872,775	0.2473
17	MORELOS	83,042	303,838	0.2733
18	NAYARIT	43,052	210,188	0.2048
19	NUEVO LEON	208,792	803,764	0.2598
20	OAXACA	254,985	858,283	0.2971
21	PUEBLA	284,822	1,081,573	0.2633
22	QUERETARO	51,214	224,435	0.2282
23	QUINTANA ROO	20,059	79,341	0.2528
24	SAN LUIS POTOSI	131,655	532,115	0.2474
25	SINALOA	138,189	568,427	0.2431
26	SONORA	118,580	484,277	0.2449
27	TABASCO	71,613	327,502	0.2187
28	TAMAULIPAS	167,402	624,497	0.2681
29	TLAXCALA	45,452	174,965	0.2598
30	VERACRUZ	449,434	1,796,219	0.2502
31	YUCATAN	93,555	367,825	0.2543
32	ZACATECAS	51,096	300,963	0.1698
	Mean	191,915	689,565	0.2583
	S.D.	227,924	688,928	0.0331
	C.V.	118.76	99.91	12.81
	Minimum	16,054	69,954	0.1698
	Maximum	1,201,896	3,312,581	0.3628

DEFINITION: Ratio is the economically active female population age 12+ to total economically active population, age 12+.

SOURCE: 1980 Mexican Census of Population, Volume 2, Table 12.

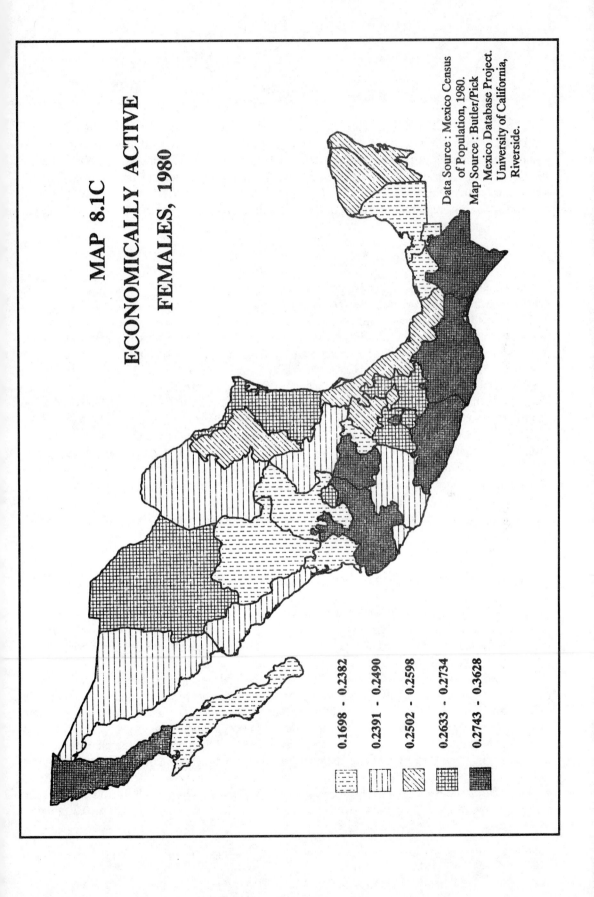

MAP 8.1C
ECONOMICALLY ACTIVE
FEMALES, 1980

Data Source : Mexico Census
  of Population, 1980.
Map Source : Butler/Pick
  Mexico Database Project.
  University of California,
  Riverside.

0.1698 - 0.2382

0.2391 - 0.2490

0.2502 - 0.2598

0.2633 - 0.2734

0.2743 - 0.3628

Occupations

Figures 8.1A, 8.1B, and 8.1C illustrate occupation by key categories for 1900, 1960, and 1980. Data for 1980 are shown because the census data for 1960 showed substantial change from earlier years. The remainder of presentation of occupations made in this section classifies occupations in 1980 as determined by the 1980 Mexican census as follows: (1) professional and technical workers, which also includes the teacher category, (2) administrative and management occupations, (3) service and support occupations, (4) agricultural occupations, and (5) all other occupations.

Professional and Technical Occupations, 1980

The percent of economically active population in professional and technical occupations, including teachers, averaged 6.1 percent for the states in 1980. There was moderate variation. As reported in Table 8.4, the major concentration of professional technical occupations is in the Federal District with a rate of 0.12. Other states with high rates are Baja California, Baja California Sur, Coahuila, Nuevo Leon, Tamaulipas, Colima and Yucatan. In addition, most remaining U.S.-Mexico border states have higher than average rates as do the state of Mexico, Morelos, and Jalisco. The state with the lowest rate of professional and technical occupations is Oaxaca with a rate of 0.03, or a rate only about a fourth that of the Federal District. Other states with very low rates are Chiapas, Hidalgo, and Michoacan.

Generally, the distribution of professional and technical occupations shown on map 8.2A corresponds to urbanization (Map 2.6A), as well as to higher income (Map 8.4B). It is not surprising that the most skilled members of the workforce are located in urban and economically prosperous settings. Two exceptions are Baja Sur and Sinaloa, for which the proportion of professional and technical workers is very much higher than urbanization. They both were 1970-80 growth states, with substantial tourism emphasis, factors which may have, in part, proven attractive to professional/technical workers and industries.

Administrative and Management Occupations, 1980

Table 8.5 indicates that in 1980, there was a statewide mean of 0.9 percent of economically active population in administrative and managerial occupations. This is substantially lower than in the U.S., which in 1980 had 10.4 of the employed labor force in executive, administrative, and managerial occupations (Bogue, 1985). There is moderate variation between states.

Map 8.2B shows that, the distribution of administrative and management occupations in 1980 has some similarities and some differences with professional and technical occupations. Similarities exist in that the Federal District, Baja California, Baja California, Baja California Sur, and in general the U.S.-Mexico border states have high rates for both occupational categories. As with professional and technical occupations, the Federal District's rate of 2.2 percent of the labor force being classified as in administrative and management positions is the highest in the country. The second highest state is Nuevo Leon (1.7 percent), which was also the case for professional and technical workers. Other states with relatively high rates are Baja, Baja Sur, Quintana Roo, and Sonora. The state with lowest rate of administrative and management occupations is Hidalgo (0.2 percent).

Occupation by Categories, Mexico

Figure 8..1A - 1980

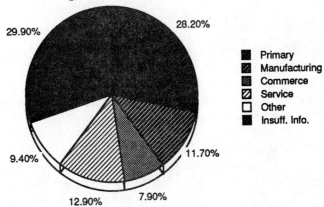

29.90% 28.20%

- ■ Primary
- ▨ Manufacturing
- ▩ Commerce
- ▨ Service
- ☐ Other
- ■ Insuff. Info.

9.40% 11.70%

12.90% 7.90%

Figure 8..1B - 1960

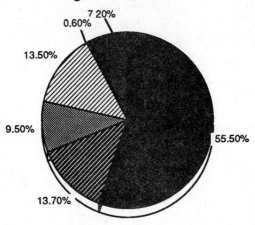

7 20%
0.60%
13.50%
9.50% 55.50%
13.70%

Figure 8.1C - 1900

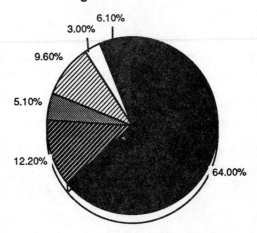

6.10%
3.00%
9.60%
5.10%
12.20% 64.00%

States with extremely low rates include Chiapas, Guerrero, Oaxaca, Puebla, Tlaxcala, and Zacatecas. All of these states are in the east central, gulf, or southern parts of Mexico.

Service and Support Occupations, 1980

The percent in service and support occupations averages 26.3 percent by state in 1980. There is considerable range of 31 percent among the states (see Table 8.6). This is comparable to the U.S. in 1980, for which 30.2 percent of the employed labor force is in service and administrative support occupations (Bogue, 1985). In geographic pattern, there is very strong resemblence to both professional/technical and administrative/management occupations.

As with the previous two occupational categories described in this section, the Federal District has the highest rate of service and support workers (45 percent). Similarly, Baja California and Baja California Sur also have a substantial proportion of the labor force in service and support occupations. The tourist state of Quintana Roo also has over a third of its labor force in service and support occupations. Other states with relatively high rates are Colima, Jalisco, the state of Mexico, and Sonora. The state with the lowest rate of service and support occupations in 1980 is Chiapas (13 percent). The next lowest state--Oaxaca--has a rate of 14 percent. Other states with relatively low rates are Hidalgo, Michoacan, and Tlaxcala. The state of Zacatecas has a low rate of service and support occupation, which contrasts with its high rate for administrative/management and low rate for professional/technical occupations (see Map 8.2C).

Agricultural Occupations, 1980

Table 8.7 shows the proportion of the ecomically active population that had an agricultural occupation from 1900 to 1980. Several trends are evident. The agricultural proportion of the economically active population remained around two thirds over the period 1900 to 1950. Since 1950, the proportion halved to 29 percent in 1980. Over the period 1900 to 1980, the total size of the agricultural labor force increased by 78 percent, a small growth relative to growth in total population. By comparison, in the U.S. over the same period, the proportion in agricultural occupations decreased from 10 percent to 3 percent. Over the same eighty year period, the geographic distribution of agricultural occupations changed very little. This constancy over time in geographic pattern is also evident for urbanization (see Map 2.6A).

In 1980, the mean proportion of the work force in agriculture was 29 percent. While Mexico is increasingly becoming urbanized, two states still have over half of their work force in agricultural occupations--Chiapas and Oaxaca. In addition, the more or less centrally located states of Zacatecas, Guerrero, Puebla, and Nayarit all have over 40 percent of their labor force in agricultural occupations. States with over a third of their work force in agricultural occupations include Michoacan, Tabasco, Veracruz, Tlaxcala, Hidalgo, and San Luis Potosi; these states are primarily located in the central and south of Mexico (see Map 8.2D). Despite being completely urbanized, the Federal District in 1980 still has six percent of its labor force in agricultural occupations.

States with 10 to 21 percent in agricultural occupations are Aguascalientes, Baja California Sur, Coahuila, Chihuahua, Jalisco, Mexico, Sonora, and Tamaulipas. Besides the Federal District, Nuevo Leon and Baja California have less than 10 percent in the agricultural labor force. Thus all border states have 21 percent or less in the agricultural labor force. Sinaloa is an anomaly since the state has extensive agricultural production but only 27 percent of its labor force is engaged in agricultural occupations.

Other Occupations, 1980

As shown in Table 8.8, labor force in occupations other than those so far discussed in this section vary substantially by state. For example, Nuevo Leon has over a third of its labor force is occupations other than professional and technical, administration and managerial, service and support, and agriculture, and the state of Mexico has almost a third of its work force in other occupations. States with a high rate of other occupations are Aguascalientes, Baja California, Coahuila, Chihuahua, Jalisco, Queretaro, Tamaulipas, and Tlaxcala. States with the lowest rate of persons in other occupations are Chiapas (9 percent), Oaxaca (9 percent), and Guerrero (11 percent); also Hidalgo and Zacatecas approximate these states in having a low percentage of their work force in other occupations.

The other occupations category corresponds closely in geographic pattern to the other non-agricultural occupational categories. It is even more closely correlated with the pattern for the manufacturing industry. Note the similarity between the "other occupations" (Map 8.2E) and the manufacturing workforce shown on Map 7.2D.

The U.S.-Mexico border states, on the average, have a higher percentage of their work force in other occupations. Many states in the south, especially the heavy agricultural states, have a relatively low percentage of their work force in other occupations. The Federal District is slightly about average.

Petroleum/Mining Workers, Oil Region, 1980

Map 8.2F shows the number of mining and petroleum workers for municipios in the oil region of Mexico, which comprises the states of Veracruz, Tabasco, and Campeche. In 1986, the region accounted for 95 percent of Mexico's 913 million barrels of crude oil production, and 77 percent of its 35.5 billion cubic meters of natural gas production. The occupational category mining and petroleum worker includes workers in the extraction, development, and exploitation of minerals which are deposited in the earth in a natural state, such as metals, coal or other non-metallic minerals, crude petroleum, and natural gas (SPP, 1984). Comparison with Pemex statistics (see Negrete, 1986) indicates that, in the oil region, this category consists largely of petroleum workers.

The municipio mean for percent petroleum/mining workers is 0.46 percent, which is much less than the 3.1 percent for the nation as a whole. The small percent in the oil region is less surprising in view the location of Pemex's headquarters and a large number of workers in Mexico City. The aggregate percent in this category for the oil region is 0.8 percent, with 2 percent for Tabasco, 0.6 percent for Veracruz, and 0.3 percent for Campeche. The small percent in Campeche may be due to the fact that Campeche's oil and gas production is nearly entirely offshore, so that offshore workers may not be residents of the state. Also, some of the onshore workers supporting the offshore operation may be resident in Tabasco, which has more oil industry facilities.

There are 12,802 petroleum/mining workers in the region. Of these, 7,832 are resident in Veracruz, 4,678 in Tabasco, and 292 in Campeche. For Veracruz, there is one large zone of concentration of workers in the north, and several smaller zones throughout the state. In addition, there is a large, nearly contiguous zone encompassing several municipios in southeast Veracruz and most of the municipios in Tabasco and Campeche. This zone, contains major oil production facilities and a large oil port, and accounts for over two thirds of the region's petroleum/mining workforce.

Table 8.4 Professional and Technical Occupations, 1980

No.	State	Professional & Technical Occupations	Teaching Occupations	Economically Active Population	Ratio
1	AGUASCALIENTES	5,453	4,631	159,943	0.0630
2	BAJA CALIFORNIA	22,295	12,363	403,279	0.0859
3	BAJA CALIFORNIA SUR	3,731	2,085	69,954	0.0831
4	CAMPECHE	5,244	3,300	134,423	0.0636
5	COAHUILA	22,762	14,033	483,898	0.0760
6	COLIMA	4,485	3,196	108,754	0.0706
7	CHIAPAS	11,696	12,422	734,047	0.0329
8	CHIHUAHUA	24,196	17,471	664,707	0.0627
9	DISTRITO FEDERAL	292,146	114,221	3,312,581	0.1227
10	DURANGO	10,864	10,289	357,163	0.0592
11	GUANAJUATO	21,339	17,814	978,013	0.0400
12	GUERRERO	12,330	17,649	719,154	0.0417
13	HIDALGO	6,129	9,538	505,091	0.0310
14	JALISCO	59,997	32,963	1,413,854	0.0657
15	MEXICO	102,161	55,526	2,410,236	0.0654
16	MICHOACAN	18,635	20,444	872,775	0.0448
17	MORELOS	14,607	6,609	303,838	0.0698
18	NAYARIT	6,040	6,667	210,188	0.0605
19	NUEVO LEON	44,098	28,184	803,764	0.0899
20	OAXACA	10,876	14,642	858,283	0.0297
21	PUEBLA	30,332	21,174	1,081,573	0.0476
22	QUERETARO	7,395	4,588	224,435	0.0534
23	QUINTANA ROO	3,227	1,794	79,341	0.0633
24	SAN LUIS POTOSI	14,787	12,910	532,115	0.0521
25	SINALOA	21,401	15,120	568,427	0.0642
26	SONORA	20,794	12,529	484,277	0.0688
27	TABASCO	10,202	7,068	327,502	0.0527
28	TAMAULIPAS	26,765	18,394	624,497	0.0723
29	TLAXCALA	3,455	4,618	174,965	0.0461
30	VERACRUZ	51,531	35,905	1,796,219	0.0487
31	YUCATAN	15,928	9,591	367,825	0.0694
32	ZACATECAS	6,131	8,128	300,963	0.0474
	Mean	28,470	17,371	689,565	0.0608
	S.D.	51,409	20,645	688,928	0.0187
	C.V.	180.57	118.85	99.91	30.72
	Minimum	3,227	1,794	69,954	0.0297
	Maximum	281,414	109,255	3,312,581	0.1179

DEFINITION: Ratio is the population with professional/technical occupations age 12+ plus the population with teaching occupations age 12+ to the economically active population age 12+.

SOURCE: 1980 Mexican Census of Population, Volume 2, Table 10 and Volume 1, Table 9.

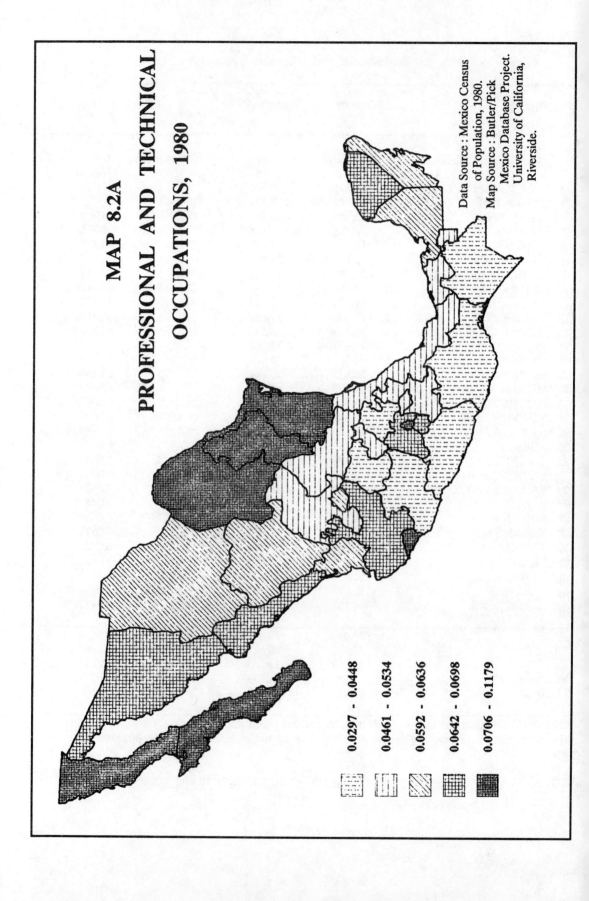

MAP 8.2A

PROFESSIONAL AND TECHNICAL

OCCUPATIONS, 1980

0.0297 - 0.0448

0.0461 - 0.0534

0.0592 - 0.0636

0.0642 - 0.0698

0.0706 - 0.1179

Data Source : Mexico Census
of Population, 1980.
Map Source : Butler/Pick
Mexico Database Project.
University of California,
Riverside.

Table 8.5 Administrative and Managerial Occupations, 1980

No.	State	Administrative/ Managerial Occupations	Economically Active Population	Ratio
1	AGUASCALIENTES	1,870	159,943	0.0117
2	BAJA CALIFORNIA	6,773	403,279	0.0168
3	BAJA CALIFORNIA SUR	919	69,954	0.0131
4	CAMPECHE	1,015	134,423	0.0076
5	COAHUILA	6,238	483,898	0.0129
6	COLIMA	1,368	108,754	0.0126
7	CHIAPAS	2,782	734,047	0.0038
8	CHIHUAHUA	7,714	664,707	0.0116
9	DISTRITO FEDERAL	74,159	3,312,581	0.0224
10	DURANGO	2,769	357,163	0.0078
11	GUANAJUATO	6,916	978,013	0.0071
12	GUERRERO	3,234	719,154	0.0045
13	HIDALGO	1,055	505,091	0.0021
14	JALISCO	17,367	1,413,854	0.0123
15	MEXICO	31,619	2,410,236	0.0131
16	MICHOACAN	5,189	872,775	0.0059
17	MORELOS	2,267	303,838	0.0075
18	NAYARIT	1,624	210,188	0.0077
19	NUEVO LEON	13,658	803,764	0.0170
20	OAXACA	1,983	858,283	0.0023
21	PUEBLA	6,803	1,081,573	0.0063
22	QUERETARO	2,154	224,435	0.0096
23	QUINTANA ROO	1,097	79,341	0.0138
24	SAN LUIS POTOSI	4,505	532,115	0.0085
25	SINALOA	5,632	568,427	0.0099
26	SONORA	6,554	484,277	0.0135
27	TABASCO	2,366	327,502	0.0072
28	TAMAULIPAS	6,506	624,497	0.0104
29	TLAXCALA	655	174,965	0.0037
30	VERACRUZ	10,330	1,796,219	0.0058
31	YUCATAN	3,110	367,825	0.0085
32	ZACATECAS	1,293	300,963	0.0043
	Mean	7,548	689,565	0.0094
	S.D.	13,397	688,928	0.0046
	C.V.	177.49	99.91	48.41
	Minimum	655	69,954	0.0021
	Maximum	74,159	3,312,581	0.0224
	Total	241,524	22,066,084	

DEFINITION: Ratio of population with administrative or managerial occupations, age 12+ to the economically active population age 12+.

SOURCE: 1980 Mexican Census of Population, Volume 1, Tables 6 and 9.

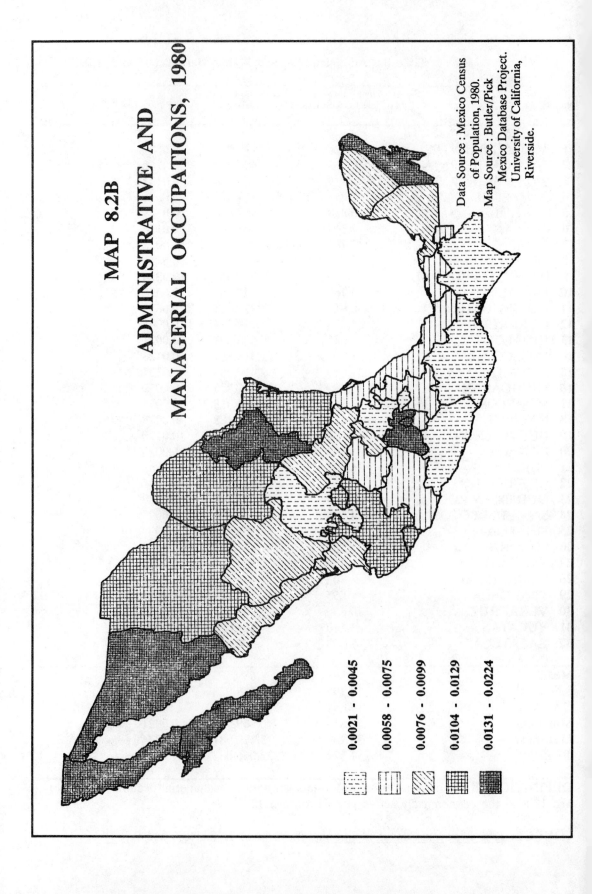

MAP 8.2B

ADMINISTRATIVE AND

MANAGERIAL OCCUPATIONS, 1980

Data Source : Mexico Census
of Population, 1980.

Map Source : Butler/Pick
Mexico Database Project.
University of California,
Riverside.

0.0021 - 0.0045

0.0058 - 0.0075

0.0076 - 0.0099

0.0104 - 0.0129

0.0131 - 0.0224

Table 8.6 Service and Support Occupations, 1980

No.	State	Service/Support Occupations	Economically Active Population	Ratio
1	AGUASCALIENTES	47,037	159,943	0.2941
2	BAJA CALIFORNIA	147,026	403,279	0.3646
3	BAJA CALIFORNIA SUR	25,417	69,954	0.3633
4	CAMPECHE	35,451	134,423	0.2637
5	COAHUILA	145,083	483,898	0.2998
6	COLIMA	34,755	108,754	0.3196
7	CHIAPAS	96,412	734,047	0.1313
8	CHIHUAHUA	195,154	664,707	0.2936
9	DISTRITO FEDERAL	1,477,332	3,312,581	0.4460
10	DURANGO	82,099	357,163	0.2299
11	GUANAJUATO	200,354	978,013	0.2049
12	GUERRERO	175,994	719,154	0.2447
13	HIDALGO	83,441	505,091	0.1652
14	JALISCO	418,938	1,413,854	0.2963
15	MEXICO	776,990	2,410,236	0.3224
16	MICHOACAN	173,293	872,775	0.1986
17	MORELOS	87,377	303,838	0.2876
18	NAYARIT	49,741	210,188	0.2367
19	NUEVO LEON	273,881	803,764	0.3407
20	OAXACA	117,942	858,283	0.1374
21	PUEBLA	229,406	1,081,573	0.2121
22	QUERETARO	54,835	224,435	0.2443
23	QUINTANA ROO	28,969	79,341	0.3651
24	SAN LUIS POTOSI	119,301	532,115	0.2242
25	SINALOA	149,786	568,427	0.2635
26	SONORA	148,518	484,277	0.3067
27	TABASCO	63,585	327,502	0.1942
28	TAMAULIPAS	201,667	624,497	0.3229
29	TLAXCALA	31,291	174,965	0.1788
30	VERACRUZ	405,797	1,796,219	0.2259
31	YUCATAN	99,472	367,825	0.2704
32	ZACATECAS	49,137	300,963	0.1633
	Mean	194,546	689,565	0.2629
	S.D.	273,730	688,928	0.0724
	C.V.	140.70	99.91	27.52
	Minimun	25,417	69,954	0.1313
	Maximum	1,477,332	3,312,581	0.4460
	Total	6,225,481	22,066,084	

DEFINITION: Ratio of population in service or support occupations age 12+ to population economically active age 12+.

SOURCE: 1980 Mexican Census of Population, Volume 1 Tables 6 & 9.

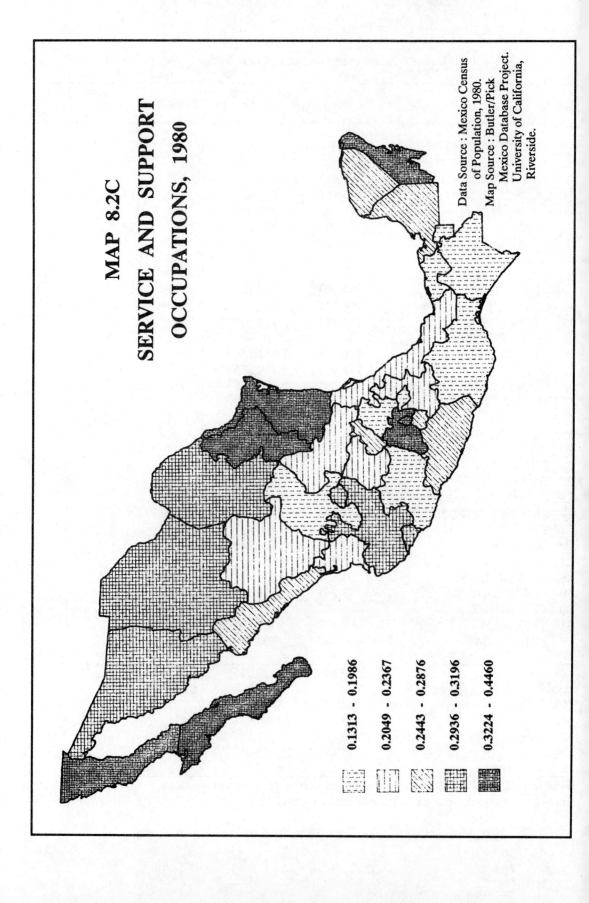

MAP 8.2C

SERVICE AND SUPPORT
OCCUPATIONS, 1980

0.1313 - 0.1986

0.2049 - 0.2367

0.2443 - 0.2876

0.2936 - 0.3196

0.3224 - 0.4460

Data Source : Mexico Census
of Population, 1980.
Map Source : Butler/Pick
Mexico Database Project.
University of California,
Riverside.

Table 8.7 Agricultural Occupations, 1900-1980

No. State	1900 Agricultural Occupations	Economically Active	Ratio	1930 Agricultural Occupations	Economically Active	Ratio
1 AGUASCALIENTES	22,077	51,982	0.4247	22,729	39,495	0.5755
2 BAJA CALIFORNIA	10,246	24,180	0.4237	11,704	19,568	0.5981
3 BAJA CALIFORNIA SUR				7,345	14,809	0.4960
4 CAMPECHE	21,203	39,906	0.5313	17,479	26,059	0.6707
5 COAHUILA	58,149	155,617	0.3737	82,587	137,979	0.5985
6 COLIMA	16,801	28,545	0.5886	12,902	20,002	0.6450
7 CHIAPAS	91,994	254,504	0.3615	134,772	166,746	0.8082
8 CHIHUAHUA	78,818	124,385	0.6337	102,413	149,794	0.6837
9 DISTRITO FEDERAL				42,465	394,097	0.1078
10 DURANGO	71,586	122,287	0.5854	99,313	129,999	0.7640
11 GUANAJUATO	241,455	443,363	0.5446	226,932	306,220	0.7411
12 GUERRERO	120,922	172,194	0.7022	175,960	196,661	0.8947
13 HIDALGO	136,415	287,548	0.4744	167,169	209,213	0.7990
14 JALISCO	275,564	589,742	0.4673	283,869	391,637	0.7248
15 MEXICO	225,170	341,403	0.6595	239,357	302,754	0.7906
16 MICHOACAN	241,620	346,096	0.6981	259,868	327,996	0.7923
17 MORELOS	42,880	59,031	0.7264	36,059	43,866	0.8220
18 NAYARIT	37,785	60,673	0.6228	41,379	55,645	0.7436
19 NUEVO LEON	54,098	140,746	0.3844	79,153	132,081	0.5993
20 OAXACA	256,954	580,746	0.4425	289,626	337,438	0.8583
21 PUEBLA	235,902	377,897	0.6242	261,120	348,527	0.7492
22 QUERETARO	61,481	93,325	0.6588	60,142	76,951	0.7816
23 QUINTANA ROO				2,342	4,118	0.5687
24 SAN LUIS POTOSI	139,121	233,322	0.5963	130,800	178,114	0.7344
25 SINALOA	68,051	169,603	0.4012	94,913	126,209	0.7520
26 SONORA	51,818	91,672	0.5653	64,112	99,951	0.6414
27 TABASCO	38,375	62,622	0.6128	52,916	63,337	0.8355
28 TAMAULIPAS	54,512	135,458	0.4024	63,316	108,236	0.5850
29 TLAXCALA	37,428	91,030	0.4112	47,807	64,264	0.7439
30 VERACRUZ	244,492	333,574	0.7329	325,996	430,258	0.7577
31 YUCATAN	81,498	119,390	0.6826	81,211	124,417	0.6527
32 ZACATECAS	99,143	158,791	0.6244	108,522	139,262	0.7793
Mean	107,433	158,432	0.5502	99,477	155,897	0.6967
S.D.	84,436	142,762	0.1170	93,915	127,328	0.1443
C.V.	78.59	90.11	21.26	94.41	81.67	20.72
Minimum	10,246	24,180	0.3615	2,342	4,118	0.1078
Maximum	275,564	589,742	0.7329	325,996	430,258	0.8947

DEFINITION: Ratio of the population with agricultural occupations to the economically active population for the same year.

NOTE: For 1900, data for Baja Sur are included with Baja California and data for Quintana Roo are included with Yucatan.

SOURCE: 1900 Mexican Census of Population; 1930, 1950, 1970 Mexican Census of Population, Resumen General; 1980 Mexican Census of Population, Volume 1, Table 9.

Table 8.7 Agricultural Occupations, 1900-1980 (Continued)

Agricultural Occupations	1950 Economically Active	Ratio	Agricultural Occupations	1970 Economically Active	Ratio	Agricultural Occupations	1980 Economically Active	Ratio
28,095	56,344	0.4986	32,095	86,332	0.3718	29,023	159,943	0.1815
34,567	77,424	0.4465	49,440	221,779	0.2229	38,245	403,279	0.0948
9,560	18,809	0.5083	12,035	34,292	0.3510	13,697	69,954	0.1958
22,248	38,967	0.5709	32,785	71,681	0.4574	41,769	134,423	0.3107
109,839	226,769	0.4844	85,760	283,351	0.3027	74,384	483,898	0.1537
21,930	37,363	0.5869	29,925	68,122	0.4393	30,831	108,754	0.2835
223,965	288,468	0.7764	293,152	413,294	0.7093	417,672	734,047	0.5690
141,920	264,016	0.5375	151,498	416,852	0.3634	134,070	664,707	0.2017
51,006	1,108,024	0.0460	49,164	2,189,521	0.0225	30,868	3,312,581	0.0093
136,854	195,203	0.7011	123,694	227,241	0.5443	108,342	357,163	0.3033
279,088	419,644	0.6651	275,644	567,774	0.4855	232,194	978,013	0.2374
232,195	291,080	0.7977	238,314	372,477	0.6398	306,031	719,154	0.4255
192,728	261,995	0.7356	184,941	307,810	0.6008	184,819	505,091	0.3659
324,660	555,713	0.5842	306,299	888,468	0.3447	270,622	1,413,854	0.1914
316,890	435,840	0.7271	300,296	965,625	0.3110	348,448	2,410,236	0.1446
319,535	439,421	0.7272	320,670	553,778	0.5791	343,472	872,775	0.3935
60,510	91,050	0.6646	73,545	166,251	0.4424	74,419	303,838	0.2449
65,302	93,711	0.6968	87,445	329,026	0.2658	84,761	210,188	0.4033
97,680	239,558	0.4078	85,149	1,060,279	0.0803	67,034	803,764	0.0834
358,349	470,915	0.7610	372,950	1,252,169	0.2978	473,935	858,283	0.5522
363,247	542,150	0.6700	380,396	1,558,904	0.2440	442,055	1,081,573	0.4087
63,576	90,564	0.7020	61,549	289,815	0.2124	65,296	224,435	0.2909
5,470	8,600	0.6360	13,374	25,262	0.5294	22,346	79,341	0.2816
186,040	270,486	0.6878	175,113	331,888	0.5276	181,423	532,115	0.3409
131,637	195,148	0.6745	177,691	343,947	0.5166	163,021	568,427	0.2868
88,927	164,281	0.5413	109,377	289,799	0.3774	101,203	484,277	0.2090
79,785	105,400	0.7570	116,147	200,232	0.5801	125,888	327,502	0.3844
122,640	234,121	0.5238	126,346	383,380	0.3296	111,232	624,497	0.1781
63,435	90,327	0.7023	58,023	104,455	0.5555	64,216	174,965	0.3670
434,878	651,872	0.6671	530,800	1,004,809	0.5283	685,302	1,796,219	0.3815
100,168	167,762	0.5971	111,076	207,538	0.5352	118,796	367,825	0.3230
157,069	199,842	0.7860	138,826	223,278	0.6218	146,008	300,963	0.4851
150,540	249,646	0.6209	145,022	479,973	0.4184	173,723	598,391	0.2901
120,138	230,547	0.1480	136,647	495,684	0.1637	160,890	728,222	0.1314
79.81	92.35	23.83	94.22	103.27	39.13	92.61	121.70	44.58
5,470	8,600	0.0460	1,035	16,251	0.0225	13,697	48,277	0.0093
434,878	1,108,024	0.7977	530,800	2,189,521	0.7093	685,302	3,312,581	0.5690

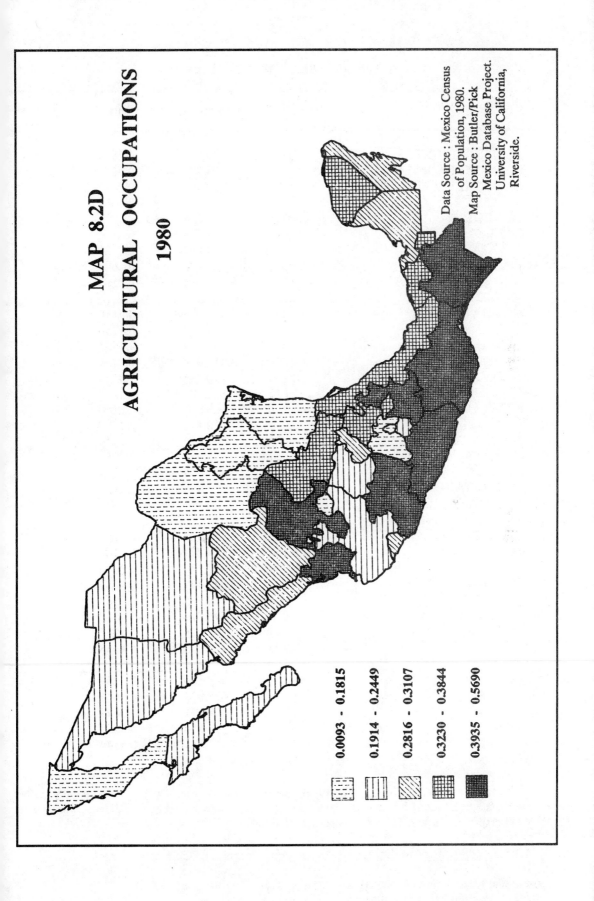

MAP 8.2D

AGRICULTURAL OCCUPATIONS

1980

Data Source : Mexico Census
of Population, 1980.
Map Source : Butler/Pick
Mexico Database Project.
University of California,
Riverside.

0.0093 - 0.1815

0.1914 - 0.2449

0.2816 - 0.3107

0.3230 - 0.3844

0.3935 - 0.5690

Table 8.8 Other Occupations, 1980

No.	State	Other Occupations	Economically Active Population	Ratio
1	AGUASCALIENTES	45,102	159,943	0.2820
2	BAJA CALIFORNIA	107,493	403,279	0.2665
3	BAJA CALIFORNIA SUR	14,172	69,954	0.2026
4	CAMPECHE	27,792	134,423	0.2068
5	COAHUILA	146,769	483,898	0.3033
6	COLIMA	22,908	108,754	0.2106
7	CHIAPAS	65,260	734,047	0.0889
8	CHIHUAHUA	172,998	664,707	0.2603
9	DISTRITO FEDERAL	849,867	3,312,581	0.2566
10	DURANGO	66,278	357,163	0.1856
11	GUANAJUATO	236,252	978,013	0.2416
12	GUERRERO	81,728	719,154	0.1136
13	HIDALGO	73,442	505,091	0.1454
14	JALISCO	386,066	1,413,854	0.2731
15	MEXICO	792,453	2,410,236	0.3288
16	MICHOACAN	147,611	872,775	0.1691
17	MORELOS	66,240	303,838	0.2180
18	NAYARIT	35,041	210,188	0.1667
19	NUEVO LEON	284,834	803,764	0.3544
20	OAXACA	81,651	858,283	0.0951
21	PUEBLA	192,703	1,081,573	0.1782
22	QUERETARO	65,841	224,435	0.2934
23	QUINTANA ROO	12,942	79,341	0.1631
24	SAN LUIS POTOSI	98,660	532,115	0.1854
25	SINALOA	99,719	568,427	0.1754
26	SONORA	105,153	484,277	0.2171
27	TABASCO	65,689	327,502	0.2006
28	TAMAULIPAS	165,947	624,497	0.2657
29	TLAXCALA	44,866	174,965	0.2564
30	VERACRUZ	325,470	1,796,219	0.1812
31	YUCATAN	71,073	367,825	0.1932
32	ZACATECAS	49,795	300,963	0.1655
	Mean	156,307	689,565	0.2139
	S.D.	193,284	688,928	0.0631
	C.V.	123.66	99.91	29.49
	Minimum	12,942	69,954	0.0889
	Maximum	849,867	3,312,581	0.3544
	Total	5,001,815	22,066,084	

DEFINITION: Ratio of the population with other occupations to the economically active population age 12+. Other occupations consists of the census categories: artists, supervisors of workers, artisans and laborer assistants to laborers.

SOURCE: 1980 Mexican Census of Population, Volume 1, Table 9.

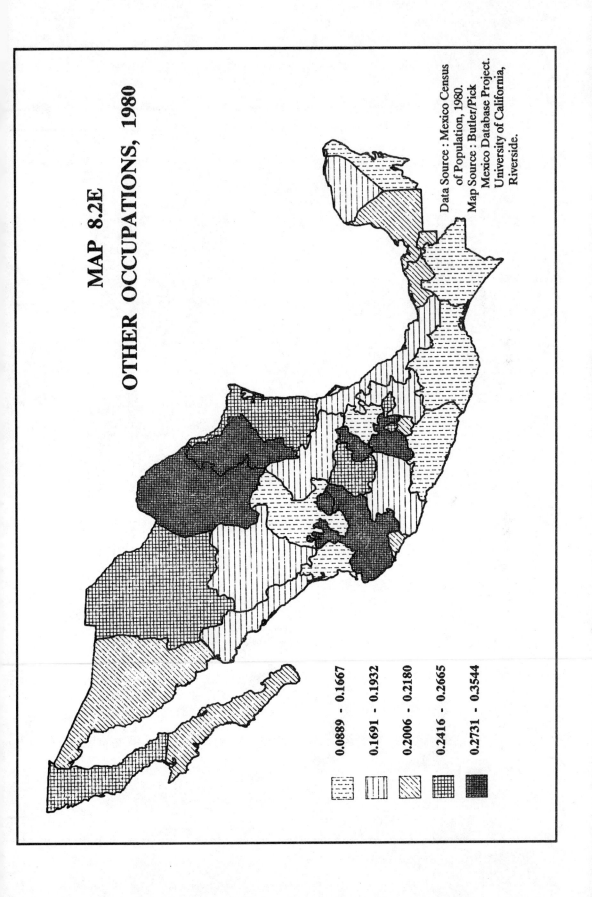

MAP 8.2E

OTHER OCCUPATIONS, 1980

Data Source : Mexico Census
of Population, 1980.
Map Source : Butler/Pick
Mexico Database Project.
University of California,
Riverside.

0.0889 - 0.1667

0.1691 - 0.1932

0.2006 - 0.2180

0.2416 - 0.2665

0.2731 - 0.3544

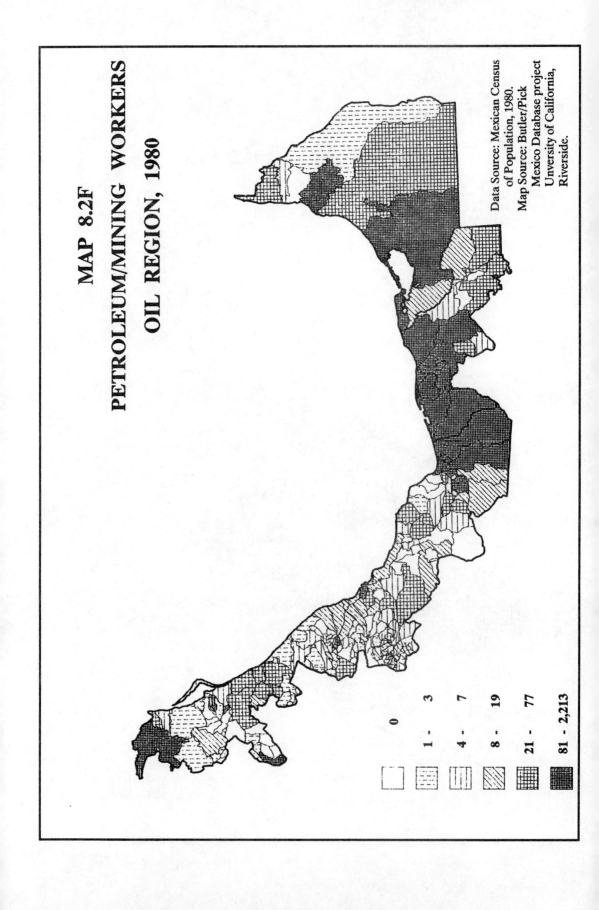

MAP 8.2F

PETROLEUM/MINING WORKERS

OIL REGION, 1980

Data Source: Mexican Census
of Population, 1980.

Map Source: Butler/Pick
Mexico Database project
Unversity of California,
Riverside.

0

1 - 3

4 - 7

8 - 19

21 - 77

81 - 2,213

Employment

Underemployment, 1980

Underemployment is the ratio of population employed more than zero hours but less than 17 hours per week to the economically active population. Mexico has substantial underemployment. In 1980, of those specifying hours worked, 9 percent were unemployed, while 28 percent worked less than 34 hours per week. The latter percent was higher for females, 32 percent, versus 26 percent for males. The text table below shows unemployment and underemployment categories, by sex.

Unemployment and Underemployment for the Economically
Active Population in Mexico, 1980, by Sex

	Males		Females		Total	
	Number	Percent	Number	Percent	Number	Percent
Unemployed	1,250.7	7.85	335.0	5.45	1,585.7	7.19
Underemployed						
0-1 hour	10.9	0.07	5.8	0.09	16.7	0.08
1-14 hours	1,223.4	7.68	548.3	8.93	1,771.7	8.03
15-24 hours	475.2	2.98	241.4	3.93	716.6	3.25
25-34 hours	540.7	3.40	322.5	5.25	863.2	3.91
35-40 hours	2,146.6	13.48	832.8	13.56	2,979.4	13.50
41-48 hours	5,759.3	36.17	1,500.4	24.43	7,259.7	32.90
49-56 hours	1,091.8	6.86	307.8	5.01	1,399.6	6.34
57+ hours	1,092.2	6.86	377.6	6.15	1,469.8	6.66
not specified	2,333.8	14.66	1,670.1	27.19	4,003.9	18.14
TOTAL	15,924.6		6,141.7		22,066.3	

NOTE: Percent of total population, including unspecified
SOURCE : 1980 Mexican Census of Population, Resumen General, Table 35.

The mean underemployment by state is 8.5 percent, with moderate variation among states (see Table 8.9). States with the highest underemployent are Guanajuato, Michoacan, and Guerrero (13 percent), whereas states with the lowest underemployment (under 5 percent), are Tamaulipas, Queretaro, and Nuevo Leon. As shown on Map 8.3A, by region, underemployment is highest in the west and gulf regions, followed by the central and gulf regions. Encircled by high underemployment, the Federal District has a low rate of 6 percent. In the pacific south, Guerrero has high underemployment, while Chiapas and Oaxaca are average, even though they are very poor states. The northeast region has very low underemployment. This is partly due to the prosperous metropolitan center of

Monterrey. The other border states are have moderate to low underemployment. Zacatecas's low underemployment of 6 percent is surprising given its low income (see Map 8.4A).

The geographic distribution of underemployment is somewhat similar to that of low income and opposite to that of urbanization. However, differences are quite apparent in the far south and Jalisco.

Unemployment, 1980

Unemployment is defined as the ratio of population employed zero hours per week to the economically active population. The aggregate unemployment for the nation was 7.2 percent, while the mean unemployment by state is 7.6 percent. The statewide coefficient of variation is moderate, but higher than for underemployment. As reported in Table 8.10 and shown on Map 8.3B, states with the highest unemployment include Zacatecas (20 percent), Guerrero (14 percent), and Durango (13 percent). While Zacatecas and Gurrero are consistently among the poorer states (for example, as measured by gross state revenues, value of corporations, and low income; see Maps 7.6A, 7.7A, 8.4A), Durango in 1980 is a state of average prosperity. The states with the lowest unemployment are Colima, Tabasco, Baja California Sur, and Campeche. Among possible explanations, Colima and Baja California Sur are tourist oriented states and rapidly-growing in the latter case, whereas Tabasco and Campeche are the most important petroleum-producing states.

The geographic distribution of employment differs from that of underemployment. Unemployment is especially high in the pacific south and southern north regions. The borderlands shows considerable variation, from 5 percent in Baja to 9 percent in Chihuahua (see Pick et al., 1987a). Unemployment in the Federal District is low (4.4 percent), while it is moderate to high (7.4 percent, on average) in the central region circling the District. The west region shows great variation, while the gulf and southeast regions are low.

Table 8.9 Underemployment, 1980

No.	State	Underemployed Population, Age 12+	Economically Active Population, Age 12+	Ratio
1	AGUASCALIENTES	12,596	159,943	0.0788
2	BAJA CALIFORNIA	33,243	403,279	0.0824
3	BAJA CALIFORNIA SUR	4,288	69,954	0.0613
4	CAMPECHE	14,005	134,423	0.1042
5	COAHUILA	36,290	483,898	0.0750
6	COLIMA	7,475	108,754	0.0687
7	CHIAPAS	63,921	734,047	0.0871
8	CHIHUAHUA	46,965	664,707	0.0707
9	DISTRITO FEDERAL	186,183	3,312,581	0.0562
10	DURANGO	35,142	357,163	0.0984
11	GUANAJUATO	131,797	978,013	0.1348
12	GUERRERO	94,270	719,154	0.1311
13	HIDALGO	45,146	505,091	0.0894
14	JALISCO	150,082	1,413,854	0.1062
15	MEXICO	219,258	2,410,236	0.0910
16	MICHOACAN	114,945	872,775	0.1317
17	MORELOS	33,746	303,838	0.1111
18	NAYARIT	12,831	210,188	0.0610
19	NUEVO LEON	40,007	803,764	0.0498
20	OAXACA	73,588	858,283	0.0857
21	PUEBLA	96,430	1,081,573	0.0892
22	QUERETARO	10,900	224,435	0.0486
23	QUINTANA ROO	5,685	79,341	0.0717
24	SAN LUIS POTOSI	45,219	532,115	0.0850
25	SINALOA	49,598	568,427	0.0873
26	SONORA	29,603	484,277	0.0611
27	TABASCO	25,618	327,502	0.0782
28	TAMAULIPAS	23,652	624,497	0.0379
29	TLAXCALA	18,205	174,965	0.1040
30	VERACRUZ	175,510	1,796,219	0.0977
31	YUCATAN	43,862	367,825	0.1192
32	ZACATECAS	17,344	300,963	0.0576
	Mean	59,294	689,565	0.0848
	S.D.	56,560	688,928	0.0245
	C.V.	95.39	99.91	28.86
	Minimum	4,288	69,954	0.0379
	Maximum	219,258	3,312,581	0.1348

DEFINITION: Underemployed population consists of population working less than 1 to 16 hours per week. The ratio represents column 1 divided by column 2. Note that these figures exclude those not specifying age.

SOURCE: 1980 Mexican Census of Population, Volume 2, Table 12.

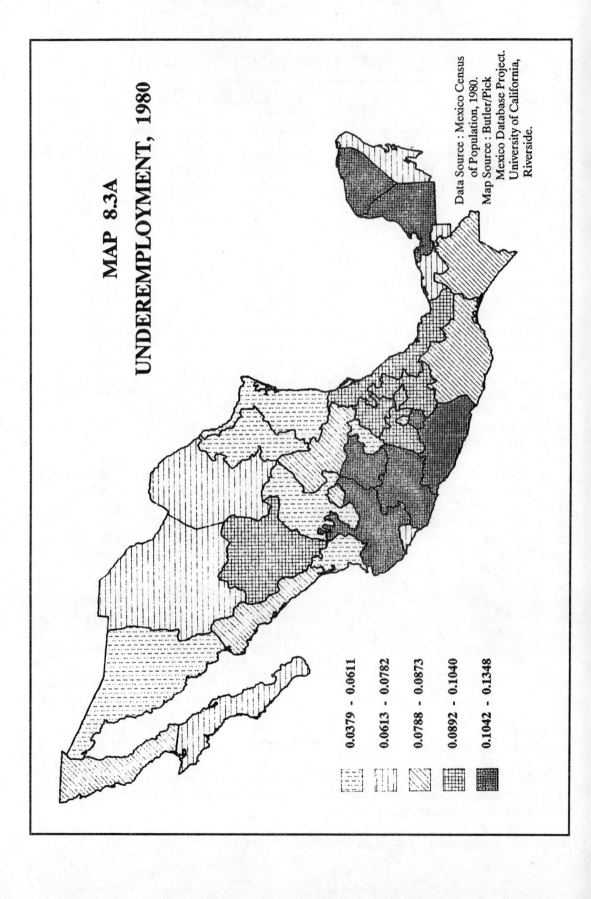

MAP 8.3A
UNDEREMPLOYMENT, 1980

Data Source : Mexico Census
  of Population, 1980.

Map Source : Butler/Pick
  Mexico Database Project.
  University of California,
  Riverside.

0.0379 - 0.0611

0.0613 - 0.0782

0.0788 - 0.0873

0.0892 - 0.1040

0.1042 - 0.1348

Table 8.10 Unemployment, 1980

No.	State	Unemployed Population Age 12+	Economically Active Population Age 12+	Ratio
1	AGUASCALIENTES	9,691	159,943	0.0606
2	BAJA CALIFORNIA	21,814	403,279	0.0541
3	BAJA CALIFORNIA SUR	3,354	69,954	0.0479
4	CAMPECHE	6,653	134,423	0.0495
5	COAHUILA	25,972	483,898	0.0537
6	COLIMA	3,861	108,754	0.0355
7	CHIAPAS	53,144	734,047	0.0724
8	CHIHUAHUA	62,895	664,707	0.0946
9	DISTRITO FEDERAL	145,082	3,312,581	0.0438
10	DURANGO	47,520	357,163	0.1300
11	GUANAJUATO	86,016	978,013	0.0879
12	GUERRERO	101,903	719,154	0.1417
13	HIDALGO	37,317	505,091	0.0739
14	JALISCO	102,431	1,413,854	0.0724
15	MEXICO	154,564	2,410,236	0.0641
16	MICHOACAN	84,472	872,775	0.0968
17	MORELOS	21,252	303,838	0.0699
18	NAYARIT	13,015	210,188	0.0619
19	NUEVO LEON	42,483	803,764	0.0529
20	OAXACA	85,176	858,283	0.0992
21	PUEBLA	70,382	1,081,573	0.0651
22	QUERETARO	15,962	224,435	0.0711
23	QUINTANA ROO	4,016	79,341	0.0560
24	SAN LUIS POTOSI	48,288	532,115	0.0907
25	SINALOA	49,152	568,427	0.0865
26	SONORA	32,011	484,277	0.0661
27	TABASCO	13,613	327,502	0.0416
28	TAMAULIPAS	46,084	624,497	0.0738
29	TLAXCALA	17,519	174,965	0.1001
30	VERACRUZ	99,716	1,796,219	0.0555
31	YUCATAN	19,899	367,825	0.0541
32	ZACATECAS	60,474	300,963	0.2009
	Mean	49,554		0.0757
	S.D.	40,483		0.0335
	C.V.	81.70		44.25
	Minimum	3,354		0.0355
	Maximum	154,564		0.2009

DEFINITION: Unemployed population consists of persons age 12+ working 0 hours per week. Ratio is the unemployed population to the population economically active age 12+. Note that these figures exclude those not specifying age.

SOURCE: 1980 Mexican Census of Population, Volume 1, Tables 6 & 7.

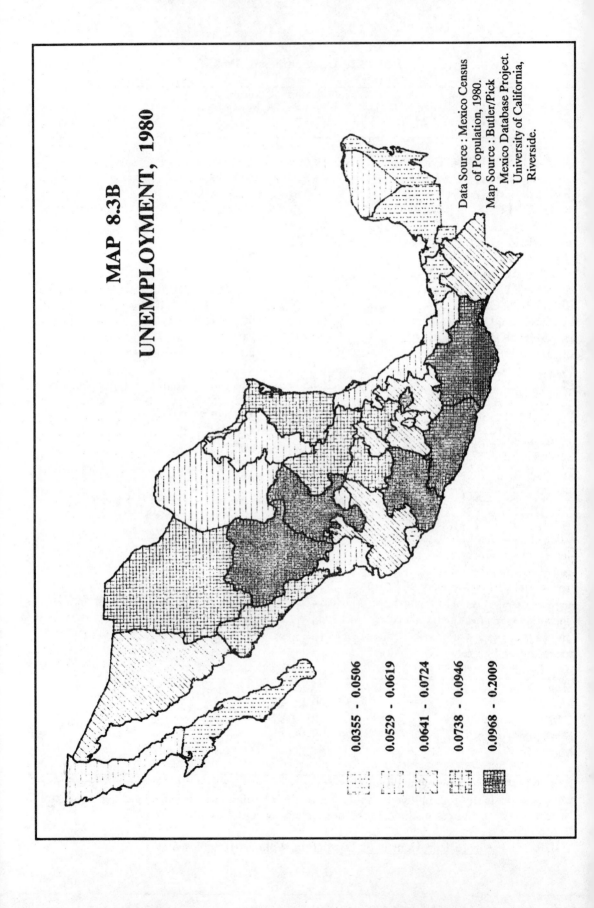

MAP 8.3B
UNEMPLOYMENT, 1980

0.0355 - 0.0506

0.0529 - 0.0619

0.0641 - 0.0724

0.0738 - 0.0946

0.0968 - 0.2009

Data Source : Mexico Census
of Population, 1980.
Map Source : Butler/Pick
Mexico Database Project.
University of California,
Riverside.

Income

Since 1980 there has been a very large peso devaluation effect on income levels. For example, in mid-1988 the value of the peso was 2,281, whereas it was about 23 in 1980. Therefore the 1980 monthly level of 1,081 pesos would be equivalent to about 107,436 pesos in 1988. However, the value of the present variable does not reflect devaluation change since it represents the percentage of the economically active population falling into this category as of 1980.

Population with Low Monthly Income, 1980

The mean value for low income that is, less than 1,081 pesos in 1980 is 9.4 percent (see Table 8.11). The coefficient of variation is 43. Thus there is moderate variation by state in low income levels. A similar extent of variation also apply for moderate and high monthly income. The Federal District has the lowest level of low level income of 3.2 percent. This is not surprising given the capital's very high economic productivity and proportion economically active. Also, many poverty areas in the central metropolis lie on its periphery, outside the Federal District. High rates of non-response to the income questions of the Census tend to lower values for this variable, since non-respondents tend to be poorer (Pick, Tellis, and Butler, 1987b). Baja California, Baja California Sur, and Nuevo Leon are next lowest. Reasons for low income levels include presence of large economically productive border cities and higher income levels keyed to a dollar-based economy in the binational borderlands. The highest value for percent low income is for Yucatan. This is somewhat surprising since Yucatan has medium values on most other economic variables. Next in descending order are Hidalgo, Puebla, Oaxaca, and Tlaxcala. These states are more commonly considered economically weak.

Low income areas are very distinct on Map 8.4A, and they overlap the standard regions. There is a six state zone of very high percent low income, encompassing Oaxaca, Puebla, Tlaxcala, Veracruz, Hidalgo, and San Luis Potosi. The west, south, and southwest contain other states of high percent low income. However, the predominantly high proportion low income in the south of the nation is punctuated by the very high values in the central zone. Northern regions generally have moderate to low proportions low income. This is due in part to proximity to the border's dollar-based economy.

The distribution of low monthy income is strongly associated with serval other major dimensions, including agricultural labor force and occupation, indigenous language population, population native to state, and percent having no meat or eggs. In addition, it has a strong association to dependency ratio and sex ratio. On the other hand, its pattern is strongly opposite to those for urbanization, urbanization change 1950-80, literacy, education, and administrative, service, and other occupations. These relationships are largely reversed for moderate monthly income.

Population with at Least a Moderate Monthly Income, 1980

For our purposes, a moderate monthly income was considered being above 6,610 pesos. As pointed out in the introduction to this section, the peso criterion used here was 23 per U.S. dollar in 1980. As reported in Table 8.12, the Federal District has the highest percentage of persons with at least a moderate income (39.1 percent), while Baja California, Baja California Sur, and Nuevo Leon all have over 30 percent of the population with moderate or better incomes.

As with so many other characteristics in Mexico, there is a clear north-south axis with all northern states having a relatively high percentage of the population having at least a moderate monthly income (see Map 8.4B). This is apparently consistent even though the border states also are those with high unemployment rates. Other states with relatively high percentages of moderate or better incomes are Mexico, Sonora, and Tamaulipas. The major exceptions to the north-south axis are the states of Mexico and the Federal District which are surrounded by states with low or extremely low percentages of persons with at least a moderate income. Further south of the Federal District, only Tabasco and Quintana Roo have a relatively high percentage of their population with moderate or better incomes. The geographic pattern for moderate and high monthly incomes are significantly opposite to that for low monthly income. The distribution and data for high monthly incomes are not included here because of the extreme comparability in distribution of medium and high incomes.

Table 8.11 Population with Low Monthly Income (1-1,080 Pesos), 1980

No.	State	Low Income Population	Economically Active Population	Ratio
1	AGUASCALIENTES	11,243	140,059	0.0803
2	BAJA CALIFORNIA	13,770	327,620	0.0420
3	BAJA CALIFORNIA SUR	2,577	60,331	0.0427
4	CAMPECHE	10,665	104,382	0.1022
5	COAHUILA	28,198	416,512	0.0677
6	COLIMA	5,972	102,735	0.0581
7	CHIAPAS	61,901	572,875	0.1081
8	CHIHUAHUA	33,997	555,727	0.0612
9	DISTRITO FEDERAL	95,020	2,967,660	0.0320
10	DURANGO	25,400	290,666	0.0874
11	GUANAJUATO	78,018	774,103	0.1008
12	GUERRERO	61,203	530,391	0.1154
13	HIDALGO	76,186	413,535	0.1842
14	JALISCO	90,320	1,176,808	0.0767
15	MEXICO	121,799	1,999,714	0.0609
16	MICHOACAN	79,162	711,158	0.1113
17	MORELOS	22,793	250,223	0.0911
18	NAYARIT	17,034	197,435	0.0863
19	NUEVO LEON	32,128	706,461	0.0455
20	OAXACA	87,900	655,536	0.1341
21	PUEBLA	137,501	899,928	0.1528
22	QUERETARO	18,889	208,582	0.0906
23	QUINTANA ROO	5,815	66,097	0.0880
24	SAN LUIS POTOSI	65,278	515,987	0.1265
25	SINALOA	30,917	466,795	0.0662
26	SONORA	21,381	409,613	0.0522
27	TABASCO	25,050	287,184	0.0872
28	TAMAULIPAS	40,247	530,678	0.0758
29	TLAXCALA	17,642	137,944	0.1279
30	VERACRUZ	181,521	1,431,621	0.1268
31	YUCATAN	60,561	286,668	0.2113
32	ZACATECAS	28,127	282,606	0.0995
Mean		49,632	577,426	0.0935
S.D.		42,022	593,201	0.0397
C.V.		84.67	102.73	42.50
Minimum		2,577	60,331	0.0320
Maximum		181,521	2,967,660	0.2113
National Total		1,588,215	18,477,634	

DEFINITION: Low income population consists of persons age 12+ with monthly income less than 1,081 pesos. Ratio is the low income population to the economically active population age 12+. Note that persons not specifying age or income are excluded from these figures.

SOURCE: 1980 Mexican Census of Population, Volume 1, Tables 6 & 10.

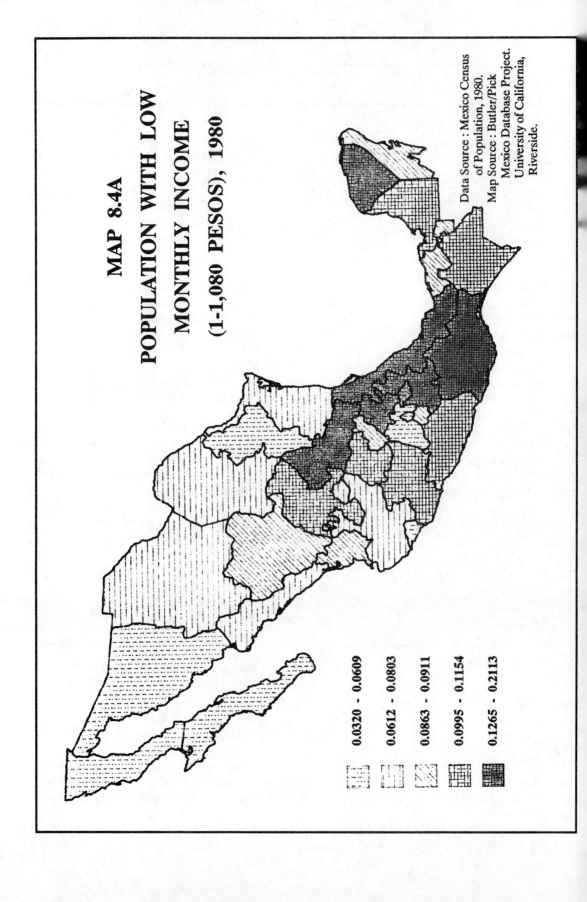

MAP 8.4A

POPULATION WITH LOW
MONTHLY INCOME
(1-1,080 PESOS), 1980

Data Source : Mexico Census
of Population, 1980.

Map Source : Butler/Pick
Mexico Database Project.
University of California,
Riverside.

0.0320 - 0.0609

0.0612 - 0.0803

0.0863 - 0.0911

0.0995 - 0.1154

0.1265 - 0.2113

Table 8.12 Population With At Least Moderate Monthly Income (Above 6,610 Pesos)

No. State	At Least Moderate Income	Economically Active	Ratio	High Income	Economically Active	Ratio
1 AGUASCALIENTES	19,090	140,059	0.1363	5,937	140,059	0.0424
2 BAJA CALIFORNIA	117,731	327,620	0.3594	42,429	327,620	0.1295
3 BAJA CALIFORNIA SUR	22,876	60,331	0.3792	7,185	60,331	0.1191
4 CAMPECHE	19,912	104,382	0.1908	5,163	104,382	0.0495
5 COAHUILA	102,140	416,512	0.2452	32,574	416,512	0.0782
6 COLIMA	22,640	102,735	0.2204	6,233	102,735	0.0607
7 CHIAPAS	49,067	572,875	0.0857	14,015	572,875	0.0245
8 CHIHUAHUA	115,111	555,727	0.2071	37,840	555,727	0.0681
9 DISTRITO FEDERAL	1,160,117	2,967,660	0.3909	445,503	2,967,660	0.1501
10 DURANGO	40,978	290,666	0.1410	12,505	290,666	0.0430
11 GUANAJUATO	92,800	774,103	0.1199	30,329	774,103	0.0392
12 GUERRERO	49,664	530,391	0.0936	12,975	530,391	0.0245
13 HIDALGO	44,797	413,535	0.1083	11,241	413,535	0.0272
14 JALISCO	235,707	1,176,808	0.2003	72,760	1,176,808	0.0618
15 MEXICO	500,668	1,999,714	0.2504	174,170	1,999,714	0.0871
16 MICHOACAN	77,688	711,158	0.1092	22,495	711,158	0.0316
17 MORELOS	41,683	250,223	0.1666	12,128	250,223	0.0485
18 NAYARIT	28,018	197,435	0.1419	7,340	197,435	0.0372
19 NUEVO LEON	229,515	706,461	0.3249	84,135	706,461	0.1191
20 OAXACA	38,032	655,536	0.0580	9,784	655,536	0.0149
21 PUEBLA	97,473	899,928	0.1083	29,201	899,928	0.0324
22 QUERETARO	35,657	208,582	0.1709	11,366	208,582	0.0545
23 QUINTANA ROO	15,570	66,097	0.2356	4,716	66,097	0.0713
24 SAN LUIS POTOSI	48,283	515,987	0.0936	14,413	515,987	0.0279
25 SINALOA	95,699	466,795	0.2050	30,346	466,795	0.0650
26 SONORA	111,091	409,613	0.2712	37,767	409,613	0.0922
27 TABASCO	60,596	287,184	0.2110	20,252	287,184	0.0705
28 TAMAULIPAS	131,679	530,678	0.2481	43,484	530,678	0.0819
29 TLAXCALA	11,721	137,944	0.0850	2,407	137,944	0.0174
30 VERACRUZ	228,401	1,431,621	0.1595	71,739	1,431,621	0.0501
31 YUCATAN	37,881	286,668	0.1321	11,188	286,668	0.0390
32 ZACATECAS	22,982	282,606	0.0813	5,994	282,606	0.0212
Mean	122,040		0.1853	41,550		0.0587
S.D.	209,525		0.0885	79,829		0.0339
C.V.	171.69		47.73	192.12		57.66
Minimum	11,721		0.0580	2,407		0.0149
Maximum	1,160,117		0.3909	445,503		0.1501

DEFINITION: Population with at least moderate income consists of persons age 12+ with monthly income greater than 6,610 pesos. Ratio is the at least moderate income population to the economically active population age 12+. High income population consists of persons age 12+ with monthly income greater than 12,110 pesos. Ratio is the high income population to the economically active population age 12+. Note that the values shown exclude persons not specifying income or age.

SOURCE: 1980 Mexican Census of Population, Volume 1, Tables 6 & 10.

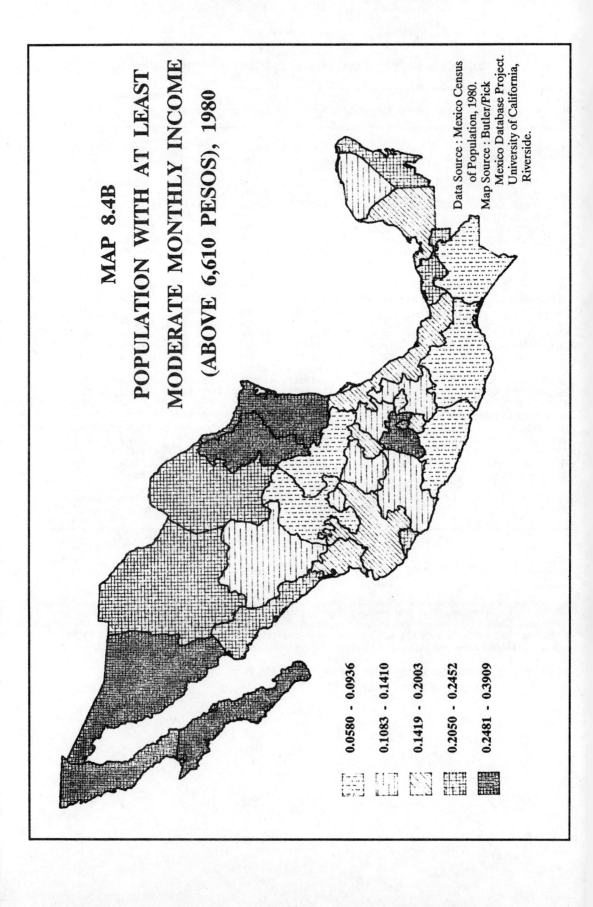

MAP 8.4B
POPULATION WITH AT LEAST
MODERATE MONTHLY INCOME
(ABOVE 6,610 PESOS), 1980

Data Source : Mexico Census
of Population, 1980.
Map Source : Butler/Pick
Mexico Database Project.
University of California,
Riverside.

0.0580 - 0.0936
0.1083 - 0.1410
0.1419 - 0.2003
0.2050 - 0.2452
0.2481 - 0.3909

9
TRANSPORTATION AND COMMUNICATION

Introduction

This chapter examines transportation and communication in Mexico. Related information in Chapter 6 illustrated gasoline consumption, films, and households with television.

In the first part of the chapter, data on major highways and vehicles, length of major highways, and fatal vehicle accidents are presented. Two air transportation dimensions of international airports and commercial air passengers are shown and discussed. Also there is a focus on major seaports. An historical series illustrates the development of railroads in Mexico, beginning in 1880 and concluding in 1980. Then, telephone and radio and television stations per capita are presented. The information in this chapter was primarily abstracted from anuarios; however, the Mexican census and various other official and unofficial documents, reports, and books were consulted. As previously, the dimensions and the time periods illustrated are only a portion of those available.

Highways and Vehicles

Registered Owned Vehicles, 1984

Registered privately-owned vehicles per capita shows moderate to large variation among states with a coefficient of variation of 75. The statewide mean of 0.10 implies that there is one registered owned vechicle for every 10 Mexicans (see Table 9.1). This ratio considerably less than the ratio of one vechicle to 1.8 persons in the United States (U.S. Bureau of the Census, 1988). Map 9.1A shows the strong north-south axis, with north states having higher than average rates. By far the highest rate is in Baja California, with Baja California Sur, the Federal District, Colima, and Chihuahua also having substantially higher rates that the rest of Mexico. The lowest rates are in Oaxaca and Chiapas with Campeche, Durango, Guanajuato, Guerrero, Hidalgo, Michoacan, Nayarit, Queretaro, San Luis Potosi, Sinaloa, Veracruz, and Zacatecas also having very low rates. All states in the northern regions have high or relatively high rates while all states south of the Federal District have extremely low rates, or at best intermediate rates such as in Yucatan and Quintana Roo.

Other than for the high levels in the border region and the low levels in the gulf and pacific south regions, there appears to be little correspondence between standard regions and registered privately-owned vehicles per capita. In geographic pattern, this variable closely resembles urbanization in 1980 (Map 2.6A) and per capita gasoline consumption (Map 6.5A), as well as the communications dimensions in this chapter of telephones and radio/TV stations.

Major Highways, 1985

Table 9.2 reports that while the rate of registered owned motor vehicles is greater in the north than the south, major highways in Mexico in 1985, were located primarily in the middle of the country. As shown on Map 9.1B, in the northern part of the country major highways primarily follow a north-south direction paralleling the major mountain ranges, Sierra Madre Occidental and Sierra Madre Oriental. The impact that topographical features have on population movement and other aspects of social life in Mexico are very clear. For example, the major flow of migrants in Mexico to Baja California is northward on the western side of the country rather from the middle or east (Butler et al., 1987a). This migration flow follows the mountain ranges, which in turn, influenced the location of major highways. Thus, it is not too surprising that there are relatively few east-west major traffic arteries in the northern section of Mexico. In the northwest and north, major highways and railroads substantially follow the same patterns (see Maps 9.1B and 9.4A-F).

The middle flank of the country, including the west, central, and gulf regions, has a high concentration of highways. The tight knot of major highways in the center of the nation corresponds to the Mexico City metropolitan zone. Major highways are less prevalent in the states of Chiapas, Tabasco, Campeche, and Quintana Roo. Chiapas is economically underdeveloped and has rough terrain including the Sierra Madre de Chiapas mountain range, while Campeche and Quintana Roo have low population densities. In the middle flank and more southern sections of Mexico, major highway routes again correspond to railroad lines.

Length of Highways Per Square Kilometer, 1985

There is a moderately large coefficient of variation implying that there is variation in length of highways among the various Mexican states (see Table 9.2). As with the location of major highways, length of major highways per square kilometer is not related substantially with registered owned vehicles per capita (Map 9.1A). All northern regions and states have a high per capita rate of personal vehicles but have the lowest length of highways, as measured on a per square kilometer basis. The highest ratios in length of highways are in the central part of the country with the Federal District, Tlaxcala and Morelos leading the way, and with all of their surrounding states having high ratios. Also, Aguascalientes and Colima have high ratios. Low ratios are prevalent towards the southeast, in the states of Chiapas, Tabasco, Campeche, and Quintana Roo. Clearly, the central part of the country is substantially more developed insofar as having major highways and greater length of highways per square kilometer than the southern and especially the northern regions (see Map 9.1C).

Fatal Vehicle Accidents, 1984

The national mean for fatal vehicle accidents per one thousand population is 0.10. There is a moderate coefficient of variation among states (CV=38). Table 9.3 shows that the highest rates of fatal vehicle accidents are in Quintana Roo (0.19), Sinaloa (0.17), and Tabasco (0.16). Other states with high rates are Baja California, Baja California Sur, Colima, Nayarit, Queretaro, Sonora, and Tlaxcala. The Federal District has the lowest rate of 0.04, while the states of Chiapas, Oaxaca, Puebla, and Veracruz also have very low rates. In general northern states have higher rates than southern states, although there is a certain amount of inconsistency that is difficult to explain. The most urbanized state has the lowest rate, i.e. the Federal District, but Jalisco and Nuevo Leon with very large cities have fairly high rates. Similarly, there appears to be an inconsistency among other states regarding fatal vehicle accidents. There is however a consistency by year in fatal vehicle accidents that occur by state thus making an explanation ever more problematic (see Map 9.1D).

At the national level, fatal motor vehicle accidents are about equally likely to take place in the rural as opposed to an urban location (Anuario Estadistico, 1986). The spatial distribution of fatal motor vehicle accidents is opposite to that of population in 1980 (Map 2.1A), but corresponds to population growth 1970-80 (Map 2.2). This implies that motor vehicles fatalities tend to be higher in small but rapidly growing states. Fatal motor vehicle accidents are also related to the air transportation variables in the next section as well as to hotels and pensions (Map 10.1).

Table 9.1 Registered Owned Vehicles, 1984

No.	State	Vehicles 1979	Vehicles 1984	Total Population 1985	Ratio
1	AGUASCALIENTES	44,287	53,999	587,967	0.0918
2	BAJA CALIFORNIA	350,908	483,999	1,342,358	0.3606
3	BAJA CALIFORNIA SUR	37,793	70,739	244,335	0.2895
4	CAMPECHE	16,876	36,302	477,109	0.0761
5	COAHUILA	132,685	222,254	1,768,549	0.1257
6	COLIMA	29,546	86,233	393,001	0.2194
7	CHIAPAS	52,741	70,492	2,363,422	0.0298
8	CHIHUAHUA	222,200	409,237	2,282,143	0.1793
9	DISTRITO FEDERAL	1,455,066	1,684,891	10,101,582	0.1668
10	DURANGO	60,585	100,828	1,337,291	0.0754
11	GUANAJUATO	203,142	187,814	3,402,546	0.0552
12	GUERRERO	48,749	74,080	2,388,542	0.0310
13	HIDALGO	77,029	75,529	1,752,592	0.0431
14	JALISCO	530,204	457,318	4,960,253	0.0922
15	MEXICO	320,232	453,854	8,577,892	0.0529
16	MICHOACAN	114,588	179,407	3,249,685	0.0552
17	MORELOS	71,536	131,617	1,075,520	0.1224
18	NAYARIT	25,238	48,300	821,740	0.0588
19	NUEVO LEON	209,496	323,860	2,858,577	0.1133
20	OAXACA	43,293	88,777	2,687,506	0.0330
21	PUEBLA	136,164	257,346	3,791,942	0.0679
22	QUERETARO	32,628	48,945	835,578	0.0586
23	QUINTANA ROO	10,872	20,072	255,801	0.0785
24	SAN LUIS POTOSI	74,503	91,413	1,894,215	0.0483
25	SINALOA	92,633	123,192	2,096,380	0.0588
26	SONORA	166,590	187,592	1,721,219	0.1090
27	TABASCO	22,516	79,006	1,202,396	0.0657
28	TAMAULIPAS	209,559	352,439	2,188,354	0.1611
29	TLAXCALA	16,023	51,761	629,932	0.0822
30	VERACRUZ	181,885	297,056	6,122,945	0.0485
31	YUCATAN	59,131	71,092	1,211,414	0.0587
32	ZACATECAS	23,934	64,536	1,282,458	0.0503
	National Total	5,072,632	6,883,980		
	Mean	158,520	215,124		0.0987
	S.D.	259,540	297,144		0.0743
	C.V.	163.73	138.1266		75.2257
	Minimum	10,872	20,072		0.0298
	Maximum	1,455,066	1,684,891		0.3606

DEFINITION: Ratio is the number of registered privately owned vehicles 1984 to the total population 1985.

SOURCE: 1980 Anuario Estadistico, Table 2.1.11; 1984 Anuario Estadistico, Table 2.1.18.

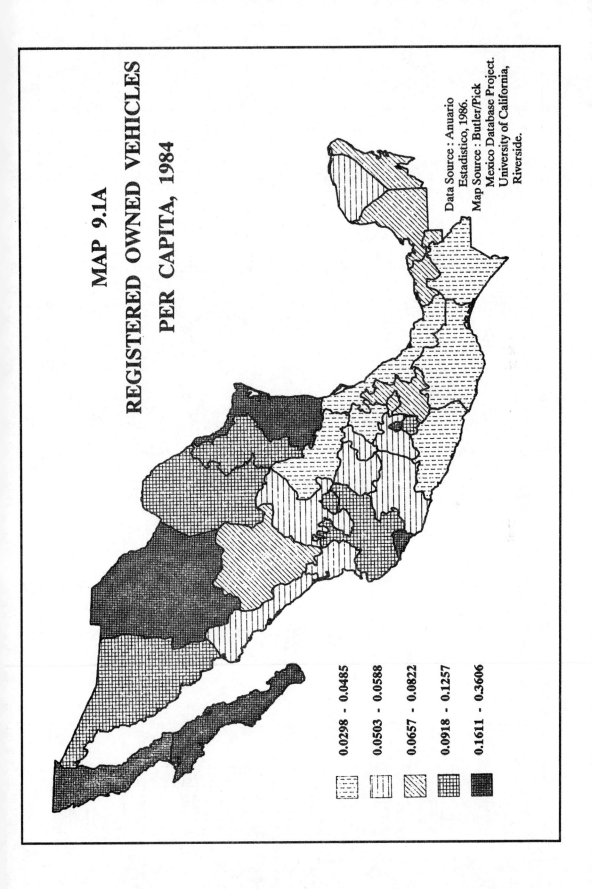

MAP 9.1A

REGISTERED OWNED VEHICLES
PER CAPITA, 1984

Data Source : Anuario
Estadistico, 1986.

Map Source : Butler/Pick
Mexico Database Project.
University of California,
Riverside.

0.0298 - 0.0485

0.0503 - 0.0588

0.0657 - 0.0822

0.0918 - 0.1257

0.1611 - 0.3606

Table 9.2 Length of Federal Highways Per Square Kilometer, 1985

No. State	Land Area in Square Kilometers	Kilometers of Local and Rural Roads	Ratio	Kilometers of State Highways	Ratio	Kilometers of Federal Highways	Ratio
1 AGUASCALIENTES	5,471	1,129	0.2064	628	0.1148	352	0.0643
2 BAJA CALIFORNIA	69,921	4,127	0.0590	1,005	0.0144	1,672	0.0239
3 BAJA CALIFORNIA SUR	73,475	2,933	0.0399	1,521	0.0207	1,327	0.0181
4 CAMPECHE	50,812	1,504	0.0296	639	0.0126	1,245	0.0245
5 COAHUILA	149,982	6,185	0.0412	2,327	0.0155	1,569	0.0105
6 COLIMA	5,191	772	0.1487	475	0.0915	343	0.0661
7 CHIAPAS	74,211	5,649	0.0761	2,416	0.0326	2,259	0.0304
8 CHIHUAHUA	244,938	4,643	0.0190	2,388	0.0097	2,422	0.0099
9 DISTRITO FEDERAL	1,479					151	0.1021
10 DURANGO	123,181	5,478	0.0445	1,071	0.0087	2,135	0.0173
11 GUANAJUATO	30,491	2,574	0.0844	2,175	0.0713	1,317	0.0432
12 GUERRERO	64,281	5,804	0.0903	790	0.0123	2,223	0.0346
13 HIDALGO	20,813	3,163	0.1520	1,998	0.0960	1,072	0.0515
14 JALISCO	80,836	5,017	0.0621	2,832	0.0350	2,286	0.0283
15 MEXICO	21,355	3,166	0.1483	4,510	0.2112	1,079	0.0505
16 MICHOACAN	59,928	5,572	0.0930	2,231	0.0372	2,471	0.0412
17 MORELOS	4,950	1,106	0.2234	794	0.1604	458	0.0925
18 NAYARIT	26,979	1,414	0.0524	708	0.0262	776	0.0288
19 NUEVO LEON	64,924	2,878	0.0443	1,998	0.0308	1,625	0.0250
20 OAXACA	93,952	7,226	0.0769	1,335	0.0142	3,089	0.0329
21 PUEBLA	33,902	4,272	0.1260	1,610	0.0475	1,507	0.0445
22 QUERETARO	11,449	2,092	0.1827	733	0.0640	653	0.0570
23 QUINTANA ROO	50,212	1,655	0.0330	1,061	0.0211	1,009	0.0201
24 SAN LUIS POTOSI	63,068	4,149	0.0658	1,310	0.0208	1,650	0.0262
25 SINALOA	58,328	6,083	0.1043	3,668	0.0629	930	0.0159
26 SONORA	182,052	5,445	0.0299	4,150	0.0228	1,635	0.0090
27 TABASCO	25,267	2,117	0.0838	2,402	0.0951	570	0.0226
28 TAMAULIPAS	79,384	6,742	0.0849	2,929	0.0369	2,140	0.0270
29 TLAXCALA	4,016	1,944	0.4841	440	0.1096	585	0.1457
30 VERACRUZ	71,699	5,794	0.0808	3,071	0.0428	2,953	0.0412
31 YUCATAN	38,402	3,488	0.0908	1,140	0.0297	1,184	0.0308
32 ZACATECAS	73,252	6,568	0.0897	1,694	0.0231	1,510	0.0206
National Total	1,958,201	120,689		56,049		46,197	
Mean	61,193.7813	3,893.1935		1,808.0323		1,443.6563	
S.D.	52,856.5437	1,915.4065		1,070.0583		762.5671	
C.V.	86.38	49.20		59.18		52.82	
Minimum	1,479	772		440		151	
Maximum	244,938	6,742		4,510		3,089	

DEFINITION: Ratio is the 1985 length of highways in kilometers to area in square kilometers.

SOURCE: 1986 Anuario Estadistico, Table 2.1.17.

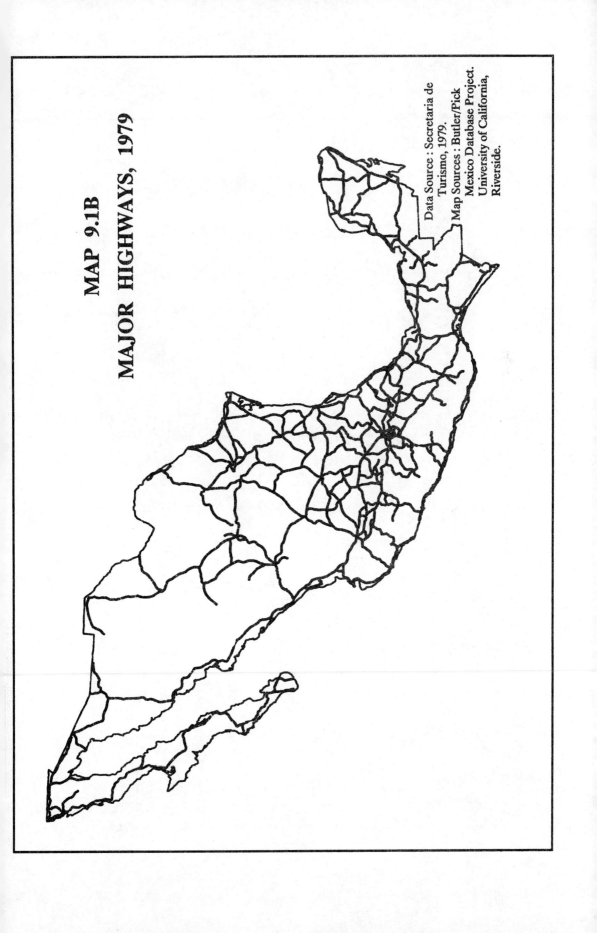

MAP 9.1B

MAJOR HIGHWAYS, 1979

Data Source : Secretaria de
Turismo, 1979.
Map Sources : Butler/Pick
Mexico Database Project.
University of California,
Riverside.

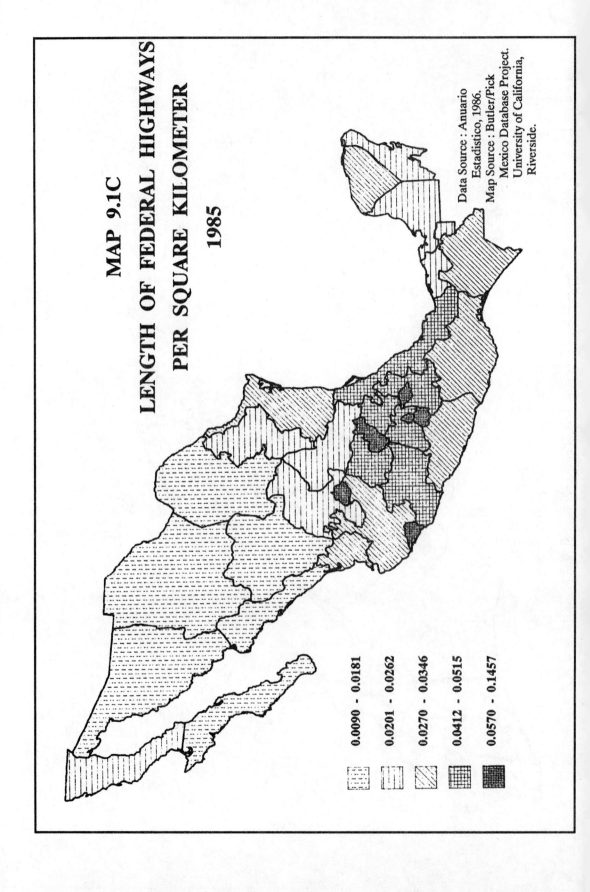

MAP 9.1C

LENGTH OF FEDERAL HIGHWAYS
PER SQUARE KILOMETER

1985

0.0090 - 0.0181

0.0201 - 0.0262

0.0270 - 0.0346

0.0412 - 0.0515

0.0570 - 0.1457

Data Source : Anuario
Estadistico, 1986.

Map Source : Butler/Pick
Mexico Database Project.
University of California,
Riverside.

Table 9.3 Fatal Vehicle Accidents, 1984

No.	State	Fatal Accidents 1979	Fatal Accidents 1984	Total Population 1985	Ratio
1	AGUASCALIENTES	77	63	587,967	0.1071
2	BAJA CALIFORNIA	166	195	1,342,358	0.1453
3	BAJA CALIFORNIA SUR	42	34	244,335	0.1392
4	CAMPECHE	50	37	477,109	0.0776
5	COAHUILA	178	162	1,768,549	0.0916
6	COLIMA	65	51	393,001	0.1298
7	CHIAPAS	137	141	2,363,422	0.0597
8	CHIHUAHUA	164	208	2,282,143	0.0911
9	DISTRITO FEDERAL	528	402	10,101,582	0.0398
10	DURANGO	105	120	1,337,291	0.0897
11	GUANAJUATO	200	282	3,402,546	0.0829
12	GUERRERO	233	190	2,388,542	0.0795
13	HIDALGO	131	117	1,752,592	0.0668
14	JALISCO	361	335	4,960,253	0.0675
15	MEXICO	457	567	8,577,892	0.0661
16	MICHOACAN	386	242	3,249,685	0.0745
17	MORELOS	123	79	1,075,520	0.0735
18	NAYARIT	123	97	821,740	0.1180
19	NUEVO LEON	189	230	2,858,577	0.0805
20	OAXACA	188	161	2,687,506	0.0599
21	PUEBLA	316	196	3,791,942	0.0517
22	QUERETARO	72	88	835,578	0.1053
23	QUINTANA ROO	63	49	255,801	0.1916
24	SAN LUIS POTOSI	242	183	1,894,215	0.0966
25	SINALOA	320	347	2,096,380	0.1655
26	SONORA	280	219	1,721,219	0.1272
27	TABASCO	175	197	1,202,396	0.1638
28	TAMAULIPAS	256	205	2,188,354	0.0937
29	TLAXCALA	32	73	629,932	0.1159
30	VERACRUZ	493	340	6,122,945	0.0555
31	YUCATAN	108	89	1,211,414	0.0735
32	ZACATECAS	129	105	1,282,458	0.0819
Mean		200	181		0.0957
S.D.		131	118		0.0363
C.V.		65.75	65.16		37.93
Minimum		32	34		0.0398
Maximum		528	567		0.1916

DEFINITION: Ratio is the number of fatal vehicle accidents 1984 to total population 1985 multiplied by 0.001.

SOURCE: 1980 Anuario Estadistico, Table 3.7.2; 1986 Anuario Estadistico, Table 3.5.9.

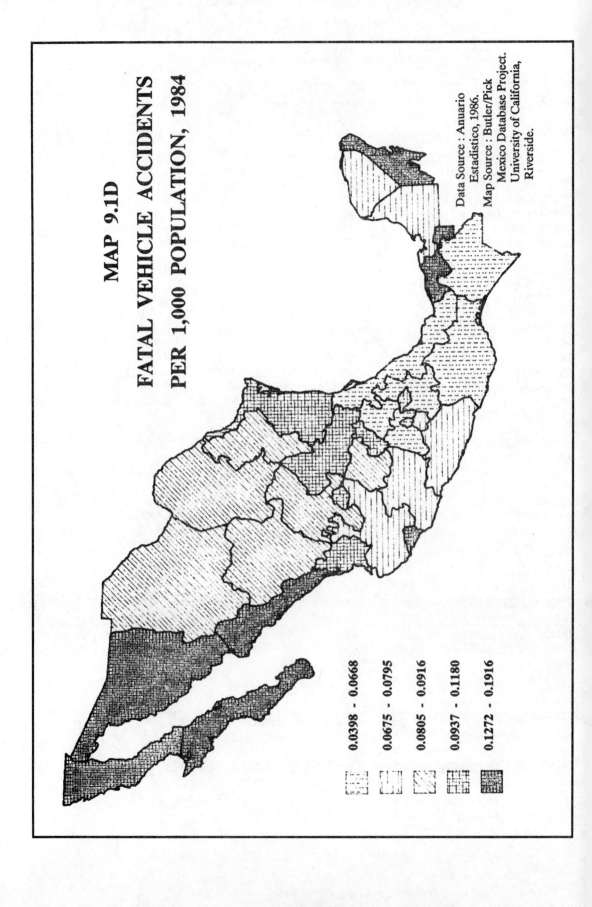

MAP 9.1D

FATAL VEHICLE ACCIDENTS
PER 1,000 POPULATION, 1984

0.0398 - 0.0668
0.0675 - 0.0795
0.0805 - 0.0916
0.0937 - 0.1180
0.1272 - 0.1916

Data Source : Anuario
Estadistico, 1986.
Map Source : Butler/Pick
Mexico Database Project.
University of California,
Riverside.

Air Transportation

International Airports, 1985

The international airports of Mexico are shown on Map 9.2A. About half of these international airports are primarily for tourists. Six of the international airports are located along the Mexico-U.S. border and one on the southern border. Baja California has two international airports while and Tamaulipas has four international airports, all of which serve both tourist and business interests. Baja California Sur has three international airports, almost exclusively tourist oriented. Guerrero's two airports located at Acapulco and Ixtapa-Zihuatanjo also are tourist oriented. Similarly, the three airports in Quintana Roo at Cozumel, Chetumal, and Cancun are primarily for the tourist industry. Jalisco has two airports, with the airport at Puerto Vallarta being primarily tourist oriented, and the international airport at Guadalajara serving both tourist and business activities. The Mexico City international airport, serving business and tourism, is the major one in the highly populous central region. Generally it must be concluded that most international airports in Mexico are tourist oriented. In fact, some of them were built only for that purpose, e.g. Puerto Vallarta, and Cozumel. Between 1979 and 1985, six more international airports were built in Mexico bringing the total to 35 (see Table II.1.43, Anuario, 1986).

In addition to international airports, there are many other major airports in Mexico scattered throughout the country (see Table 9.4 for total of national and international airports). Also, there are 1,335 other airports scattered throughout the country that are not considered as international or national airports (aerodromos), with every state containing at least two, with Chiapas, Chihuahua, and Veracruz having over 100 such airports (Anuario Estadistico, 1986).

Commercial Air Passengers, Per Capita, 1985

There are extreme differences in commercial air passengers by state on a per capita basis; the mean is 0.6, with an extremely substantial coefficent of variation of 218 (see Table 9.4). Part of this substantial variation is attributable to the fact that four states do not have a commercial airport-- Hidalgo, Morelos, Queretaro, and Tlaxcala. All of these states are located near or adjacent to the Federal District whose international airport undoubtedly also serves these states. However, the other obvious substantial contributor to the great variation in commercial air passengers is the location of international airports in the major tourist states of Quintana Roo, Baja California Sur, and Guerrero. Each of these states, it was noted in the previous section, has several airports that serve the tourist industry. Thus, by far the highest rate of 7.6 commercial air passengers per capita is for the state of Quintana Roo; this is followed by Baja California Sur with a rate of 2.8, and Baja California, the Federal District, and Guerrero with rates of 1.0-1.3 (see Map 9.2B). All other states have rates less than 1.0 and four states listed above have no commercial air passengers. In terms of raw numbers of passengers, the Federal District is by far the largest, accounting for about one third of the nation's 32 million air passengers. For the states, there is a substantial relationship between the tourist industry and commercial air passengers per capita (Butler et al., 1987b).

Table 9.4 Commercial Air Transportation Per Capita, 1985

No.	State	Total Passengers	Passengers Per Capita	Total Flights	Flights Per Capita	Total Airports	Airports Per 10,000 Pop.
1	AGUASCALIENTES	159,515	0.2713	3,454	0.0059	1	0.0170
2	BAJA CALIFORNIA	1,682,066	1.2531	15,915	0.0119	4	0.0298
3	BAJA CALIFORNIA SUR	694,601	2.8428	19,611	0.0803	5	0.2046
4	CAMPECHE	275,274	0.5770	22,082	0.0463	2	0.0419
5	COAHUILA	283,675	0.1604	7,851	0.0044	5	0.0283
6	COLIMA	285,958	0.7276	5,061	0.0129	2	0.0509
7	CHIAPAS	387,843	0.1641	5,449	0.0023	2	0.0085
8	CHIHUAHUA	634,351	0.2780	15,106	0.0066	2	0.0088
9	DISTRITO FEDERAL	12,088,183	1.1967	126,880	0.0126	1	0.0010
10	DURANGO	168,217	0.1258	6,533	0.0049	1	0.0075
11	GUANAJUATO	208,204	0.0612	4,212	0.0012	3	0.0088
12	GUERRERO	2,457,671	1.0289	29,310	0.0123	2	0.0084
13	HIDALGO	0	0.0000	0	0.0000	0	0.0000
14	JALISCO	4,176,671	0.8420	71,714	0.0145	2	0.0040
15	MEXICO	18,733	0.0022	909	0.0001	3	0.0035
16	MICHOACAN	103,483	0.0318	5,584	0.0017	3	0.0092
17	MORELOS	0	0.0000	0	0.0000	0	0.0000
18	NAYARIT	30,497	0.0371	4,553	0.0055	1	0.0122
19	NUEVO LEON	1,381,176	0.4832	18,716	0.0065	2	0.0070
20	OAXACA	467,430	0.1739	8,613	0.0032	2	0.0074
21	PUEBLA	3,950	0.0010	424	0.0001	2	0.0053
22	QUERETARO	0	0.0000	0	0.0000	0	0.0000
23	QUINTANA ROO	1,943,658	7.5983	35,604	0.1392	4	0.1564
24	SAN LUIS POTOSI	108,436	0.0572	2,601	0.0014	2	0.0106
25	SINALOA	1,364,715	0.6510	44,740	0.0213	3	0.0143
26	SONORA	615,355	0.3575	22,189	0.0129	5	0.0290
27	TABASCO	454,770	0.3782	9,161	0.0076	1	0.0083
28	TAMAULIPAS	873,146	0.3990	12,662	0.0058	5	0.0228
29	TLAXCALA	0	0.0000	0	0.0000	0	0.0000
30	VERACRUZ	605,341	0.0989	7,797	0.0013	4	0.0065
31	YUCATAN	617,135	0.5094	13,449	0.0111	1	0.0083
32	ZACATECAS	126,957	0.0990	2,429	0.0019	1	0.0078
	Mean	1,006,782	0.6377	16,332	0.0136	2	0.0228
	S.D.	2,174,243	1.3919	24,904	0.0278	2	0.0435
	C.V.	215.96	218.27	152.49	204.41	68.29	190.79
	Minimum	0	0.0000	0	0.0000	0	0.0000
	Maximum	12,088,183	7.5983	126,880	0.1392	5	0.2046

DEFINITION: Per capita values were calculated using 1985 total population. National and International airports are both included in the airport total.

SOURCE: 1986 Anuario Estadistico, Tables 2.1.41, 2.1.43.

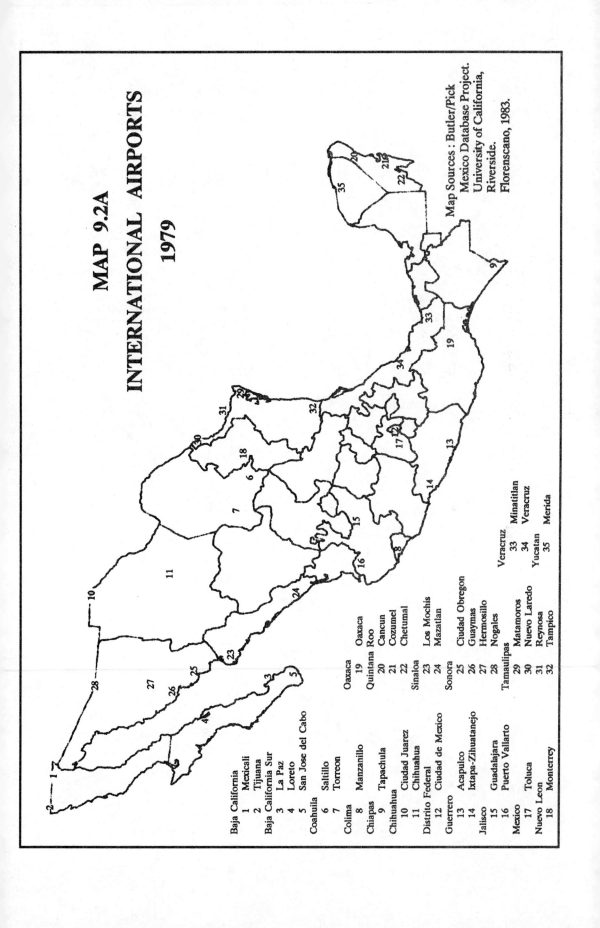

MAP 9.2A
INTERNATIONAL AIRPORTS
1979

Map Sources : Butler/Pick
Mexico Database Project.
University of California,
Riverside.
Florenscano, 1983.

Baja California
1   Mexicali
2   Tijuana
Baja California Sur
3   La Paz
4   Loreto
5   San Jose del Cabo
Coahuila
6   Saltillo
7   Torreon
Colima
8   Manzanillo
Chiapas
9   Tapachula
Chihuahua
10 Ciudad Juarez
11 Chihuahua
Distrito Federal
12 Ciudad de Mexico
Guerrero
13 Acapulco
14 Ixtapa-Zihuatanejo
Jalisco
15 Guadalajara
16 Puerto Vallarto
Mexico
17 Toluca
Nuevo Leon
18 Monterrey

Oaxaca
19 Oaxaca
Quintana Roo
20 Cancun
21 Cozumel
22 Chetumal
Sinaloa
23 Los Mochis
24 Mazatlan
Sonora
25 Ciudad Obregon
26 Guaymas
27 Hermosillo
28 Nogales
Tamaulipas
29 Matamoros
30 Nuevo Laredo
31 Reynosa
32 Tampico

Veracruz
33 Minatitlan
34 Veracruz
Yucatan
35 Merida

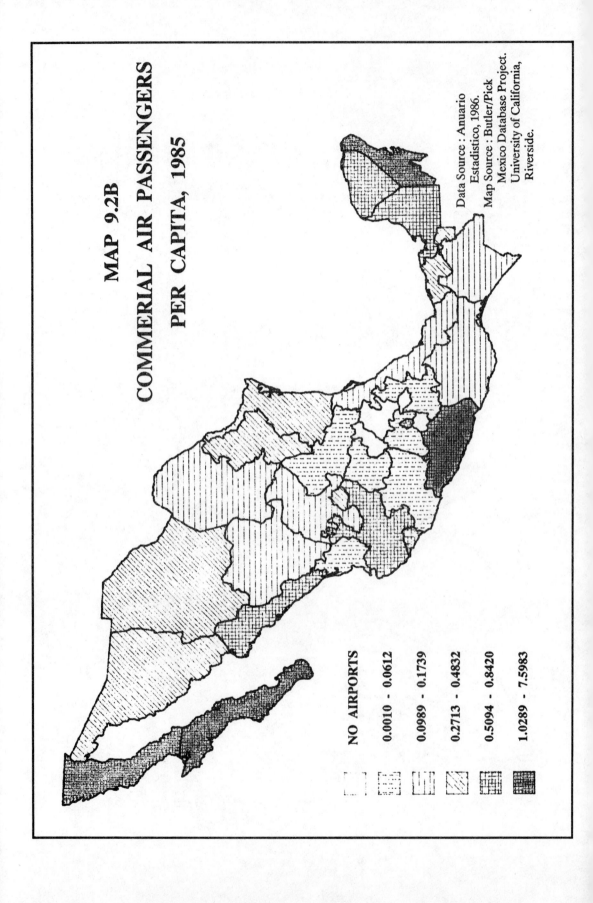

MAP 9.2B

COMMERIAL AIR PASSENGERS
PER CAPITA, 1985

Data Source : Anuario
Estadistico, 1986.
Map Source : Butler/Pick
Mexico Database Project.
University of California,
Riverside.

NO AIRPORTS

0.0010 - 0.0612

0.0989 - 0.1739

0.2713 - 0.4832

0.5094 - 0.8420

1.0289 - 7.5983

Major Seaports and Tonnage, 1985

Map 9.3 shows 12 major seaports in Mexico, as measured by total international tonnage of one million or more in 1985 (Anuario, 1986). The state of Veracruz contained three of these major seaports at Coatzacoalcos, Tuxpan, and Veracruz. Two other major seaports are located in the gulf -- Dos Bocas, Tabasco and Cuidad de Carmen, Campeche. Thus five of the twelve major seaports in Mexico are located in the three oil region states (see Pick et al., 1987b). Seven of the other major seaports are located on the pacific rim and the remaining major seaport is located in northeast Mexico at Tampico, Tamaulipas.

As shown in Table 9.5, tonnage handled by these major seaports is highly variable. Coatzacoalcos (29 million tons) and Ciudad de Carmen (23 million tons) in the gulf region handle substantially more tonnage than all other major seaports combined. Dos Bocas in the state of Tabasco also handled over two times more tonnage than any of the remaining major seaports. While there has been some variability over the past several years in the tonnage passing through these major seaports, they have remained substantially in the same rank order as far as total tonnage is concerned (Anuario Estadistico, 1986). Only two other seaports disembarked and embarked a total of more than .33 million tons in 1985--Mazatlan, Sinaloa (.53 million tons) and Progresso (Merida), Yucatan (.36 million tons).

Table 9.5 Major Seaports and Tonnage, 1985

No.	Major Seaports	International Tonnage Embarking	Debarking	Total	% nation	Domestic Tonnage Embarking	Debarking
	PACIFIC COAST	14,316,987	3,681,597	17,998,584	18.99	15,633,150	19,643,865
1	Isla de Cedros, Baja California	5,104,970	0	5,104,970	5.39	3,962	5,601,554
2	Santa Rosalia, Baja California Sur	1,917,554	18,026	1,935,580	2.04	30,310	92,371
3	Guaymas, Sonora	398,214	1,033,788	1,432,002	1.51	642,634	2,298,113
4	Manzanillo, Colima	184,154	1,293,197	1,477,352	1.56	782,561	3,044,915
5	Lazaro Cardenas, Michoacan	273,031	748,953	1,021,985	1.08	9,799	334,572
6	Salina Cruz, Oaxaca	6,363,056	22,798	6,385,854	6.74	7,043,659	527,429
	Manzatlan, Sinaloa	44,298	483,650	527,947	0.56	283,151	2,053,278
	Other	31,710	81,185	112,894	0.12	6,837,074	5,691,633
	GULF AND CARIBBEAN COAST	69,821,769	6,937,241	76,759,011	81.01	15,342,900	7,121,425
7	Tampico, Tamaulipas	2,860,187	1,756,924	4,617,111	4.87	4,345,298	1,201,871
8	Tuxpan, Veracruz	604,048	640,015	1,244,063	1.31	28,914	1,953,969
9	Veracruz, Veracruz	838,422	2,514,141	3,352,562	3.54	34,659	2,145,959
10	Coatzacoalcos, Veracruz	27,946,108	1,512,059	29,458,167	31.09	7,151,255	1,389,524
11	Dos Bocas, Tabasco	14,439,449	0	14,439,449	15.24	1,442,498	0
12	Ciudad del Carmen, Campeche	23,052,535	177,617	23,230,152	24.52	524,246	350,401
	Progreso, Yucatan	30,494	326,040	356,534	0.38	0	79,701
	Other	50,526	10,445	60,973	0.06	1,816,030	4,210,760
	National Total	84,138,756	10,618,838	94,757,595		30,976,050	30,976,050
	Mean	5,258,672	663,677	5,922,349	6.25	1,936,003	1,936,003
	S.D.	8,508,055	738,980	8,533,481	9.01	2,659,573	1,813,626
	C.V.	161.7909	111.3462	144.0894	144.0894	137.3744	93.67888
	Minimum	30,494	0	60,973	0.06	0	0
	Maximum	27,946,108	2,514,141	29,458,167	31.09	7,151,255	5,691,633

DEFINITION: Total international tonnage is the sum of embarking cargo at Mexican ports, in tons.

SOURCE: 1986 Anuario Estadistico, Table 2.1.36.

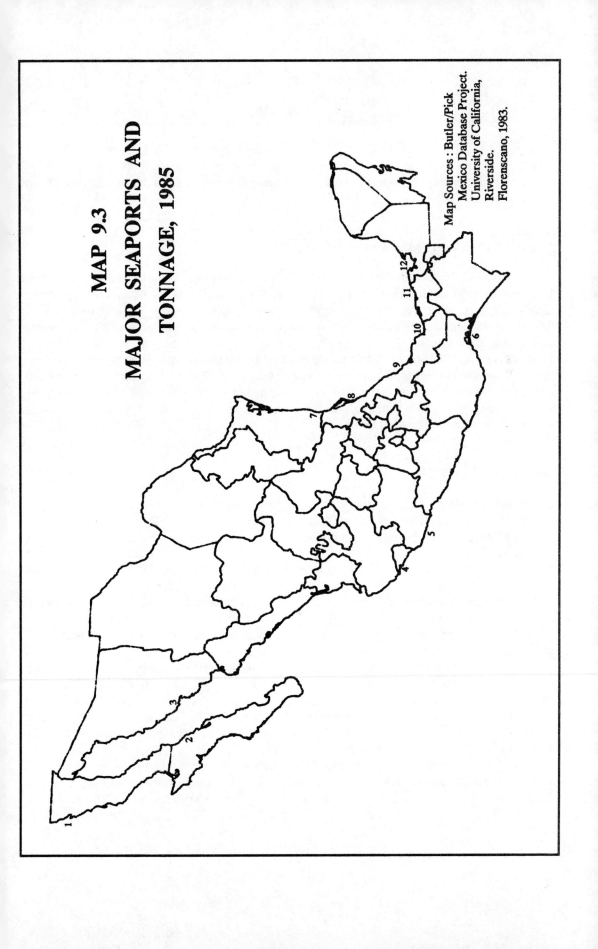

MAP 9.3
MAJOR SEAPORTS AND
TONNAGE, 1985

Map Sources : Butler/Pick
Mexico Database Project.
University of California,
Riverside.
Florenscano, 1983.

Railroads

Maps 9.4A-9.4E illustrate the growth of railroads in Mexico over the 100 years between 1880 and 1980. Railroads from the very beginning substantially followed the topography of the country. Thus, most major lines lie in a north-south direction and follow substantially the same routes as major highways (Map 9.1B).

Length of Railroads Per Square Kilometer, 1985

As shown in Table 9.6, the Federal District had among the fewest miles of railways in 1985 but had the highest ratio of length of railways per square kilometer (0.21). No other state approached such a high ratio. In fact, the next highest ratios were for Tlaxcala (0.09) and Morelos (0.06). Table 9.7 shows that Baja California Sur and Quintana Roo had no railway mileage in 1985. The Federal District and its surrounding states, along with Aguascalientes and Colima have the highest length of railroads per square kilometer. Most pacific south and southeast states have very low rates of railroads as measured by length of railways per square kilometer. Part of this distribution may be attributable to the smaller land area of the states with higher ratios (see Map 9.4A). In comparing the 1985 length of railroads with length in 1980, it is obvious that virtually no railroad construction took place in the first half of the 1980s.

Railroads, 1980 and 1910

As shown on Maps 9.4B-D, most major railroad lines in Mexico were completed by 1910, with interstitial and connecting lines only being completed between 1910 and 1980. Most rail lines in 1910, as in 1980, were in a north-south direction. Few railroads, even in 1985 are in an east-west direction. Five of the major lines terminate at the U.S. border and one railroad ends at the Guatemala border in the south. The Federal District is the focal point for many railroads; this focal point was established by 1910 and enhanced by more lines over the subsequent years (see Map 9.4E).

In 1910 there were several railroad lines in the Yucatan Peninsula, but they did not connect with the rest of Mexico. Another line crossed Mexico near its southern tip in Chiapas and also connected with a line to Mexico City. Thus, except for the Yucatan, by 1910 the southern states were linked to Mexico City by a railroad. Most railroads in 1910 were located in the center of the country. No railroad connected the rest of Mexico with Baja California in 1910 although subsequently there was a connection to Mexicali and then partially through the U.S. to Tijuana. In 1910, one major line ran up the northwest region, without an east-west connector. Another major parallel line ran up the center of the north region, with an east-west connector running east across the Sierra Madre Oriental mountains to Nuevo Leon. By 1980 these two major lines were connected by an east-west link across the Sierra Madre Occidental.

In 1910, there was no linkage between Mexico City and the states in the northwest region. This linkage was established between 1910 and 1980 so currently it is possible to travel from the rest of Mexico to the northwest states by rail. Also a linkage was established between 1910 and 1985 between the rest of Mexico and the Yucatan Peninsula, so it became possible to travel by rail from the southeast to the northwest and border regions.

Railroads, 1898, 1884 and 1880

Around 1880 there were three short railroads in Mexico, as seen in Map 9.4B. An extremely short railroad completed in 1881 connected Progresso with Merida in the state of Yucatan (Diccionario Porrua, 1964). Another very short railroad in the north central eventually joined a railroad link to the Federal District.

In January of 1873, the railroad line between Mexico City and Veracruz was inaugurated (Diccionario Porrua, 1964). While there were short railroad lines completed before 1880, series of main lines and connectors were completed by 1884 (see Map 9.4C). One railroad connected Nogales, Sonora on the U.S. border with the seaport of Guaymas, Sonora, in the Gulf of California. Another completed railroad linked the El Paso and Ciudad Juarez metropolitan area with Mexico City, which in turn connected to the seaport of Veracruz. Two short lines in Coahuila and Nuevo Leon connected to the U.S. but not to other railroads in Mexico. A variety of short lines not connected with other railroads were being built, one of which was being underway in the gulf and pacific south linking the gulf and Pacific Ocean. Other small links were under construction in the Yucatan.

By the turn of the century, the Yucatan was linked to Campeche but neither were yet connected to the rest of Mexico by railroad (see Map 9.4D). The link between Puerto Mexico on the Gulf in Veracruz and Salina Cruz in Oaxaca was completed. The line from Ciudad Juarez to Mexico City now had a series of connecting lines, including those completed earlier in Coahuila. Four of the eventual six railroad lines to the U.S. were completed during this era. Baja California's line remained to be built and connected to those linking the rest of Mexico. In railroad terms, the major two areas of Mexico not yet linked to the rest of the country at the turn of the century were Baja California and the Yucatan Peninsula. Baja California Sur and Quintana Roo still are not linked with the rest of Mexico by railroads as of 1985.

Table 9.6 Railroads, 1985

No.	State	Railroad Kilometers 1980	Railroad Kilometers 1985	Land Area in Square Kilometers	Ratio
1	AGUASCALIENTES	212	214	5,471	0.0391
2	BAJA CALIFORNIA	200	205	69,921	0.0029
3	BAJA CALIFORNIA SUR	0	0	73,475	0.0000
4	CAMPECHE	391	397	50,812	0.0078
5	COAHUILA	2,121	2,184	149,982	0.0146
6	COLIMA	192	199	5,191	0.0383
7	CHIAPAS	547	542	74,211	0.0073
8	CHIHUAHUA	2,581	2,642	244,938	0.0108
9	DISTRITO FEDERAL	343	313	1,479	0.2116
10	DURANGO	1,215	1,233	123,181	0.0100
11	GUANAJUATO	1,050	1,072	30,491	0.0352
12	GUERRERO	104	106	64,281	0.0016
13	HIDALGO	743	752	20,813	0.0361
14	JALISCO	1,010	1,036	80,836	0.0128
15	MEXICO	1,177	1,126	21,355	0.0527
16	MICHOACAN	1,127	1,144	59,928	0.0191
17	MORELOS	337	274	4,950	0.0554
18	NAYARIT	384	389	26,979	0.0144
19	NUEVO LEON	1,055	1,096	64,924	0.0169
20	OAXACA	672	684	93,952	0.0073
21	PUEBLA	993	1,026	33,902	0.0303
22	QUERETARO	298	301	11,449	0.0263
23	QUINTANA ROO	0	0	50,212	0.0000
24	SAN LUIS POTOSI	1,159	1,145	63,068	0.0182
25	SINALOA	1,175	1,229	58,328	0.0211
26	SONORA	1,879	1,965	182,052	0.0108
27	TABASCO	305	302	25,267	0.0120
28	TAMAULIPAS	864	938	79,384	0.0118
29	TLAXCALA	353	361	4,016	0.0899
30	VERACRUZ	1,765	1,755	71,699	0.0245
31	YUCATAN	600	607	38,402	0.0158
32	ZACATECAS	658	672	73,252	0.0092
	Mean	797	810		0.0270
	S.D.	622	639		0.0386
	C.V.	77.96	78.93		142.96
	Minimum	0	0		0.0000
	Maximum	2,581	2,642		0.2116

DEFINITION: Ratio is the 1985 kilometers length of railroads to the land area in square kilometers.

SOURCE: <u>1980 Anuario Estadistico</u>, Table 2.1.12; <u>1986 Anuario Estadistico</u>, Table 2.1.27.

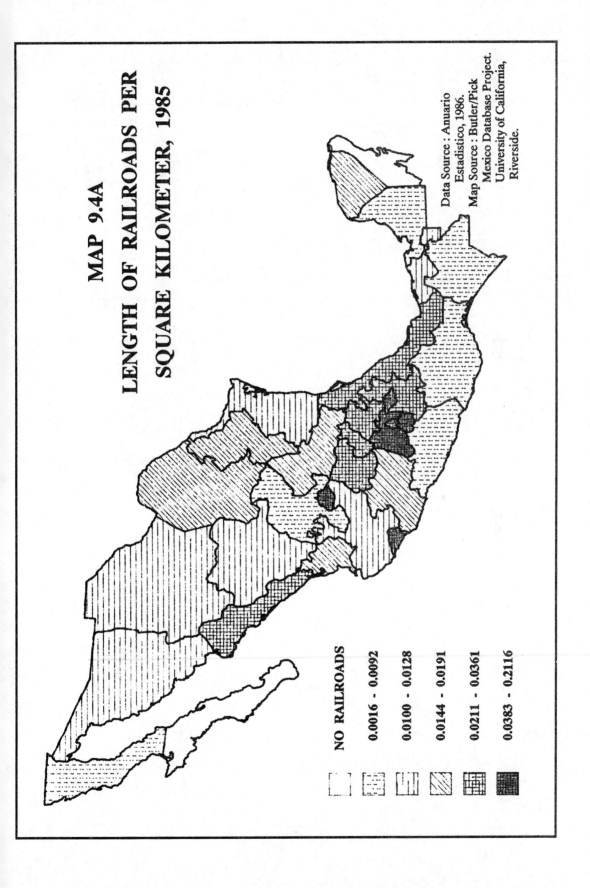

MAP 9.4A

LENGTH OF RAILROADS PER

SQUARE KILOMETER, 1985

Data Source : Anuario
    Estadistico, 1986.
Map Source : Butler/Pick
    Mexico Database Project.
    University of California,
    Riverside.

NO RAILROADS

0.0016 - 0.0092

0.0100 - 0.0128

0.0144 - 0.0191

0.0211 - 0.0361

0.0383 - 0.2116

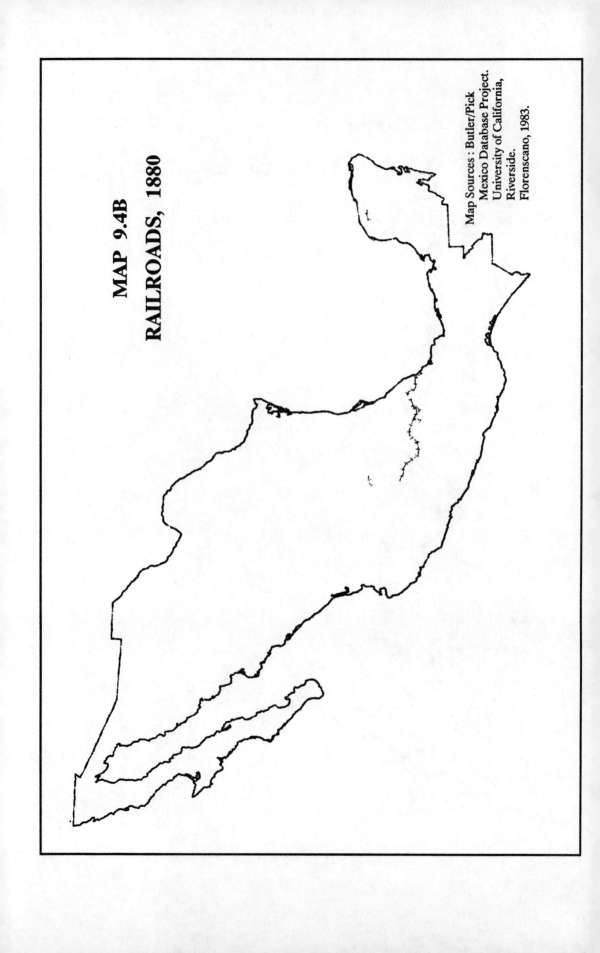

MAP 9.4B
RAILROADS, 1880

Map Sources : Butler/Pick
Mexico Database Project.
University of California,
Riverside.
Florenscano, 1983.

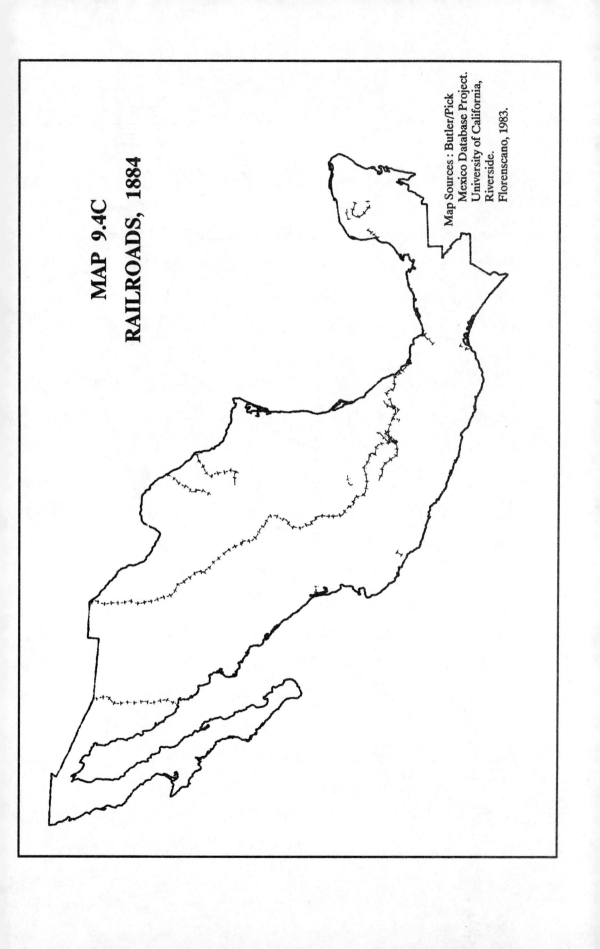

MAP 9.4C
RAILROADS, 1884

Map Sources : Butler/Pick
Mexico Database Project.
University of California,
Riverside.
Florenscano, 1983.

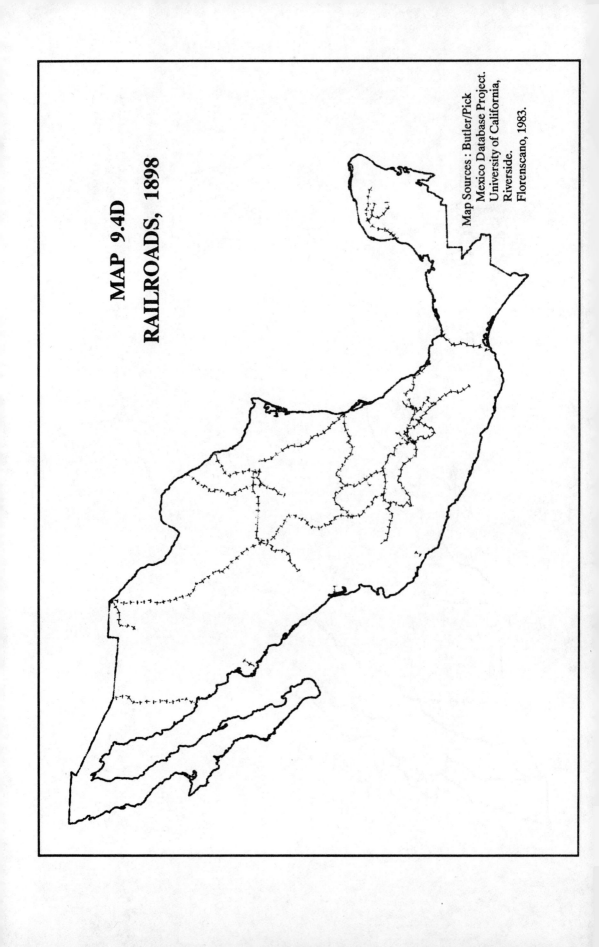

MAP 9.4D
RAILROADS, 1898

Map Sources : Butler/Pick
Mexico Database Project.
University of California,
Riverside.
Florenscano, 1983.

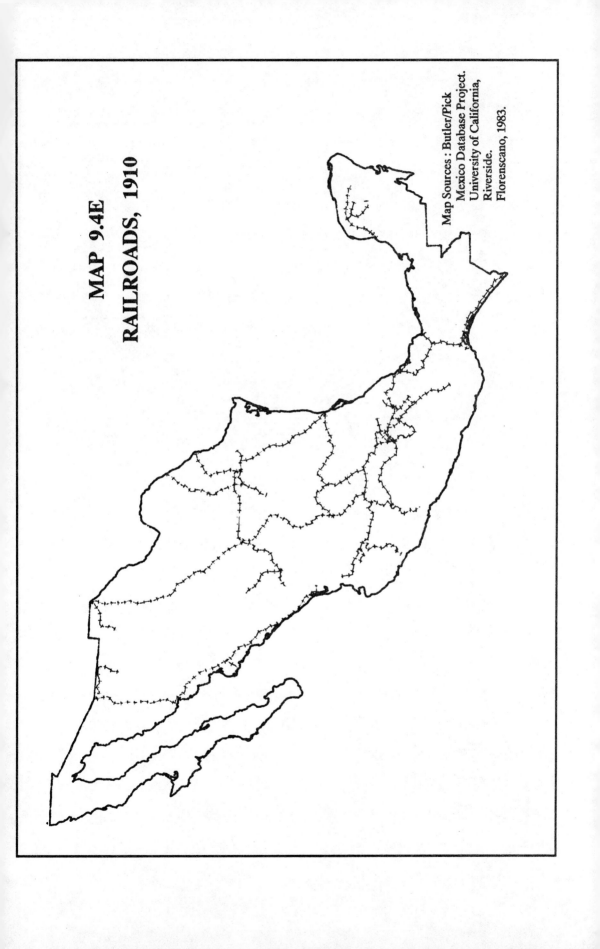

MAP 9.4E
RAILROADS, 1910

Map Sources : Butler/Pick
Mexico Database Project.
University of California,
Riverside.
Florescano, 1983.

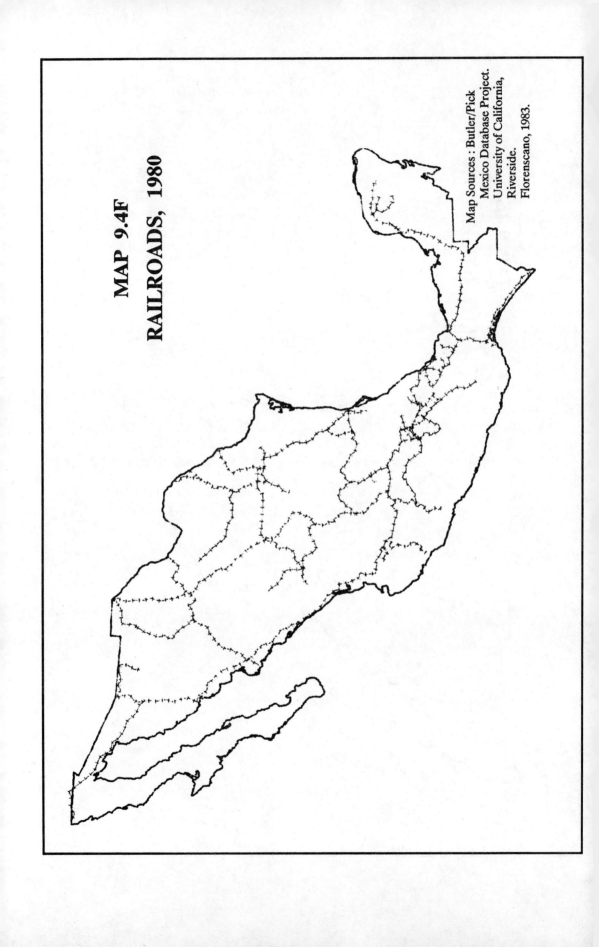

MAP 9.4F
RAILROADS, 1980

Map Sources : Butler/Pick
Mexico Database Project.
University of California,
Riverside.
Florenscano, 1983.

Telephones, 1985

The mean value for telephones per capita in 1985 is 0.08, or one telephone for approximately every 12 persons. This is compared to a mean value of 0.06 in 1980, or one telephone for every 16 persons (Anuario Estadistico, 1986). There is a moderate coefficient of variation among states. The Federal District, by far, has the highest rate of telephones in service in Mexico (0.23). The only other states approaching the Federal District in rate of telephones are Baja California Sur (0.20) and Nuevo Leon (0.16). Other states with rates 0.10 are Coahuila, Colima, Chihuahua, Jalisco, Morelos, Quintana Roo, Sonora, and Tamaulipas. States with the lowest rates of telephones per capita are Campeche, Chiapas, Guerrero, Hidalgo, Michoacan, Nayarit, Oaxaca, Tlaxcala, and Zacatecas (see Table 9.7 and Map 9.5).

Overall, the heaviest concentration of telephones in service by region is along the U.S.-Mexico border with five of the six border states having higher rates than all of the other states and regions in Mexico except for the Federal District. The only border state with an intermediate rate is Baja California. Most states in the center of the country have an intermediate rate of telephones per capita, as does Yucatan. Excluding the extremely high rate of telephones per capita in the Federal District, clearly Baja California Sur and the states on the U.S.-Mexico border are those with the most adequate telephone service in Mexico. On the other hand, the south region has the lowest level of telephone service.

Telphones per capita in 1985 is very strongly related with urbanization in 1980 (Map 2.6A), and to other urban-related characteristics. It is strongly associated with other technology-related dimensions, such as households with television (Map 6.7E), vehicles (Map 9.1A), and air passengers (Map 9.2B).

Table 9.7 Telephones, 1980-1985

No.	State	1980 Total Telephones	1980 Telephones Per Capita	1985 Total Telephones	1985 Telephones Per Capita	Per Capita % Change 1980-85
1	AGUASCALIENTES	37,543	0.0723	54,913	0.0934	29.18
2	BAJA CALIFORNIA	56,240	0.0477	121,124	0.0902	89.10
3	BAJA CALIFORNIA SUR	26,198	0.1218	48,563	0.1988	63.22
4	CAMPECHE	14,122	0.0336	21,493	0.0450	33.93
5	COAHUILA	148,953	0.0957	199,734	0.1129	17.97
6	COLIMA	25,636	0.0740	40,132	0.1021	37.97
7	CHIAPAS	50,118	0.0240	79,871	0.0338	40.83
8	CHIHUAHUA	166,572	0.0831	246,437	0.1080	29.96
9	DISTRITO FEDERAL	1,850,000	0.2095	2,325,950	0.2303	9.93
10	DURANGO	41,678	0.0353	78,071	0.0584	65.44
11	GUANAJUATO	141,434	0.0470	225,219	0.0662	40.85
12	GUERRERO	92,631	0.0439	127,115	0.0532	21.18
13	HIDALGO	47,153	0.0305	74,955	0.0428	40.33
14	JALISCO	357,419	0.0818	542,140	0.1093	33.62
15	MEXICO	351,300	0.0464	620,698	0.0724	56.03
16	MICHOACAN	102,170	0.0356	175,391	0.0540	51.69
17	MORELOS	77,041	0.0813	108,993	0.1013	24.60
18	NAYARIT	25,722	0.0354	42,617	0.0519	46.61
19	NUEVO LEON	300,740	0.1197	463,295	0.1621	35.42
20	OAXACA	44,376	0.0187	72,073	0.0268	43.32
21	PUEBLA	143,941	0.0430	233,595	0.0616	43.26
22	QUERETARO	31,500	0.0426	56,163	0.0672	57.75
23	QUINTANA ROO	11,767	0.0521	33,153	0.1296	148.75
24	SAN LUIS POTOSI	63,919	0.0382	109,754	0.0579	51.57
25	SINALOA	112,278	0.0607	177,955	0.0849	39.87
26	SONORA	165,878	0.1096	206,705	0.1201	9.58
27	TABASCO	38,510	0.0362	67,134	0.0558	54.14
28	TAMAULIPAS	165,941	0.0862	247,953	0.1133	31.44
29	TLAXCALA	11,868	0.0213	19,677	0.0312	46.48
30	VERACRUZ	235,818	0.0438	368,690	0.0602	37.44
31	YUCATAN	58,283	0.0548	99,393	0.0820	49.64
32	ZACATECAS	27,412	0.0241	39,560	0.0308	27.80
	Mean	157,005	0.0609	229,016	0.0846	44.03
	S.D.	318,216	0.0393	404,734	0.0472	24.75
	C.V.	202.68	64.53	176.73	55.79	56.22
	Minimum	11,767	0.0187	19,677	0.0268	9.58
	Maximum	1,850,000	0.2095	2,325,950	0.2303	148.75

DEFINITION: Per capita values are the number of telephones to the total population of the year shown. Per Capita Percent Change was calculated by subtracting the 1980 Per Capita rate from the 1985 Per Capita rate and dividing by the 1980 Per Capita rate multiplied by 100.

SOURCE: 1980 Anuario Estadistico, Table 2.1.7; 1986 Anuario Estadistico, Table 2.1.11.

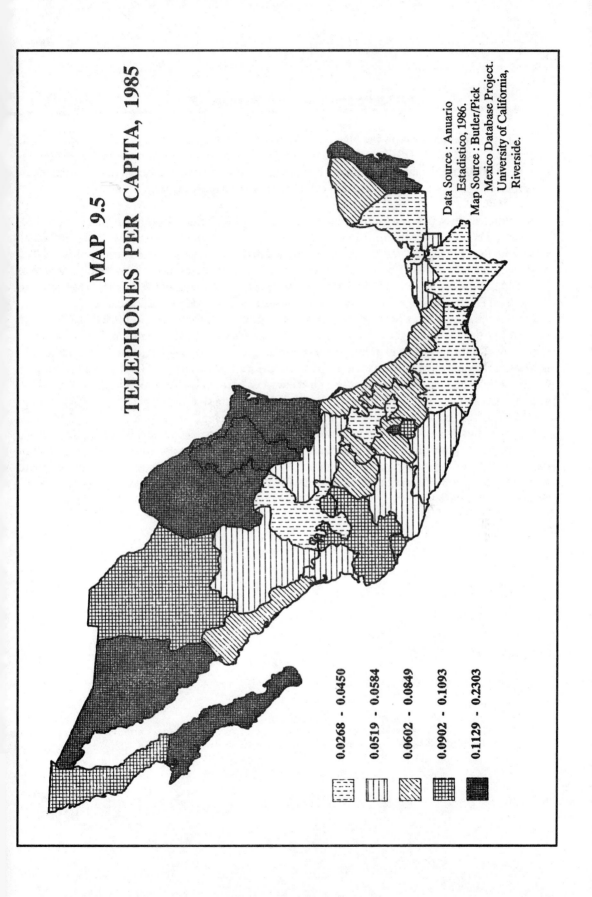

MAP 9.5

TELEPHONES PER CAPITA, 1985

Data Source : Anuario
Estadistico, 1986.

Map Source : Butler/Pick
Mexico Database Project.
University of California,
Riverside.

0.0268 - 0.0450

0.0519 - 0.0584

0.0602 - 0.0849

0.0902 - 0.1093

0.1129 - 0.2303

Radio and Television Stations, 1985

In Chapter 6, an illustration was given of households with television sets in 1977 (Map 6.7E), as determined by the World Fertility Survey. Here a description of the rate of radio and television stations per 10,000 population is presented. Not unexpectedly, the two characteristics are significantly correlated. There is moderate variation in the rates of radio and television stations on a per capita basis (CV=54).

As with telephones, the major regional concentration of high rates is along the U.S.-Mexico border, with all border states except Nuevo Leon having a very high rate (see Table 9.8). In fact, all states with the very highest rates, except one, are located in the U.S. - Mexico border region. The only exception is Quintana Roo, a major tourist state. Several states have an extremely low rate of radio and television stations. The lowest rates are reported in the states of Hidalgo and Mexico with the Federal District, Oaxaca, Puebla, and Tlaxcala also having extremely low rates.

One of the lowest rates of radio and television stations is in the Federal District (0.07) yet the Federal District has the highest proportion of households owning a television set. On the other hand, Baja California has an extremely high rate of households owning a television set and in addition has the highest rate of all states for radio and television stations (0.31). Several other states with few households having a television set also have low rates of radio and television stations, e.g., Hidalgo and Oaxaca. The geographic pattern of radio and television stations shown on Map 9.6 is strongly related to that urbanization, although less so than for telephones. It is also associated with urban-related variables, including literacy, education, high income, and administrative and service occupations. It shows an opposite pattern to those for rural dimensions such as agricultural labor force and occupation, and rural-related dependency ratio, low income, and population native to state. Like telephones, it is strongly associated with other technological dimensions such as airports, air flights, and vehicles.

Table 9.8 Radio and Television Stations, 1985

No.	State	1980 Total Stations	1980 Stations Per Capita	1985 Total Stations	1985 Stations Per Capita	Per Capita % Change 1980-85
1	AGUASCALIENTES	15	0.2888	12	0.2041	-29.33
2	BAJA CALIFORNIA	46	0.3905	42	0.3129	-19.87
3	BAJA CALIFORNIA SUR	7	0.3254	6	0.2456	-24.52
4	CAMPECHE	13	0.3091	13	0.2725	-11.84
5	COAHUILA	53	0.3403	47	0.2658	-21.89
6	COLIMA	9	0.2599	7	0.1781	-31.47
7	CHIAPAS	24	0.1151	24	0.1015	-11.82
8	CHIHUAHUA	64	0.3191	53	0.2322	-27.23
9	DISTRITO FEDERAL	76	0.0861	70	0.0693	-19.51
10	DURANGO	11	0.0930	13	0.0972	4.52
11	GUANAJUATO	46	0.1530	45	0.1323	-13.53
12	GUERRERO	27	0.1280	23	0.0963	-24.77
13	HIDALGO	7	0.0452	7	0.0399	-11.73
14	JALISCO	66	0.1510	62	0.1250	-17.22
15	MEXICO	14	0.0185	12	0.0140	-24.32
16	MICHOACAN	36	0.1220	36	0.1108	-9.18
17	MORELOS	11	0.1161	12	0.1116	-3.88
18	NAYARIT	15	0.2066	13	0.1582	-23.43
19	NUEVO LEON	46	0.1830	44	0.1539	-15.90
20	OAXACA	23	0.0971	20	0.0744	-23.38
21	PUEBLA	24	0.0717	27	0.0712	-0.70
22	QUERETARO	12	0.1622	10	0.1197	-26.20
23	QUINTANA ROO	6	0.2655	7	0.2737	3.09
24	SAN LUIS POTOSI	24	0.1434	23	0.1214	-15.34
25	SINALOA	39	0.2108	33	0.1574	-25.33
26	SONORA	52	0.3435	49	0.2847	-17.12
27	TABASCO	15	0.1411	14	0.1164	-17.51
28	TAMAULIPAS	64	0.3326	51	0.2331	-29.92
29	TLAXCALA	4	0.0719	4	0.0635	-11.68
30	VERACRUZ	79	0.1466	78	0.1274	-13.10
31	YUCATAN	21	0.1974	17	0.1403	-28.93
32	ZACATECAS	14	0.1231	13	0.1014	-17.63
	Mean	30	0.1862	28	0.1502	-17.52
	S.D.	22	0.1013	20	0.0782	9.22
	C.V.	73.28	54.39	70.79	52.06	-52.61
	Minimum	4	0.0185	4	0.0140	-31.47
	Maximum	79	0.3905	78	0.3129	4.52

DEFINITION: Per capita values are the number of radio and television stations to the total population of the year shown. Per Capita Percent Change was calculating by subtracting the 1980 Per Capita rate from the 1985 Per Capita rate and dividing by the 1980 Per Capita multiplied by 100.

SOURCE: 1980 Anuario Estadistico, Table 2.1.9; 1986 Anuario Estadistico, Table 2.1.16.

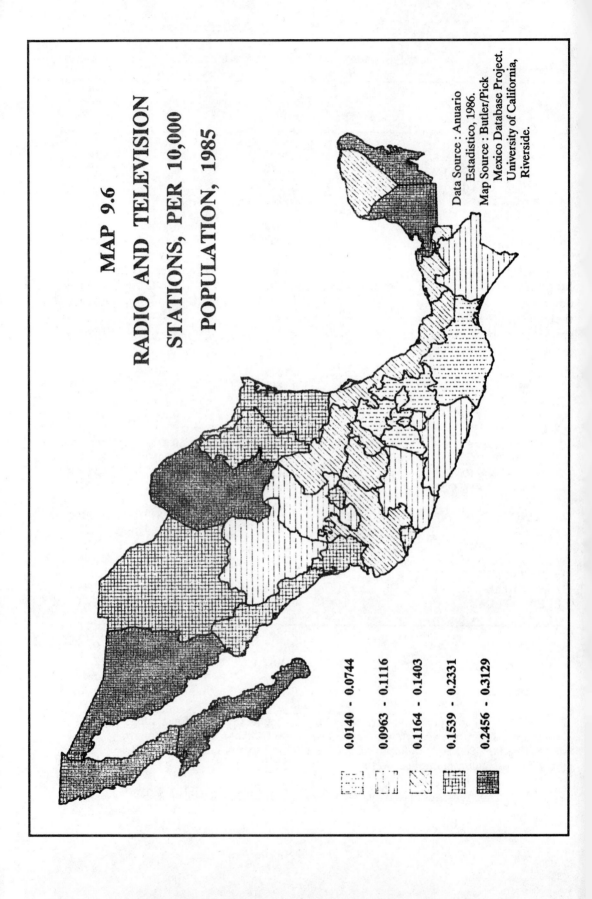

MAP 9.6

RADIO AND TELEVISION
STATIONS, PER 10,000
POPULATION, 1985

Data Source : Anuario
Estadistico, 1986.
Map Source : Butler/Pick
Mexico Database Project.
University of California,
Riverside.

0.0140 - 0.0744

0.0963 - 0.1116

0.1164 - 0.1403

0.1539 - 0.2331

0.2456 - 0.3129

10

MISCELLANEOUS

Introduction

Chapter 10 serves as a reminder that there is extensive other information and data available on Mexican states and municipios from a variety of sources that can be illustrated and analyzed in a descriptive and sophisticated manner. For example, information presented in this chapter is from the <u>Estadisticas Basicas de la Actividad Turistica</u> (1985), the Mexican census, <u>anuarios,</u> and from various unofficial and official documents relating to presidential elections in Mexico. As this chapter amply illustrates, these available data are both historical and contemporary.

Hotels, 1985

There were 6,761 hotels in Mexico in 1985, equivalent to one hotel per 11,614 persons, based on projected 1985 population (SPP, 1983). As shown in Table 10.1, about half of the hotels are concentrated in the six states of Veracruz, Federal District, Jalisco, Guerrero, Baja California, and Michoacan. All these states contain major urban centers and/or are major ocean tourist locations. The statewide mean of hotels and pensions per 100 persons is 0.014, with large variation (CV=110). The highest per capita value by far of 0.084 is for Quintana Roo, a state with major developing tourist resorts and high growth. Other high states on a per capita basis are Colima (0.039) and Baja California Sur (0.036), while the lowest states are Mexico (0.013), Tlaxcala (0.005), and the Federal District (0.005).

Map 10.1 reveals that higher levels of hotels per capita tend to occur in exterior states adjacent to the United States or oceans, while interior states generally have lower levels. This pattern does not correspond to standard regions.

Hotels per capita are strongly associated with personal service labor force, construction labor force, airports, air passengers, foreign tourism, alcoholic establishments, and movies. The relationships likely involve the effects of tourism and leisure activities. There is a strong relationship with hospitals and clinics per capita (see Map 5.2A). There are strong positive and inverse relationships with population growth in the 70s and population native to state respectively. In other words, hotels tend to be associated with high growth and inmigration.

Table 10.1 Hotels, 1985

No.	State	Total Hotels	Hotels Per 100 Population
1	AGUASCALIENTES	44	0.0075
2	BAJA CALIFORNIA	336	0.0250
3	BAJA CALIFORNIA SUR	88	0.0360
4	CAMPECHE	71	0.0149
5	COAHUILA	111	0.0063
6	COLIMA	152	0.0387
7	CHIAPAS	191	0.0081
8	CHIHUAHUA	244	0.0107
9	DISTRITO FEDERAL	537	0.0053
10	DURANGO	85	0.0064
11	GUANAJUATO	190	0.0056
12	GUERRERO	400	0.0167
13	HIDALGO	117	0.0067
14	JALISCO	548	0.0110
15	MEXICO	115	0.0013
16	MICHOACAN	386	0.0119
17	MORELOS	157	0.0146
18	NAYARIT	129	0.0157
19	NUEVO LEON	78	0.0027
20	OAXACA	218	0.0081
21	PUEBLA	151	0.0040
22	QUERETARO	108	0.0129
23	QUINTANA ROO	214	0.0837
24	SAN LUIS POTOSI	152	0.0080
25	SINALOA	252	0.0120
26	SONORA	182	0.0106
27	TABASCO	80	0.0067
28	TAMAULIPAS	260	0.0119
29	TLAXCALA	32	0.0051
30	VERACRUZ	890	0.0145
31	YUCATAN	137	0.0113
32	ZACATECAS	106	0.0083
	Mean	211	0.0138
	S.D.	176	0.0152
	C.V.	83.27	110.15
	Minimum	32	0.0013
	Maximum	890	0.0837

DEFINITION: Hotel establishments per 100 population was calculated using 1985 total population multiplied by 0.01.

SOURCE: 1986 Anuario Estadistico, Table 4.4.5.

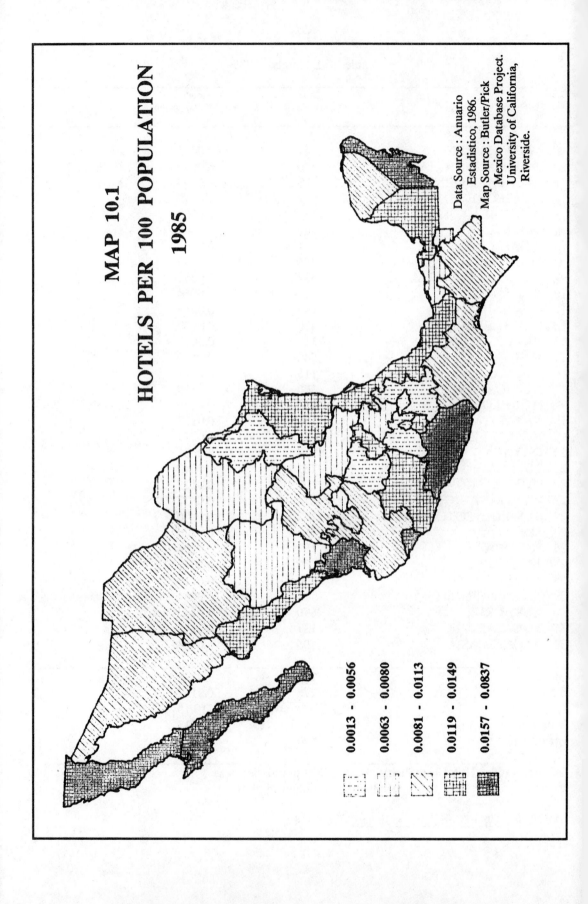

MAP 10.1

HOTELS PER 100 POPULATION

1985

Data Source : Anuario
Estadistico, 1986.

Map Source : Butler/Pick
Mexico Database Project.
University of California,
Riverside.

0.0013 - 0.0056

0.0063 - 0.0080

0.0081 - 0.0113

0.0119 - 0.0149

0.0157 - 0.0837

Foreign Tourism, 1984

This dimension measures the proportion foreign tourists among those who visit museums, archeological zones, and cultural sites administrered by the Instituto Nacional de Antropologia e Historia (for more extensive analysis of foreign and national tourism, see Butler, Fukurai, and Pick, 1989). The data described here were obtained from Estadisticas Basicas de la Actividad Turistica (1985).

There were 8.3 million tourists in Mexico during 1984, of which 2.4 million, or 29 percent, are foreign (see Table 10.2). Five states account for 83 percent of foreign tourists, namely Mexico (29 percent), the Federal District (24 percent), Yucatan (12 percent), Oaxaca (9 percent), and Quintana Roo (9 percent). It is important to note that data are unavailable for six states, including highly touristic Baja and Sonora. On the other hand, a somewhat different set of six states accounts for 77 percent of domestic tourists. These states are the Federal District (31 percent), Mexico (18 percent), Puebla (9 percent), Oaxaca (8 percent), Veracruz (6 percent), and Morelos (5 percent). For foreign as well as domestic tourists, the central metropolitan zone accounts for half of the volume.

The actual variable mapped, i.e. the proportion foreign (see Map 10.2), has a state mean value of 25 percent, reflects that over one-fourth of the tourists were foreign. Variation is moderate. States attracting the highest percentages of foreign tourists in 1980 are the northwest state of Baja California Sur (55 percent), the central state of Mexico (50 percent), Jalisco (50 percent) and Colima (49 percent) in the west, and the southeast state of Yucatan (51 percent). On the other hand, Queretaro, San Luis Potosi, Guanajuato, Veracruz, and Zacatecas all have less than ten percent foreign tourists. Coahuila (13 percent), Hidalgo (10 percent), and Puebla (13 percent) also have far fewer foreign than domestic tourists.

The geographic pattern closely resembles that for hotels and pensions, with the states of the nation's exterior tending to have higher values than interior states. An exception is the state of Mexico. A notable difference between the two patterns is Yucatan, which has a very high percent of foreign tourists, but a low per capita rate of hotels and pensions. On the other hand, Morelos has a below average percent of foreign tourists but a very high rate of hotels. The overall closeness of the two patterns would indicate that the concentrations of hotels are more keyed to foreign than domestic tourism. Since the two variables are strongly correlated, many of the relationships with other dimensions noted for hotels and pensions (see Map 10.1) also hold true for foreign tourism.

Table 10.2 Foreign Tourism, 1984

No.	State	Foreign Tourists	National Tourists	Total Tourists	Percent Foreign
1	AGUASCALIENTES	NA	NA	NA	NA
2	BAJA CALIFORNIA	NA	NA	NA	NA
3	BAJA CALIFORNIA SUR	6,162	5,133	11,295	0.5456
4	CAMPECHE	31,352	82,137	113,489	0.2763
5	COAHUILA	1,499	10,334	11,833	0.1267
6	COLIMA	8,965	9,184	18,149	0.4940
7	CHIAPAS	22,527	68,465	90,992	0.2476
8	CHIHUAHUA	3,756	8,125	11,881	0.3161
9	DISTRITO FEDERAL	580,711	1,815,137	2,395,848	0.2424
10	DURANGO	NA	NA	NA	NA
11	GUANAJUATO	17,845	214,826	232,671	0.0767
12	GUERRERO	13,559	34,292	47,851	0.2834
13	HIDALGO	11,820	101,166	112,986	0.1046
14	JALISCO	11,885	11,697	23,582	0.5040
15	MEXICO	682,271	1,061,917	1,744,188	0.3912
16	MICHOACAN	19,983	115,024	135,007	0.1480
17	MORELOS	64,102	274,634	338,736	0.1892
18	NAYARIT	7,596	32,467	40,063	0.1896
19	NUEVO LEON	52,826	83,592	136,418	0.3872
20	OAXACA	220,559	464,665	685,224	0.3219
21	PUEBLA	82,831	537,937	620,768	0.1334
22	QUERETARO	5,541	101,169	106,710	0.0519
23	QUINTANA ROO	213,393	216,013	429,406	0.4969
24	SAN LUIS POTOSI	826	12,628	13,454	0.0614
25	SINALOA	NA	NA	NA	NA
26	SONORA	NA	NA	NA	NA
27	TABASCO	87	478	565	0.1540
28	TAMAULIPAS	NA	NA	NA	NA
29	TLAXCALA	3,522	21,674	25,196	0.1398
30	VERACRUZ	35,802	386,658	422,460	0.0847
31	YUCATAN	274,350	267,228	541,578	0.5066
32	ZACATECAS	75	1,138	1,213	0.0618
	National Total	2,373,845	5,937,718	8,311,563	6.5350
	Mean	91,302	228,374	319,676	0.2513
	S.D.	172,469	393,026	550,991	0.1575
	C.V.	188.90	172.10	172.36	62.66
	Minimum	75	478	565	0.0519
	Maximum	682,271	1,815,137	2,395,848	0.5456

DEFINITION: Foreign tourists are the number of foreigners who, in 1984, visited museums, archeological zones, and cultural sites administered by the Instituto Nacional de Antropologia e Historia. National tourists are the number of Mexican nationals, who visited such places in 1984.

NOTE: NA = not available.

SOURCE: Estadisticas Basicas de La Actividad Turistica, 1985.

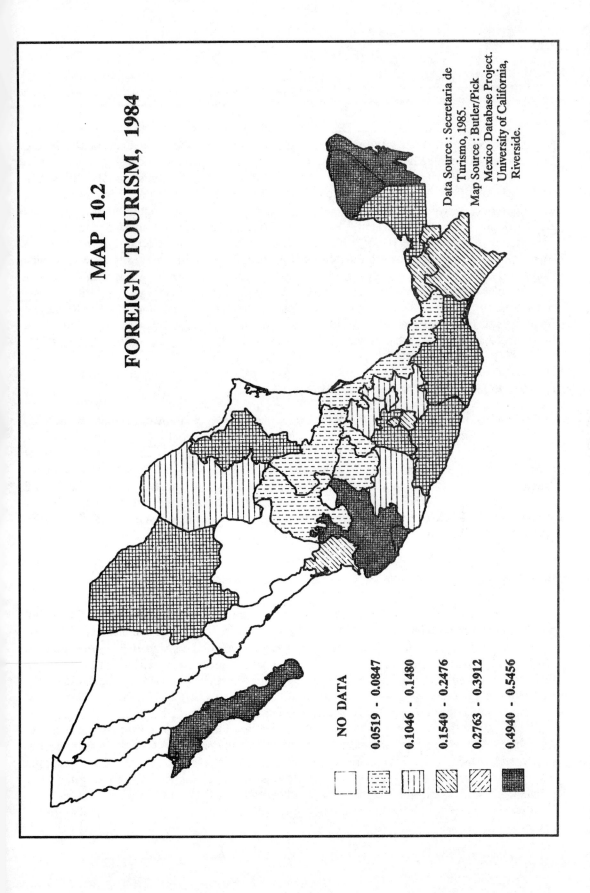

MAP 10.2

FOREIGN TOURISM, 1984

Data Source : Secretaria de
Turismo, 1985.

Map Source : Butler/Pick
Mexico Database Project.
University of California,
Riverside.

NO DATA

0.0519 - 0.0847

0.1046 - 0.1480

0.1540 - 0.2476

0.2763 - 0.3912

0.4940 - 0.5456

Presidential Election, 1988

Prior to the Mexican presidential election of 1988, there was widespread discontent with the political process in Mexico. With the PAN on the right, and the emergence of the Frente Democratico Nacional (FDN) on the center-left, virtually everyone knowledgeable about Mexico expected more formidable opposition to the dominant party in the 1988 presidential election than in prior years. Official election results of July, 1988, illustrated that Mexico indeed, in some respects, was undergoing radical shifts insofar as electoral politics was concerned, but in other respects the election continued trends delineated as early as 1940 (for a more extensive analysis of the material presented in this section see Butler, Pick, and Tellis, 1989). The 1988 election subsequently has been reported as setting the stage for the development of a pluralistic party structure in Mexico (Reyna, 1988). Of course, these conclusions may be premature. However, it is clear that a new course of electoral politics has been established in Mexico; one which holds vast implications for the country's future, its internal stability, and its relationship with the U.S. and other nations (Reyna and Butler, 1989). In this section, official election results are presented for the three major parties and voter participation in the 1988 presidential election (Proceso Electoral Federal, 1988; El Dia, 1988).

Presidential Election, Voter Participation, 1988

Of particular interest in any election is the extent of voter participation, or turnout. In the 1988 election, the official voter participation rate was just over 50 percent (¿Que Paso?, 1988: 31). However, as Table 10.3 and Map 10.3A illustrate, there was wide variation among states in turnout rates. The range was from a high of 58.2 percent in Queretaro to a low of 37.9 percent in Coahuila. There was no discernable regional pattern in voter turnout except that states around the Federal District generally had higher voter participation rates than the rest of the country, and the border region generally had lower rates. There was virtually no relationship between levels of voter turnout and voting for PAN, PRI, or FDN (see Butler, Pick, and Tellis, 1989).

Presidential Vote, PRI, 1988

As in past elections, the 1988 presidential election demonstrated that support for PRI and opposition parties varies considerably by state, municipio, urban-rural areas, and districts. The percentage of the PRI vote was shown in Table 10.3 and is illustrated on Map 10.3B. According to official election results, the PRI candidate Carlos Salinas de Gortari carried 27 of the 32 states. In three states he had a plurality but not a majority--Aguascalientes, Guanajuato, and Jalisco. The major support for Salinas was from the southern states of Campeche, Chiapas, Puebla, Tabasco and Yucatan, as well as from Nuevo Leon, San Luis Potosi, and Sonora.

The two major factors associated with the PRI are dimensions one would expect to be negatively associated with each other--urbanization and agricultural labor force. Other important dimensions correlated with the PRI vote are education (the higher the level of education in a state, the lower the PRI vote), literacy, all occupational categories except agricultural are negatively associated, and low income which is positively correlated with the PRI vote.

Presidential Vote, PAN, 1988

The distribution of the PAN vote was reported in Table 10.3 and is shown on Map 10.3C. The PAN did not win a single state in the 1988 election and its overall vote was similar to that in earlier elections. Apparently the PAN was unable to mobilize any greater popular support in 1988 than in previous elections. Eight states remained virtually static in support for the PAN, while eight states actually reduced their support for the PAN. On the other hand, the PAN and its candidate Clouthier had strong support in Aguascalientes, Chihuahua, the Federal District, Guanajuato, Jalisco, and Sinaloa, with possible future growth in Nuevo Leon and Yucatan.

In contrast to PRI, the PAN vote is negatively associated with agricultural occupations and has high positive correlations with education, literacy, and medium and higher level incomes. Further, population growth areas are more likely to be PAN oriented than non-growth areas. The PAN vote also is positively linked to measures of corporate structure such as the number of corporations per capita and value of corporations.

Presidential Vote, FDN, 1988

As seen in Map 10.3D and reported in Table 10.3, the FDN and its candidate, Cardenas, carried the adjoining states of Mexico, Morelos, and Michoacan, the candidate's home state. In the Federal District, FDN vote was a plurality and nearly a majority (49.2 percent). The FDN was also strong in Baja California and Colima. FDN was the weakest (3.8 percent) in the industrial/metropolitan state of Nuevo Leon. Geographical patterns by standard region are not apparent.

The few variables strongly associated with the FDN vote are as follows: growth states, more dense areas, and outmigration (1979 to 1980 and lifetime) all of which are positively associated with the FDN vote, while there is a negative relationship with native to state population. The impression from the results is that the FDN vote is strongest in areas undergoing population change. A detailed examination of the FDN vote also suggest that much of the lack of relationship between the FDN vote and various demographic and social characteristics is linked to the fact that the FDN vote is made up of various political parties and interest groups that are often times associated with demographic and social characteristics in very contrasting ways (Butler, Pick, and Tellis, 1989). If this conclusion is an accurate one, it will be extremely difficult for the FDN to maintain itself as an important opposition party or become a majority party in the future.

Table 10.3 Presidential Election Voting, 1988

No.	State	Total Vote	Percent of Voting Population	Percent Vote For PRI	Percent Vote For FDN	Percent Vote For PAN	Percent Vote For Other
1	AGUASCALIENTES	168,899	50.43	50.21	18.67	28.42	2.70
2	BAJA CALIFORNIA	413,953	50.64	36.66	37.19	24.39	1.77
3	BAJA CALIFORNIA SUR	85,643	56.96	54.02	25.87	19.00	1.10
4	CAMPECHE	116,107	50.49	70.88	16.30	12.37	0.46
5	COAHUILA	328,239	37.89	54.27	29.95	15.34	0.43
6	COLIMA	97,316	44.63	47.83	35.74	14.80	1.63
7	CHIAPAS	658,195	55.36	89.91	6.45	3.39	0.24
8	CHIHUAHUA	521,995	40.31	54.58	6.77	38.19	0.46
9	DISTRITO FEDERAL	2,904,169	57.00	27.25	49.22	22.01	1.52
10	DURANGO	356,446	52.24	63.63	18.82	16.99	0.56
11	GUANAJUATO	726,312	46.18	44.03	22.01	29.93	4.03
12	GUERRERO	510,797	42.54	60.53	35.80	2.44	1.23
13	HIDALGO	421,893	51.94	64.72	28.26	5.84	1.19
14	JALISCO	1,194,247	47.49	42.57	23.87	30.76	2.80
15	MEXICO	2,331,479	55.64	29.79	51.58	16.33	2.30
16	MICHOACAN	614,899	40.18	23.21	64.16	10.28	2.35
17	MORELOS	278,208	47.67	33.74	57.65	7.44	1.17
18	NAYARIT	205,214	50.63	56.56	36.80	5.72	0.91
19	NUEVO LEON	704,156	46.65	72.08	3.83	23.70	0.39
20	OAXACA	628,155	46.03	63.81	30.25	4.63	1.30
21	PUEBLA	1,091,658	64.39	71.55	17.69	9.87	0.89
22	QUERETARO	238,058	58.15	63.34	15.81	19.43	1.42
23	QUINTANA ROO	94,322	50.12	65.70	24.14	9.69	0.47
24	SAN LUIS POTOSI	380,418	43.81	68.25	8.81	21.15	1.79
25	SINALOA	623,904	56.01	50.81	16.75	32.07	0.37
26	SONORA	410,386	45.64	68.59	9.98	20.85	0.59
27	TABASCO	268,071	42.24	74.30	19.94	5.25	0.51
28	TAMAULIPAS	470,309	41.98	59.33	30.15	9.91	0.61
29	TLAXCALA	184,000	55.44	60.21	31.00	5.88	2.92
30	VERACRUZ	1,516,257	49.78	62.59	31.05	5.21	1.16
31	YUCATAN	307,657	51.10	67.08	1.61	31.19	0.12
32	ZACATECAS	293,650	48.72	66.17	22.31	10.77	0.76
	Mean	598,282	49.32	56.82	25.89	16.04	1.25
	S.D.	615,775	6.00	14.87	14.91	9.78	0.92
	C.V.	102.92	12.17	26.17	57.59	61.01	73.05
	Minimum	85,643	37.89	23.21	1.61	2.44	0.12
	Maximum	2,904,169	64.39	89.91	64.16	38.19	4.03

DEFINITION: Percent of official vote.

SOURCE: Proceso Electoral Federal, July 7, 1988.

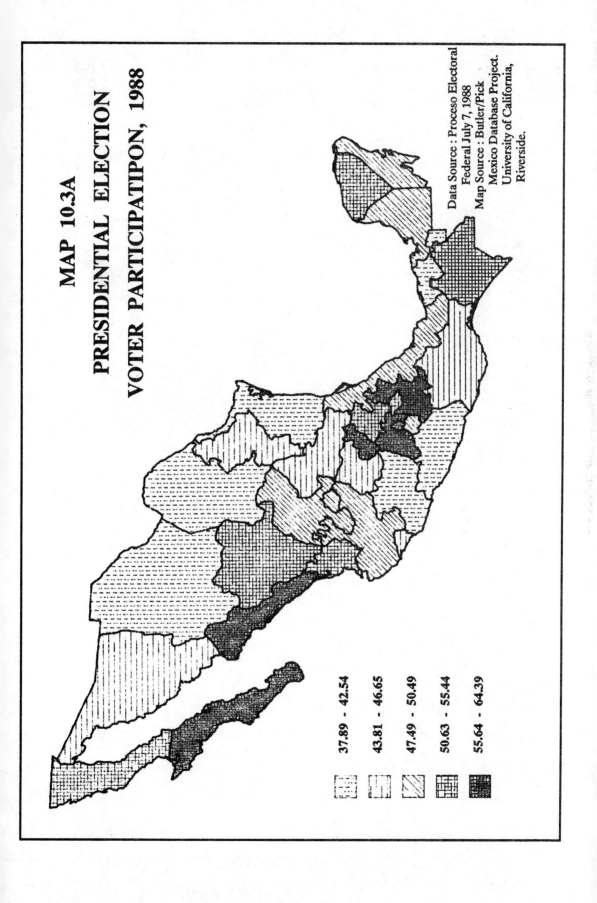

MAP 10.3A

PRESIDENTIAL ELECTION

VOTER PARTICIPATIPON, 1988

Data Source : Proceso Electoral
Federal July 7, 1988
Map Source : Butler/Pick
Mexico Database Project.
University of California,
Riverside.

37.89 - 42.54

43.81 - 46.65

47.49 - 50.49

50.63 - 55.44

55.64 - 64.39

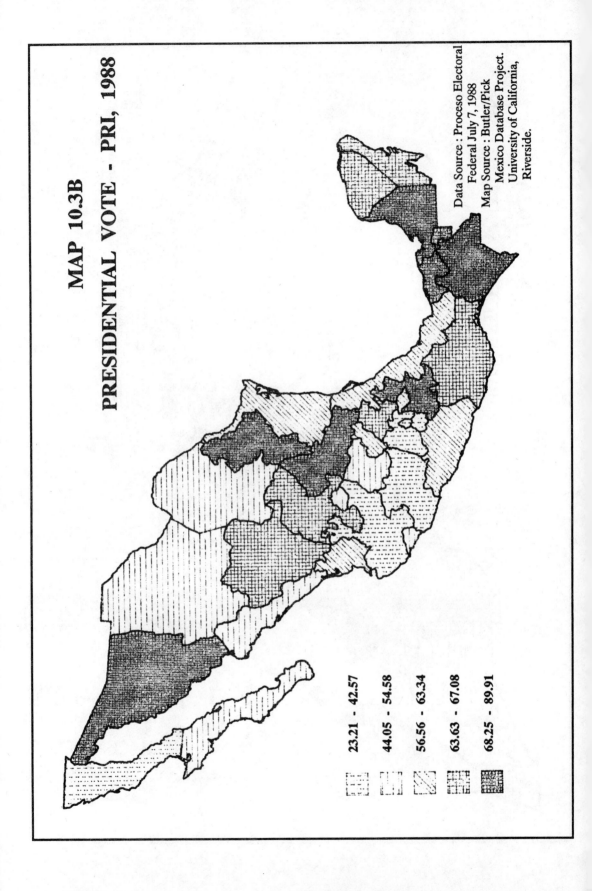

MAP 10.3B

PRESIDENTIAL VOTE - PRI, 1988

23.21 - 42.57

44.05 - 54.58

56.56 - 63.34

63.63 - 67.08

68.25 - 89.91

Data Source : Proceso Electoral
Federal July 7, 1988
Map Source : Butler/Pick
Mexico Database Project.
University of California,
Riverside.

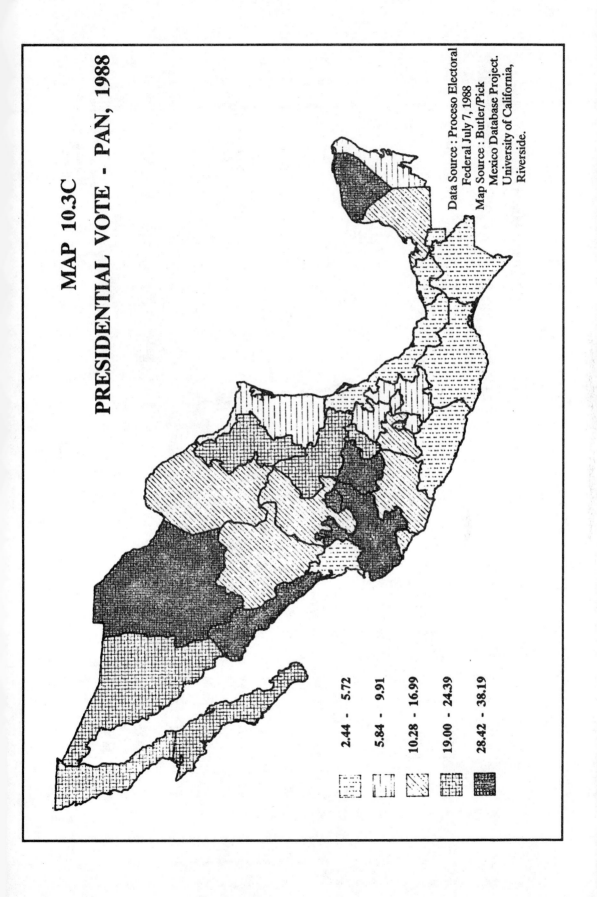

MAP 10.3C
PRESIDENTIAL VOTE - PAN, 1988

2.44 - 5.72

5.84 - 9.91

10.28 - 16.99

19.00 - 24.39

28.42 - 38.19

Data Source : Proceso Electoral
Federal July 7, 1988
Map Source : Butler/Pick
Mexico Database Project.
University of California,
Riverside.

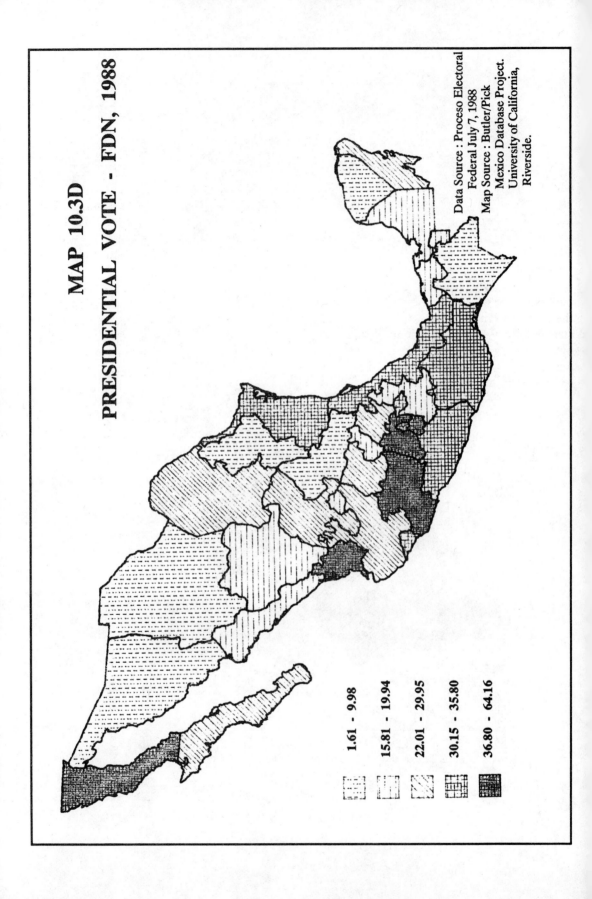

MAP 10.3D

PRESIDENTIAL VOTE - FDN, 1988

1.61 - 9.98

15.81 - 19.94

22.01 - 29.95

30.15 - 35.80

36.80 - 64.16

Data Source : Proceso Electoral
Federal July 7, 1988
Map Source : Butler/Pick
Mexico Database Project.
University of California,
Riverside.

PRI and Opposition Vote: 1934 - 1988

Figures 10.1A and 10.1B and Table 10.4 illustrate the PRI and opposition vote in presidential elections from 1934 through the 1988 election. An analysis of these election results on a state by state basis results in the conclusion that support for opposition parties in 1988 came from areas in which PRI's strength already was in decline. Opposition states in the 1988 election could have been identified as early as 1940 (see Butler, Pick, and Tellis, 1989). While parties may have changed their name and/or orientation, and areas may have changed in demographic and social characteristics, states that voted for the opposition in 1940 remained relatively stable in their opposition between 1940 and 1988. Thus, while the magnitude of the relationship varied between the PRI and opposition vote, opposition states remained remarkably similar for almost 50 years.

As the text table below indicates, when comparing areas which voted for PRI in 1988 are compared to those states that voted for PRI in elections back in time to the 1934 presidential election, the 1934 election was an anomaly. In any case, opposition to the major party has been consistent by state but not necessarily in strength. There is, then , a substantial consistency in opposition voting by state over a fifty year time period in Mexico. The fluctuations can be explained based upon the degree of contested election, candidate personalities, and/or structural conditions related to a specific election, e.g., electoral reform.

Correlation between 1988 and Earlier Presidential Election Results

Year	Correlation with 1988 Election Results
1934	-0.16
1940	0.36
1946	0.52
1952	0.67
1958	0.28
1964	0.47
1970	0.55
1976	0.41
1982	0.69

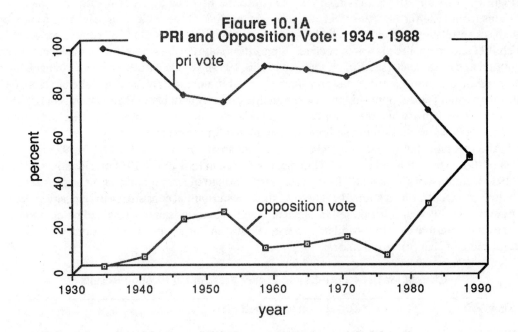

Figure 10.1A
PRI and Opposition Vote: 1934 - 1988

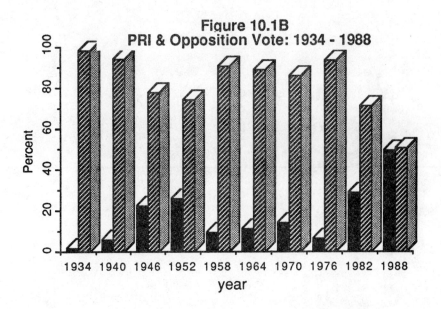

Figure 10.1B
PRI & Opposition Vote: 1934 - 1988

Table 10.4 Presidential Election Results: 1934-1982

No.	State	1934	1940	1946	1952	1958	1964	1970	1976	1982
1	AGUASCALIENTES	95.96	93.89	70.36	67.92	89.25	91.23	87.38	93.81	75.60
2	BAJA CALIFORNIA	97.18	93.92	63.26	61.74	60.67	81.39	74.35	92.42	56.35
3	BAJA CALIFORNIA SUR	99.59	-	91.68	82.25	93.42	96.83	68.09	94.23	74.11
4	CAMPECHE	0.00	98.06	75.08	86.98	87.73	95.94	98.07	99.62	90.04
5	COAHUILA	93.54	95.06	81.36	80.79	94.88	93.40	91.20	99.76	68.07
6	COLIMA	94.77	95.33	66.83	80.10	89.66	87.33	90.74	97.29	90.48
7	CHIAPAS	0.00	98.05	87.26	90.53	98.00	98.89	98.91	99.55	92.07
8	CHIHUAHUA	99.82	97.09	75.66	63.86	64.60	78.72	81.10	89.34	65.50
9	DISTRITO FEDERAL	97.32	71.99	57.01	51.39	78.87	74.86	69.25	80.38	52.09
10	DURANGO	99.66	96.75	65.37	65.02	84.73	90.00	86.73	98.79	75.94
11	GUANAJUATO	98.71	95.94	63.96	64.12	89.49	79.60	80.82	97.99	67.29
12	GUERRERO	99.98	95.43	85.06	82.48	98.19	96.95	95.68	98.74	84.17
13	HIDALGO	99.99	99.46	90.35	88.69	98.09	98.36	97.16	96.48	84.49
14	JALISCO	99.09	98.71	78.89	64.70	88.95	87.02	82.76	93.85	59.79
15	MEXICO	99.78	94.86	84.05	81.06	98.92	91.72	84.66	90.57	59.09
16	MICHOACAN	98.83	92.90	67.33	55.37	87.20	86.00	86.77	97.77	78.19
17	MORELOS	99.76	98.13	57.31	68.46	95.83	94.21	90.29	92.21	76.75
18	NAYARIT	99.99	96.98	85.27	97.33	98.68	91.62	96.49	97.06	80.61
19	NUEVO LEON	84.45	89.32	70.40	80.83	90.33	84.26	84.18	90.45	72.66
20	OAXACA	99.95	99.36	90.20	79.76	95.62	96.64	96.57	99.73	84.53
21	PUEBLA	99.26	98.83	81.85	80.87	95.24	93.65	85.50	95.46	83.93
22	QUERETARO	-	95.72	91.42	95.25	79.88	96.58	98.21	97.65	92.18
23	QUINTANA ROO	99.46	98.75	84.30	82.00	89.50	91.29	90.74	97.07	78.29
24	SAN LUIS POTOSI	99.92	98.18	80.15	88.90	94.33	91.57	90.23	97.76	84.14
25	SINALOA	97.65	89.51	89.89	68.27	98.09	98.07	94.57	97.93	79.23
26	SONORA	99.91	92.42	81.49	81.09	97.28	98.36	93.50	99.55	76.14
27	TABASCO	0.00	99.83	95.58	79.33	98.85	99.33	98.85	99.57	92.57
28	TAMAULIPAS	97.15	88.09	72.41	69.53	94.78	96.51	91.62	96.08	77.64
29	TLAXCALA	99.61	95.64	81.09	81.22	98.39	98.43	94.31	99.98	82.13
30	VERACRUZ	99.06	94.80	90.54	91.53	97.63	96.80	92.67	98.50	83.01
31	YUCATAN	99.39	88.08	75.94	81.48	77.38	85.38	85.27	92.59	80.27
32	ZACATECAS	93.82	94.32	67.63	71.78	91.73	79.48	90.75	98.57	86.16
	Nacional	98.19	93.89	77.91	74.32	90.56	88.62	85.80	93.60	71.00

DEFINITION: Percent of official vote for PRI candidate.

SOURCE: La Fundacion Javier Barros Sierra Al (1987).

Elections in Sonora

Figure 10.2 illustrates the PRI and PAN vote for gubernatorial elections between 1973 and 1985. The figure demonstrates that the PAN vote is variable but a stronger in 1979 and increased in 1982 with a slight decline in 1985. Maps 10.4A and 10.4B present the Sonoran municipio presidential vote and gubernatorial vote for PRI in 1985. While there is some slight variation, basically the vote for governor and municipio president parallel each other. The vote for the PAN gubernatorial candidate is shown on Map 10.4C. As might be expected, the areas are substantially opposite from those voting for the PRI candidate. Strong PAN vote is associated with urbanization, as is seen by comparison with Map 2.6A. In any case, these maps demonstrate that there also is variation <u>within</u> states as well as among states in voting for majority and opposition party candidates.

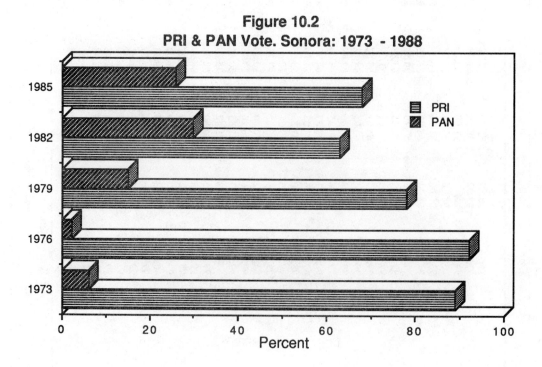

Figure 10.2
PRI & PAN Vote. Sonora: 1973 - 1988

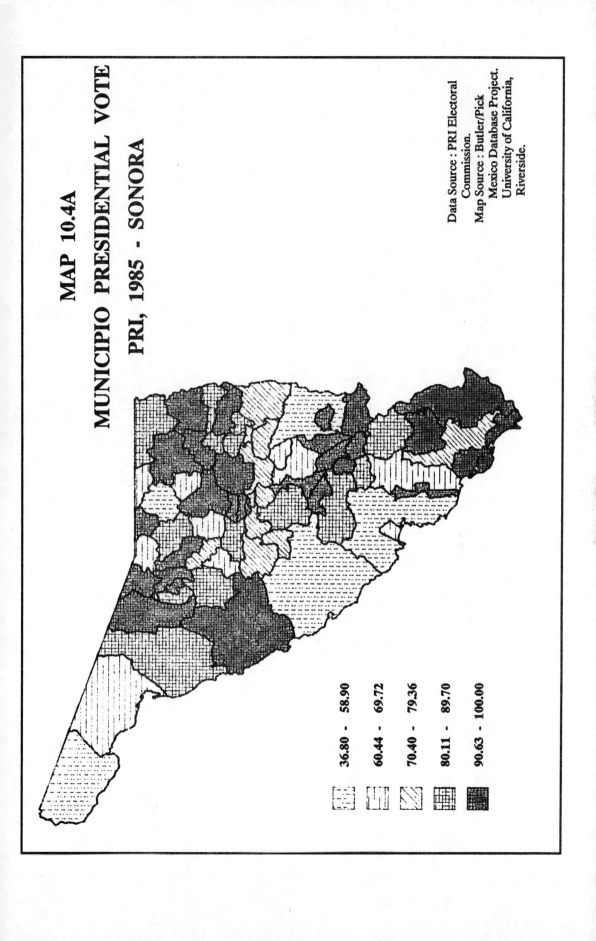

MAP 10.4A

MUNICIPIO PRESIDENTIAL VOTE

PRI, 1985 - SONORA

Data Source : PRI Electoral
    Commission.
Map Source : Butler/Pick
    Mexico Database Project.
    University of California,
    Riverside.

36.80 - 58.90

60.44 - 69.72

70.40 - 79.36

80.11 - 89.70

90.63 - 100.00

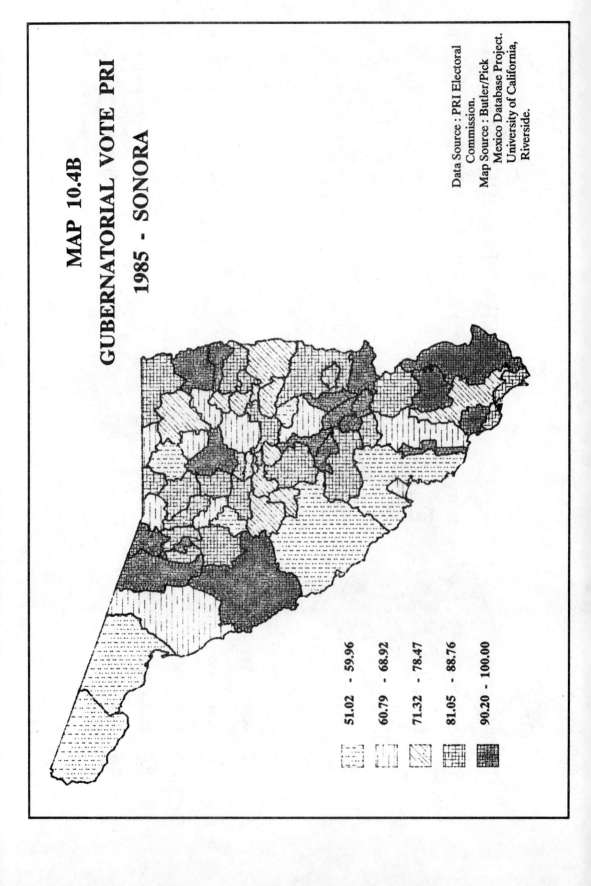

MAP 10.4B

GUBERNATORIAL VOTE PRI

1985 - SONORA

Data Source : PRI Electoral
Commission.
Map Source : Butler/Pick
Mexico Database Project.
University of California,
Riverside.

51.02 - 59.96

60.79 - 68.92

71.32 - 78.47

81.05 - 88.76

90.20 - 100.00

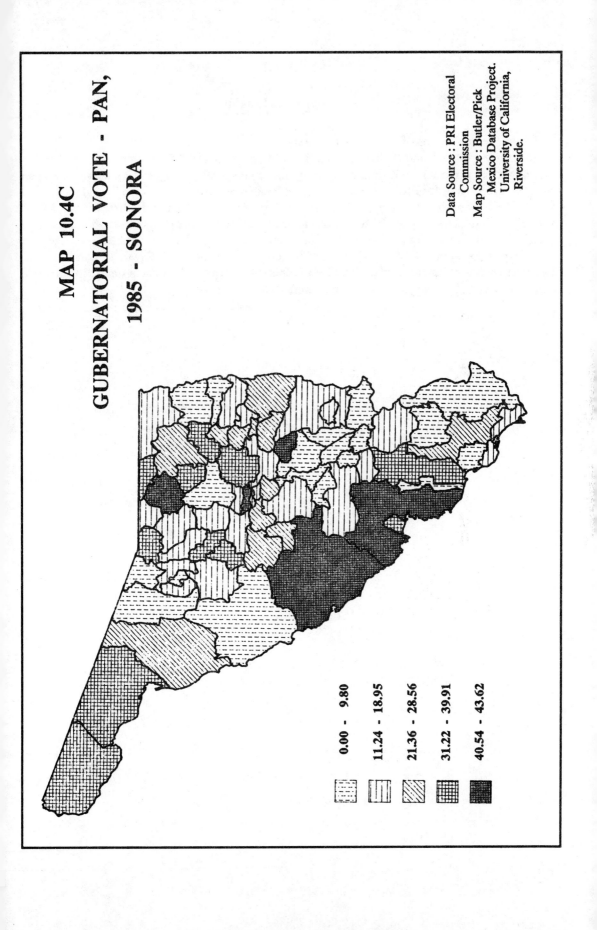

MAP 10.4C
GUBERNATORIAL VOTE - PAN,
1985 - SONORA

0.00 - 9.80

11.24 - 18.95

21.36 - 28.56

31.22 - 39.91

40.54 - 43.62

Data Source : PRI Electoral
Commission
Map Source : Butler/Pick
Mexico Database Project.
University of California,
Riverside.

Elections in Chihuahua

Further demonstration of variation within a state in voting behavior for the PRI and PAN parties is shown in Maps 10.5A and 10.5B of substantial election results in 1985. Within state voting variation in Mexico is substantial with one cluster of municipios in southwestern Chihuahua having an over 90 percent vote for PRI, and another cluster located nearby with between 87 and 90 percent vote for PRI. Both clusters are highly rural, as shown in Map 2.10C. Similarly, there are municipios with over a third of the vote for PAN, e.g., all municipios on or near the U.S. - Mexico border, as well as an urban strip in the central-south. In contrasting Sonora and Chihuahua, there appears to be much more geographic clustering of votes in Chihuahua than in Sonora. Given the consistency of electoral votes at the state level over a fifty year period, undoubtedly there is similar longitudinal consistency among municipios and districts within states.

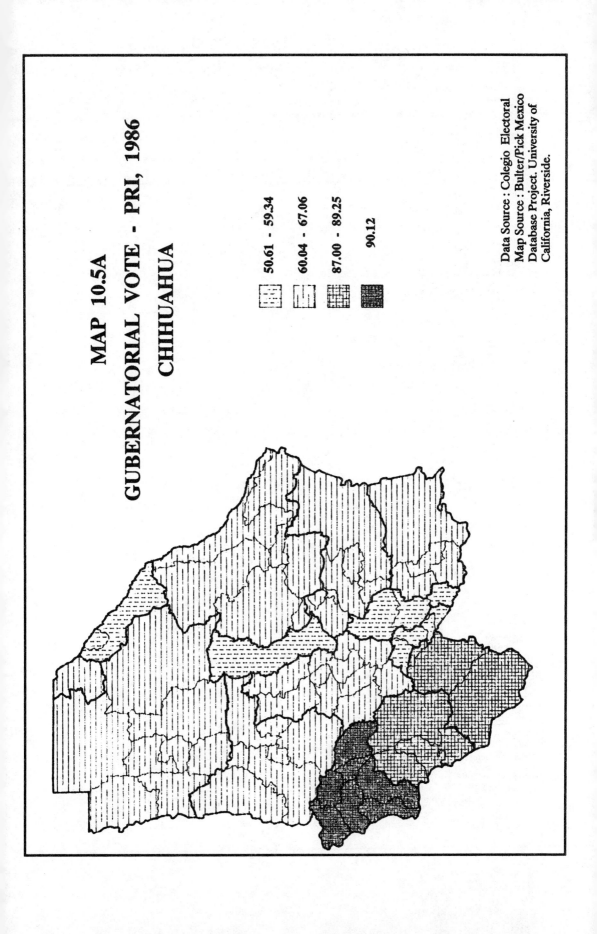

MAP 10.5A
GUBERNATORIAL VOTE - PRI, 1986
CHIHUAHUA

50.61 - 59.34

60.04 - 67.06

87.00 - 89.25

90.12

Data Source : Colegio Electoral
Map Source : Bulter/Pick Mexico
Database Project. University of
California, Riverside.

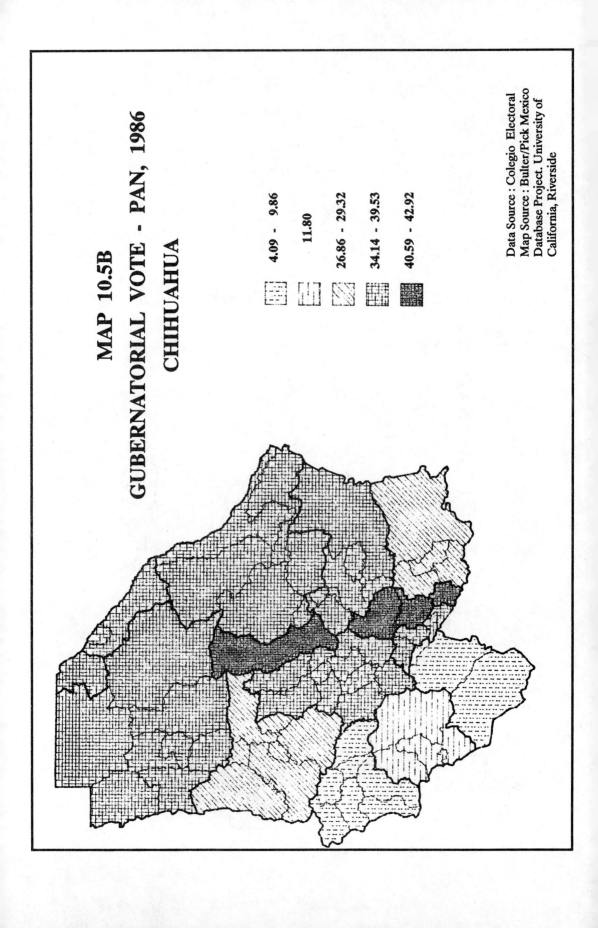

MAP 10.5B
GUBERNATORIAL VOTE - PAN, 1986
CHIHUAHUA

4.09 - 9.86

11.80

26.86 - 29.32

34.14 - 39.53

40.59 - 42.92

Data Source : Colegio Electoral
Map Source : Bulter/Pick Mexico
Database Project. University of
California, Riverside

APPENDIX

Relevent Unspecified Population From the
Mexican Census of Population, 1980

Relevant Unspecified Populations From the
Mexican Census of Population, 1980

No.	State	Population Not Specifying Age:		
		Total	Males	Females
1	AGUASCALIENTES	221	110	111
2	BAJA CALIFORNIA	1,300	646	654
3	BAJA CALIFORNIA SUR	130	71	59
4	CAMPECHE	391	187	204
5	COAHUILA	1,094	544	550
6	COLIMA	199	94	105
7	CHIAPAS	48,229	22,443	25,785
8	CHIHUAHUA	3,457	1,667	1,790
9	DISTRICTO FEDERAL	3,857	1,861	1,996
10	DURANGO	6,576	3,076	3,500
11	GUANAJUATO	5,241	2,569	2,672
12	GUERRERO	6,005	3,129	2,876
13	HILDAGO	1,877	957	920
14	JALISCO			
15	MEXICO	11,327	5,602	5,725
16	MICHOACAN	3,555	1,733	1,822
17	MORELOS	1,430	690	740
18	NAYARIT	227	102	125
19	NUEVO LEON	1,196	547	649
20	OAXACA	11,963	5,650	6,313
21	PUEBLA	22,366	10,681	11,685
22	QUERETARO	288	140	148
23	QUINTANA ROO	388	194	194
24	SAN LUIS POTOSI	1,703	872	831
25	SINALOA	3,049	1,529	1,520
26	SONORA	1,137	570	567
27	TABASCO	935	453	482
28	TAMAULIPAS	1,371	662	709
29	TLAXCALA	1,011	464	547
30	VERACRUZ	8,602	4,254	4,348
31	YUCATAN	2,107	1,031	1,076
32	ZACATECAS	1,927	850	1,077

NOTE: These populations are not included in any age specific variables.

SOURCE: 1980 Mexican Census of Population, Volume 1, Table 1.

Relevant Unspecified Populations From the
Mexican Census of Population, 1980

No.	State	Unspecified Industry Or Occupation	Unspecified Income Or Work Hours	Males Work Hours Unspecified	Females Work Hours Unspecified
1	AGUASCALIENTES	25,756	19,884	14,166	9,068
2	BAJA CALIFORNIA	66,642	75,659	45,655	23,859
3	BAJA CALIFORNIA SUR	9,576	9,623	8,898	3,589
4	CAMPECHE	19,126	30,041	18,702	10,451
5	COAHUILA	70,892	67,386	20,393	5,579
6	COLIMA	10,758	6,019	7,035	5,928
7	CHIAPAS	126,230	161,172	83,979	79,425
8	CHIHUAHUA	107,453	108,980	78,438	43,598
9	DISTRICTO FEDERAL	590,709	344,921	237,714	235,686
10	DURANGO	73,932	66,497	40,609	26,586
11	GUANAJUATO	256,713	203,910	117,294	92,539
12	GUERRERO	118,061	188,763	92,561	82,966
13	HILDAGO	144,064	91,556	51,769	39,123
14	JALISCO			152,535	98,582
15	MEXICO	288,319	410,522	236,605	148,054
16	MICHOACAN	158,325	161,617	103,593	68,595
17	MORELOS	50,214	53,615	34,101	21,765
18	NAYARIT	25,307	12,753	14,501	9,673
19	NUEVO LEON	85,711	97,303	123,427	81,572
20	OAXACA	154,211	202,748	109,395	109,056
21	PUEBLA	154,956	181,645	107,361	89,607
22	QUERETARO	23,123	15,853	14,739	11,123
23	QUINTANA ROO	8,655	1,344	8,703	6,176
24	SAN LUIS POTOSI	97,582	96,128	64,044	43,105
25	SINALOA	109,357	101,632	77,499	39,649
26	SONORA	85,941	74,664	61,812	28,277
27	TABASCO	51,452	40,316	35,527	27,871
28	TAMAULIPAS	89,794	93,819	75,361	40,893
29	TLAXCALA	24,905	37,021	19,947	15,198
30	VERACRUZ	274,843	364,598	216,227	149,485
31	YUCATAN	48,285	81,157	52,160	28,785
32	ZACATECAS	37,227	18,357	22,687	15,695

NOTE: Due to the summary nature of the unspecified population figures, they are often found in more than one table. In most cases, the tables specified are the ones used to extract the relevant specific data.

SOURCE: <u>1980 Mexican Census of Population</u>, Volume 1, Tables 7 and 9; Volume 1, Table 10; Volume 2, Table 12 (both male & female populations).

Relevant Unspecified Populations From the
Mexican Census of Population, 1980

No.	State	Unspecified Third Level Education	Unspecified Education Level Age 14+	Unspecified Education Level Age 17+	Unspecified Education Level Age 15-29
1	AGUASCALIENTES	65	24,586	22,700	8,689
2	BAJA CALIFORNIA	200	97,816	90,205	38,109
3	BAJA CALIFORNIA SUR	27	11,852	10,971	4,697
4	CAMPECHE	62	37,989	34,905	14,530
5	COAHUILA	222	92,295	85,153	23,982
6	COLIMA	68	9,498	8,832	3,291
7	CHIAPAS	197	222,787	201,997	100,102
8	CHIHUAHUA	227	120,290	110,644	46,099
9	DISTRICTO FEDERAL	1,612	264,224	246,320	108,025
10	DURANGO	160	79,630	72,748	29,666
11	GUANAJUATO	312	300,682	275,772	113,023
12	GUERRERO	252	262,500	241,407	92,734
13	HILDAGO	169	113,393	103,059	207,437
14	JALISCO	611	350,606	323,453	
15	MEXICO	1,169	555,644	381,636	209,076
16	MICHOACAN	240	162,255	139,780	425,790
17	MORELOS	152	84,048	61,663	26,838
18	NAYARIT	82	17,651	16,674	5,418
19	NUEVO LEON	385	123,478	115,410	43,506
20	OAXACA	225	241,983	224,564	83,628
21	PUEBLA	273	274,106	253,556	96,181
22	QUERETARO	83	29,189	26,873	10,536
23	QUINTANA ROO	32	18,352	16,809	8,356
24	SAN LUIS POTOSI	126	138,399	128,293	46,622
25	SINALOA	215	136,016	126,328	48,173
26	SONORA	181	87,196	81,272	30,735
27	TABASCO	122	63,611	57,954	26,333
28	TAMAULIPAS	389	126,173	117,239	44,918
29	TLAXCALA	109	53,422	50,769	17,789
30	VERACRUZ	480	563,003	518,935	206,920
31	YUCATAN	113	131,270	120,838	50,099
32	ZACATECAS	52	21,698	20,017	7,123

SOURCE: <u>1980 Mexican Census of Population</u>, Volume 2, Table 7; Volume 1, Table 5.

Relevant Unspecified Populations From the
Mexican Census of Population, 1980

No.	State	# Rooms & # Residents	Population Not Specifying: Meat/Eggs For Age <5	Potable Water	Language Skills
1	AGUASCALIENTES	1,308	14,991	549	539
2	BAJA CALIFORNIA	3,586	24,330	1,571	1,219
3	BAJA CALIFORNIA SUR	741	5,863	358	95
4	CAMPECHE	1,704	14,036	542	5,308
5	COAHUILA	3,788	39,933	1,757	1,596
6	COLIMA	1,363	5,531	546	461
7	CHIAPAS	38,999	83,716	5,357	32,454
8	CHIHUAHUA	6,650	41,580	2,289	4,179
9	DISTRICTO FEDERAL	16,320	113,025	7,251	13,354
10	DURANGO	3,890	44,281	1,540	1,370
11	GUANAJUATO	14,680	108,392	6,381	3,421
12	GUERRERO	44,337	82,442	6,683	15,953
13	HILDAGO	13,607	55,154	2,470	18,739
14	JALISCO	14,080			
15	MEXICO	30,337	193,425	13,332	23,458
16	MICHOACAN	14,083	88,705	5,017	8,540
17	MORELOS	3,618	25,939	1,504	2,119
18	NAYARIT	1,942	11,101	528	843
19	NUEVO LEON	5,752	58,274	1,999	2,326
20	OAXACA	39,918	101,896	7,347	48,483
21	PUEBLA	21,520	125,980	4,327	25,801
22	QUERETARO	2,096	14,564	573	962
23	QUINTANA ROO	2,350	8,948	559	3,680
24	SAN LUIS POTOSI	11,625	60,237	2,396	9,955
25	SINALOA	7,966	53,637	3,501	2,723
26	SONORA	3,560	35,358	1,584	3,701
27	TABASCO	9,638	35,601	2,010	3,502
28	TAMAULIPAS	6,664	47,785	2,722	2,143
29	TLAXCALA	2,317	23,754	860	2,003
30	VERACRUZ	61,861	184,050	12,765	38,215
31	YUCATAN	10,648	41,145	2,734	23,404
32	ZACATECAS	1,796	17,833	479	933

SOURCE: 1980 Mexican Census of Population, Volume 2, Table 18; Volume 1, Table 17; Volume 1, Table 22; Volume 1, Table 15.

Relevant Unspecified Populations From the
Mexican Census of Population, 1980

No.	State	Populations Not Specifying:	
		Hours Worked Per Week	Native To State
1	AGUASCALIENTES	23,234	3,057
2	BAJA CALIFORNIA	69,514	75,659
3	BAJA CALIFORNIA SUR	12,487	1,627
4	CAMPECHE	29,153	6,148
5	COAHUILA	25,972	11,942
6	COLIMA	12,963	1,763
7	CHIAPAS	163,404	85,003
8	CHIHUAHUA	122,036	19,067
9	DISTRICTO FEDERAL	473,400	59,012
10	DURANGO	67,195	17,002
11	GUANAJUATO	209,833	39,901
12	GUERRERO	175,547	44,368
13	HILDAGO	90,892	21,016
14	JALISCO	251,117	
15	MEXICO	384,659	80,279
16	MICHOACAN	172,188	28,763
17	MORELOS	55,866	10,978
18	NAYARIT	24,174	2,692
19	NUEVO LEON	41,855	13,184
20	OAXACA	218,451	54,225
21	PUEBLA	196,968	51,188
22	QUERETARO	25,862	3,462
23	QUINTANA ROO	14,879	2,634
24	SAN LUIS POTOSI	107,149	19,516
25	SINALOA	117,148	19,730
26	SONORA	90,089	10,894
27	TABASCO	63,398	12,424
28	TAMAULIPAS	116,254	15,238
29	TLAXCALA	35,145	7,340
30	VERACRUZ	365,712	84,512
31	YUCATAN	80,945	22,357
32	ZACATECAS	38,382	5,733

SOURCE: 1980 Mexican Census of Population, Volume 2, Table 12; Volume 1, Table 11.

References

Afifi, A. A. and S. P. Azen. Statistical Analysis: A Computer Oriented Approach. New York: Academic Press, 1972.

Aguirre, Alejandro and Sergio Camposortega. "Evaluacion de la Informacion Basica Sobre Mortalidad Infantil en Mexico," in Lecturas en Materia de Seguridad Social, Planeacion Familiar, y Cambio Demografico, Mexico, D.F., IMSS, 1982.

Bassols Batalla Angel. "La Division Economica Regional de Mexico." Investigacion Economica 24:387-413, 1961.

Beegle, J. Alan, Harold F. Goldsmith, and Charles P.Loomis. "Demographic Characteristics of the United States-Mexican Border." Rural Sociology 25:107-161, 1960.

Blalock, Hubert M. Social Statistics (second edition), New York; McGraw-Hill, 1979.

Bogue, Donald J. The Population of the United States. New York: The Free Press, 1985.

Bronfman, Mario, Elsa Lopez, and Rodolfo Tuiran. "Practica Anticonceptiva y Clases Sociales en Mexico: La Experiencia Reciente." Estudios Demograficos y Urbanos 1(2):165-203, 1986.

Bruch, Hans A., Silera B. Hartman, and Jose Sanchez-Crespo. "The Health and Vital Statistics Systems in Mexico." Chap. 2 in DHHS Pub. No. (PHS) 81-1353. Hyattsville, Maryland: National Center for Health Statistics, 1980.

Brunn, Stanley D. Jack F. Williams. Cities of the World: World Regional Urban Development. New York: Harper and Row. 1983.

Butler, Edgar W. and James B. Pick. Geothermal Energy Development. New York: Plenum Publishing Co. 1982.

Butler, Edgar W., James B. Pick, Hiroshi Fukurai, and Glenda Tellis. "Migration to Baja California: 1900-1980." The Center for Inter-American and Border Studies, the University of Texas at El Paso, Research Paper Series, 54pp., 1987a.

Butler, Edgar W., Hiroshi Fukurai, and James B.Pick. "Tourism and the Economies of Mexican States." Proceedings of the American Statistical Association, Social Statistics Section, 1987b.

Butler, Edgar W., Glenda Telis, and James B.Pick. "An Evaluation of 1980 Mexican Census Data: The State of Oaxaca." Paper presented at the Western Social Science Association, El Paso, Texas, April 23, 1987c.

Butler, Edgar W., James B. Pick, and Hiroshi Fukurai. "A Systematic Approach to a Socioeconomic Geographical Information System for Mexico." Paper presented at the Western Social Science Association, Denver, Colorado, April 28, 1987d.

Butler, Edgar W., James B.Pick, and Glenda Tellis. "An Empirical Examation of the Official Results of the 1988 Mexican Presential Election," in Sucesion Presidencial: Bi-National Reflections, Edgar W.Butler and Jorge Bustamante (eds.), Boulder, Colorado: Westview Press, 1989.

Butler, Edgar W., Hiroshi Fukurai, and James B.Pick "Tourism and the Economies of Mexican States," in Hooshang Kuklan (ed.), 1989 BALAS Proceedings, Business Association of Latin American Studies, 1989. Reviewed version of earlier paper.

C.I.A. The World Factbook. Washington, D.C.; Central Intelligence Agency. 1986-88.

360

CONAPO. "Encuesta Nacional Demografica." Mexico, D.F.: Consejo Nacional de Poblacion and Secretaria de Programacion y Presupuesto, 1982.

CPNPF. "Encuesta Nacional de Prevalencia en el Uso de Metodos Anticonceptivos." Mexico, D.F.: Coordinacion del Programa Nacional de Planificacion Familiar, 1980.

Camposortega, Sergio. "Evaluacion y Correction de la Poblacion Mexicana Censada en 1970." Revista de Estadistica y Geografia 3(10). Mexico, D.F., Secretaria de Programacion y Presupuesto, 1982.

Cantu Gutierrez Juan Jose. "La Migracion Internacional y Sus Effectos en La Frontera Norte: Retos Para La Accion Publica." Paper presented at Conference on the Northern Border Municipios, Tijuana, B.C., April 23-26, 1986.

Coplamar. "Minimos de Bienestar, Vol. 4 Salud. Mexico, D.F.: Presidencia de la Republica de Mexico. 1979.

Dagodog, W. Tim. "Illegal Mexican Immigration to California from Western Mexico," in Jones, Richard C. (ed.), Patterns of Undocumented Migration, Totowa, New Jersey, Littlefield Adams and Co. 1984.

Davis, Diane E. "Rank-Size Distribution and Economic Development: the Case of Mexico." Studies in Comparative International Development 16:84-107, 1981.

Delfina Ramirez Maria. "Las Desigualdades Interregionales en Mexico, 1970-1980." Estudios Demograficos y Urbanos 1(3):351-374, 1986.

Diccionario Porrua, Mexico, D.F.: Editorial Porrua, 1971.

Dillman, C. Daniel. "Border Industrialization," in Stoddard, Ellwyn et al. (eds.), Borderlands Sourcebook, Norman, Oklahoma, University of Oklahoma Press, 1983a.

Dillman, C. Daniel. "Border Urbanization," in Stoddard, Ellwyn et al. (eds.), Borderlands Sourcebook, Norman, Oklahoma, University of Oklahoma Press, 1983b.

El Dia, July 7, 1988.

ESRI. Arc/Info Geographic Information System. Redlands, California: Environmental Systems Research Institute, 1985.

Florescano, Enrique. Atlas Historico de Mexico. Mexico, D.F.: Siglo XXI Editores. 1983.

Fukurai, Hiroshi, James B. Pick, Edgar W. Butler, and Swapan Nag. "An Analysis of the Interstate Migration in Mexico." Mexican Studies/Estudios Mexicanos 3(2):365-395, 1987a.

Fukurai, Hiroshi, James B. Pick, and Edgar W. Butler. "Interstate Migration in Mexico, 1980: A Spatial Analysis." Sociology and Social Research 71(4):313-322, 1987b.

Fukurai, Hiroshi, James B. Pick, Edgar W. Butler, and Glenda Tellis. "An Examination of Regional Migration Patterns in Mexico: New and Old Mexican Regions." Genus, in press. 1988.

Garcia y Garma, Irma Olaga. "Diferenciales de Fecundidad en Mexico, 1970." Demografia y Economia 13(1):49-81, 1979.

Garza, Gustavo. El Proceso de Industrializacion en La Ciudad de Mexico: 1821-1970. Mexico, D.F.: El Colegio de Mexico. 1985.

Holian, John. "Fertility Differentials in Mexico: An Individual Level Analysis." Secolas Annals 14:47-60, 1983.

Holian, John. "The Effect of Female Education on Marital Fertility in Different Size Communities in Mexico." Social Biology 31(3-4):298-307, 1986.

IMF. International Financial Statistics. Washington, D.C.: International Monetary Fund. 48-88.

Jones, Richard C. "Macro-Patterns of Undocumented Migration Between Mexico and the U.S.," in Jones, Richard C. (ed.), Patterns of Undocumented Migration, Totowa, New Jersey, Littlefield, Adams, and Co., 1984.

Lezema, Jose Luis. "Migracion y Petreleo en Tabasco," Estudios Demograficos y Urbanos 2(2):231-256, 1987.

Lopez Chavez, Guidalupe. "Metodologia para la Critica de la Informacion del Censo de Poblacion y Vivienda 1980." Revista de Estadistica y Geografia 3(10), 1982.

Margulis, Mario, and Rodolfo Tuiran. "Nuevos Patrones Migratorios en La Fronter Norte: La Emigracion." Demografia y Economia 3(59):410-444, 1984.

Marlin, John T., Immanuel Ness, and Stephen T. Collins. Book of World City Rankings. New York: The Free Press. 1986.

Martinez, Jorge. The Demographic Revolution in Mexico: 1970-1980. Mexico, D.F.: Mexican Institute of Social Security, 1982.

Martinez, Oscar. "Border Cities," in Stoddard, Ellwyn et al. (eds), Borderlands Sourcebook, Norman, Oklahoma, University of Oklahoma Press, 1983.

Martinez, Oscar. Troublesome Border. Tucson, The University of Arizona Press, 1988.

Nag, Swapan. Development of a Computerized Cartographic System for Mapping Sociodemographic, Economic, and Marketing Data in Municipios of Six Mexican Border States. Masters Thesis, Graduate School of Management, University of California, Riverside, 1986.

Negrete Salas, Maria E. and Hector Salazar Sanchez. "Zonas Metropolitanas en Mexico, 1980." Estudios Demograficos y Urbanos 1(1):97-124, 1986.

PEMEX. Anuario Estadistico, 1986. Instituto Mexicano del Petreleo, 1986.

Partida, Virgilio. "Problemas en la Estimacion de la Mortalidad a Nivel Regional en Mexico," in Investigacion Demografica en Mexico-1980, Mexico, D.F., CONAPO, 1982.

Pebley, Anne R. and Noreen Goldman. "Legalizacion de Uniones Consensuales en Mexico," Estudios Demograficos y Urbanos 1(2):267-290, 1986.

Pick, James B., Edgar W. Butler, Swapan Nag, and Glenda Tellis. "Socioeconomic Effects on Fertility in Mexican Border State Municipios, 1980." Proceedings of the American Statistical Association, Social Statistics Section, 373-78, 1986.

Pick, James B., Swapan Nag, Glenda Tellis, and Edgar W. Butler. "Geographical Distribution and Variation in Selected Socioeconomic Variables for Municipios in Six Mexican Border States, 1980." Journal of Borderlands Studies 2(1):58-92, 1987a.

Pick, James B., Glenda Tellis, and Edgar W. Butler. "Socioeconomic Characteristics of the Mexican Oil Region." Proceedings of the American Statistical Association, Social Statistics Section, 483-489. 1987b.

Pick, James B., Edgar W. Butler, and Suhas Pavgi. "Socioeconomic Determinants of Fertility, Selected Mexican Regions, 1976-77." Social Biology, 35(1-2): 137-157, 1988a.

Pick, James B., Swapan Nag, and Edgar W. Butler. "A Cluster Analysis Approach to Marketing Research in the Borderlands Region of Mexico." 1988 BALAS Proceedings. Business Association of Latin American Studies, 19-25, 1988b.

Pick, James B., Glenda L. Tellis, and Edgar W. Butler. "Fertility Determinants in the Oil Region of Mexico," Social Biology, in press. 1988c.

Pick, James B., Edgar W. Butler, Swapan Nag, and Glenda Tellis. "Socioeconomic Influences on Fertility in the Mexican Borderlands Regions, 1980." Manuscript, 1988d.

Pick, James B., Glenda L. Tellis, Edgar W. Butler, and Suhas Pavgi. "Socioeconomic Determinants of Migration in Mexico," manuscript, 1988e.

Pillet, Bernard. Fertility Changes in the Early Decades of Rapid Socioeconomic Development: Recent Mexican Experience Ph.D. Dissertation, Stanford University. 1980.

362

Pirez, Pedro. "Para El Estudio de Los Municipios y La Politica Regional en Mexico." Demografia y Economia 15(3) : 344-358, 1981.

Ponce, G. Dolores and Alonso C., Antonio. FORO Mexico 2010: Internal Politics, Mexico City: Fundación Javier Barros Sierra AZ, June 20, 1987 (Mimeograph).

Population Reference Bureau. "1987 World Population Data Sheet." Washington, D.C.: Population Reference Bureau. 1987.

Population Reference Bureau. "1988 World Population Data Sheet." Washington, D.C.: Population Reference Bureau. 1988.

Preston, Samuel H., Nathan Keyfitz, and Robert Schoen. Causes of Death: Life Tables for National Populations. New York: Seminar Press, 1972.

Proceso Electoral Federal, July 7, 1988.

¿ Que Paso? Elecciones 1988. 1988. Mexico, D.F.: Editorial Diana.

Rabell, Cecilia, Marta Mier, and Teran Rocha. "Ed Descenso de la Mortalidad en Mexico de 1940 a 1980." Estudios Demograficos y Urbanos 1(1):39:72, 1986.

Reich, Peter L. Statistical Abstract of the United States-Mexico Borderlands. Los Angeles, UCLA Latin American Center Publications, Statistical Astract of Latin America, Supplement 9, 1984.

Rendon, Teresa and Carlos Salas. "La Poblacion Economicamente Active en el Censo de 1980." Estudios Demograficos y Urbanos 1(2):291-309, 1986.

Roberts, Brian R. "Urban Poverty and Public Welfare in Mexico and Britain," Comparative Urban Research 11(1-2):105-125, 1985.

Rodriguez Sala, Maria L. "La Regionalizacion de Mexico." Revista Mexicana de Sociologia 22:231-248, 1960.

Rubin-Kurtzman, Jane R. "The Socioeconomic Determinants of Fertility in Mexico: Changing Perspectives." Monograph Series, No. 23, Center for U.S.-Mexican Studies, University of California, San Diego, 1987.

SAS Institute Inc. SAS User's Guide. Cary, North Carolina: SAS Institute Inc. 1985.

SPP. Anuario Estadistico de los Estados Unidos Mexicanos, various volumes. Mexico, D.F.: Secretaria de Programacion y Presupuesto. 1976-86

SPP. Encuesta Mexicana de Fecundidad. Informe Metodologico Mexico. Mexico, D.F.: Secretaria de Programacion y Presupuesto, 1978.

SPP. Encuesta Mexicana de Fecundidad. V I. Primer Informe Nacional. Mexico, D.F.: Secretaria de Programacion y Presupuesto, 1979a.

SPP. Encuesta Mexicana de Fecundidad. V. II. Primer Informe Nacional. Mexico, D.F.: Secretaria de Programacion y Presupuesto, 1979b.

SPP. Encuesta Mexicana de Fedundidad. V. III. Tres Areas Metropolitanas. Mexico, D.F.: Secretaria de Programacion y Presupuesto, 1979c.

SPP. X Censo General de Poblacion y Vivienda, 1980. Various volumes." Mexico, D.F.: Secretaria de Programacion y Presupuesto, 1982-4.

SPP. Estadisticas Historicas de Mexico. Volumes I and II. Mexico, D.F.: Secretaria de Programacion y Presupuesto. 1985.

SPP. "Mexico Estimaciones y Proyecciones de Poblacion, 1950-2000." Mexico, D.F.: Secretaria de Programacin y Presupuesto, 1983.

SPSS Inc. SPSS X User's Guide, 2nd edition. Chicago, Illinois: SPSS Inc., 1986.

Sanchez Molina, Antonio. Sintesis Geographica de Mexico. Mexico, D.F.: Editorial Trillas, 1973.

Schteingart, Martha. "Mexico City," In Dogan, Mattei and John D. Kasarda, The Metropolis Era, Vol. 2, Mega-Cities, pp. 268-293, 1988.

Scott, Ian. Urban and Spatial Development in Mexico. Baltimore: The Johns Hopkins University Press, 1982.

Secretaria de Turismo. 1979 Turista Mapa. Mexico, D.F., Secretaria de Turismo, 1979.

Secretaria de Turismo. Estadisticas Basicas de la Actividad Turistica. Mexico, D.F.: Secretaria de Turismo, Direction General de Politica Turistica, 1985.

Seiver, Daniel A. "Recent Fertility in Mexico: Measurement and Interpretation." Population Studies 29(3):341-354, 1975.

Shryock, Henry S., Jacob S. Siegel, and Associates. The Methods and Materials of Demography. New York: Academic Press, 1976.

Silvestre, Jose, and Santiago Zorrilla. Mexico por Entidades Federativas. Mexico, D.F.: Ediciones Oceano. 1986.

Stoddard, Ellwyn R. Richard Nostrand, & Johathan P. West. Borderlands Sourcebook: A Guide to the Literature on Northern Mexico and the American Southwest. Norman, Oklahoma: University of Oklahoma Press, 1983.

Stoddard, Ellwyn R. Maquila: Assembly Plants in Northern Mexico. El Paso, Texas: Texas Western Press, 1987.

Tamayo, Jesus. Zonas Fronterizas. Mexico, D.F.: Centro de Investigacion y Docencia Economicas, 1983.

Tamayo, Jorge L. Geografia Moderna de Mexico. Mexico, D.F.: Editorial Trillas, 1985.

U.S. Bureau of the Census. Statistical Abstract of the United States: 1984. Washington, D.C.: U.S. Government Printing Office, 1984.

U.S. Bureau of the Census. Statistical Abstract of the United States. U.S. Bureau of the Census, Department of Commerce, 1988.

U.S. Dept. of Interior. Minerals Yearbook, Vol. III, Area Reports: International. Washington, D.C.: U.S. Dept. of the Interior, 1986.

Unikel, Luis. "Urbanization in Mexico: Process, Implications, Policies, and Prospects," in Goldstein and Sly (eds.), Patterns of Urbanization, Dolhain, Belgium, Ordina Editions, pp. 465-568, 1977.

Van Arsdol, Maurice, Nadia Youssef, Michel Antochiw, Dennis Berg, and John Brennan, Jr. "Migration and Population Redistribution in the State of Mexico, Republic of Mexico." ICP Work Agreement Reports, Occasional Monograph Series, 5(1), Washington, D.C.: Smithsonian Institution, 133-176, 1976.

WFS. "The Mexican Fertility Survey, 1976-1977: A Summary of Findings." Voorburg, Netherlands: International Statistical Institute, 1980.

Whetten, Nathan, and Robert G. Burnight. "Internal Migration in Mexico." Rural Sociology 21:140-156, 1956.

Wilkie, James W. The Mexican Revolution: Federal Expenditure and Social Change Since 1910, Second Edition. Berkeley, University of California Press, 1970.

Wilkie, James W. Statistical Abstract of Latin America, Volume 23. Los Angeles: UCLA Latin American Center Publications, 1986.

Wilkie, Richard W. Latin American Population and Urbanization Analysis: Maps and Statistics, 1950-82. Los Angeles: UCLA Latin American Center Publications, 1984.

Winnie, William. "Componentes del Crecimiento y Redistribucion de la Poblacion Mexicana, Resultados del Censo, 1980." Demografia y Economia 15(3):359-376, 1981.

Zambrano Lupi, Jorge H. "Fecundidad y Escolaridad en la Ciudad de Mexico." Demografia y Economia 13(4):405-448, 1979.

Index